10.90

THE VERRINE ORATIONS

I

CICERO

THE VERRINE ORATIONS

WITH AN ENGLISH TRANSLATION BY
L. H. G. GREENWOOD, M.A.
FELLOW OF EMMANUEL COLLEGE, CAMBRIDGE
UNIVERSITY LECTURER IN CLASSICS

IN TWO VOLUMES

I

AGAINST CAECILIUS

AGAINST VERRES : PART ONE
PART TWO, BOOKS I AND II

CAMBRIDGE, MASSACHUSETTS
HARVARD UNIVERSITY PRESS
LONDON
WILLIAM HEINEMANN LTD
MCMLXXVIII

American
ISBN 0-674-99243-1

British
ISBN 0 434 99221 6

First printed 1928
Reprinted 1948, 1953, 1959, 1966, 1978

Printed in Great Britain

CONTENTS OF VOLUME ONE

PREFACE

This edition of the Verrine Orations is not intended as a serious contribution to the improvement of the text. The textual notes have therefore purposely been kept as few and short as possible. The present text is, however, not identical with any already published. It is printed, with many changes, from that of Nobbe. As against Nobbe, the consensus of C. F. W. Müller's Teubner edition and Sir W. Peterson's Oxford edition has usually been accepted without comment; but not always, nor without consideration. I have admitted one or two conjectures of my own; these are carefully noted. Peterson's book remains indispensable for all those who are concerned to assure themselves of the " best readings " and the reasons for them. I have not adopted by any means all his changes; nor, I hope, either adopted or rejected any of them without due consideration ; and the more important of them I have acknowledged. The short account of the manuscript authorities, in my Introduction, is based upon his Latin introduction to his

edition and on his numerous articles on the subject in the *Classical Review* and elsewhere. My punctuation often differs slightly from his, but still more often and more widely from Müller's, as any modern English edition must, in this respect, differ from any German one.

For the explanatory notes I am considerably indebted to Long's edition (1862), especially in the otherwise almost wholly neglected first three books of the *actio secunda*.

INTRODUCTION

In the late summer of the year 70 B.C. Gaius Verres, governor of Sicily during the three preceding years, was prosecuted at Rome by Cicero, on behalf of the Sicilian people. Technically the charge was one of extortion. The province, like a plaintiff in a purely civil suit, sued for the restitution of some £400,000, and brought its claim before the *quaestio de pecuniis repetundis*, "the (court of) inquiry into moneys claimed back." But in effect the case was a criminal prosecution for general misgovernment and oppression. The accused, if convicted, would not only have to pay damages; he would be sentenced to the loss of his *caput*, his rights as a Roman citizen.

It is not strange that such cases were no new thing in Rome. During the actual term of office of a Roman provincial governor, he could not be removed. No one in his province could dispute his authority; and the control that could be exercised over him from Rome was little in theory and less in practice. Once out of office, he could be brought to justice; but the chances, even for the worst offender, of avoiding this, or at least of securing acquittal, were always too great, and the deterrent was not serious. It is less surprising that oppression was common than that it was not still commoner. The case of Verres excited unusual interest in Rome; but this was not due either

to the nature of his misconduct or to its magnitude. It was due partly to the personal struggle between the advocates, in which Cicero tried, and, as it proved, tried successfully, to wrest from the older Hortensius his acknowledged pre-eminence among Roman pleaders. It was due, far more, to the bearing of the case on a political crisis of this year, a crisis that forms an interesting episode in the constitutional history of the Republic.

The main body of Roman citizens, though in theory the sovereign power in the Roman state, was never to any great extent sovereign in practice. From the time of the first Punic War the real control of government lay with the Senate, and more and more as time went on, for over a century. Constitutionally the Senate was no more than an advisory committee to help the executive magistrates; in practice, the magistrates acted, and the popular assemblies voted, in accordance with its decrees. Its members were members of the great ancient Roman families, patrician or plebeian, which were only slowly added to, or in part replaced, by other families that rose to wealth as the empire extended. These other families for the most part remained outside the senatorial class; their members neither held the higher magistracies nor sat in the Senate; their political powers were, ostensibly, only those of all Roman citizens. But their class, the *equester ordo*, possessed collectively, and they possessed individually, great financial and social importance; and in the series of attacks upon senatorial ascendancy which opened with the attempted reforms of Tiberius Gracchus and culminated in the Marian revolution, the Knights counted for much. Their motive was

jealousy of the powers and privileges of the senatorial class; they were not moved, any more than the various leaders of the opposition were moved, by any belief in or desire for real democracy. But the rule of the Senate and the senatorial magistrates was sufficiently incapable and corrupt to give the opposition plausible justification for its assaults.

One of those measures of Tiberius Gracchus which remained effective was the re-constitution of the Extortion Courts. These were already in more or less permanent existence to try claims and charges brought against the senatorial governors of provinces. Membership of them was now confined to the equestrian order. It was reasonably held that senatorial offenders should not be tried by senatorial judges for offences which those judges had had, or would like in future to have, the opportunity of committing themselves; and that equestrian judges would be more likely to punish, and so to discourage, oppression of provincials by governors. In practice, there was little or no improvement; senatorial governors and equestrian financiers combined to fleece the provincials on the basis of a division of the plunder, and the equestrian court was never likely to convict a governor who had taken the natural steps to secure an acquittal. Though, therefore, the senatorial order would have liked to recover control of the Extortion Courts, want of will as well as want of power made them acquiesce for some fifty years in the tenure of this judicial power by the Knights alone.

Ten years before the prosecution of Verres, the constitution imposed on Rome by Sulla the dictator had given to the Senate, in theory now as well as in

practice, almost complete supremacy in the state. It was only one detail of his settlement that membership of the Extortion Court, as of the new criminal courts which he instituted, was confined to senators. Justice in the Extortion Court was administered no better for the change. Oppression in the provinces was less, not more, severely punished, and therefore increased rather than diminished. This fact would not of itself cause great discontent in Rome ; what mattered was that the Knights had lost more by the change than the Senators had gained. As soon as the opportunity arose, the senatorial monopoly was sure to be challenged, and by the year 70 the opportunity had arisen.

The permanence of Sulla's settlement could only be secured if all senators, however powerful, wealthy and ambitious, would sacrifice their personal aims to the common maintenance of the supremacy of their order. It is doubtful if Sulla himself expected this to happen ; in any case, he was hardly dead before it became clear that this would not happen. Under the open or secret leadership of ambitious persons like Pompeius and Crassus and Caesar, senators deserting for their own ends the cause of the Senate, the " popular " opposition began to revive. Unity of purpose, coupled with effective control of the legions, would have enabled the Senate to crush, one by one as they arose, the attempts made to reverse this or that detail of the Sullan constitution. Possessing neither advantage, the Senate was soon revealed less autocratic in fact than in theory. The election of Pompeius and Crassus as consuls for the year 70 was the first striking success of the opposition. A second followed promptly : with the support of the

consuls, the great powers of the tribunes of the plebs, reduced by Sulla almost to nothing, were restored to them. A third was being threatened when Cicero addressed the senatorial Extortion Court as prosecutor of Verres : a bill was already " promulgated " providing that membership of the criminal courts, the Extortion Court included, was no longer to be the monopoly of senators, who were only to constitute one-third of the whole. The menaced privilege was in itself, for reasons already given, not a thing for which the senatorial majority were ready to fight to the last ; but they were ready to do much to retain it, both for its own sake and because of what its loss would signify in the party struggle. This was the crisis that gave the case of Verres exceptional interest. The court may or may not have been composed, as Cicero naturally declares it is composed, of unusually honest men eager to punish and remedy grave injustice. The important fact was that it was composed of members of that senatorial order whose supremacy was being threatened, at that moment, as it had never been threatened since Sulla's death. In the issue now pending, the verdict might turn the scale ; Cicero insists that it certainly would. He pays compliments to the high character of the judges, but his appeal is to their interests. He urges, again and again, that if this court does not convict this governor, the people will be forced to conclude that no court composed of senators will ever convict any governor, however guilty, who has money to spend on bribery ; and that the consequence will be the loss by the Senate of its present monopoly control of the courts.

That this danger was real the sequel proved ;

INTRODUCTION

Verres was not acquitted, but the already promulgated bill became law nevertheless, and the Senate's monopoly was ended. The court had, to be sure, no very fine opening for a display of its incorruptibility. The case was too hopelessly black against the accused for either himself or his advocate to care to face it out, and he condemned himself to exile, flying from Rome to Massilia before the court could condemn him. Even had he been willing to await the verdict, the nation's opinion of senatorial courts might well have remained unchanged ; it might well have been thought that the acquittal of such a man would have been so unspeakable a scandal that his conviction could bring his judges no great credit. Cicero himself expresses no confidence that a conviction will prevent the bill's passing, but only his certainty that an acquittal will ensure its passing ; the chance, he implies, is a slender one, though not on that account to be thrown away.

Concerning the man whom circumstances made, for the moment, so notable a personage, we know nothing more than Cicero tells us, except the bare facts of his flight, condemnation, and exile, and his death, as an exile still, among those proscribed by Mark Antony in 43. To summarize those facts here seems needless. Except his father and his son, we know of no one who bore his name of Verres. We do not know whether this name was his *nomen* or his *cognomen* ; if it was the latter, we do not know what his *nomen* was. His father was a senator ; apart from that, not a word of his antecedents is given us. Undoubtedly a bad magistrate and a bad man, he was no doubt something less incredible than the monster depicted by his prosecutor. His passion for

Greek art was not the insincere and foolish pretence that Cicero would have it believed; nor was he exceptionally incompetent and silly. Of course Cicero says the worst possible of him at every turn; allowances and deductions must be made. When all is done, he cuts a sorry figure; and it is strange that he was suffered to oppress Sicily for three years, and that political considerations gained him, even in that age, so many responsible and respectable supporters.

Of the various schemes adopted to secure his acquittal Cicero gives us a full account. One of them led to the *Divinatio*, four months before the trial began. Supported by all the Sicilian cities but Syracuse and Messina, Cicero applied for leave to prosecute only to find that he must first establish his superior fitness against Caecilius, a rival prosecutor, put forward by Verres' own supporters, and meant to fail, either through lack of competence, or by playing into the hands of the defence, or both together. The court that decided between the two claimants simply heard the speeches of each on his own behalf, and settled the issue by " guess-work "; the word *divinatio*, properly describing the mental process by which it reached its verdict, was extended to cover the whole procedure, and narrowed again to describe the speech made by each claimant. The danger of Cicero's having to give way to his rival may or may not have been serious; we have no means of estimating it. In any case, it was surmounted.

Having failed to set up a rival prosecutor, Verres' friends next set up a rival prosecution. Delay would be valuable, for many circumstances pointed to a better chance of success for them if the case could

be postponed to the following year. It was decided to prosecute, on a similar charge before the same court, an ex-governor of the province of Achaea, and by being ready to begin this case before Cicero was ready with his, to secure the time of the court for the rest of the year. Plainly, the prosecutor could require the hearing to begin as soon as he liked; and Cicero was ready so long before his opponents had expected that their own preparations had barely begun.

One last resource was open to them. They could not delay the opening of the case, but they might delay its conclusion ; and if no verdict were reached that year, a completely fresh trial would be required before a fresh court the year following. To meet this danger, Cicero had to depart from the usual procedure, and to do a thing which it is plain he was legally entitled to do, and for which he tells the court that he can plead actual precedent. There is some obscurity about the exact nature of his innovation.

In the usual procedure, the prosecutor opened with a long speech, which was answered by a long speech for the defence. Each of these speeches may have been followed by speeches from the junior counsel (*subscriptores*) on the same side : we know little of the way in which such persons took part in the proceedings. When all the speeches on both sides were over, the witnesses gave their evidence ; first those for the prosecution, then those for the defence. Each of the advocates was allowed to cross-examine his opponent's witnesses ; and there was also a debate (*altercatio*) between the opposing advocates, but where this occurred—whether before or after all the evidence was given, or even perhaps after the evidence of each separate witness—we

xvi

INTRODUCTION

cannot tell. There was then an adjournment, *comperendinatio*; the name implies an interval of one day, but this may not have been the actual fact. The *actio secunda* began, like the *actio prima*, with long speeches from both advocates; after which, the hearing of further evidence was certainly possible, whether usual or not; and it may be that all the features of the *actio prima* were or might be reproduced. Then the verdict followed.

What Cicero was able to do, whether in virtue of recognized usage or by special favour of Glabrio the president of the court, was to rearrange the procedure of the *actio prima*. He broke up his long consecutive speech into a series of short ones, each of which dealt with one specific charge; and after each of these he called the witnesses concerned to give their evidence. He thus debarred Hortensius from making a long opening speech, but gave him in exchange the chance of making a similar series of short speeches, not merely later on when calling his own witnesses, but also, it would seem, immediately, by replying to Cicero's short speeches as well as by cross-examining Cicero's witnesses. In the *actio secunda* the procedure was to be the normal one; it was only the *actio prima* that would be affected.

The advantages of this plan to Cicero he himself states candidly (*Actio Prima*, §§ 53, 54). (1) The whole time occupied by the trial would be shortened, so that a verdict could be reached within the present year. It is not quite plain how the time would be shortened; for it may seem that the time saved by dropping the two continuous opening speeches might be spent on the short speeches, on both sides, in connexion with the separate charges and the wit-

nesses' evidence on them. We can only suppose that a closer knowledge of the recognized procedure would show that the shortening of the time did follow as a necessary consequence. If there was no legal limit to the length of time that might be spent on the continuous opening speeches, it would be an advantage to prevent the defence spinning theirs out to an altogether abnormal length.[a] (2) The defence would not be able to reply, for the first time, after a long recess, when Cicero's arguments were already half-forgotten and the emotion aroused by his eloquence had subsided. (3) Cicero counted upon public opinion to keep the judges in the path of honesty ; and this opinion would be reinforced in August by the crowds of summer visitors to Rome, drawn there by the census, by the elections, and by the festivals. And, though Cicero naturally does not say so, he may have thought that (4) the evidence of his witnesses would be so overwhelming that the defence would be abandoned, as did in fact happen.

The consequence for us of this new procedure is that the *actio prima* speech preserved to us is merely a short explanatory preface to the *actio* proper. The short speeches that introduced the separate blocks of evidence, though they did not only state, but also commented upon, the particular charges, depended too much on the evidence itself to be worth preserving, especially as the ground is covered, partly if not wholly, by the *actio secunda* speech. There is no reason to suppose that the *divinatio* and *actio prima* speeches are not substantially the speeches actually delivered by Cicero. We cannot tell how

[a] This seems to be hinted at in § 31, "deinde se ducturos et dicendo et excusando facile ad ludos Victoriae."

far he, or any other ancient orator, when revising his speeches for publication, would allow himself to change or improve what he had in fact said.

Since not even the *actio prima* was completed, of course no *actio secunda* took place ; the condemnation and assessment of damages followed Verres' flight immediately. Therefore the *actio secunda* speech, though it may represent in its general contents the short speeches, some of which were actually delivered in the *actio prima*, was never delivered as the connected whole which is what we have. But it does not follow that it was entirely composed "as a rhetorical exercise." Cicero may have hoped that such a speech would never be needed, but he could not be sure of this. He must therefore have composed a rough draft of it before the *actio prima* began ; and unless he could count on a long enough *comperendinatio* to give him time for his "fair copy," he must have gone far towards making that too. In the speech as actually published, he has been careful to keep up the similitude of a speech actually delivered ; this was inevitable if the form of a speech was to be kept at all. It may be granted that a certain air of unreality is given by the necessary though fictitious assumption that Verres had not fled but continued to stand his trial. But this is a superficial detail ; in substance and even in form, the *secunda* speech was composed, in advance, for delivery in court ; and the substance of some of it was delivered, in detached pieces, as part of the *actio prima*. Its interest is therefore surely not greatly lessened by the fact that it was never delivered in court just as it stands. We should have lost more than we should have gained by its conversion into a historical monograph.

INTRODUCTION

THE TEXT AND MANUSCRIPTS

The manuscript authorities for the text may be classified in four groups as follows :

1. The Vatican Palimpsest (*V*), written in the 3rd century or a little later. This is extant in some 50 fragments, none more than 12 sections long, and most of them about 3 or 4 sections long, of the *Actio Secunda*. As much our oldest authority, it is of high value, in spite of many imperfections.

2. (i.) The Cluni or Holkham MS. (*C*), of the 9th century. This only covers three passages of *Actio Secunda*, Book ii., about a quarter of the whole book. For these it is the best authority ; but its value goes further. It originally contained all Books ii. and iii., and was used by the writer of

(ii.) the Lagomarsinian MS. 42 (*O*) of the 15th century, which is consequently valuable for these two books, though not for the rest of the speeches ; and also by

(iii.) "Nannius," "Fabricius," and "Metellus," 16th century scholars whose work, now available, allows us to infer, in many doubtful passages, what the Cluni MS. readings (*c*) were.

3. The "Italian" group : the two best of these, covering all the speeches, are

(i.) *Parisinus* 7776 (*p*) of the 11th century, and

(ii.) the good, though late, *Lagomarsinianus* 29 (*q*), of the 15th century, which is closely related to *p*. The earliest printed editions were made from inferior manuscripts of this group.

4. The "Gallican" group. Of these the earliest and best is

(i.) *Regius Parisinus* 7774A (*R*) of the 9th century : from which, or from a closely similar MS., was made

(ii.) *Parisinus* 7775 (*S*) of the 13th century : from which in its turn was made

(iii.) *Parisinus* 7823 (*D*) of the 15th century ; a careful piece of work, which (except for a small part of *Actio Secunda* i.) is the best authority in this group for everything except the last 2 books, which alone have survived in R. Several other manuscripts of this group have little value.

The improvements effected in Peterson's edition are due mainly to his establishment of the importance of the first two of the above groups, of the second in particular, and to his collation of *p* in the third group.

The following table shows the portions of the wl ole text represented by the four groups.

	1	2		3	4		
	V	C	c (O)	p, q	R	S	D
Divinatio . . .				+			+
Actio Prima . . .				+			+
Actio Secunda, i. 1-89 .				+			+
90-111	(+)			+		+	+
111-end	(+)			+			+
ii. 1-30 .	(+)	+	+	+			+
31-111	(+)		+	+			+
112-117	(+)	+	+	+			+
118-156	(+)		+	+			+
157-183	(+)	+	+	+			+
184-end	(+)		+	+			+
iii. . .	(+)		+	+			+
iv. . .	(+)			+	+	+	+
v. . .	(+)			+	+	+	+

LIST OF CICERO'S WORKS

SHOWING THEIR DIVISION INTO VOLUMES IN THIS EDITION

LIST OF CICERO'S WORKS

LIST OF CICERO'S WORKS

LIST OF CICERO'S WORKS

SPEECH DELIVERED AGAINST
QUINTUS CAECILIUS NIGER

IN Q. CAECILIUM ORATIO QUAE
DIVINATIO DICITUR

1 I. Si quis vestrum, iudices, aut eorum qui adsunt, forte miratur me, qui tot annos in causis iudiciisque publicis ita sim versatus ut defenderim multos, laeserim neminem, subito nunc mutata voluntate ad accusandum descendere : is, si mei consilii causam rationemque cognoverit, una et id quod facio probabit, et in hac causa profecto neminem praeponendum esse mihi actorem putabit.

2 Cum quaestor in Sicilia fuissem, iudices, itaque ex ea provincia decessissem ut Siculis omnibus iucundam diuturnamque memoriam quaesturae nominisque mei relinquerem, factum est uti cum summum in veteribus patronis multis, tum nonnullum etiam in me praesidium suis fortunis constitutum esse arbitrarentur. Quare nunc populati atque vexati cuncti ad me publice saepe venerunt, ut suarum fortunarum om-

SPEECH DELIVERED AGAINST QUINTUS CAECILIUS NIGER

(MAINTAINING CICERO'S OWN GREATER FITNESS TO PROSECUTE VERRES)

I. It may be, gentlemen, that some of you, or some 1
of the audience, are surprised that I have departed
from the line of action which I have pursued for all
these years with regard to criminal proceedings ; that
having defended many accused persons, and attacked
nobody, I have now suddenly changed my policy,
and entered the arena as a prosecutor. But anyone
whom this surprises has only to understand the
motives that govern my action, and he will not only
recognize that I am doing right, but will certainly
take the view that no one can be held better fitted
than myself to conduct the case before us.

Gentlemen, I served in Sicily as quaestor, and so 2
discharged my duties there as to leave behind me,
in the minds of all Sicilians, lasting and agreeable
memories of my year of office and of myself. The
result was that, while they regarded a number of
their ancient champions as the main bulwark of
their fortunes, they felt they had gained something of the sort in myself as well. Thus it is that
now, plundered and despoiled, they have all, repeatedly and officially, approached me, to get me to

nium causam defensionemque susciperem. Me saepe
esse pollicitum, saepe ostendisse dicebant, si quod
tempus accidisset quo tempore aliquid a me require-
3 rent, commodis eorum me non defuturum. Venisse
tempus aiebant, non iam ut commoda sua, sed ut
vitam salutemque totius provinciae defenderem : sese
iam ne deos quidem in suis urbibus ad quos con-
fugerent habere, quod eorum simulacra sanctissima
C. Verres ex delubris religiosissimis sustulisset : quas
res luxuries in flagitiis, crudelitas in suppliciis, avaritia
in rapinis, superbia in contumeliis efficere potuisset,
eas omnes sese hoc uno praetore per triennium
pertulisse : rogare et orare ne illos supplices asper-
narer quos me incolumi nemini supplices esse
oporteret.
4   II. Tuli graviter et acerbe, iudices, in eum me
locum adduci ut aut eos homines spes falleret qui
opem a me atque auxilium petissent, aut ego, qui me
ad defendendos homines ab ineunte adulescentia de-
dissem, tempore atque officio coactus ad accusandum
traducerer. Dicebam habere eos actorem Q. Caecilium, qui praesertim quaestor in eadem provincia post
me quaestorem fuisset. Quo ego adiumento sperabam hanc a me posse molestiam demoveri, id mihi
erat adversarium maxime ; nam illi multo mihi hoc
facilius remisissent, si istum non nossent, aut si iste
5 apud eos quaestor non fuisset. Adductus sum,
iudices, officio, fide, misericordia, multorum bonorum

4

undertake the cause of defending their common fortunes. They have been telling me that I made
many professions and promises not to fail to forward
their interests, if the time should ever come when
they needed me. They have declared that now the 3
time has come for me, not merely to forward their
interests, but to stand up for the life and existence
of the whole province : that now they have not even
the gods left in their cities to fly to for protection,
since Verres has carried off the holy images of the
gods from their most sacred shrines. During the
three years in which this man has been their praetor,
they have endured, they say, every outrage and
torture, every spoliation and disgrace, that vice,
cruelty, greed, and insolence could inflict. And they
pray and beseech me not to spurn the appeal for help
of men who, so long as I am alive, should have no
need to appeal for help to anyone.

II. I found myself thrust into a painfully un- 4
comfortable position, gentlemen. Either I must
disappoint these people who had come to me for
help and succour, or circumstances were forcing
upon me the duty of turning prosecutor, after having
given myself from my earliest youth to the task of
defending the prosecuted. I told them that they
could get Caecilius to manage their case, and that
he had the advantage of having served as quaestor
in the province. That fact, which I had been hoping
would help me out of an annoying situation, really
told against me more than anything else : the Sicilians
would have been far readier to let me off if they
had known nothing of Caecilius, or if he had not
served as quaestor among them. Duty, honour, 5
feelings of pity, the noble example of many others,

exemplo, vetere consuetudine institutoque maiorum,
ut onus hoc laboris atque officii non ex meo sed ex
meorum necessariorum tempore mihi suscipiendum
putarem.

Quo in negotio tamen illa me res, iudices, consolatur, quod haec quae videtur esse accusatio mea
non potius accusatio, quam defensio est existimanda.
Defendo enim multos mortales, multas civitates, provinciam Siciliam totam. Quam ob rem, quia mihi
unus est accusandus, prope modum manere in instituto meo videor, et non omnino a defendendis
hominibus sublevandisque discedere.

6 Quodsi hanc causam tam idoneam, tam illustrem,
tam gravem non haberem ; si aut hoc a me Siculi
non petissent aut mihi cum Siculis causa tantae necessitudinis non intercederet, et hoc quod facio me
reipublicae causa facere profiterer—ut homo singulari
cupiditate, audacia, scelere praeditus, cuius furta
atque flagitia non in Sicilia solum, sed in Achaia,
Asia, Cilicia, Pamphylia, Romae denique ante oculos
omnium maxima turpissimaque nossemus, me agente
in iudicium vocaretur—quis tandem esset qui meum
consilium aut factum posset reprehendere ? III.

7 Quid est, pro deum hominumque fidem, in quo ego
reipublicae plus hoc tempore prodesse possim ? Quid
est quod aut populo Romano gratius esse debeat, aut
sociis exterisque nationibus optatius esse possit, aut

and the established traditional practice of our ancestors—all these, gentlemen, forced me to the same conclusion. Not in my own interests, but in those of my friends, I was bound to shoulder this heavy and toilsome task.

At the same time, this business brings me one consolation. In form, it is an act of prosecution: but it may fairly be regarded as equally an act of defence. I am, in fact, defending a number of individuals, and a number of communities ; I am defending the entire province of Sicily ; and therefore, in prosecuting only one single man, I feel that I am almost remaining true to my established custom —that I am not wholly abandoning my mission as rescuer and helper.

But suppose it otherwise. Suppose the reasons 6 for my action less suitable, less creditable, and less cogent than in fact they are. Suppose that the Sicilians had not made this request to me, or that I were not affected by the strong tie of friendship that binds me to them. Suppose that I were to say that what I am doing I do for the sake of my country. Here is a human monster of unparalleled greed, impudence, and wickedness. We know the vast scale of his vile robberies and outrages—not merely in Sicily, but in Achaia and Asia and Cilicia and Pamphylia, and even in Rome before the eyes of us all. If I bring this man to judgement, who can find fault with me for doing this, or with my purpose in doing it ? III. Tell me, in the name of all that is just 7 and holy, what better service I can do my country at this present time. Nothing should be more acceptable to the people of this country. Nothing can be more eagerly desired by our allies and by foreign

saluti fortunisque omnium magis accommodatum sit ?
Populatae, vexatae, funditus eversae provinciae :
socii stipendiariique populi Romani afflicti, miseri,
iam non salutis spem sed exitii solatium quaerunt.
8 Qui iudicia manere apud ordinem senatorium volunt
queruntur accusatores se idoneos non habere ; qui
accusare possunt iudiciorum severitatem desiderant.
Populus Romanus interea, tametsi multis incommodis
difficultatibusque affectus est, tamen nihil aeque in
republica atque illam veterem iudiciorum vim gravi-
tatemque requirit. Iudiciorum desiderio tribunicia
potestas efflagitata est ; iudiciorum levitate ordo
quoque alius ad res iudicandas postulatur ; iudicum
culpa atque dedecore etiam censorium nomen, quod
asperius antea populo videri solebat. id nunc poscitur,
9 id iam populare atque plausibile factum est. In hac
libidine hominum nocentissimorum, in populi Romani
cotidiana querimonia, iudiciorum infamia, totius
ordinis offensione, cum hoc unum his tot incommodis
remedium esse arbitrarer, ut homines idonei atque
integri causam reipublicae legumque susciperent,

8

nations. Nothing is likely to contribute more to
the general safety and prosperity of us all. Our
provinces have been ravaged and plundered and
utterly ruined ; the allies and dependents of the
Roman nation have been brought down to the
lowest pitch of wretchedness ; they no longer enter-
tain any hope of deliverance, and are only looking for
some comfort in the midst of calamity. Those who 8
are anxious to see our courts of law still reserved
for the senatorial order are complaining that they
cannot get the right men to act as prosecutors.
Those who might act as prosecutors look in vain to
see strict justice done in our courts of law. The
people of this country meanwhile have been visited
with many hardships and many disabilities : yet in
all the national life there is nothing whose loss they
feel so much as the energy and sense of responsibility that our law-courts showed in times gone by.
It is because they feel the lack of such courts that
the agitation arose for restoring the tribunes' powers.
It is the untrustworthiness of our courts that has
excited the further demand for another class of
citizens to serve on them. It is through the disgraceful conduct of our judges that the censorship,
which in former times was seldom popular, is now
being clamoured for, and has already come to be
held an excellent and democratic institution. When 9
criminals of the worst sort can now do what they
like ; when day by day we hear expressions of
popular discontent ; when the law-courts are dis-
graced, and the whole senatorial order detested : for
all this evil state of things, there is, I have been
feeling, only one possible remedy—capable and
honest men must take up the cause of their country

fateor me salutis omnium causa ad eam partem accessisse reipublicae sublevandae quae maxime laboraret.

10   Nunc, quoniam quibus rebus adductus ad causam accesserim demonstravi, dicendum necessario est de contentione nostra, ut in constituendo accusatore quid sequi possitis habeatis. Ego sic intellego, iudices : cum de pecuniis repetundis nomen cuiuspiam deferatur, si certamen inter aliquos sit cui potissimum delatio detur, haec duo in primis spectari oportere : quem maxime velint actorem esse ii quibus factae esse dicantur iniuriae, et quem minime velit is qui 11 eas iniurias fecisse arguatur. IV. In hac causa, iudices, tametsi utrumque esse arbitror perspicuum, tamen de utroque dicam, et de eo prius quod apud vos plurimum debet valere, hoc est de voluntate eorum quibus iniuriae factae sunt, quorum causa iudicium de pecuniis repetundis est constitutum.

Siciliam provinciam C. Verres per triennium depopulatus esse, Siculorum civitates vastasse, domos exinanisse, fana spoliasse dicitur. Adsunt, queruntur Siculi universi ; ad meam fidem, quam habent spectatam iam et diu cognitam, confugiunt ; auxilium sibi per me a vobis atque a populi Romani legibus petunt ; me defensorem calamitatum suarum, me

10

and their country's laws. And therefore I will admit that it is the safety of the whole country that has brought me forward to help her where she most needs help.

Having now explained the motives that led me to 10 ome for ward in this case, I am bound to deal with the contest between Caecilius and myself, so as to give you something to go upon in your choice of prosecutor. The way in which I understand the matter, gentlemen, is this. When anyone is to be prosecuted for extortion, there are two main considerations to be borne in mind, if there is any competition for the right to prosecute. Whom do the sufferers by the alleged injustice most desire to have conducting their case for them ? And whom does the alleged doer of the injustice desire least ? IV. In the case before us, gentlemen, the answer to 11 each of these questions seems to me obvious. However, I will deal with each of them : and I will deal first with that one which you are bound to regard as the more important of the two, I mean the wishes of those to whom the injustice has been done, those, in fact, for whose benefit this Extortion Court has been appointed.

The charge against Gaius Verres is that during a period of three years he has laid waste the province of Sicily : that he has plundered Sicilian communities, stripped bare Sicilian homes, and pillaged Sicilian temples. Here before you, here with their tale of wrong, stand the whole Sicilian people. I am the man to whose honour, having proved it in the past and not found it wanting, they now fly for refuge. Through me are they seeking help from you and from the law of Rome. It is I, I and no other, whom

11

ultorem iniuriarum, me cognitorem iuris sui, me
12 actorem causae totius esse voluerunt. Utrum, Q.
Caecili, hoc dices, me non Siculorum rogatu ad causam
accedere ? an optimorum fidelissimorumque sociorum
voluntatem apud hos gravem esse non oportere ? Si
id audebis dicere quod C. Verres, cui te inimicum esse
simulas, maxime existimari vult, Siculos hoc a me non
petisse, primum causam inimici tui sublevabis, de quo
non praeiudicium sed plane iudicium iam factum
putatur, quod ita percrebruit, Siculos omnes actorem
13 suae causae contra illius iniurias quaesisse. Hoc si
tu, inimicus eius, factum negabis, quod ipse cui
maxime haec res obstat negare non audet, videto ne
nimium familiariter inimicitias exercere videare.
Deinde sunt testes viri clarissimi nostrae civitatis,
quos omnes a me nominari non est necesse : eos qui
adsunt appellabo, quos, si mentirer, testes esse impudentiae meae minime vellem. Scit is qui est in
consilio, C. Marcellus, scit is quem adesse video,
Cn. Lentulus Marcellinus ; quorum fide atque praesidio Siculi maxime nituntur, quod omnino Marcel-
14 lorum nomini tota illa provincia adiuncta est. Hi
sciunt hoc non modo a me petitum esse, sed ita
saepe et ita vehementer esse petitum ut aut causa
mihi suscipienda fuerit aut officium necessitudinis

they have chosen to protect them in their calamities and avenge their wrongs, to champion their rights and manage their case throughout. Will you assert, 12 Caecilius, that it is not at the request of the Sicilians that I come forward in this case ? Or that this court need pay no serious attention to the wishes of these good and loyal allies of ours ? If you dare to assert that the Sicilians have not asked me to come forward—a thing which your pretended enemy Verres would particularly like us to believe—then the first thing I have to say is that you will be backing up your enemy's case. It is just this widely-known fact, that all the Sicilians *have* been looking for someone to maintain their cause against his outrages, which makes people feel that not only a preliminary but a definite and final verdict has already been given against him. Now, heavily as this fact tells 13 against him, he dares not deny it : and if you, his enemy, do deny it, I am afraid people will think you treat your enemies in rather too friendly a fashion. In the next place, the truth of the fact is confirmed by some of the leading men in the country. I need not name them all : I will appeal to those who are present in court, since if I were lying I should not like to have them exposing my impudence. The fact is known to C. Marcellus, who is here as a member of the court, and to Cn. Lentulus Marcellinus, who I see is also present. These are men in whose honour the Sicilians particularly trust for protection, since Sicily as a whole is closely connected in all respects with their family. They are aware that 14 this request has not only been made to me, but made so often, and so earnestly, that I had either to take up the case or to disown the obligations of

repudiandum. Sed quid ego his testibus utor, quasi
res dubia aut obscura sit ? Adsunt homines ex tota
provincia nobilissimi, qui praesentes vos orant atque
obsecrant, iudices, ut in actore causae suae deligendo
vestrum iudicium ab suo iudicio ne discrepet. Omnium civitatum totius Siciliae legationes adsunt
praeter duas civitates ; quarum duarum si adessent,
duo crimina vel maxima minuerentur quae cum his
15 civitatibus C. Verri communicata sunt. At enim cur
a me potissimum hoc praesidium petiverunt ? Si
esset dubium petissent a me praesidium necne,
dicerem cur petissent. Nunc vero, cum id ita perspicuum sit ut oculis iudicare possitis, nescio cur hoc
mihi detrimento esse debeat, si id mihi obiciatur, me
16 potissimum esse delectum. Verum id mihi non sumo,
iudices, et hoc non modo in oratione mea non pono,
sed ne in opinione quidem cuiusquam relinquo, me
omnibus patronis esse praepositum. Non ita est ;
sed unius cuiusque temporis, valetudinis, facultatis
ad agendum ducta ratio est. Mea fuit semper haec
in hac re voluntas et sententia, quemvis ut hoc
mallem de iis qui essent idonei suscipere quam me,
me ut mallem, quam neminem.
17 V. Reliquum est iam ut illud quaeramus, cum hoc
constet, Siculos a me petisse, ecquid hanc rem apud

ᵃ These two cities (Messana and Syracuse) have not kept
away because they object to Cicero as their champion, but
because, if they did appear, though they would no doubt help
thereby to establish their own innocence, they would also
help to establish that of Verres, and they care more for
revenge on him than for their own good name.

ᵇ *obiciatur* is ironical, like Pitt's " atrocious crime of being
a young man."

friendship. Yet after all, I need not appeal to their
testimony as though the fact itself could be challenged or misunderstood. Men of high rank, who
have come here from every part of the province,
stand before you, gentlemen, to beg and pray that
when you choose the man to manage their case
for them, there may be no variance between your
judgement and their own. Deputations are present
from every community in Sicily except two : and had
they come from these two also, it would but mitigate
the force of two extremely serious charges against
Verres, relating to matters in which he has made
these two communities his accomplices.[a] It may 15
be asked why they have petitioned me, of all people,
for this protection. Well, if there were any doubt
whatever about the fact, I should be ready to tell
you the reason for the fact. But the fact, as your
own eyes can tell you, being perfectly obvious, I
cannot see how the charge [b] of having been specially
chosen can properly be held to tell against my
claim. However, I do not venture to pretend that 16
they have thought me a better man than any of
their other supporters ; I will not say so in this
speech, and I will not even allow anyone to think
so, for it is not true. But with each of these others
they have had to consider whether it would suit
him, whether his health would allow him, and whether
he was really able, to act for them. What I have
all along felt and wished about the case is just this :
I would rather that any suitable person undertook
the case instead of me, but I would prefer myself
to nobody at all.

V. There is, then, no doubt that the Sicilians have 17
appealed to me, and we have only to ask how far

vos animosque vestros valere oporteat, ecquid auctoritatis apud vos in suo iure repetundo socii populi
Romani, supplices vestri, habere debeant. De quo
quid ego plura commemorem ? Quasi vero dubium
sit quin tota lex de pecuniis repetundis sociorum
18 causa constituta sit. Nam civibus cum sunt ereptae
pecuniae, civili fere actione et privato iure repetuntur. Haec lex socialis est ; hoc ius nationum
exterarum est ; hanc habent arcem, minus aliquanto
nunc quidem munitam quam antea, verum tamen si qua
reliqua spes est quae sociorum animos consolari possit,
ea tota in hac lege posita est. Cuius legis non modo
a populo Romano, sed etiam ab ultimis nationibus,
19 iampridem severi custodes requiruntur. Quis ergo
est qui neget oportere eorum arbitratu lege agi
quorum causa lex sit constituta ? Sicilia tota si una
voce loqueretur, hoc diceret : " Quod auri, quod
argenti, quod ornamentorum in meis urbibus, sedibus,
delubris fuit, quod in una quaque re beneficio
senatus populique Romani iuris habui, id mihi tu,
C. Verres, eripuisti atque abstulisti ; quo nomine abs
te sestertium milliens ex lege repeto." Si universa,
ut dixi, provincia loqui posset, hac voce uteretur ;
quoniam id non poterat, harum rerum actorem quem
20 idoneum esse arbitrata est ipsa delegit. In eius modi
re quisquam tam impudens reperietur, qui ad alienam

16

this fact should influence you, and how far you are
bound to consider the views of these allies of Rome,
who come to you humbly seeking redress for their
wrongs. About this I need surely say very little.
There is of course no question that the whole Extortion Law was framed for the benefit of our allies.
For when our own citizens are robbed of their 18
money, they can usually bring *civil* actions to recover
it, in accordance with the *civil* law. *This* law is for
our allies. This is the foreigners' charter of rights.
This is their strong tower ; somewhat less strong
now, certainly, than it once was ; but still, if our
allies have any hope left with which to comfort their
sad hearts, it must all rest on this law alone. Not
the people of Rome only, but the most distant
nations of the earth, look to find men who shall
maintain this law in all its strictness ; and they
have long been looking in vain. Then can anyone 19
deny that those for whose benefit the law was made
should be able to choose the method of procedure
under it ? Could all Sicily speak with a single voice,
this is what she would say : " All the gold, all the
silver, all the beautiful things that once were in my
cities, houses, and temples : all the various privileges
of which, by the favour of the Roman senate and
people, I was once possessed : all these things you,
Verres, have plundered and stolen from me : and on
this account I sue you in accordance with the law
for the sum of one million pounds." These, as I
say, are the words all Sicily would utter, if she
could speak with a single voice : and as she cannot,
she has chosen the man whom she herself thinks the
right man to conduct her case for her. When such 20
is the issue, what incredible impudence, that a man

17

causam, invitis iis quorum negotium est, accedere aut
aspirare audeat? VI. Si tibi, Q. Caecili, hoc Siculi
dicerent: " Te non novimus, nescimus qui sis, numquam te antea vidimus; sine nos per eum nostras
fortunas defendere cuius fides est nobis cognita ":
nonne id dicerent quod cuivis probare deberent? Nunc
hoc dicunt, utrumque se nosse, alterum se cupere defensorem esse fortunarum suarum, alterum plane nolle.

21 Cur nolint, etiamsi tacent, satis dicunt; verum non
tacent: tamen his invitissimis te offeres? tamen in
aliena causa loquere? tamen eos defendes qui se ab
omnibus desertos potius quam abs te defensos esse
malunt? tamen iis operam tuam pollicebere qui te
neque velle sua causa nec, si cupias, posse arbitrantur? Cur eorum spem exiguam reliquarum fortunarum, quam habent in legis et in iudicii severitate
positam, vi extorquere conaris? cur te interponis
invitissimis iis quibus maxime lex consultum esse
vult? cur, de quibus in provincia non optime es
meritus, eos nunc plane fortunis omnibus conaris
evertere? cur iis non modo persequendi iuris sui, sed
etiam deplorandae calamitatis, adimis potestatem?

22 Nam te actore quem eorum adfuturum putas, quos

18

should dare to undertake or hope to undertake the cause of other people, when those others, those whose interests are concerned, will not have him ! VI. Suppose the Sicilians were saying to you, Caecilius, " We have no knowledge of you, we do not know who you are, we have never seen you before to-day. Allow us to defend our fortunes by means of a man whose good faith we have learned to trust." They would only be saying, surely, what everyone would have to recognize as just. What they actually are saying is that they know both of us, and that they are eager to have one of us to champion their interests, and will not have the other at all. *Why* 21 they will not have the other they let us know plainly ; their silence would be enough, but they are not silent. In spite of this, will you thrust yourself on them against their will ? In spite of this, will you plead in a cause that does not concern you? Defend people who would rather be abandoned by everyone than defended by you ? And promise your assistance to people who believe that you neither desire to serve them nor could serve them if you would ? Why do you seek to tear away from them the slender hope of future happiness that they still have, founded on the strictness of the law and those who administer the law ? Why do you force yourself in, against all the wishes of those whose wishes the law is particularly anxious to consider ? Why, after doing none too well by them as an official among them, do you now seek to achieve nothing less than their utter ruin ? Why would you make it impossible for them not only to work for their rights but even to lament their wrongs ? You 22 must know that if you take charge of their case not

19

intellegis non ut per te alium sed ut per aliquem te
ipsum ulciscantur laborare ?

VII. At enim solum id est, ut me Siculi maxime
velint : alterum illud, credo, obscurum est, a quo
Verres minime se accusari velit. Ecquis umquam
tam palam de honore, tam vehementer de salute sua
contendit quam ille atque illius amici ne haec mihi
delatio detur ? Sunt multa quae Verres in me esse
arbitratur, quae scit in te, Q. Caecili, non esse ;
quae cuius modi in utroque nostrum sint paulo post
23 commemorabo ; nunc tantum id dicam quod tacitus
tu mihi assentiare, nullam rem in me esse quam ille
contemnat, nullam in te quam pertimescat. Itaque
magnus ille defensor et amicus eius tibi suffragatur,
me oppugnat ; aperte ab iudicibus petit ut tu mihi
anteponare, et ait hoc se honeste sine ulla invidia ac
sine ulla offensione contendere. " Non enim " inquit
" illud peto quod soleo, cum vehementius contendi,
impetrare ; reus ut absolvatur non peto, sed ut
potius ab hoc quam ab illo accusetur, id peto. Da
mihi hoc ; concede quod facile est, quod honestum,
quod non invidiosum ; quod cum dederis, sine ullo

---

^a In §§ 30-33 Cicero gives some details of the conduct of
Caecilius in Sicily that go to prove his having been the accomplice of Verres in Sicily.

^b *i.e.*, Caecilius, even unheard, is not an impressive person :
let him reveal his incompetence by speaking, and Cicero's
judgement will be further confirmed.

^c The singular number is used, to suggest that Hortensius
is appealing to each member of the court individually.

one of them will appear in it. You must know that
they are anxious not to use you to be revenged on
someone else, but to use someone to be revenged
on you.[a]

VII. Well, but this, you may argue, says only that
I am the man whom the Sicilians most wish to have
as prosecutor. The other point is, By whom does
Verres particularly wish *not* to be prosecuted ? That
no doubt is a very hard point to settle ! Did any
man ever struggle so openly and so savagely to win
an election, or to save his own life, as Verres and
his friends have struggled to prevent the assignment
of this prosecution to me ? Verres believes me,
Caecilius, to possess many qualities that he knows
well you do not possess. As to how we are both
qualified in these respects, I shall have something
to say a little later ; for the moment I will merely 23
say—and you may support me in this without opening your lips [b]—that there is nothing in me that
Verres can afford to despise, and nothing in you
to make him feel very anxious. That is why his
great friend and defender is canvassing on your
behalf and working against me. He is openly asking
the court to give you the preference over me. It is
a perfectly proper request to make, he says, and it
can involve nobody in any unpopularity or dislike.
" I am not asking," he says, " for what I do usually
get if I exert myself more than usual to get it. I
am not asking that the accused should be acquitted ;
I am simply asking that one of two men, and not
the other, should be his prosecutor. Allow [c] me
this ; make me a simple and justifiable concession
which nobody will blame you for making ; and by
so doing you will at the same time be allowing me,

tuo periculo, sine infamia illud dederis, ut is absolva-
24 tur cuius ego causa laboro." Et ait idem, ut aliquis
metus adiunctus sit ad gratiam, certos esse in consilio quibus ostendi tabellas velit (id esse perfacile) ;
non enim singulos ferre sententias, sed universos
constituere : ceratam uni cuique tabellam dari cera
legitima, non illa infami ac nefaria. Atque is non
tam propter Verrem laborat quam quod eum minime
res tota delectat. Videt enim, si a pueris nobilibus,
quos adhuc elusit, si a quadruplatoribus, quos non
sine causa contempsit semper ac pro nihilo putavit,
accusandi voluntas ad viros fortes spectatosque
homines translata sit, sese in iudiciis diutius dominari
non posse.

25 VIII. Huic ego homini iam ante denuntio, si a me
causam hanc vos agi volueritis, rationem illi defen-
dendi totam esse mutandam ; et ita mutandam ut,
meliore et honestiore conditione quam qua ipse esse
vult, imitetur homines eos quos ipse vidit amplissimos,
L. Crassum et M. Antonium, qui nihil se arbitrabantur ad iudicia causasque amicorum praeter fidem
et ingenium adferre oportere. Nihil erit quod me

---

[a] Two precautions (to ensure secrecy of ballot) which
Hortensius bids those judges whom he has bribed, or in-
timidated, to nullify by showing their tablets to his agents
among them.

[b] *Cf.* i § 40.

[c] The tablets will be all alike, without distinguishing
marks or colours on the wax.

without incurring any risk or discredit yourself, to secure the acquittal of the gentleman in whose behalf I am working." At the same time, he appeals 24 in some measure to your fears as well as to your kindness. There are, he tells you, certain members of the court to whom he wishes the voting-tablets to be shown (as can quite easily be done), because the votes are to be recorded not one by one but simultaneously,[a] and moreover each voter is receiving a tablet waxed properly, as the law requires,[b] and not in the scandalous and shocking way that you may remember.[c] Not that he is so very deeply concerned on Verres' account; it is rather that he dislikes the whole turn affairs are taking. Hitherto some of the prosecutors have been boys of good social standing: and these he has been able to outwit. Others have been mere profit-hunters : and these, with good reason, he has always despised and neglected. He now sees that courageous men, persons of established reputation, are willing to prosecute : and he is aware, that if this change takes place, his own supremacy in the courts will be at an end.

VIII. I give this gentleman fair warning well be- 25 forehand, that, if you decide that I am to conduct this case, he will have to make a radical change in his methods of defence. He will find himself forced into a sounder and more respectable position than he at all desires to take up. He will have to follow the example of eminent men like L. Crassus and M. Antonius, whom he once knew : men who did not hold themselves justified in bringing into court any means of helping their friends except their own honesty and talent. If *I* conduct the case, he will

agente arbitretur iudicium sine magno multorum
26 periculo posse corrumpi. Ego in hoc iudicio mihi
Siculorum causam receptam, populi Romani susceptam esse arbitror ; ut mihi non unus homo improbus
opprimendus sit, id quod Siculi petiverunt, sed
omnino omnis improbitas, id quod populus Romanus
iamdiu flagitat, exstinguenda atque delenda sit. In
quo ego quid eniti aut quid efficere possim malo in
aliorum spe relinquere quam in oratione mea ponere.
27 Tu vero Caecili, quid potes ? Quo tempore aut
qua in re non modo specimen ceteris aliquod dedisti,
sed tute tui periculum fecisti ? In mentem tibi non
venit quid negotii sit causam publicam sustinere,
vitam alterius totam explicare, atque eam non modo
in animis iudicum sed etiam in oculis conspectuque
omnium exponere, sociorum salutem, commoda provinciarum, vim legum, gravitatem iudiciorum defendere ? IX. Cognosce ex me, quoniam hoc primum
tempus discendi nactus es, quam multa esse oporteat
in eo qui alterum accuset ; ex quibus si unum aliquod
in te cognoveris, ego iam tibi ipse istuc quod expetis
mea voluntate concedam.

Primum integritatem atque innocentiam singu-

have no reason to think that the court can be bribed
without serious danger to a large number of people.
I, feeling that in this trial I have, certainly, con- 26
sented to undertake the cause of the Sicilians, but
have also chosen to undertake the cause of the
Roman nation—I have not only to do what the
Sicilians ask of me, not only to crush one particular
rascal, but also to do what the people of this country
has long been demanding should be done—I have to
extinguish and exterminate all rascality of every
kind. How far I can succeed, how far I can achieve
this end, I will rather leave to the hopes of others
than declare with my own lips.

And now, Caecilius, I ask what *you* can possibly 27
do. When or where have you done anything to
make other people believe in you, or even tested
yourself on your own account? It has probably
never occurred to you what it means to bear on
your shoulders the whole weight of a criminal trial.
You must set forth in detail the whole history of
another man's life. You must not only make it clear
to the understanding of the court : you must draw
the picture so vividly that the whole of the audience
can see it with their own eyes. You have to maintain the security of our allies and the prosperity of
our dominions, the efficacy of our laws and the
authority of our law-courts. IX. Let me instruct
you, this being your first opportunity of gaining
such instruction, as to the many qualifications a
prosecutor must possess : and if you find that you
possess any single one of them, you may have what
you are seeking, for I shall be willing to withdraw
in your favour.

First, a prosecutor must possess a particularly

larem ; nihil est enim quod minus ferendum sit quam
rationem ab altero vitae reposcere eum qui non possit
28 suae reddere.   Hic ego de te plura non dicam ; unum
illud credo omnes animadvertere, te adhuc a nullis
nisi ab Siculis potuisse cognosci ; Siculos hoc dicere,
cum eidem sint irati cui tu te inimicum esse dicis, sese
tamen te actore ad iudicium non adfuturos.   Quare
negent ex me non audies ; hos patere id suspicari
quod necesse est.   Illi quidem, ut est hominum genus
nimis acutum et suspiciosum, non te ex Sicilia litteras
in Verrem deportare velle arbitrantur, sed, quod
isdem litteris illius praetura et tua quaestura con-
signata sit, asportare te velle ex Sicilia litteras
suspicantur.

29   Deinde accusatorem firmum verumque esse oportet.
Eum ego si te putem cupere esse, facile intellego esse
non posse.   Nec ea dico quae, si dicam, tamen infirmare non possis : te antequam de Sicilia decesseris
in gratiam redisse cum Verre : Potamonem, scribam
et familiarem tuum, retentum esse a Verre in provincia cum tu decederes : M. Caecilium, fratrem
tuum, lectissimum atque ornatissimum adulescentem,
non modo non adesse neque tecum tuas iniurias
persequi, sed esse cum Verre et cum illo familiaris-

upright and blameless personal character ; nothing
could be more intolerable than that a man whose
own conduct will not stand criticism should proceed
to criticize the conduct of someone else. I will not 28
say much about you in this connexion ; but there is
one fact that I imagine nobody has failed to notice.
The Sicilians are the only people who have hitherto
had the opportunity of knowing much about you ;
and although the hostility of the Sicilians is directed
against the man whose enemy you profess yourself
to be, yet what they say is that, if you are to conduct the case, they will not appear at the trial.
Why they say so you shall not be told by me ; let
these gentlemen surmise what they cannot help
surmising. The opinion of the Sicilians, certainly,
is not that you are anxious to procure from their
country documentary evidence against Verres. They
are an unduly shrewd and suspicious race : and what
they suspect is that you are anxious to get certain
documents safely out of Sicily that contain, under
one and the same seal, evidence not only about
Verres' praetorship but about your quaestorship also.

In the next place, a prosecutor must show firmness 29
and honesty. Even if I thought you were anxious
to show such qualities, it is easy to see that you
cannot. I do not assert certain facts which nevertheless you could not call in question if I did. I do
not assert that before you left Sicily you made
friends with Verres again : nor that your secretary
and intimate friend Potamo was retained in Sicily
by Verres when you left it : nor that your accomplished and brilliant young brother Marcus has not
only failed to come here with you and help you to
avenge your wrongs, but is actually in Verres' com-

sime atque amicissime vivere. Sunt et haec et alia
in te falsi accusatoris signa permulta, quibus ego nunc
non utor ; hoc dico, te, si maxime cupias, tamen
30 verum accusatorem esse non posse. Video enim
permulta esse crimina quorum tibi societas cum Verre
eius modi est ut ea in accusando attingere non audeas

X. Queritur Sicilia tota C. Verrem ab aratoribus,
cum frumentum sibi in cellam imperavisset et cum
esset tritici modius HS II, pro frumento in modios
singulos duodenos sestertios exegisse. Magnum
crimen, ingens pecunia, furtum impudens, iniuria non
ferenda. Ego hoc uno crimine illum condemnem
31 necesse est : tu, Caecili, quid facies ? Utrum hoc
tantum crimen praetermittes an obicies ? Si obicies,
idne alteri crimini dabis quod eodem tempore in
eadem provincia tu ipse fecisti ? Audebis ita accusare alterum ut quo minus tute condemnere recusare
non possis ? Sin praetermittes, qualis erit tua ista
accusatio, quae domestici periculi metu certissimi et
maximi criminis non modo suspicionem,[1] verum etiam
mentionem ipsam pertimescat ?

32   Emptum est ex senatus consulto frumentum ab
Siculis praetore Verre, pro quo frumento pecunia

---

[1] suspicionem *is the* MS. *reading* : *Peterson emends to*
sponsionem : subscriptionem *and* susceptionem *have also
been suggested.*

pany and associating with him on thoroughly intimate and friendly terms. You display all these marks of the counterfeit prosecutor, and many others besides. But I will make no use of them at present. All I maintain is that, however anxious you might be to be a genuine prosecutor, it is simply impossible for you to be one. For I observe 30 that a great many of the charges against Verres concern matters wherein you have been associated with him in such a way that you dare not refer to them as prosecutor.

X. It is a general complaint of the Sicilians that Verres, having requisitioned corn from the farmers for his private maintenance, exacted 12 sesterces a bushel from them in lieu of the corn, when the value of a bushel of wheat was 2 sesterces. A serious charge ; a huge sum of money ; a shameless theft ; an intolerable wrong. I could not fail to secure his condemnation on this ground alone ; but what will you do about it, Caecilius ? Will you pass over a charge 31 of this importance, or bring it up against him ? If you bring it up, are you prepared to charge another man with the guilt of doing what you have done yourself at the same time and place ? Will you dare to conduct your prosecution of another man in such a way as to leave you no defence against being condemned yourself ? If on the other hand you pass this charge over, what can be your value as a prosecutor ? Serious and well-grounded as the charge is, the personal risk to yourself will deter you not merely from any suggestion of its truth, but even from any allusion to its existence.

Again, during Verres' praetorship a quantity of 32 corn was by decree of the Senate bought from Sicilian

omnis soluta non est. Grave est hoc crimen in
Verrem—grave me agente, te accusante nullum ; eras
enim tu quaestor, pecuniam publicam tu tractabas ;
ex qua, etiamsi cuperet praetor, tamen ne qua de-
ductio fieret magna ex parte tua potestas erat. Huius
quoque igitur criminis te accusante mentio nulla fiet ;
silebitur toto iudicio de maximis et notissimis illius
furtis et iniuriis. Mihi crede, Caecili, non potest in
accusando socios vere defendere is qui cum reo
criminum societate coniunctus est.

33 Mancipes a civitatibus pro frumento pecuniam
exegerunt. Quid ? hoc Verre praetore factum est
solum ? non, sed etiam quaestore Caecilio. Quid
igitur ? daturus es huic crimini quod et potuisti
prohibere ne fieret et debuisti, an totum id relinques ?
Ergo id omnino Verres in iudicio suo non audiet,
quod, cum faciebat, quemadmodum defensurus esset
non reperiebat.

XI. Atque ego haec quae in medio posita sunt
commemoro : sunt alia magis occulta furta, quae ille,
ut istius, credo, animos atque impetus retardaret,
34 benignissime cum quaestore suo communicavit. Haec
tu scis ad me esse delata ; quae si velim proferre,
facile omnes intellegent vobis inter vos non modo

growers : and part of the purchase money has never
been paid. This is a serious charge against Verres—
serious, that is, if I bring it, but nothing at all, if *you*
are to be the prosecutor. For you were his quaestor ;
you handled this public money ; and to a large
extent it was in your power to see that none of it was
withheld, however anxious your praetor might be to
withhold it. Here, then, is another charge, of which,
if *you* prosecute, no mention will be made. Throughout the trial not a word will be said about the most
serious and notorious of Verres' acts of dishonesty
and injustice. Believe me, Caecilius, no man can
honestly defend our allies as a prosecutor if he has
been the ally and accomplice of the person prosecuted.

Further, the corn-contractors have exacted money 33
from various communities instead of corn. Well, it
may be said, has this happened only with Verres as
praetor ? No, to be sure : also with Caecilius as
quaestor. Then, Caecilius, are you likely to include
in the charges against him an offence which you
could have and should have prevented ? Or will
you let it pass altogether ? So then, Verres at his
trial is simply not to hear mentioned a misdeed for
which, at the very time when he was committing it,
he could think of no possible future defence.

XI. Now these facts to which I refer are all such
as have been brought into the light of day. There
are other more secret robberies, in which Verres
has had the kindness to let his quaestor have a
share, no doubt in order to mitigate the violence of
his quaestor's animosity against him. You are aware 34
that these latter have been reported to me. If I
care to expose them, it will at once be made plain to
everyone that your dealings with each other have

voluntatem fuisse coniunctam, sed ne praedam quidem
adhuc esse divisam. Quapropter si tibi indicium
postulas dari quod tecum una fecerit, concedo, si id
lege permittitur ; sin autem de accusatione dicimus,
concedas oportet iis qui nullo suo peccato impediun-
tur quo minus alterius peccata demonstrare possint.
35 Ac vide quantum interfuturum sit inter meam tuam-
que accusationem. Ego etiam quae tu sine Verre
commisisti Verri crimini daturus sum, quod te non
prohibuerit cum summam ipse haberet potestatem :
tu contra ne quae ille quidem fecit obicies, ne qua
ex parte coniunctus cum eo reperiare.

Quid ? illa, Caecili, contemnendane tibi videntur
esse, sine quibus causa sustineri, praesertim tanta,
nullo modo potest ? aliqua facultas agendi, aliqua
dicendi consuetudo, aliqua in foro, iudiciis, legibus
36 aut ratio aut exercitatio ? Intellego quam scopuloso
difficilique in loco verser. Nam cum omnis arrogantia
odiosa est, tum illa ingenii atque eloquentiae multo
molestissima. Quam ob rem nihil dico de meo
ingenio ; neque est quod possim dicere, neque, si
esset, dicerem. Aut enim id mihi satis est quod est
de me opinionis, quidquid est, aut, si id parum est,
ego maius id commemorando facere non possum.

---

[a] *i.e.*, they trusted each other too well for this to be needed.

not only involved a union of hearts, but not even, as
yet, led to a division of plunder.[a] If therefore you
demand the right of giving evidence against him
about the misdeeds in which you have helped him,
I have no objection, if it can legally be done. But
if it is the right of prosecution that we are discussing,
you must really withdraw in favour of those who are
not prevented by their own misconduct from demon-
strating the misconduct of others. Do but note the 35
vast difference there will be between your method
of prosecution and my own. I shall lay to Verres'
account even the wrong things you have done without his help, on the ground that he was in supreme
command and yet did not stop your doing them :
you, on the other hand, will not even charge him with
things he has done himself, for fear of being proved
to be more or less his accomplice.

There are other qualities, Caecilius, which you
may think of small account, but without which no
man can possibly manage any case, and especially
not one of this magnitude. He must have some
little capacity as a pleader ; some little experience
as a speaker ; some little training either in the
principles or in the practice of the Forum, the law-
courts, and the law. I am aware that I am here 36
treading on dangerous and difficult ground. Vanity
of every kind is disagreeable ; but vanity concerning
intellectual and oratorical gifts is far more detestable
than any other kind. I shall therefore say nothing
of my own intellectual capacity. There is nothing
I can say, nor, if there were, would I say it. For
either the powers, be they more or less, with which
I am credited, are sufficient for my purpose ; or, if
they are not, I can make them no greater than they

37 XII. De te, Caecili—iam mehercule hoc extra
hanc contentionem certamenque nostrum familiariter
tecum loquar—tu ipse quem ad modum existimes
vide etiam atque etiam, et tu te collige, et qui sis et
quid facere possis considera. Putasne te posse de
maximis acerbissimisque rebus, cum causam sociorum
fortunasque provinciae, ius populi Romani, gravitatem
iudicii legumque susceperis, tot res tam graves, tam
varias, voce, memoria, consilio, ingenio sustinere ?
38 Putasne te posse quae C. Verres in quaestura, quae
in legatione, quae in praetura, quae Romae, quae in
Italia, quae in Achaia Asia Pamphyliaque peccarit,
ea, quem ad modum locis temporibusque divisa sint,
sic criminibus et oratione distinguere ? Putasne te[1]
posse, id quod in huius modi reo maxime necessarium
est, facere ut quae ille libidinose, quae nefarie, quae
crudeliter fecerit, ea aeque acerba et indigna videantur esse his qui audient atque illis visa sunt qui
39 senserunt ? Magna sunt ea quae dico, mihi crede ;
noli haec contemnere. Dicenda,·demonstranda, ex-
plicanda sunt omnia ; causa non solum exponenda,
sed etiam graviter copioseque agenda est. Per-
ficiendum est, si quid agere aut perficere vis, ut
homines te non solum audiant, verum etiam libenter

---

[1] te *has no good* MS. *authority in this place.*

are by talking about them. XII. But as for you, 37
Caecilius—and I would assure you that I am now going
to speak to you as one friend to another, without
reference to the present competition between us—I
earnestly advise you to examine your own mind.
Recollect yourself. Think of what you are, and of
what you are fit for. This is a formidable and very
painful undertaking, which involves the cause of our
allies and the welfare of our province, the rights of
our own nation, and the authority of our law and
our courts of law. These are not light or simple
matters to take upon you : have you the powers
of voice and memory, have you the intelligence
and the ability to sustain such a burden ? Think 38
of the crimes that Verres has committed as quaestor,
as legate, and as praetor, at Rome and in Italy,
in Achaia and Asia and Pamphylia : do you think
yourself able to charge him with all these, arranging
and distinguishing them properly, according to the
times and places at which they respectively occurred ?
Do you think you can do what is especially necessary
in prosecuting a man on such charges as these—
make all his acts of lust and impiety and cruelty
excite as much pain, and as much indignation, in
those who are told of them here, as they excited in
those who underwent them there ? I assure you, 39
these things of which I tell you are no trifles, and you
must not think of them lightly. You have to mention everything, establish every fact, expound everything in full. You have not merely to state your
case : you have to develop it with impressive wealth
of detail. If you wish to achieve any sort of success,
you must not only make people listen to you : you
must make them listen with pleasure, with eagerness.

studioseque audiant. In quo si te multum natura adiuvaret ; si optimis a pueritia disciplinis atque artibus studuisses, et in his elaborasses ; si litteras Graecas Athenis, non Lilybaei, Latinas Romae, non in Sicilia didicisses : tamen esset magnum tantam causam, tam exspectatam, et diligentia consequi et memoria complecti et oratione exponere et voce ac viribus sustinere.

40 Fortasse dices, " Quid ergo ? haec in te sunt omnia ? " Utinam quidem essent ! verum tamen ut esse possent magno studio mihi a pueritia est elabora- tum. Quodsi ego haec propter magnitudinem rerum ac difficultatem assequi non potui, qui in omni vita nihil aliud egi, quam longe tu te ab his rebus abesse arbitrare, quas non modo antea numquam cogitasti, sed ne nunc quidem cum in eas ingrederis quae et 41 quantae sint suspicari potes ? XIII. Ego, qui, sicut omnes sciunt, in foro iudiciisque ita verser ut eiusdem aetatis aut nemo aut pauci plures causas defenderint, et qui omne tempus quod mihi ab amicorum negotiis datur in his studiis laboribusque consumam, quo paratior ad usum forensem promptiorque esse possim, tamen ita deos mihi velim propitios ut, cum illius temporis mihi venit in mentem quo die citato reo mihi dicendum sit, non solum commoveor animo, sed 42 etiam toto corpore perhorresco. Iam nunc mente et

Even had you the advantage of great natural gifts;
had you from boyhood received the best teaching
and enjoyed an elaborate and thorough education;
had you studied Greek literature at Athens instead of
at Lilybaeum, and Latin at Rome instead of in
Sicily: even so, with a case of such magnitude, a
case that has aroused such wide public interest, it
would be hard to find the industry to master it, the
memory to remember it, the eloquence to set it
forth, and the strength of voice and body to carry it
through.

"Well," you may say, "what if it be so? do you **40**
then possess all these qualities yourself?" Would
that I did, indeed. Still, I have done my best, and
worked hard from my boyhood, in order to acquire
them if I could. And if the task of acquiring them
is so immensely difficult that I, who have devoted my
whole life to the pursuit of them, have nevertheless
failed, you must see how far *you* are from possessing
them—you who have never given them a thought
till now, and have no idea of their nature and scope
even now, when the time has come to use them.
XIII. Everyone knows that my life has centred **41**
round the Forum and the law-courts; that few men,
if any, of my age have defended more cases; that
all the time I can spare from the business of my
friends I spend in the study and hard work that this
profession demands, to make myself fitter and readier
for forensic practice: yet even I so feel the need of
the special favour of heaven, that when I think of
the great day when the accused man is summoned
to appear and I have to make my speech, I am not
merely mentally perturbed but tremble physically
from head to foot. Even now I picture to myself **42**

cogitatione prospicio quae tum studia hominum, qui
concursus futuri sint ; quantam exspectationem magnitudo iudicii sit allatura ; quantam auditorum multitudinem C. Verris infamia concitatura ; quantam
denique audientiam orationi meae improbitas illius
factura sit. Quae cum cogito, iam nunc timeo quidnam pro offensione hominum qui illi inimici infensique
sunt, et exspectatione omnium et magnitudine rerum,
43 dignum eloqui possim. Tu horum nihil metuis, nihil
cogitas, nihil laboras. Si quid ex vetere aliqua
oratione, *Iovem ego optimum maximum* aut *Vellem, si
fieri potuisset, iudices* aut aliquid eiusmodi, ediscere
potueris, praeclare te paratum in iudicium venturum
arbitraris.

44 Ac si tibi nemo responsurus esset, tamen ipsam
causam, ut ego arbitror, demonstrare non posses.
Nunc ne illud quidem cogitas, tibi cum homine
disertissimo et ad dicendum paratissimo, futurum esse
certamen, quicum modo disserendum, modo omni
ratione pugnandum certandumque sit. Cuius ego
ingenium ita laudo ut non pertimescam, ita probo ut
me ab eo delectari facilius quam decipi putem posse.
XIV. Numquam ille me opprimet consilio, numquam
ullo artificio pervertet, numquam ingenio me suo
labefactare atque infirmare conabitur. Novi omnes
hominis petitiones rationesque dicendi ; saepe in
isdem, saepe in contrariis causis versati sumus. Ita

the excitement and the crowds of people, the breathless interest that will be aroused by the importance
of the trial, the vast concourse of hearers which the
evil name of Verres will bring together, the keen
attention which his misconduct will direct to the
speech I make against him. Even now the thought
of all this fills me with dread, and I wonder if I can
possibly make a speech that will satisfy the indignation of those who abhor and detest the man, or that
will be worthy of the expectations of the public and
the greatness of the occasion. *You* have no such 43
fears, no such thoughts, no such anxieties. You
imagine that, if you can learn by heart a phrase
or two out of some old speech, like " I beseech
almighty and most merciful God " or " I could wish,
gentlemen, had it only been possible," you will be
excellently prepared for your entrance into court.

Even if no one were going to reply to you, I 44
cannot believe that you would be able to establish
your own case. But in fact, though it has not occurred
to you, you will have opposed to you an eloquent
and highly-trained speaker, whom you will at one
time have to meet in argument, and at another to
fall upon and attack with every weapon available.
For myself, I can commend his ability without being
terrified by it ; I can admire him, and yet believe it
possible that he will enchant me more easily than
entrap me. XIV. He will never crush me with his
cleverness ; he will never lead me astray by any
display of ingenuity ; he will never employ his great
powers to weaken and dislodge me from my position.
I am well acquainted with all the gentleman's
methods of attack, and all his oratorical devices. We
have often appeared together, on the same side or on

39

contra me ille dicet, quamvis sit ingeniosus, ut nonnullum etiam de suo ingenio iudicium fieri arbitretur.

45 Te vero, Caecili, quem ad modum sit elusurus, quam
omni ratione iactaturus, videre iam videor ; quotiens
ille tibi potestatem optionemque facturus sit ut eligas
utrum velis, factum esse necne, verum esse an falsum :
utrum dixeris, id contra te futurum. Qui tibi aestus,
qui error, quae tenebrae, di immortales, erunt
homini minime malo ! Quid cum accusationis tuae
membra dividere coeperit, et in digitis suis singulas
partes causae constituere ? Quid cum unum quid-
que transigere, expedire, absolvere ? Ipse profecto
metuere incipies ne innocenti periculum facessieris.

46 Quid cum commiserari, conqueri et ex illius invidia
deonerare aliquid et in te traicere coeperit ? commemorare quaestoris cum praetore necessitudinem
constitutam, morem maiorum, sortis religionem—
poterisne eius orationis subire invidiam ? Vide modo,
etiam atque etiam considera. Mihi enim videtur
periculum fore ne ille non modo verbis te obruat, sed
gestu ipso ac motu corporis praestringat aciem ingenii tui, teque ab institutis tuis cogitationibusque

47 abducat. Atque huiusce rei iudicium iam continuo

40

opposing sides. However capable he may be, he will feel, when he comes to speak against me, that the trial is among other things a trial of his own capacity. But as for you, Caecilius, I can see already, in my 45 mind's eye, how he will outwit you, and make sport of you in a hundred ways ; how often he will give you the fullest freedom to choose between two alternatives—that a thing has or has not happened, that a statement is true or false ; and how, whichever you choose, your choice will tell against you. Heaven help you, poor innocent, how you will be confused, and distracted, and befogged! Think of it, when he begins to subdivide your speech for the prosecution, and tick off with his fingers the separate sections of your case ! Think of it, when he proceeds to smash them up, and clear them away, and polish them off one after the other ! Upon my word, you will begin to feel alarmed yourself at the thought that you may have set out to bring ruin upon an innocent man. Think of it when he begins to be- 46 wail his client's unhappy condition : to lighten the load of prejudice against Verres, and shift a portion of it on to your own back : to remind us of the close personal tie between a quaestor and his chief, of our national tradition in this matter and the solemn obligation the lot imposes upon them. Can you face the hostility that such arguments will arouse against you ? Take care, take care : consider the danger, I beg and implore you. I cannot help feeling the risk that he will not only beat you down with his arguments, but dazzle and confuse your senses with his mere gestures and bodily movements, till he has made you abandon the whole of your intended line of action. I note, by the way, that we shall almost 47

video futurum. Si enim mihi hodie respondere ad
haec quae dico potueris, si ab isto libro, quem tibi
magister ludi nescio qui ex alienis orationibus com-
positum dedit, verbo uno discesseris, posse te et illi
quoque iudicio non deesse et causae atque officio tuo
satisfacere arbitrabor. Sin mecum in hac prolusione
nihil fueris, quem te in ipsa pugna cum acerrimo
adversario fore putemus ?

XV. Esto ; ipse nihil est, nihil potest : at venit
paratus cum subscriptoribus exercitatis et disertis
Est tamen hoc aliquid, tametsi non est satis ; omnibus
enim rebus is qui princeps in agendo est ornatissimus
et paratissimus esse debet. Verum tamen L. Appu-
leium esse video proximum subscriptorem, hominem
non aetate sed usu forensi atque exercitatione tiro-
48 nem. Deinde, ut opinor, habet T.[1] Alienum, hunc
tamen ab subselliis ; qui quid in dicendo posset, numquam satis attendi ; in clamando quidem video eum
esse bene robustum atque exercitatum. In hoc spes
tuae sunt omnes ; hic, si tu eris actor constitutus,
totum iudicium sustinebit. At ne is quidem tantum
contendet in dicendo quantum potest, sed consulet
laudi et existimationi tuae, et ex eo quod ipse potest
in dicendo aliquantum remittet, ut tu tamen aliquid

---

[1] habet Alienum *MSS.*: *E. F. Eberhard conjectures the loss
of* T., *caused by* habet *preceding.*

---

[a] *Subsellium* may be any seat in a court. Alienus began
his career as a *claqueur.*

immediately be able to settle this question. If you show yourself to-day able to reply to what I am now saying ; if you use one single expression that is not contained in the book of extracts from other people's speeches with which some schoolmaster has presented you : then I will allow it possible that you will not be a failure at the trial too, but do justice to the case and your responsible part in it. But if you come to nothing in this preliminary skirmish with me, how can we expect you to stand up against your furious opponent in the actual battle itself ?

XV. Very well, Caecilius himself is nothing and counts for nothing ; but it is suggested that he comes provided with experienced and eloquent supporters. That is certainly something, though not enough : the man who is in chief charge of a case ought to be thoroughly well prepared and well equipped himself. Still, who are these supporters of his ? Lucius Appuleius, I see, is the first of them : and he, though not young in years, is the rawest beginner so far as forensic training and forensic experience go. The next, I take it, is Titus Alienus ; well, he gets even him from the spectators' seats[a] ; nor have I ever observed at all carefully what his powers as a speaker may be, though I am certainly aware that he is a powerful and well-trained shouter. He is the mainstay of your hopes ; if you are appointed to conduct the case, it is he who will have to bear the full weight of it. And even so, he will not be able to exert his full powers as a speaker. He will have to think of *your* credit and *your* reputation. He will be forgoing some of the success he might achieve by his own speech, in order that you may not, in spite of everything, be a complete failure.

esse videare. Ut in actoribus Graecis fieri videmus,
saepe illum qui est secundarum aut tertiarum partium,
cum possit aliquanto clarius dicere quam ipse pri-
marum, multum summittere, ut ille princeps quam
maxime excellat : sic faciet Alienus ; tibi serviet,
tibi lenocinabitur, minus aliquanto contendet quam
49 potest. Iam hoc considerate, cuius modi accusatores
in tanto iudicio simus habituri, cum et ipse Alienus
ex ea facultate, si quam habet, aliquantum detrac-
turus sit, et Caecilius tum denique se aliquid futurum
putet si Alienus minus vehemens fuerit et sibi primas
in dicendo partes concesserit. Quartum quem sit
habiturus non video, nisi quem forte ex illo grege
moratorum qui subscriptionem sibi postularunt cui-
50 cumque vos delationem dedissetis ; ex quibus alie-
nissimis hominibus ita paratus venis ut tibi hospes
aliquis sit recipiendus. Quibus ego non sum tantum
honorem habiturus ut ad ea quae dixerint certo loco
aut singillatⁱⁿ uni cuique respondeam ; sic breviter,
quoniam non consulto sed casu in eorum mentionem
incidi, quasi praeteriens satisfaciam universis. XVI.
Tantane vobis inopia videor esse amicorum ut mihi
non ex his quos mecum adduxerim, sed de populo,
subscriptor addatur ? vobis autem tanta inopia reorum est ut mihi causam praeripere conemini, potius

44

We know how Greek actors behave on the stage;
very commonly the man who has the second or third
part could speak a good deal more loudly and clearly
than the man who has the first part, but lowers his
voice considerably, in order that the superiority of
the chief actor may be as pronounced as possible.
That is what Alienus will be doing. He will subordinate himself to you, and play up to you, and
exert himself considerably less than he might. Now 49
let me ask this court to consider the sort of prosecutors we are likely to have in this important trial,
if Alienus himself is going to withhold from us a
good part of such capacity as he does possess, and
Caecilius can hope to have any sort of success himself only if Alienus moderates his own energy and
hands over the chief part as orator to *him*. Whom
he is likely to find as fourth speaker I cannot
imagine, unless it is to be one of that gang of ob-
structionists who applied for the right of supporting
the chosen prosecutor whoever he might be : worse 50
aliens than Alienus, but Caecilius comes here in such
a condition that he will have to extend his hospitality
to one of them. I shall not pay them the compliment
of reserving a definite part of my speech in which to
deal with their observations, nor shall I reply to each
of them separately. I had no intention of referring
to them at all, and I have done so quite by accident;
and I shall therefore dispose of them in a few passing
words. XVI. Do they suppose I am so badly off for
friends, that I must be furnished with a supporter
from the street instead of from among the gentlemen whom I have brought here with me ? And are
they so badly off for persons to accuse that they
must try to snatch my own case out of my hands,

quam aliquos ad columnam Maeniam[a] vestri ordinis
reos reperiatis ? " Custodem," inquit, " Tullio me
51 apponite." Quid ? mihi quam multis custodibus
opus erit, si te semel ad meas capsas admisero ? qui
non solum ne quid enunties, sed etiam ne quid
auferas, custodiendus sis. Sed de isto custode toto
sic vobis brevissime respondebo : non esse hos tales
viros commissuros ut ad causam tantam, a me
susceptam, mihi creditam, quisquam subscriptor me
invito aspirare possit ; etenim fides mea custodem
repudiat, diligentia speculatorem reformidat.

52 Verum ut ad te, Caecili, redeam : quam multa te
deficiant vides ; quam multa sint in te quae reus
nocens in accusatore suo cupiat esse profecto iam intellegis. Quid ad haec dici potest ? Non enim quaero
quid tu dicturus sis ; video mihi non te sed hunc
librum esse responsurum, quem monitor tuus hic
tenet : qui, si te recte monere volet, suadebit tibi ut
hinc discedas neque mihi verbum ullum respondeas.
Quid enim dices ? an id quod dictitas, iniuriam tibi
fecisse Verrem ? Arbitror ; neque enim esset veri
simile, cum omnibus Siculis faceret iniurias, te illi
53 unum eximium cui consuleret fuisse. Sed ceteri
Siculi ultorem suarum iniuriarum invenerunt : tu,

---

[a] In the Forum : presumably a lounging-place of the
" lower orders."

instead of finding themselves victims of their own
social standing in the neighbourhood of the Maenian
Column a ? " Set me to keep watch on Tullius,"
says one of them. Upon my word, I shall want a 51
good many people to keep watch, if I ever let *you*
have access to my cupboards. *You* will certainly
want watching, or you will not only let out my
secrets but go off with my property. However, in
answer to these gentlemen's proposal to watch me,
a few words will be enough. This great case has
been undertaken by me and entrusted to me : and
a court of the present character is not likely to
allow anyone to aspire to the honour of assisting
me as prosecutor, unless I am willing to have him :
the fact being that my integrity repudiates the need
for watchers, and my caution warns me against spies.

But to return to yourself, Caecilius. You see how 52
many qualifications you lack : you must certainly
by this time be aware how much you are what any
guilty man would wish his prosecutor to be. Well,
what reply can be made to all this ? Note that I
do not ask what reply *you* are likely to make. I
know well that your reply will not come from you,
but from that book which I see in the hands of your
adviser there, who, if he wants to give you a really
good piece of advice, will insist on your leaving the
court without attempting a single word in reply to
me. For what reply will you make ? Perhaps what
you are always repeating, that Verres has wronged
you. I can well believe that. He has wronged
everyone in Sicily, and it would be too much to
expect that he should make you a special exception
by forwarding your interests. But while the rest of 53
the Sicilians have found themselves a man to avenge

dum tuas iniurias per te, id quod non potes, persequi
conaris, id agis ut ceterorum quoque iniuriae sint
impunitae atque inultae. Et hoc te praeterit, non id
solum spectari solere, qui debeat, sed etiam illud,
qui possit ulcisci ; in quo utrumque sit, eum supe-
riorem esse ; in quo alterutrum,[1] in eo non quid is
54 velit, sed quid facere possit, quaeri solere. Quod si ei
potissimum censes permitti oportere accusandi potestatem cui maximam C. Verres iniuriam fecerit :
utrum tandem censes hoc iudices gravius ferre oportere, te ab illo esse laesum, an provinciam Siciliam
esse vexatam ac perditam ? Opinor, concedes multo
hoc et esse gravius et ab omnibus ferri gravius oportere. Concede igitur ut tibi anteponatur in accusando provincia ; nam provincia accusat, cum is agit
causam quem sibi illa defensorem sui iuris, ultorem
iniuriarum, actorem causae totius adoptavit.

55 XVII. At eam tibi C. Verres fecit iniuriam quae
ceterorum quoque animos posset alieno incommodo
commovere. Minime. Nam id quoque ad rem
pertinere arbitror, qualis iniuria dicatur quae causa
inimicitiarum proferatur. Cognoscite ex me ; nam
iste eam profecto, nisi plane nihil sapit, numquam
proferet. Agonis quaedam est Lilybaetana,[2] liberta

---

[1] alterutrum *Peterson with the best MSS.*: alterum *some
MSS. and most editors.*
[2] *Peterson, with good MS. and archaeological support,
reads* Lilybitana.

their wrongs, you are trying to get satisfaction yourself for your own, a thing which you cannot do, and
in attempting which you are going the right way to
prevent also the infliction of punishment and vengeance for the wrongs of all the others. You forget
that it is usual for people to ask not merely who
should, but also who can, avenge them. The man
who has both qualities is better than any other ; but
if a man has only one of these things, it is usual to
inquire rather what he can do than what he would
like to do. If, however, you really think that the 54
right to prosecute Verres should be conceded to the
greatest sufferer from his wrongdoing, which fact,
after all, do you think should excite the greater
indignation in the minds of this court—that he has
injured you, or that he has ravaged and ruined our
province of Sicily ? You will, I presume, allow that
the latter is the more serious, and deserves to excite,
in every mind, the more serious indignation. You
must therefore also allow the province to have preference over you in the privilege of prosecuting—for
the province it is that prosecutes, when her case is
conducted by the man whom she has definitely
chosen to maintain her rights, to avenge her wrongs,
and to conduct her case throughout.

XVII. You may object that the wrong Verres 55
has done you is serious enough to stir deeply the
feelings of all others, even though it does not touch
them directly. I deny this. It is not, I take it,
beside the point to ask what sort of wrong is alleged
as the reason for a personal enmity. I will therefore
tell the court what the wrong is : for unless Caecilius
is a downright fool he will certainly never allege
it himself. There is a certain woman of Lily-

Veneris Erycinae, quae mulier ante hunc quaestorem
copiosa plane et locuples fuit. Ab hac praefectus
Antonii quidam symphoniacos servos abducebat per
iniuriam, quibus se in classe uti velle dicebat. Tum
illa, ut mos in Sicilia est omnium Veneriorum et
eorum qui a Venere se liberaverunt, ut praefecto illi
religionem Veneris nomine obiceret, dixit et se et
56 sua Veneris esse. Ubi hoc quaestori Caecilio, viro
optimo et homini aequissimo, nuntiatum est, vocari
ad se Agonidem iubet : iudicium dat statim *Si paret
eam se et sua Veneris esse dixisse.* Iudicant recupera-
tores id quod necesse erat ; neque enim erat cuiquam
dubium quin illa dixisset. Iste in possessionem
bonorum mulieris intrat ; ipsam Veneri in servitutem
adiudicat ; deinde bona vendit, pecuniam redigit.
Ita dum pauca mancipia Veneris nomine Agonis ac
religione retinere vult, fortunas omnes libertatemque
suam istius iniuria perdidit. Lilybaeum Verres venit
postea ; rem cognoscit, factum improbat ; cogit
quaestorem suum pecuniam, quam ex Agonidis bonis
redegisset, eam mulieri omnem adnumerare et red-
57 dere. Est adhuc, id quod vos omnes admirari video,
non Verres sed Q. Mucius. Quid enim facere potuit

---

a The father of Mark Antony. He had a general
commission to suppress piracy.

b In these formulae, the apodosis of the *si* clause is
condemnato.

c Or possibly " into the public account."

d Q. Mucius Scaevola, the eminent jurist, proconsular
governor of Asia 94 B.C., where his just rule made his name
a synonym for an upright governor.

baeum, named Agonis, formerly a slave of Venus of Eryx. This woman, in the days before Caecilius was quaestor, had very considerable wealth and property. An admiral serving under Antonius [a] wronged her by carrying off a number of her slave musicians, whom he said he required for service in the navy. She thereupon followed the regular practice of those Sicilians who belong to Venus, or who having belonged to her have since become free. She used the name of Venus to make the admiral afraid of committing sacrilege, and stated that she, and all that belonged to her, were the property of the goddess. When this was reported to Caecilius 56 as quaestor, that excellent man and paragon of justice sent for Agonis, and at once appointed a court with instructions to decide " Whether [b] she was guilty of having said that she and her property were the property of Venus." The members of the court gave the only decision possible : for no one had the least doubt that Agonis had spoken thus. Caecilius took possession of the woman's property, and adjudged the woman herself to be the slave of Venus : then he sold her property, and paid the money he got for it into his account.[c] Thus Agonis, just for using the sacred name of Venus in order to keep possession of a few slaves, was most unjustly deprived by Caecilius of all her property, and of her freedom as well. Later on, Verres arrived at Lilybaeum. He investigated the matter, annulled the judgement, and obliged his quaestor to pay over to Agonis the full sum he had realized by the sale of her property. So far, as I see you all note with sur- 57 prise, Verres is not Verres but a perfect Scaevola.[d] Could he have added more gracefully to his public

elegantius ad hominum existimationem, aequius ad
levandam mulieris calamitatem, vehementius ad
quaestoris libidinem coercendam ? Summe haec
omnia mihi videntur esse laudanda. Sed repente e
vestigio ex homine tamquam aliquo Circaeo poculo
factus est Verres ; redit ad se atque ad mores suos.
Nam ex illa pecunia magnam partem ad se vertit,[1]
mulieri reddidit quantulum visum est.

58   XVIII. Hic tu si laesum te a Verre esse dices,
patiar et concedam : si iniuriam tibi factam quereris,
defendam et negabo. Denique de iniuria quae tibi
facta sit neminem nostrum graviorem vindicem esse
oportet quam te ipsum cui facta dicitur. Si tu cum
illo postea in gratiam redisti, si domi illius aliquotiens
fuisti, si ille apud te postea cenavit, utrum te perfidiosum an praevaricatorem existimari mavis ? Video
esse necesse alterutrum ; sed ego tecum in eo non
59 pugnabo quo minus utrum velis eligas. Quodsi ne
iniuriae quidem quae tibi ab illo facta sit causa
remanet, quid habes quod possis dicere quam ob rem
non modo mihi, sed cuiquam, anteponare ? Nisi forte
illud, quod dicturum te esse audio, quaestorem illius
fuisse. Quae causa gravis esset, si certares mecum
uter nostrum illi amicior esse deberet : in contentione
suscipiendarum inimicitiarum ridiculum est putare
causam necessitudinis ad inferendum periculum ius-

---

[1] *The* MS. *reading* : avertit, verrit, averrit *have been
suggested.*

---

[a] *Verres* means " boar."

reputation, or relieved a poor woman in distress more equitably, or checked his wanton subordinate more energetically? The whole of his actions here seem to deserve the highest commendation. But suddenly, as though he had drunk of Circe's goblet, he turned in one flash from a man into a Verres,[a] became the hog that his name suggests, and resumed his proper character. He appropriated a considerable part of that sum of money, only returning a modest fraction to the woman herself.

XVIII. Now if you maintain that in this matter 58 Verres has injured you, very good; I will allow that. But if you complain that he has done you a wrong, I say no, he has not. And finally, if any wrong has been done you, none of us should resent the matter more gravely than yourself, the alleged sufferer. But if you subsequently made friends with him again, if you visited him several times at his house, if later he dined with you—well, which would you have us consider you, a traitor to your friend or a traitor to justice? One or the other it is plain to me you must be: but I do not propose to argue the point with you—you may choose which alternative you will.

Now if your plea that Verres has wronged you 59 fails as the others have failed, what good reason can you produce for being preferred to me, or indeed to anyone? Possibly one that I am told you do intend to produce, the fact that you were his quaestor. Such a reason would have much force, if the dispute between us were as to which of us was bound to have the more friendly feelings towards him. But we are in fact competing for the right of attacking him as an enemy; and it is absurd to suppose that a good reason for behaving to him as a friend can also be

60 tam videri oportere. Etenim si plurimas a tuo
praetore iniurias accepisses, tamen eas ferendo maiorem laudem quam ulciscendo mererere ; cum vero
nullum illius in vita rectius factum sit quam id quod
tu iniuriam appellas, hi statuent hanc causam, quam
ne in alio quidem probarent, in te iustam ad necessitudinem violandam videri ? Qui si summam iniuriam
ab illo accepisti, tamen, quoniam quaestor eius fuisti,
non potes eum sine ulla vituperatione accusare ; si
vero non ulla tibi facta est iniuria, sine scelere eum
accusare non potes. Quare, cum incertum sit de
iniuria, quemquam esse horum putas qui non malit te
sine vituperatione quam cum scelere discedere ?

61 XIX. Ac vide quid differat inter meam opinionem
ac tuam. Tu cum omnibus rebus inferior sis, hac una
in re te mihi anteferri putas oportere, quod quaestor
illius fueris : ego, si superior ceteris rebus esses, hanc
unam ob causam te accusatorem repudiari putarem
oportere. Sic enim a maioribus nostris accepimus,
praetorem quaestori suo parentis loco esse oportere ;
nullam neque iustiorem neque graviorem causam
necessitudinis posse reperiri quam coniunctionem
sortis, quam provinciae, quam officii, quam publici
62 muneris societatem. Quam ob rem si iure eum posses
accusare, tamen, cum is tibi parentis numero fuisset,

a good reason for attempting to secure his downfall. The truth is that even if your praetor had done you 60 a number of wrongs, you would gain yourself more credit by bearing them patiently than by seeking revenge for them : and since he has, in point of fact, never in all his life behaved better than when he did you what you call a wrong, how can this court hold that a reason which they would not admit valid even for someone else can justify you in being false to a personal obligation ? Even if he has wronged you deeply, yet, having been his quaestor, you cannot prosecute him without incurring some blame : and if he has not wronged you at all, you cannot prosecute him without incurring criminal guilt. Consequently, the alleged wrong not being proved, can you imagine that there is any member of this court who would not rather you came out of the affair free from blame than guilty of a crime ?

XIX. Just think how very differently you and I 61 regard this matter. You, who are worse qualified than myself in all other respects, hold that your claim is better than mine, on the sole ground that you have been Verres' quaestor : I should hold, even if you were better qualified in all other respects, that your claim to prosecute should be rejected on this one ground alone. We have inherited from our ancestors the tradition that a praetor and his quaestor must be like father and son ; that no tie of friendship can be imagined more inevitable and more solemnly binding than their close association in the sphere of duty which the lot assigns them and their intimate connexion as servants of the public. It 62 follows that, as Verres has stood in a parental relation towards you, you could not prosecute him without

id pie facere non posses ; cum vero neque iniuriam
acceperis et praetori tuo periculum crees, fatearis
necesse est te illi iniustum impiumque bellum inferre
conari.   Etenim ista quaestura ad eam rem valet, ut
elaborandum tibi in ratione reddenda sit quam ob
rem eum cui quaestor fueris accuses, non ut ob eam
ipsam causam postulandum sit ut tibi potissimum
accusatio detur.   Neque fere umquam venit in contentionem de accusando qui quaestor fuisset, quin
63 repudiaretur.   Itaque neque L. Philoni in C. Servilium
nominis deferendi potestas est data, neque M. Aurelio
Scauro in L. Flaccum, neque Cn. Pompeio in T.
Albucium ;   quorum nemo propter indignitatem re-
pudiatus est, sed ne libido violandae necessitudinis
auctoritate iudicum comprobaretur.   Atque ille Cn.
Pompeius ita cum C. Iulio contendit ut tu mecum ;
quaestor enim Albucii fuerat, ut tu Verris ;   Iulius
hoc secum auctoritatis ad accusandum afferebat,
quod, ut hoc tempore nos ab Siculis, sic tum ille ab
Sardis rogatus ad causam accesserat.

Semper haec causa plurimum valuit, semper haec
ratio accusandi fuit honestissima, pro sociis, pro salute
provinciae, pro exterarum nationum commodis inimicitias suscipere, ad periculum accedere, operam,

being guilty of unnatural conduct, even though you were legally justified in doing so : and since you are in fact trying to secure the downfall of your own superior officer without his having wronged you at all, you cannot deny that your intended assault upon him is both unnatural and unjust. Indeed the effect of your quaestorship is to make it exceedingly hard for you to justify your prosecuting the man whose quaestor you were, and not to constitute a ground for your claiming to be specially selected as his prosecutor. Hardly ever has a man's quaestor competed for the right of prosecuting him and not been rejected. For this reason Lucius Philo was not 63 allowed to prosecute Gaius Servilius; Marcus Aurelius Scaurus was not allowed to prosecute Lucius Flaccus; Gnaeus Pompeius was not allowed to prosecute Titus Albucius. None of them were rejected because they were thought incapable : the court's object was to avoid endorsing, with its authority, the wilful disregard of the obligations of friendship. I may remark that the competition between Gnaeus Pompeius and Gaius Julius was much like the present one between you and myself. For Pompeius had been quaestor to Albucius, just as you have been quaestor to Verres : and Julius as prosecutor was much strengthened by having undertaken his case at the request of the Sardinians, just as I have undertaken mine at the request of the Sicilians.

No prosecutor has ever been held to be better justified, nor to have more honourable reasons for his action, than when he has incurred hostility, faced danger, and spared himself neither pains nor enthusiasm nor hard work, in behalf of our allies, in defence

64 studium, laborem interponere. XX. Etenim si probabilis est eorum causa qui iniurias suas persequi
volunt—qua in re dolori suo, non rei publicae commodis serviunt—, quanto illa causa honestior, quae
non solum probabilis videri sed etiam grata esse
debet, nulla privatim accepta iniuria sociorum atque
amicorum populi Romani dolore atque iniuriis commoveri ? Nuper cum in P. Gabinium vir fortissimus
et innocentissimus L. Piso delationem nominis postularet, et contra Q. Caecilius peteret, isque se veteres
inimicitias iam diu susceptas persequi diceret, cum
auctoritas et dignitas Pisonis valebat plurimum, tum
illa erat causa iustissima, quod eum sibi Achaei
patronum adoptarant.

65   Etenim cum lex ipsa de pecuniis repetundis sociorum atque amicorum populi Romani patrona sit, iniquum est non eum legis iudiciique actorem idoneum
maxime putari quem actorem causae suae socii
defensoremque fortunarum suarum potissimum esse
voluerunt. An quod ad commemorandum est honestius, id ad probandum non multo videri debet
aequius ? Utra igitur est splendidior, utra illustrior
commemoratio, " Accusavi eum cui quaestor fueram,
quicum me sors consuetudoque maiorum, quicum
me deorum hominumque iudicium coniunxerat " an
58

of our dominions or for the good of foreign peoples.
XX. The truth is that the motive of a man who 64
seeks to avenge his own wrongs may be unobjectionable, though he is then prompted by his own resentment, and not by desire for his country's good;
but surely the motive is far nobler, surely it should be
felt not merely unobjectionable but welcome, when
a man who has suffered no personal wrong is moved
to indignation by the wrongs and miseries inflicted
upon our nation's allies and friends. Not along ago
that gallant and honourable gentleman Lucius Piso
applied for the right to prosecute Publius Gabinius.
Quintus Caecilius, making a counter-application,
said that he was prompted thereto by the personal
enmity that had long existed between him and
Gabinius. The personal influence and character of
Piso had much to do with his success: still, the
strongest reason was that the Achaeans had chosen
him as their champion.

After all, the Extortion Law itself is meant to 65
champion the allies and friends of the Roman nation;
surely, therefore, when our allies have decided that
they wish for a particular man to conduct their case
and defend their interests for them, the merest justice
requires us to believe that that man is the right one
to conduct the case in court. Can it be denied that
the more creditable motive for a man to mention is far
the stronger argument in support of his plea? Very
well then, which of these two motives is the more
creditable and distinguished for a man to mention?
" I prosecuted the man whom I served as quaestor,
with whom I was associated intimately by the
verdict of the lot, by ancient tradition, by the solemn
judgement of heaven and earth ? " or " I prosecuted

59

"Accusavi rogatu sociorum atque amicorum, delectus sum ab universa provincia qui eius iura fortunasque defenderem "? Dubitare quisquam potest quin honestius sit eorum causa apud quos quaestor fueris, quam eum cuius quaestor fueris accusare ?

66 Clarissimi viri nostrae civitatis temporibus optimis hoc sibi amplissimum pulcherrimumque ducebant, ab hospitibus clientibusque suis, ab exteris nationibus quae in amicitiam populi Romani dicionemque essent, iniurias propulsare eorumque fortunas defendere. M. Catonem illum Sapientem, clarissimum virum et prudentissimum, cum multis graves inimicitias gessisse accepimus propter Hispanorum, apud quos con-

67 sul fuerat, iniurias. Nuper Cn. Domitium scimus M. Silano diem dixisse propter unius hominis, Aegritomari, paterni amici atque hospitis, iniurias. XXI. Neque enim magis animos hominum nocentium res umquam ulla commovit quam haec maiorum consuetudo longo intervallo repetita ac relata, sociorum querimoniae delatae ad hominem non inertissimum, susceptae ab eo qui videbatur eorum fortunas fide

68 diligentiaque sua posse defendere. Hoc timent homines ; hoc laborant ; hoc institui, atque adeo institutum referri ac renovari, moleste ferunt. Putant fore uti, si paulatim haec consuetudo serpere ac prodire coeperit, per homines honestissimos virosque fortissimos, non imperitos adulescentulos aut illius

him at the request of our allies and friends, I was
chosen by the entire province to protect its rights and
interests." Is there room for doubt, that it is more
creditable in a prosecutor to be *helping* the people
among whom he served, than to be *attacking* the
man *under* whom he served ?

The most eminent men in the country, during the 66
best period of our history, counted it among their
most honourable and splendid achievements to protect
from injury, and to maintain in prosperity, those
guests and retainers of theirs, the foreign nations
who had been received as friends into the Roman
Empire. That wise and distinguished man Marcus
Cato Sapiens, history tells us, made many bitter
and lasting enemies by standing up for the unfortunate Spaniards, among whom he had served as
consul. More recently, we may remember, Gnaeus 67
Domitius prosecuted Marcus Silanus in connexion
with the wrongs of a single friend and guest of his
father's, one Aegritomarus. XXI. Nothing, indeed,
has ever alarmed the tyrant and oppressor more
than the revival and reintroduction, after long
disuse, of this tradition of our forefathers, by which
our allies' grievances have been brought before a
man not notably inactive, and taken up by a man
whom they believed honourable and painstaking
enough to defend their interests successfully. It is 68
just this that is causing, in certain quarters, alarm
and anxiety. It is just this custom the introduction
of which is resented, or rather—for it was introduced
before—its recovery and renewal. They anticipate
that, with its gradual extension and advance, the law
and the law-courts will pass into the hands of honourable and fearless gentlemen, and out of the hands

61

modi quadruplatores, leges iudiciaque administrentur.

69 Cuius consuetudinis atque instituti patres maiores-
que nostros non paenitebat tum cum P. Lentulus,
is qui princeps senatus fuit, accusabat M'. Aquilium
subscriptore C. Rutilio Rufo, aut cum P. Africanus,
homo virtute, fortuna, gloria, rebus gestis amplis-
simus, posteaquam bis consul et censor fuerat, L.
Cottam in iudicium vocabat. Iure tum florebat populi
Romani nomen ; iure auctoritas huius imperii civita-
tisque maiestas gravis habebatur. Nemo mirabatur
in Africano illo, quod in me nunc, homine parvis
opibus ac facultatibus praedito, simulant sese mirari,

70 cum moleste ferunt : " Quid sibi iste vult ? accusa-
toremne se existimari, qui antea defendere consue-
verat, nunc praesertim, ea iam aetate, cum aedilitatem petat ? " Ego vero et aetatis non modo meae
sed multo etiam superioris et honoris amplissimi puto
esse et accusare improbos et miseros calamitososque
defendere. Et profecto aut hoc remedium est aegro-
tae ac prope desperatae rei publicae, iudiciisque corruptis ac contaminatis paucorum vitio ac turpitudine,
homines ad legum defensionem iudiciorumque auctoritatem quam honestissimos et integerrimos diligen-
tissimosque accedere ; aut, si ne hoc quidem prodesse

of raw youths and profit-hunters like our friends yonder. This custom, this practice, was the pride 69 of our fathers and grandfathers, in the days when Publius Lentulus, senior member of the Senate, prosecuted Manius Aquilius, and Gaius Rutilius Rufus supported him; the days when Lucius Cotta was summoned to stand his trial by Publius Africanus, at a time when that great and fortunate man had already been consul twice, and also censor, and was at the zenith of his brilliant and successful career. In those days this country had a great name, and deserved to have it : the importance and prestige of the Roman empire were, and deserved to be, tremendous. No one thought it strange then that Africanus should do what people to-day pretend to think strange when done by a man of such moderate wealth and modest capacity as myself. " What is 70 that fellow up to ? " they grumble. " He has always been on the side of the defence so far : why does he want to get a reputation as a prosecutor, particularly now that he is old enough to be a candidate for the aedileship ? " Well, I hold that the prosecution of bad men, and the defence of those in misery and distress, is appropriate to men of my own age, and to men far older than I am ; I hold that it is appropriate to men holding the highest offices in the country. And most surely, now that our public life is in a state of serious and almost fatal decay, and the degraded villainy of certain members of our courts has infected and contaminated them as a whole, either the remedy is that the most honourable, incorruptible, and industrious men available should come forward to defend our laws and uphold our courts ; or else, if even this can do

63

poterit, profecto nulla umquam medicina his tot
71 incommodis reperietur. Nulla salus rei publicae maior
est quam eos qui alterum accusant non minus de
laude, de honore, de fama sua quam illos qui accusan-
tur de capite ac fortunis suis pertimescere. Itaque
semper ii diligentissime laboriosissimeque accusarunt
qui se ipsos in discrimen existimationis venire arbi-
trati sunt.

XXII. Quam ob rem hoc statuere, iudices, debetis,
Q. Caecilium, de quo nulla umquam opinio fuerit
nullaque in hoc ipso iudicio exspectatio futura sit,
qui neque ut ante collectam famam conservet neque
uti reliqui temporis spem confirmet laborat, non nimis
hanc causam severe, non nimis accurate, non nimis
diligenter acturum. Habet enim nihil quod in offensione deperdat ; ut turpissime flagitiosissimeque dis-
cedat, nihil de suis veteribus ornamentis requiret.
72 A nobis multos obsides habet populus Romanus, quos
ut incolumes conservare, tueri, confirmare ac recuperare possimus, omni ratione erit dimicandum.
Habet honorem quem petimus ; habet spem quam
propositam nobis habemus ; habet existimationem
multo sudore, labore vigiliisque collectam ; ut, si in
hac causa nostrum officium ac diligentiam probaveri-
mus, haec quae dixi retinere per populum Romanum
incolumia ac salva possimus ; si tantulum offensum
titubatumque sit, ut ea quae singillatim ac diu collecta

no good, then most surely no cure for all these
grave evils can ever be devised. Nothing can form 71
a better safeguard of the country's interests, than
that the prosecutor should be as deeply concerned
for his credit and honour as the man he prosecutes is
concerned for his life and property. That is why
the most energetic and painstaking prosecutors have
always been men who feel that their own reputations
are at stake.

XXII. Therefore, gentlemen, the conclusion forced
upon you is this. No one has ever thought anything of Quintus Caecilius, and no one will have any
expectation of him in the present case. He has no
earlier reputation that he is anxious to preserve,
no hope for the future that he is concerned to justify.
He is consequently not likely to display any great
severity, or any great care, or any great industry,
in handling this case. For he has nothing to lose if
he fails: he may come out of the business branded
as an infamous scoundrel, and yet not find that he
has lost any of his former distinctions. I have given 72
many hostages to the Roman people; and if I am
to preserve them unharmed, to protect them, to secure
them, to have them restored to me, I must fight
with every weapon at my disposal. What are these
hostages? The office to which I seek election; the
ambition that I cherish in my heart; the reputation
which I have risen early and toiled in the heat to
gain. If I can show, in this case, that I have done
my duty to the best of my power, I shall, by the favour
of my countrymen, be able to keep those precious
things unharmed and safe. But I have only to fail,
only to take one little false step, and I shall lose in
a moment all the good things that I have acquired,

73 sunt uno tempore universa perdamus. Quapropter, iudices, vestrum est deligere quem existimetis facillime posse magnitudinem causae ac iudicii sustinere fide, diligentia, consilio, auctoritate. Vos si mihi Q. Caecilium anteposueritis, ego me dignitate superatum non arbitrabor: populus Romanus ne tam honestam, tam severam diligentemque accusationem neque vobis placuisse neque ordini vestro placere arbitretur, providete.

one by one, through a long period of years. It 73
rests with you, then, gentlemen, to choose the man
whom you think best qualified by good faith, industry,
sagacity and weight of character to maintain this
great case before this great court. If you give
Quintus Caecilius the preference over me, I shall
not think I have been beaten by the better man :
but Rome may think that an honourable, strict, and
energetic prosecutor like myself was not what you
desired, and not what Senators ever would desire.
Gentlemen, see that this does not happen.

IN C. VERREM ACTIO PRIMA

1 I. Quod erat optandum maxime, iudices, et quod unum ad invidiam vestri ordinis infamiamque iudiciorum sedandam maxime pertinebat, id non humano consilio sed prope divinitus datum atque oblatum vobis summo reipublicae tempore videtur. Inveteravit enim iam opinio perniciosa reipublicae nobisque periculosa, quae non modo Romae sed etiam apud exteras nationes omnium sermone percrebuit, his iudiciis quae nunc sunt pecuniosum hominem, quam-**2** vis sit nocens, neminem posse damnari. Nunc in ipso discrimine ordinis iudiciorumque vestrorum, cum sint parati qui contionibus et legibus hanc invidiam senatus inflammare conentur, reus in iudicium adductus est C. Verres, homo vita atque factis omnium iam opinione damnatus, pecuniae magnitudine sua spe ac praedicatione absolutus. Huic ego causae, iudices, cum summa voluntate et exspectatione populi Romani actor accessi, non ut augerem invidiam

FIRST PART OF THE SPEECH AGAINST GAIUS VERRES AT THE FIRST HEARING

I. Gentlemen of the Court : At this great political 1
crisis, there seems to have been offered to you, not
through man's wisdom but almost as the direct gift
of heaven, the very thing that was most to be desired ;
a thing that will help, more than anything else, to
mitigate the unpopularity of your Order and the
discredit attaching to these Courts of Law.   A
belief has by this time established itself, as harmful
to the whole nation as it is perilous to yourselves,
and everywhere expressed not merely by our own
people but by foreigners as well : the belief that
these Courts, constituted as they now are, will
never convict any man, however guilty, if only he
has money.   And now, at the moment of supreme 2
danger for your Order and your judicial privileges,
when preparations have been made for an attempt,
by means of public meetings and proposals for
legislation, to fan the flames of senatorial unpopularity, Gaius Verres appears, to stand his trial
before you : a man already condemned, in the world's
opinion, by his life and deeds ; already acquitted,
according to his own confident assertions, by his
vast fortune.   In this case, gentlemen, I appear as
prosecutor, backed by the strong approval and keen
interest of the nation ; not to increase the un-

ordinis, sed ut infamiae communi succurrerem. Adduxi enim hominem in quo reconciliare existimationem iudiciorum amissam, redire in gratiam cum populo Romano, satis facere exteris nationibus possetis ; depeculatorem aerarii, vexatorem Asiae atque Pamphyliae, praedonem iuris urbani, labem atque

3 perniciem provinciae Siciliae. De quo si vos severe ac religiose iudicaveritis, auctoritas ea quae in vobis remanere debet haerebit : sin istius ingentes divitiae iudiciorum religionem veritatemque perfregerint, ego hoc tamen assequar, ut iudicium potius reipublicae quam aut reus iudicibus aut accusator reo defuisse videatur.

II. Equidem ut de me confitear, iudices, cum multae mihi a C. Verre insidiae terra marique factae sint, quas partim mea diligentia devitarim, partim amicorum studio officioque reppulerim, numquam tamen neque tantum periculum mihi adire visus sum neque

4 tanto opere pertimui, ut nunc in ipso iudicio. Neque tantum me exspectatio accusationis meae concursusque tantae multitudinis, quibus ego rebus vehementissime perturbor, commovet quantum istius insidiae nefariae, quas uno tempore mihi, vobis, M'. Glabrioni praetori, populo Romano,[1] sociis, exteris

---

[1] *The reading here follows a suggestion of Peterson's not adopted in his text.*

---

[a] President of the Extortion Court.

popularity of your Order, but to help in allaying the discredit which is mine as well as yours. The character of the man I am prosecuting is such, that you may use him to restore the lost good name of these Courts, to regain favour at home, and to give satisfaction abroad : he has robbed the Treasury, and plundered Asia and Pamphylia ; he has behaved like a pirate in his city praetorship, and like a destroying pestilence in his province of Sicily. You have only to pronounce against this man an upright and conscientious verdict, and you will continue to possess that public respect which ought always to belong to you. If, however, the vastness of his wealth shatters the conscience and the honesty of the judges in these Courts, I shall achieve one thing at least : it will be felt that the nation lacked the right judges in this case, and not that the judges lacked the right prisoner to convict, or the prisoner the right man to prosecute him.

II. May I make you a personal confession, gentlemen ? Many are the stealthy attacks that Verres has delivered against me by land and sea, some of which I have eluded by my own carefulness, repelling the rest with the help of my energetic and loyal friends. Yet never have I felt myself facing such grave danger, nor been so thoroughly alarmed, as now when the trial has begun. And it is not the eagerness with which my speech for the prosecution is awaited, nor the huge crowd assembled here, that thus affects me, profoundly disturbing as these things are to me : it is rather the unscrupulous assault that Verres is secretly attempting to launch, at once against myself, and you, and the praetor Manius Glabrio,[a] and the Roman nation, and their allies, and

nationibus, ordini, nomini denique senatorio facere
conatur ; qui ita dictitat, iis esse metuendum qui
quod ipsis solis satis esset surripuissent, se tantum
rapuisse ut id multis satis esse possit ; nihil esse tam
sanctum quod non violari, nihil tam munitum quod
non expugnari pecunia possit.

5   Quodsi quam audax est ad conandum tam esset
obscurus in agendo, fortasse aliqua in re nos aliquando
fefellisset.   Verum hoc adhuc percommode cadit,
quod cum incredibili eius audacia singularis stultitia
coniuncta est.   Nam ut apertus in corripiendis
pecuniis fuit, sic in spe corrumpendi iudicii perspicua
sua consilia conatusque omnibus fecit.   Semel ait se
in vita pertimuisse, tum cum primum reus a me factus
sit ; quod, cum e provincia recens esset, invidiaque et
infamia non recenti sed vetere ac diuturna flagraret,
tum ad iudicium corrumpendum tempus alienum
6 offenderet.   Itaque cum ego diem inquirendi in
Siciliam perexiguam postulavissem, invenit iste qui
sibi in Achaiam biduo breviorem diem postularet ;
non ut is idem conficeret diligentia et industria sua
quod ego meo labore et vigiliis consecutus sum;
etenim ille Achaicus inquisitor ne Brundisium quidem
pervenit, ego Siciliam totam quinquaginta diebus sic

72

the foreign world, and the senatorial order, and all
that the Senate means and is. He goes about saying
that people have reason to fear the consequences
of filching enough for themselves only, but that he
himself has carried off enough for a great many
people ; that no sanctuary is too holy for money
to defile it, no fortress too strong for money to
capture it.

If only the audacity of his designs were equalled **5**
by his secrecy in carrying them out, he might perhaps
have contrived, at some time or in some detail, to
hide them from me. But it has very fortunately come
about, hitherto, that his incredible audacity has been
accompanied by unparalleled folly. Just as he has
been quite open in amassing his stolen wealth, so he
has revealed quite clearly to everybody the plans
and schemes by which he aims at corrupting his
judges. He says he was really frightened once in
his life—on the day when I first issued the summons
against him ; not only because he had newly arrived
from his province to face a blaze of hatred and
dislike, which, so far from being new, had burnt
steadily for a long time past, but also because he had
stumbled upon a time unsuitable for corrupting the
Court. That is why, when I had applied for a very **6**
short space of time in which to go and collect my
evidence in Sicily, he found himself another man to
apply for a period shorter by two days in which to do
the like in Achaea ; not with any idea that the latter
should effect by his carefulness and energy what I
have achieved by my own hard work and watchfulness—indeed, this collector of evidence in Achaea
never got even so far as Brundisium ; whereas I
covered the whole of Sicily in fifty days, so effectively,

obii ut omnium populorum privatorumque litteras
iniuriasque cognoscerem : ut perspicuum cuivis esse
posset hominem ab isto quaesitum esse, non qui reum
suum adduceret, sed qui meum tempus obsideret.

7   III. Nunc homo audacissimus atque amentissimus
hoc cogitat.   Intellegit me ita paratum atque instruc-
tum in iudicium venire ut non modo in auribus
vestris, sed in oculis omnium, sua furta atque flagitia
defixurus sim.   Videt senatores multos esse testes
audaciae suae, videt multos equites Romanos ;
frequentes praeterea cives atque socios, quibus ipse
insignes iniurias fecerit ; videt etiam tot tam
graves ab amicissimis civitatibus legationes cum
8 publicis auctoritatibus convenisse. Quae cum ita sint,
usque eo de omnibus bonis male existimat, usque
eo senatoria iudicia perdita profligataque esse
arbitratur, ut hoc palam dictitet, non sine causa
se cupidum pecuniae fuisse, quoniam in pecunia
tantum praesidium experiatur esse : sese, id quod
difficillimum fuerit, tempus ipsum emisse iudicii sui,
quo cetera facilius emere postea posset ; ut, quoniam
criminum vim subterfugere nullo modo poterat, pro-
9 cellam temporis devitaret. Quodsi non modo in
causa, verum in aliquo honesto praesidio aut in
alicuius eloquentia aut gratia, spem aliquam col-

---

that I took cognizance of the wrongs, and the documents recording the wrongs, of all the communities and individuals concerned : so that anyone could see quite clearly that Verres secured the man not to prosecute his own victim but to block the way for me.[a]

III. Let me tell you of the impudent and insane 7 plan that is now in his mind. It is plain to him that I am approaching this case so well equipped and prepared for it that I shall be able to pin him down as a robber and a criminal, not merely in the hearing of this Court, but before the eyes of the whole world. He sees how many senators, and how many Roman knights, have come to testify to his evil violence ; he sees also the throng of those, citizens of our own and of allied states, to whom he has himself done conspicuous wrong ; he sees, too, from communities that are among our best friends, how many deputations, formed of responsible men and armed with official documents, are assembled here against him. But in spite of this, he holds so low 8 an opinion of the whole upper class, he believes the senatorial Courts to be so utterly abandoned and corrupt, that he goes about remarking openly what good reason he had to set his heart on making money, since he finds his money such a tower of strength to him ; how he bought himself the hardest thing to buy, the right date for his own trial, so that he might be able to buy all else the more easily afterwards, and since he could not possibly escape the rough waters of prosecution, might at least avoid the gales of the stormy season. And yet if he 9 could have placed any trust, I do not say in the strength of his case, but in any honourable kind of defence, in the eloquence, or in the popularity, of

locasset, profecto non haec omnia colligeret atque
aucuparetur ; non usque eo despiceret contemne-
retque ordinem senatorium, ut arbitratu eius de-
ligeretur ex senatu qui reus fieret, qui, dum hic quae
opus essent compararet, causam interea ante eum
diceret.

10   Quibus ego rebus quid iste speret et quo animum
intendat facile perspicio ; quam ob rem vero se
confidat aliquid perficere posse, hoc praetore et hoc
consilio,intellegere non possum. Unum illud intellego,
quod populus Romanus in reiectione iudicum iudicavit,
ea spe istum fuisse praeditum ut omnem rationem
salutis in pecunia constitueret, hoc erepto praesidio
ut nullam sibi rem adiumento fore arbitraretur.

IV. Etenim quod est ingenium tantum, quae tanta
facultas dicendi et copia, quae istius vitam, tot vitiis
flagitiisque convictam, iam pridem omnium voluntate
iudicioque damnatam, aliqua ex parte possit defen-
11 dere? Cuius ut adulescentiae maculas ignominiasque
praeteream ; quaestura, primus gradus honoris, quid
aliud habet in se nisi Cn. Carbonem spoliatum a
quaestore suo pecunia publica, nudatum et proditum
consulem, desertum exercitum, relictam provinciam,
sortis necessitudinem religionemque violatam? cuius

---

^a The accused in the rival prosecution already mentioned
(§ 6).
^b See Book I. of the *Actio Secunda* for full details of the
earlier career of Verres, here only summarized.

any of his supporters, he would certainly not have
been driving and hunting such game as that; he
would not have held a view of the senatorial order
so low and contemptuous as to set about the selection
of a senator,[a] chosen by his own caprice, to be the
object of a prosecution, and to stand his trial first,
while he himself meanwhile was making the preparations he needed.

Now, in all this, I can see easily enough what his **10**
hopes are, and what ends he has in view : but with
such a court and such a president of the court as we
now have sitting here, I do fail to understand how
he can expect to gain his ends at all. One thing
alone I do understand—and the people of Rome
were convinced of this when the challenging of the
judges took place : his hopes were of such a kind that
he looked upon his money as his only possible means
of escape, and never supposed that, if this support
were taken from him, anything else could help him.

IV. And indeed what brain could be powerful
enough, what eloquence ready or rich enough, to
defend with even partial success the career of Verres,
a career convicted already of countless vices and
countless crimes, and condemned long ago by the
feelings, and by the judgement, of all the world? I **11**
pass over the stained and shameful record of his
youthful days : what is the story of his quaestorship,
the first stage in his official career ?[b] It is the
story of how Gnaeus Carbo was robbed, by his own
quaestor, of money belonging to the state : the
story of a consular superior left helpless and deserted,
of an army abandoned to its fate, of duty left undone,
of the violation of the personal tie that the lot had
imposed and hallowed. His term of service as

legatio exitium fuit Asiae totius et Pamphyliae;
quibus in provinciis multas domos, plurimas urbes,
omnia fana depeculatus est, tum cum in Cn. Dolabellam suum scelus illud pristinum renovavit et instau-
ravit quaestorium, cum eum, cui et legatus et pro
quaestore fuisset, et in invidiam suis maleficiis adduxit
et in ipsis periculis non solum deseruit sed etiam
12 oppugnavit ac prodidit; cuius praetura urbana
aedium sacrarum fuit publicorumque operum depopu-
latio, simul in iure dicundo bonorum possessionumque
contra omnium instituta addictio et condonatio.

Iam vero omnium vitiorum suorum plurima et
maxima constituit monumenta et indicia in provincia
Sicilia; quam iste per triennium ita vexavit ac perdidit ut ea restitui in antiquum statum nullo modo
possit, vix autem per multos annos innocentesque
praetores aliqua ex parte recreari aliquando posse
13 videatur. Hoc praetore Siculi neque suas leges
neque nostra senatus consulta neque communia iura
tenuerunt; tantum quisque habet in Sicilia quantum
hominis avarissimi et libidinosissimi aut imprudentiam
subterfugit aut satietati superfuit. V. Nulla res
per triennium nisi ad nutum istius iudicata est; nulla

---

[a] *suum* is perhaps to be stressed: ". . . of the peculiarly
Verrine wickedness that had . . ."

adjutant was a disaster to the whole of the provinces
of Asia and Pamphylia, where few private houses,
very few cities, and not one single sanctuary escaped
his depredations. It was now that he carried out,
at Gnaeus Dolabella's expense, a fresh performance
of the [a] wickedness that had already distinguished
his quaestorship, bringing discredit through his own
misconduct on a man whom he had served not only
as adjutant but as acting-quaestor also, and not
merely failing to support him in the hour of danger,
but deliberately attacking and betraying him. His 12
city praetorship was occupied in a plundering
onslaught upon sanctuaries and public buildings,
and in awarding, or failing to award, in the civil
courts, personal and real property in violation of all
legal precedents.

But nowhere did he multiply and magnify the
memorials and the proofs of all his evil qualities so
thoroughly as in his governorship of Sicily ; which
island for the space of three years he devastated
and ruined so effectually that nothing can restore
it to its former condition, and it hardly seems
possible that a long lapse of years and a succession
of upright governors can in time bring it a partial
revival of prosperity. So long as Verres was govern- 13
ing it, its people were protected neither by their
own laws, nor by the decrees of the Roman Senate,
nor by the rights that belong to all nations alike.
None of them has anything left to-day, except
what either escaped the notice of this avaricious and
intemperate ruffian, or remained over when his greed
was glutted. V. For the space of three years, the
law awarded nothing to anybody unless Verres

res tam patria cuiusquam atque avita fuit quae non
ab eo, imperio istius, abiudicaretur. Innumerabiles
pecuniae ex aratorum bonis novo nefarioque instituto
coactae ; socii fidelissimi in hostium numero existi-
mati ; cives Romani servilem in modum cruciati
et necati ; homines nocentissimi propter pecunias
iudicio liberati, honestissimi atque integerrimi, absentes rei facti, indicta causa, damnati et eiecti ;
portus munitissimi, maximae tutissimaeque urbes,
piratis praedonibusque patefactae ; nautae militesque
Siculorum, socii nostri atque amici, fame necati ;
classes optimae atque opportunissimae cum magna
ignominia populi Romani amissae et perditae.
14 Idem iste praetor monumenta antiquissima, partim
regum locupletissimorum, quae illi ornamento urbibus
esse voluerunt, partim etiam nostrorum imperatorum,
quae victores civitatibus Siculis aut dederunt aut
reddiderunt, spoliavit nudavitque omnia. Neque hoc
solum in statuis ornamentisque publicis fecit, sed
etiam delubra omnia sanctissimis religionibus con-
secrata depeculatus est ; deum denique nullum
Siculis, qui ei paullo magis adfabre atque antiquo
artificio factus videretur, reliquit. In stupris vero et
flagitiis nefarias eius libidines commemorare pudore
deterreor ; simul illorum calamitatem commemorando augere nolo quibus liberos coniugesque suas
80

chose to agree; and nothing was so undoubtedly
inherited from a man's father or grandfather that
the courts would not cancel his right to it, if Verres
bade them do so. Countless sums of money, under
a new and unprincipled regulation, were wrung
from the purses of the farmers; our most loyal allies
were treated as if they were national enemies;
Roman citizens were tortured and executed like
slaves; the guiltiest criminals bought their legal
acquittal, while the most honourable and honest
men would be prosecuted in absence, and condemned
and banished unheard; strongly fortified harbours,
mighty and well-defended cities, were left open to
the assaults of pirates and buccaneers; Sicilian
soldiers and sailors, our allies and our friends, were
starved to death; fine fleets, splendidly equipped,
were to the great disgrace of our nation destroyed
and lost to us. Famous and ancient works of art, 14
some of them the gifts of wealthy kings, who intended them to adorn the cities where they stood,
others the gifts of Roman generals, who gave or
restored them to the communities of Sicily in the
hour of victory—this same governor stripped and
despoiled every one of them. Nor was it only the
civic statues and works of art that he treated thus;
he also pillaged the holiest and most venerated
sanctuaries; in fact, he has not left the people of
Sicily a single god whose workmanship he thought
at all above the average of antiquity or artistic merit.
As to his adulteries and the like vile offences, a sense
of decency makes me afraid to repeat the tale of
his acts of wanton wickedness: and besides, I would
not wish, by repeating it, to add to the calamities of
those who have not been suffered to save their

integras ab istius petulantia conservare non licitum
15 est.　At enim haec ita commissa sunt ab isto ut non
cognita sint ab omnibus.　Hominem esse arbitror
neminem, qui nomen istius audierit, quin facta quoque
eius nefaria commemorare possit ; ut mihi magis
timendum sit ne multa crimina praetermittere quam
ne qua in istum fingere existimer.　Neque enim mihi
videtur haec multitudo, quae ad audiendum convenit,
cognoscere ex me causam voluisse, sed ea quae scit
mecum recognoscere.

VI. Quae cum ita sint, iste homo amens ac perditus alia mecum ratione pugnat.　Non id agit, ut
alicuius eloquentiam mihi opponat ; non gratia, non
auctoritate cuiusquam, non potentia nititur.　Simulat
his se rebus confidere ; sed video quid agat, neque
enim agit occultissime.　Proponit inania mihi nobilitatis, hoc est hominum arrogantium, nomina—qui
non tam me impediunt quod nobiles sunt quam ad-
iuvant quod noti sunt ; simulat se eorum praesidio
confidere, cum interea aliud quiddam iam diu ma-
16 chinetur.　Quam spem nunc habeat in manibus et
quid moliatur breviter iam, iudices, vobis exponam :
sed prius ut ab initio res ab eo constituta sit, quaeso,
cognoscite.

Ut primum e provincia rediit, redemptio est huius
iudicii facta grandi pecunia.　Mansit in condicione
atque pacto usque ad eum finem dum iudices re-

---

children and their wives from outrage at the hands
of this lecherous scoundrel. Is it alleged that he did 15
these things so secretly that they were not known
everywhere ? I do not believe that one human being
lives, who has heard the name of Verres spoken,
and cannot also repeat the tale of his evil doings.
I have therefore more reason to fear criticism for
passing over charges of which he is guilty, than for
inventing against him charges of which he is innocent.
And indeed the purpose of the great audience that
has gathered to attend this trial is not, I conceive,
to learn the facts of the case from me, but to join me
in reviewing the facts that it knows already.

VI. The knowledge of all these things has led this
abandoned madman to adopt a new method of
fighting me. It is not his real purpose to find an
eloquent advocate to oppose me. He relies upon no
man's popularity or influence or power. He does
indeed pretend that it is here his confidence lies ;
but I can see what his purpose is, of which, to be sure,
he makes no great secret. He displays against me
a hollow show of titled names, the names of a very
arrogant set of persons, who harm my cause by their
being noble less than they forward it by their being
known : and he pretends to put his trust in their
protection, while all the time he has been engineer-
ing a quite different scheme. I will explain briefly 16
to you, gentlemen, the hope that now possesses him,
and the object of his present exertions : but before
coming to that, I will ask you to note what he was
aiming at in the earlier stages of this affair.

No sooner was he back from his province than he
bought up this Court for a large sum of money.[a] The
terms of the contract held good as arranged, until the

iecti sunt : posteaquam reiectio iudicum facta est, quod et in sortitione istius spem fortuna populi Romani, et in reiiciendis iudicibus mea diligentia istorum impudentiam vicerat, renuntiata est tota
17 condicio. Praeclare se res habebat. Libelli nominum vestrorum consiliique huius in manibus erant omnium ; nulla nota, nullus color, nullae sordes videbantur his sententiis adlini posse ; cum iste repente ex alacri atque laeto sic erat humilis atque demissus ut non modo populo Romano, sed etiam sibi ipse, condemnatus videretur. Ecce autem repente his diebus paucis, comitiis consularibus factis, eadem illa vetera consilia pecunia maiore repetuntur, eaedemque vestrae famae fortunisque omnium insidiae per eosdem homines comparantur. Quae res primo, iudices, pertenui nobis argumento indicioque patefacta est : post aperto suspicionis introitu ad omnia intima istorum consilia sine ullo errore pervenimus.

18   VII. Nam ut Hortensius consul designatus domum reducebatur e campo cum maxima frequentia ac multitudine, fit obviam casu ei multitudini C. Curio ; quem ego hominem honoris potius quam contumeliae causa nominatum volo, etenim ea dicam quae ille, si com-

---

[a] The court thus left was too honest to be bribed for the sum promised.

[b] For Cicero and justice.

[c] *Divinatio*, § 24 note.

[d] The Campus Martius, where the elections were held.

[e] Consul 76 B.C. : father of Caesar's famous supporter.

challenging took place. When the challenging had taken place—since the good destiny of our country had prevailed over Verres' hopes when the lots were cast, and when the members of the Court were challenged my carefulness prevailed over the effrontery of him and his supporters—the contractor threw up his undertaking entirely.[a] Everything now promised well.[b] The list of your names, as members **17** of this Court, was accessible to everyone : this verdict, it seemed, could be given without any fear that special signs, colours, or smudges could be marked upon the voting-tablets.[c] Verres, from looking lively and cheerful, had been plunged suddenly into so gloomy a state of depression, that he was looked on as an already condemned man by everyone in Rome, himself included. And now behold, equally suddenly, within these last few days, since the result of the consular elections has been known, the same old methods are being set going again, and more money than before is being spent upon them : the same insidious attacks are being organized, by the same agents, upon your good name, gentlemen, and upon the well-being of the community at large. This fact was first revealed to me by a slender thread of circumstantial evidence ; but once the door was opened to admit suspicion, a direct path led me to the inmost secrets of Verres and his friends.

VII. What happened was this. Hortensius had **18** just been declared consul-elect, and was being escorted home from the Campus [d] by a large crowd of his supporters, when it chanced that they were met by Gaius Curio.[e] (I do not wish my reference to this gentleman to be taken as disparaging him, but rather the reverse. If he had wished that the remark I am

memorari noluisset, non tanto in conventu tam aperte
palamque dixisset; quae tamen a me pedetentim
cauteque dicentur, ut et amicitiae nostrae et digni-
19 tatis illius habita ratio esse intellegatur. Videt ad
ipsum fornicem Fabianum in turba Verrem; appellat
hominem et ei voce maxima gratulatur; ipsi Hortensio, qui consul erat factus, propinquis necessariisque
eius, qui tum aderant, verbum nullum facit; cum hoc
consistit, hunc amplexatur, hunc iubet sine cura esse.
" Renuntio " inquit " tibi te hodiernis comitiis esse
absolutum." Quod cum tam multi homines honestissimi audissent, statim ad me defertur; immo vero,
ut quisque me viderat narrabat. Aliis illud indignum,
aliis ridiculum videbatur: ridiculum iis qui istius
causam in testium fide, in criminum ratione, in iudicum potestate, non in comitiis consularibus, positam
arbitrabantur; indignum iis qui altius perspiciebant
et hanc gratulationem ad iudicium corrumpendum
20 spectare videbant. Etenim sic ratiocinabantur, sic
honestissimi homines inter se et mecum loquebantur,
aperte iam ac perspicue nulla esse iudicia. Qui reus
pridie iam ipse se condemnatum putabat, is posteaquam defensor eius consul est factus absolvitur?
Quid igitur? quod tota Sicilia, quod omnes Siculi,
omnes negotiatores, omnes publicae privataeque
litterae Romae sunt, nihilne id valebit? nihil, invito

---

[a] In the Via Sacra.
[b] *Renuntio* is the regular word for making official
announcements, such as election results.

going to quote should not be repeated, he would not
have made it so openly in the hearing of so large a
gathering. None the less, what I am going to say
shall be said with cautious hesitation, showing that I
am mindful of his high rank, and of the personal
friendship between us.) Just near the· Arch of 19
Fabius,[a] he noticed Verres among the crowd, called out
to him, and congratulated him loudly. He said not a
word to the newly-elected consul Hortensius himself,
nor to the relatives and friends of Hortensius who were
there at the time. No, it was Verres with whom he
stopped to talk, Verres whom he embraced and told
to put aside all anxiety. " I hereby inform [b] you,"
he said, "that to-day's election means your acquittal."
This remark, being overheard by a number of honest
gentlemen, was forthwith reported to me ; or I
should rather say, everyone told me of it as soon as he
saw me. Some found it distressing, others absurd :
it was absurd to those who regarded the issue of the
case as depending on the credit of the witnesses, the
methods of the prosecution, and the Court's power to
decide, not on the consular election ; distressing to
those who could look further beneath the surface, and
saw that this speech of congratulation pointed to the
corruption of the members of the Court. For they 20
argued thus, and honest gentlemen kept saying so to
one· another and to me, that it was at last unmistakably plain that our law-courts were worthless. An
accused man one day regards his own condemnation
as an accomplished fact, and the next day is acquitted
by the election of his advocate to the consulship ?
Why, is the presence at Rome of all Sicily and its
inhabitants, of all its business men, of all its public
and private records—is all this, then, to count for

consule designato. Quid? iudices non crimina, non testes, non existimationem populi Romani sequentur? Non ; omnia in unius potestate ac moderatione vertentur. VIII. Vere loquar, iudices : vehementer me haec res commovebat. Optimus enim quisque ita loquebatur, "Iste quidem tibi eripietur, sed nos non tenebimus iudicia diutius ; etenim quis poterit Verre 21 absoluto de transferendis iudiciis recusare?" Erat omnibus molestum ; neque eos tam istius hominis perditi subita laetitia quam hominis amplissimi nova gratulatio commovebat. Cupiebam dissimulare me id moleste ferre ; cupiebam animi dolorem vultu tegere et taciturnitate celare.

Ecce autem illis ipsis diebus, cum praetores designati sortirentur et M. Metello obtigisset ut is de pecuniis repetundis quaereret, nuntiatur mihi tantam isti gratulationem esse factam ut is domum quoque 22 mitteret qui uxori suae nuntiarent. Sane ne haec quidem res mihi placebat ; neque tamen tanto opere quid in hac sorte metuendum mihi esset intellegebam. Unum illud ex hominibus certis, ex quibus omnia comperi, reperiebam : fiscos complures cum pecunia Siciliensi a quodam senatore ad equitem Romanum esse translatos, ex his quasi x. fiscos ad senatorem illum relictos esse comitiorum meorum nomine, divisores omnium tribuum noctu ad istum vocatos.

---

[a] To decide the sphere of office each was to occupy.
[b] For the aedileship. The electors were to be bribed to vote against him.

nothing ? No, not if the consul-elect will not have it
so. Why, will the Court have no regard for the statements of the prosecution, the evidence of the witnesses,
the credit of the Roman nation ? No ; everything is
to be steered and directed by the hand of one powerful
man. VIII. I will speak frankly, gentlemen. This
circumstance disturbed me profoundly. Everywhere
the soundest men were saying, " Verres will certainly
escape your clutches, but the law-courts will be in our
keeping no longer ; for who can possibly hesitate about
transferring them to other hands, if Verres is acquitted ? " Everyone was distressed ; less disturbed, 21
however, by this scoundrel's sudden exultation, than
by this unheard-of speech of congratulation from a
man of such high position. I did my best to pretend
that I felt no uneasiness myself ; I did my best, with
the help of calm looks and silence, to mask and conceal
the anguish that I felt.

But to my surprise, only a few days later, when the
praetors-elect were casting lots,[a] and it fell to Marcus
Metellus to be president of the Extortion Court, I
received the news that Verres had been so warmly
congratulated on this that he even sent off slaves to
his house to carry the news to his wife. Now I admit 22
that the way the lot had fallen was a new source of
regret to me : but still, I could not see what special
reason I had to be alarmed by it. One thing I did
learn from certain persons who were my regular
detectives : that a number of baskets of Sicilian
money had been transferred from a particular senator
to a particular knight, that some ten or more of these
baskets were left at this senator's house for a purpose
connected with my own candidature,[b] and that a meeting of the bribery-agents for all the tribes was held

23 Ex quibus quidam, qui se omnia mea causa debere
arbitrabatur, eadem illa nocte ad me venit ; demonstrat, qua iste oratione usus esset ; commemorasse
istum quam liberaliter eos tractasset, et iam antea
cum ipse praeturam petisset, et proxumis consularibus praetoriisque comitiis : deinde continuo esse
pollicitum quantam vellent pecuniam si me aedilitate
deiecissent. Hic alios negasse audere, alios respon-
disse non putare id perfici posse ; inventum tamen
esse fortem amicum ex eadem familia, Q. Verrem
Romilia, ex optima divisorum disciplina, patris istius
discipulum atque amicum, qui HS quingentis mil-
libus depositis id se perfecturum polliceretur ; et
fuisse tamen nonnullos qui se una facturos esse dicerent. Quae cum ita essent, sane benivolo animo
me ut magno opere caverem praemonebat.

24   IX. Sollicitabar rebus maximis uno atque eo per-
exiguo tempore. Urgebant comitia, et in his ipsis
oppugnabar grandi pecunia : instabat iudicium ; ei
quoque negotio fisci Sicilienses minabantur. Agere
quae ad iudicium pertinebant libere comitiorum metu deterrebar ; petitioni toto animo servire propter
iudicium non licebat ; minari denıque divisoribus
ratio non erat, propterea quod eos intellegere videbam me hoc iudicio districtum atque obligatum
25 futurum. Atque hoc ipso tempore Siculis denuntia-
tum esse audio primum ab Hortensio domum ad illum

---

[a] By threatening to prosecute them for their conduct in
either connexion.

one night at Verres' house. One of these agents, a 23
man who felt bound to give me all the help he could,
called on me that same night, and told me what
Verres had been saying to them : he had reminded
them how liberally he had dealt with them, both when
he was himself a candidate for the praetorship some
time ago, and at the recent elections of consuls and
praetors ; and then had at once proceeded to promise
them what they chose to ask for turning me out of my
aedileship. At this, some of them had said they would
not dare to try it, others had replied that they did not
believe it could be managed ; however, a stout ally
turned up from among his own kinsmen, Quintus
Verres of the Romilian tribe, a fine old specimen of
the bribery-agent, who had been the pupil and friend
of Verres' father ; this man undertook to manage the
business for £5000 down, and some of the others said
after all that they would join him. In view of all
this my friend very kindly warned me to take every
possible precaution.

IX. Within the same short space of time I had now 24
to face more than one pressing anxiety. My election
was upon me ; and here, as in the trial, a great sum
of money was fighting against me. The trial was
approaching ; and in this matter also those baskets
of Sicilian gold were threatening me. I was deterred
by concern for my election from giving my mind freely
to the business of the trial ; the trial prevented my
devoting my whole attention to my candidature ; and
to crown all, there was no sense in my trying to intimidate the bribery-agents,[a] since I could see they
were aware that the conduct of this present trial
would tie my hands completely. It was just at this 25
moment that I heard for the first time how Hortensius

ut venirent ; Siculos sane in eo liberos fuisse, qui quam ob rem arcesserentur cum intellegerent, non venisse. Interea comitia nostra, quorum iste se, ut ceterorum hoc anno comitiorum, dominum esse arbitrabatur, haberi coepta sunt. Cursare iste homo potens cum filio blando et gratioso circum tribus ; paternos amicos, hoc est divisores, appellare omnes et convenire. Quod cum esset intellectum et animadversum, fecit animo libentissimo populus Romanus ut, cuius divitiae me de fide deducere non potuissent, ne eiusdem pecunia de honore deicerer.

26 Posteaquam illa petitionis magna cura liberatus sum, animo coepi multo magis vacuo ac soluto nihil aliud nisi de iudicio agere et cogitare. Reperio, iudices, haec ab istis consilia inita et constituta, ut, quacumque opus esset ratione, res ita duceretur ut apud M. Metellum praetorem causa diceretur. In eo esse haec commoda : primum M. Metellum amicissimum ; deinde Hortensium consulem non solum, sed etiam Q. Metellum, qui quam isti sit amicus, attendite ; dedit enim praerogativam suae voluntatis eius modi ut isti pro praerogativis iam reddidisse

27 videatur. An me taciturum tantis de rebus existimavistis ? et me, in tanto reipublicae existimationisque meae periculo, cuiquam consulturum potius quam officio et dignitati meae ?—Arcessit alter consul

---

ᵃ Lit. " (tribes, or centuries) voting first," and by their example influencing the votes of those that followed. Verres had bribed the tribes, and perhaps the *centuriae praerogativae* most heavily, to vote for Q. Metellus as one consul.

ᵇ Cicero seems to address Verres and his supporters.

had sent the Sicilians word to call on him at his house
—and how they had behaved like free and independent men, refusing to go when they understood
why they were being sent for. And now began my
election, which Verres supposed to be under his own
control like all the other elections of this year. He
flew about, this great potentate, with his amiable and
popular son, canvassing the tribes, and interviewing
the family friends—to wit, the bribery-agents—and
summoning them to the fray. As soon as this was
noticed and understood, the people of Rome, with
prompt enthusiasm, ensured my not being thrust out
of my office by the money of a man whose wealth had
failed to lure me out of my honour.

Once relieved of the heavy anxieties of my candida- 26
ture, I began, with a mind much less occupied and
distracted, to devote my thoughts and energies to
the trial alone. I now discovered, gentlemen, that
the plan of action formed and adopted by Verres and
his friends was this : so to prolong proceedings, by
whatever method might be necessary, that the trial
should take place under the presidency of Marcus
Metellus as praetor. This would have several
advantages. First, the strong friendly support of
Marcus Metellus. Next, not only Hortensius would
be consul, but Quintus Metellus too, the strength of
whose friendship for Verres I will ask you to note : he
has indeed given so clear a preliminary token of
goodwill that Verres feels himself already paid in
full for those preliminary votes ^a at the election.
Indeed? did you ^b count on my saying nothing of so 27
serious a matter? on my caring for anything, when the
country and my own reputation are in such danger,
except my duty and my honour? The second

designatus Siculos ; veniunt nonnulli, propterea quod L. Metellus esset praetor in Sicilia. Cum iis ita loquitur : se consulem esse ; fratrem suum alterum Siciliam provinciam obtinere, alterum esse quaesiturum de pecuniis repetundis ; Verri ne noceri possit 28 multis rationibus esse provisum. X. Quid est, quaeso, Metelle, iudicium corrumpere, si hoc non est, testes, praesertim Siculos, timidos homines et adflictos, non solum auctoritate deterrere, sed etiam consulari metu et duorum praetorum potestate ? Quid faceres pro homine innocente et propinquo, cum propter hominem perditissimum atque alienissimum de officio ac dignitate decedis, et committis ut quod ille dictitat alicui qui te ignorat verum esse videatur ? 29 Nam hoc Verrem dicere aiebant, te non fato, ut ceteros ex vestra familia, sed opera sua, consulem factum.—Duo igitur consules et quaesitor erunt ex illius voluntate. " Non solum effugiemus " inquit " hominem in quaerendo nimium diligentem, nimium servientem populi existimationi, M'. Glabrionem ; accedet nobis etiam illud. Iudex est M. Caesonius, collega nostri accusatoris, homo in rebus iudicandis spectatus et cognitus, quem minime expediat esse in eo consilio quod conemur aliqua ratione corrumpere, propterea quod iam antea, cum iudex in Iuniano consilio fuisset, turpissimum illud facinus non solum

---

^a The verse *Fato Metelli Romae fiunt consules* was attributed, by a doubtful tradition, to the poet Naevius.

^b As aedile elect.

consul-elect sent for the Sicilians, and some of them came, remembering that Lucius Metellus was now praetor in Sicily. He talked to them in this sort of way : " I am consul ; one of my brothers is governing Sicily, the other is going to preside over the Extortion Court ; many steps have been taken to secure that no harm can happen to Verres." X. 28 To attempt to intimidate witnesses, especially these timorous and calamity-stricken Sicilians, not merely by your personal influence, but by appealing to their awe of you as consul, and to the power of the two praetors—if this is not judicial corruption, Metellus, I should be glad to know what is. What would you not do for an innocent kinsman, if you forsake duty and honour for an utter rascal who is no kin of yours at all, and make it possible for those who do not know you to believe in the truth of his allegations concerning you ? For Verres was reported to have been saying that you 29 were made consul, not, like the rest of your family, by fate,[a] but by his own exertions. Well then, he will have the two consuls, and the president of the Court, to suit him. He says to himself : " We shall not only escape having Manius Glabrio as President of the Court—a man who is far too conscientious and too subservient to considerations of the national honour. We shall also gain in the following ways. At present one of the judges is Marcus Caesonius, who is the colleague [b] of our prosecutor, and whose behaviour as a judge has already been publicly tested and approved ; a man whom it would be most undesirable to have as member of any court that we may try in any way to corrupt ; for before this, when he was a judge in the court over which Junius presided, he did not simply take to heart the scandalous wickedness then com-

95

graviter tulit, sed etiam in medium protulit. Hunc
iudicem ex Kalendis Ianuariis non habebimus;
30 Q. Manlium et Q. Cornificium, duos severissimos
atque integerrimos iudices, quod tribuni plebis tum
erunt, iudices non habebimus; P. Sulpicius, iudex
tristis et integer, magistratum ineat necesse est
Nonis Decembribus; M. Crepereius, ex acerrima
illa equestri familia et disciplina, L. Cassius, ex
familia cum ad ceteras res tum ad iudicandum severis-
sima, Cn. Tremellius, homo summa religione et
diligentia, tres hi homines veteres tribuni militares
sunt designati; ex Kalendis Ianuariis non iudicabunt.
Subsortiemur etiam in M. Metelli locum, quoniam is
huic ipsi quaestioni praefuturus est. Ita secundum
Kalendas Ianuarias, et praetore et prope toto consilio commutato, magnas accusatoris minas magnam-
que iudicii exspectationem ad nostrum arbitrium libi-
31 dinemque eludemus. Nonae sunt hodie Sextiles; hora
octava convenire coepistis; hunc diem iam ne nume-
rant quidem. Decem dies sunt ante ludos votivos
quos Cn. Pompeius facturus est; hi ludi dies quindecim auferent; deinde continuo Romani conse-
quentur. Ita prope xl. diebus interpositis tum denique se ad ea quae a nobis dicta erunt responsuros
esse arbitrantur; deinde se ducturos et dicendo et

ᵃ A majority of the *iudices*, bribed by Aulus Cluentius
the prosecutor, found his stepfather Oppianicus guilty of
attempted poisoning.

mitted,[a] but took steps to expose it publicly   We
shall not have this man as a judge after the 1st of
January ; nor shall we have Quintus Manlius and 30
Quintus Cornificius, two judges of entirely scrupulous
and upright character, because they will then be
Tribunes of the Plebs ; that stern and upright judge
Publius Sulpicius will have to enter upon his
magistracy on the 5th of December ; Marcus
Crepereius, who belongs to an equestrian family of
the strictest traditions. Lucius Cassius, whose family
has shown the highest integrity in judicial as in all
other matters, and Gnaeus Tremellius, who is a
particularly scrupulous and conscientious man—these
three men of the fine old school have all been
designated for military tribuneships, and after the
1st of January will not be judges.   We shall also be
having a supplementary ballot to fill the place of
Marcus Metellus, since he is to preside over this
actual Court.   So that after the 1st of January, both
the president and practically the whole of the Court
will be changed ; and thus we shall baffle the
formidable threats of the prosecutor, and the wide-
spread hopes that are centred upon this trial, just as
we think best and feel most inclined." To-day. the 31
5th of August, the Court did not assemble till three
o'clock : they are already reckoning that to-day does
not count at all.   It is only ten days to the Votive
Games that Gnaeus Pompeius is to hold ; these
games will occupy fifteen days, and will be followed
emmediately by the Roman Games.   Thus it is not
till after an interval of nearly forty days that they
expect to begin their reply, at last, to the charges
that we on this side shall have brought against them.
They count on being able then, with the help of long

excusando facile ad ludos Victoriae; cum his plebeios esse coniunctos, secundum quos aut nulli aut pauci dies ad agendum futuri sunt. Ita defessa ac refrigerata accusatione rem integram ad M. Metellum praetorem esse venturam. Quem ego hominem, si eius fidei diffisus essem, iudicem non retinuissem; 32 nunc tamen eo animo sum ut eo iudice quam praetore hanc rem transigi malim, et iurato suam quam iniurato aliorum tabellas committere.

XI. Nunc ego, iudices, iam vos consulo quid mihi faciendum putetis; id enim consilii mihi profecto taciti dabitis quod egomet mihi necessario capiendum intellego. Si utar ad dicendum meo legitimo tempore, mei laboris industriae diligentiaeque capiam fructum, et ex accusatione perficiam ut nemo umquam post hominum memoriam paratior, vigilantior, compositior ad iudicium venisse videatur. Sed in hac laude industriae meae reus ne elabatur summum periculum est. Quid est igitur quod fieri possit? non obscurum, 33 opinor, neque absconditum. Fructum istum laudis qui ex perpetua oratione percipi potuit in alia tempora reservemus: nunc hominem tabulis, testibus,

speeches and technical evasions, to prolong the trial till the Games of Victory begin. These games are followed without a break by the Plebeian Games, after which there will be very few days, or none at all, on which the Court can sit. In this way they reckon that all the impetus of the prosecution will be spent and exhausted, and that the whole case will come up afresh before Marcus Metellus as president of the Court. Now so far as this gentleman is concerned, I should not have retained him as a member of the Court, if I had had any doubts of his honesty ; but even so, my 32 feeling is that I would prefer this issue to be decided while he is only a member of the Court, and not when he is presiding over it ; I would rather trust him under oath with his own voting-tablet, than not under oath with the voting-tablets of other persons.

XI. And now, gentlemen, I should really like to ask you what, in your opinion, I ought to do : for I am sure the unspoken advice that you give me will be to do just that which my own understanding shows me I am bound to do. If I spend upon my speech the full time allotted me by law, I shall indeed secure some return to myself for all my toilsome and concentrated exertions ; my conduct of this prosecution will show that no man in all history ever came into court more ready and watchful and well-prepared than I come now. But there is the gravest danger that, while I am thus reaping the credit due to my hard work, the man I am prosecuting will slip through my fingers. What, then, can be done ? A thing that is surely plain and obvious enough. The harvest of fame that 33 might have been gathered by making a long continuous speech let us reserve for another occasion, and let us now prosecute our man by means of documents

privatis publicisque litteris auctoritatibusque accusemus. Res omnis mihi tecum erit, Hortensi. Dicam aperte. Si te mecum dicendo ac diluendis criminibus in hac causa contendere putarem, ego quoque in accusando atque in explicandis criminibus operam consumerem. Nunc, quoniam pugnare contra me instituisti non tam ex tua natura quam ex istius tempore et causa, necesse est istius modi rationi

34 aliquo consilio obsistere. Tua ratio est ut secundum binos ludos mihi respondere incipias : mea, ut ante primos ludos comperendinem. Ita fiet ut tua ista ratio existimetur astuta, meum hoc consilium necessarium.

XII. Verum illud quod institueram dicere, mihi rem tecum esse, huius modi est. Ego cum hanc causam Siculorum rogatu recepissem, idque mihi amplum at praeclarum existimassem, eos velle meae fidei diligentiaeque periculum facere qui innocentiae abstinentiaeque fecissent : tum, suscepto negotio, maius mihi quiddam proposui, in quo meam in rempublicam voluntatem populus Romanus perspicere

35 posset. Nam illud mihi nequaquam dignum industria conatuque meo videbatur, istum a me in iudicium iam omnium iudicio condemnatum vocari,

and witnesses, the written statements and official pronouncements of private persons and public bodies. It is you, Hortensius, with whom I shall have to reckon throughout. I will speak frankly. If I could suppose that, in this case, your method of opposing me was that of fair speech in palliation of the charges I am bringing, I too would be for devoting my energies to a speech for the prosecution setting forth the charges in full. But since, as it is, you have chosen to fight me in a way less well suited to your own personal character than to the emergency in which Verres finds himself and to the badness of Verres' case, tactics such as you have adopted must somehow or other be countered. Your plan is, 34 that you should not begin your speech for the defence till both the festivals are over. My plan is, to reach the adjournment of the case before the first festival begins. It amounts to this, that you will have the credit of planning an ingenious move, and I of making the inevitable reply to it.

XII. But with regard to what I began just now to speak of—that it is you with whom I have to reckon—what I mean is this. Although, when I undertook this case at the request of the Sicilians, I felt that there was a full measure of honour for me in the fact that the people who had made trial of my integrity and self-control were willing now to make trial of my good faith and energy : yet the task once undertaken, I put before myself a still greater object, whereby to let the Roman people perceive my loyalty to my country. For I reflected that to prosecute in court a man who 35 already stood condemned by the court of humanity was a task very far from worthy of the toil and effort it would cost me, were it not that your intolerably

nisi ista tua intolerabilis potentia, et ea cupiditas qua
per hosce annos in quibusdam iudiciis usus es, etiam
in istius hominis desperati causa interponeretur.
Nunc vero, quoniam haec te omnis dominatio reg-
numque iudiciorum tanto opere delectat, et sunt
homines quos libidinis infamiaeque suae neque pudeat
neque taedeat, qui quasi de industria in odium
offensionemque populi Romani irruere videantur,
hoc me profiteor suscepisse magnum fortasse onus et
mihi periculosum, verum tamen dignum in quo omnes
nervos aetatis industriaeque meae contenderem.
36 Quoniam totus ordo paucorum improbitate et audacia
premitur et urgetur infamia iudiciorum, profiteor huic
generi hominum me inimicum accusatorem, odiosum,
assiduum, acerbum adversarium. Hoc mihi sumo,
hoc mihi deposco, quod agam in magistratu, quod
agam ex eo loco, ex quo me populus Romanus ex
Kalendis Ianuariis secum agere de republica ac de
hominibus improbis voluit ; hoc munus aedilitatis
meae populo Romano amplissimum pulcherrimumque
polliceor. Moneo, praedico, ante denuntio : qui aut
deponere aut accipere aut recipere aut polliceri aut
sequestres aut interpretes corrumpendi iudicii solent
esse, quique ad hanc rem aut potentiam aut impuden-

---

^a The aediles were expected to provide entertainments on
a large scale for the Roman public.
^b There is some doubt about the technical meaning of
accipere and *polliceri* here.

despotic power, and the self-seeking that you have
exhibited in more than one trial of recent years, were
being engaged once more in the defence of that
desperate scoundrel yonder. But as things now
stand, since you take so much pleasure in all this
tyrannical domination of our courts of law, and since
men do exist who find nothing shameful, nothing
disgusting, in their own wanton deeds and vile
reputations, but appear to challenge, as though of
set purpose, the hatred and anger of the people of
Rome : I will declare boldly, that the burden I have
shouldered may indeed be heavy and dangerous for
myself, but is nevertheless such that my manhood
and determination may fitly strain every muscle to
bear it. Since the whole of our poorer class is being **36**
oppressed by the hand of recklessness and crime,
and groaning under the infamy of our law-courts, I
declare myself to these criminals as their enemy and
their accuser, as their pertinacious, bitter, and un-
relenting adversary. It is this that I choose, this
that I claim, as my duty in my public office, as my
duty in that position in which the people of Rome
have willed that, from the first day of next January,
I should take counsel with them for the public welfare
and the punishment of evil men. This is the most
splendid and noble spectacle that I can promise to
bestow during my aedileship on the people of Rome.[a]
I here issue this warning, this public notice, this preliminary proclamation : To all those who are in the
habit of depositing or receiving deposits [b] for bribery,
of undertaking to offer or offering [b] bribes, or of acting
as agents or go-betweens for the corruption of judges
in our courts, and to all those who have offered to make
use of their power or their shamelessness for these

tiam suam professi sunt, abstineant in hoc iudicio
37 manus animosque ab hoc scelere nefario. XIII. Erit
tum consul Hortensius cum summo imperio et
potestate, ego autem aedilis, hoc est, paulo amplius
quam privatus : tamen haec huius modi res est
quam me acturum esse polliceor, ita populo Romano
grata atque iucunda, ut ipse consul in hac causa prae
me minus etiam, si fieri possit, quam privatus esse
videatur.

Omnia non modo commemorabuntur, sed etiam
expositis certis rebus agentur, quae inter decem
annos, posteaquam iudicia ad senatum translata sunt,
in rebus iudicandis nefarie flagitioseque facta sunt.
38 Cognoscet ex me populus Romanus quid sit quam
ob rem, cum equester ordo iudicaret, annos prope
quinquaginta continuos in nullo, iudices,[1] equite
Romano iudicante ne tenuissima quidem suspicio
acceptae pecuniae ob rem iudicandam constituta sit ;
quid sit quod, iudiciis ad senatorium ordinem trans-
latis, sublataque populi Romani in unum quemque
vestrum potestate, Q. Calidius damnatus dixerit
minoris HS triciens praetorium hominem honeste non
posse damnari ; quid sit quod, P. Septimio senatore
damnato Q. Hortensio praetore de pecuniis repetundis, lis aestimata sit eo nomine quod ille ob rem
39 iudicandam pecuniam accepisset ; quod in C. Heren-
nio, quod in C. Popilio, senatoribus, qui ambo peculatus damnati sunt, quod in M. Atilio, qui de maiestate

---

[1] *The MSS. read* continuos nullo iudice equite . . . :
Zumpt proposed in nullo : *Peterson accepts this and changes*
iudice (*an almost impossible tautology*) *to the vocative* iudices.

---

[a] *i.e.*, the treachery of voting for the condemnation of a
member of one's own class could only be justified by a
really heavy bribe.

purposes : in this present trial, take care that your
hands and your minds are kept clear of this vile crime.
XIII. Hortensius will then be consul, endowed with 37
supreme command and authority, while I shall be
an aedile, nothing much grander than an ordinary
citizen : yet the thing that I now promise to do is of
such a kind, so welcome and acceptable to the people
of Rome, that the consul himself must seem even less
than an ordinary citizen, if that were possible, when
matched against me on this issue.

The whole story shall not only be recalled, but set
forth and corroborated in detail, the story of all the
judicial crimes and villainies that have been committed during the ten years since the transfer of the
law-courts to the Senate.   The people of Rome shall 38
learn from me how it is that, so long as the law-courts
were in the hands of the Equestrian Order, for nearly
fifty years together, not even the faintest suspicion
rested upon one single Roman knight, gentlemen,
when sitting as a judge, of accepting a bribe to give a
particular verdict ; how it is that, when the courts had
been transferred to the Senatorial Order, and the
power of the people over you as individuals had been
taken away, Quintus Calidius observed, upon being
convicted, that a man of praetorian rank could not
decently be convicted for less than thirty thousand
pounds [a]; how it is that, when Quintus Hortensius
was president of the Extortion Court, the penalty
inflicted on the condemned senator Publius Septimius
was assessed with express reference to the fact of his
having received a bribe as judge ; that in the cases 39
of the senators Gaius Herennius and Gaius Popilius,
who were both found guilty of embezzlement, and of
Marcus Atilius, who was found guilty of treason, the

damnatus est, hoc planum factum est, eos pecuniam
ob rem iudicandam accepisse ; quod inventi sunt
senatores qui C. Verre praetore urbano sortiente
exirent in eum reum quem incognita causa condemnarent ; quod inventus est senator qui, cum iudex
esset, in eodem iudicio et ab reo pecuniam acciperet
quam iudicibus divideret et ab accusatore ut reum
40 damnaret. Iam vero quo modo illam labem ignominiam calamitatemque totius ordinis conquerar, hoc
factum esse in hac civitate, cum senatorius ordo
iudicaret, ut discoloribus signis iuratorum hominum
sententiae notarentur ? Haec omnia me diligenter
severeque acturum esse polliceor.

XIV. Quo me tandem animo fore putatis, si quid
in hoc ipso iudicio intellexero simili aliqua ratione
esse violatum atque commissum ? cum praesertim
planum facere multis testibus possim C. Verrem in
Sicilia, multis audientibus, saepe dixisse se habere
hominem potentem cuius fiducia provinciam spoliaret ;
neque sibi soli pecuniam quaerere, sed ita triennium
illud praeturae Siciliensis distributum habere ut
secum praeclare agi diceret si unius anni quaestum
in rem suam converteret, alterum patronis et defensoribus traderet, tertium illum uberrimum quae-
stuosissimumque annum totum iudicibus reservaret.
41 Ex quo mihi venit in mentem illud dicere quod apud

---

[a] This meaning of *exirent in* is conjectural.
[b] This implies that (1) the secrecy of the voting was
violated, (2) that it was done because the judges had been
bribed, (3) that the takers of bribes could not be trusted.
See *Divinatio*, § 24, and this speech, § 17.

fact was established that they had taken bribes as
judges ; that when Gaius Verres was presiding at a
trial as City Praetor, senators were found to vote
against [a] a man whom they were condemning without
having attended his trial ; that a senator was once
found who, when sitting as a judge, in one and the
same case received money from the accused man
with which to bribe the other judges, and from the
prosecutor to vote for the accused man's condemnation.   And now, what words can I find to deplore that 40
foul and disastrous blot upon the honour of our whole
Order, the fact that in this land of ours, with the law-
courts in the Senatorial Order's hands, such a thing
happened as that the voting-tablets, given to judges
who were under oath, were marked with wax of
different colours ? [b] With all these facts I promise
you I will deal sternly and faithfully.

XIV. And now what do you conceive that my
feelings will be, if in this very trial I shall find that
any offence of this description has been committed ?
For you must note that I can bring many witnesses
to prove that Gaius Verres, when in Sicily, has frequently said, in the presence of many listeners, that
he had a powerful friend in whose protection he
trusted while plundering the province ; and that he
was not trying to make money for himself alone, but
had those three years of his Sicilian praetorship so
parcelled out as to feel he would do well if he might
apply the profits of one year to increasing his own
fortune, hand over those of the second year to his
advocates and defenders, and reserve the whole of
the great third year, the richest and most profitable
of the three, for his judges.   And this suggests to 41
me the repetition of a remark which I made before

M'. Glabrionem nuper cum in reiciendis iudicibus
commemorassem intellexi vehementer populum
Romanum commoveri : me arbitrari fore uti nationes
exterae legatos ad populum Romanum mitterent ut
lex de pecuniis repetundis iudiciumque tolleretur ;
si enim iudicia nulla sint, tantum unum quemque
ablaturum putant quantum sibi ac liberis suis satis
esse arbitretur : nunc, quod eius modi iudicia sint,
tantum unumquemque auferrequantum sibi,patronis,
advocatis, praetori, iudicibus satis futurum sit ; hoc
profecto infinitum esse : se avarissimi hominis
cupiditati satisfacere posse, nocentissimi victoriae
42 non posse. O commemoranda iudicia praeclaramque
existimationem nostri ordinis, cum socii populi
Romani iudicia de pecuniis repetundis fieri nolunt,
quae a maioribus nostris sociorum causa comparata
sunt ! An iste umquam de se bonam spem habuisset,
nisi de vobis malam opinionem animo imbibisset ?
Quo maiore etiam, si fieri potest, apud vos odio esse
debet quam est apud populum Romanum, cum in
avaritia, scelere, periurio vos sui similes esse
arbitretur.
43   XV Cui loco, per deos immortales, iudices, consulite ac providete. Moneo praedicoque id quod
intellego, tempus hoc vobis divinitus datum esse ut
odio, invidia, infamia, turpitudine totum ordinem

---

a The exact sense of *loco* is doubtful : it may be (i.)
" critical situation " (*tempori,* καιρῷ), (ii.) " weak spot " in
your defences, (iii.) " assumption " (so Long translates),
" line of argument."

Manius Glabrio recently when the challenging of judges was taking place, and which I could see made a profound impression upon the people of Rome. I said that I believed the day would come when our foreign subjects would be sending deputations to our people, asking for the repeal of the existing law and the abolition of the Extortion Court. Were there no such Court, they imagine that any one governor would merely carry off what was enough for himself and his family : whereas with the courts as they now are, each governor carries off what will be enough to satisfy himself, his advocates and supporters, and his judges and their president : and this is a wholly unlimited amount. They feel that they may meet the demands of a greedy man's cupidity, but cannot meet those of a guilty man's acquittal. How illustrious are our Courts of Law, how splen-42 did is the reputation of our Order, if the allies of Rome desire the abolition of that very Extortion Court which our ancestors established for those allies' benefit ! Would Verres, indeed, ever have cherished fair hopes for himself, had his mind not been saturated with this foul opinion of you ? An opinion that should make him yet more loathsome, if that be possible, to you than to the Roman people, this man who believes you to be as avaricious, as criminal, as false and perjured as he is himself.

XV. Now I entreat you, gentlemen, in God's 43 name to take thought, and to devise measures, to meet this state of affairs.[a] I would warn you and solemnly remind you of what is clear to me, that heaven itself has granted you this opportunity of delivering our whole Order from unpopularity and hatred, from dishonour and disgrace. Men reckon

liberetis. Nulla in iudiciis severitas, nulla religio, nulla denique iam existimantur esse iudicia. Itaque a populo Romano contemnimur, despicimur : gravi 44 diuturnaque iam flagramus infamia. Neque enim ullam aliam ob causam populus Romanus tribuniciam potestatem tanto studio requisivit ; quam cum poscebat, verbo illam poscere videbatur, re vera iudicia poscebat. Neque hoc Q. Catulum, hominem sapientissimum atque amplissimum, fugit, qui Cn. Pompeio, viro fortissimo et clarissimo, de tribunicia potestate referente cum esset sententiam rogatus, hoc initio est summa cum auctoritate usus, patres conscriptos iudicia male et flagitiose tueri : quodsi in rebus iudicandis populi Romani existimationi satis facere voluissent, non tanto opere homines fuisse tribuni 45 ciam potestatem desideraturos. Ipse denique Cn. Pompeius cum primum contionem ad urbem consul designatus habuit, ubi (id quod maxime exspectari videbatur) ostendit se tribuniciam potestatem restitu turum, factus est in eo strepitus et grata contionis admurmuratio. Idem in eadem contione cum dixisset populatas vexatasque esse provincias, iudicia autem turpia et flagitiosa fieri ; ei rei se providere ac consulere velle : tum vero non strepitu, sed maximo

that our courts of law have no strictness left, no conscience—nay, by now, no existence worth the name. The result is that we are contemned and despised by the people of Rome. We have been groaning, and that for many years, under a heavy load of infamy. Let me tell you that it was for this reason, **44** and for no other, that the people of Rome have expressed so strong a desire for the restoration of the powers of the tribunes. Their demand for that was but nominally and apparently a demand for the thing itself: their real demand was for honest law-courts. This fact was not missed by that wise and eminent man Quintus Catulus. When our distinguished general Gnaeus Pompeius introduced his measure to restore the powers of the tribunes, Catulus, on being called upon to speak, began his speech with a most impressive declaration, that the members of that House were proving ineffective and immoral guardians of our courts of justice ; and that had they only chosen, in their capacity as judges, to maintain the honour of Rome, people would not have felt so acutely their loss of the tribunes' powers. In fact, when Gnaeus Pompeius himself, as consul- **45** elect, for the first time addressed a public meeting near the city, and, in accordance with what appeared to be a very general expectation, declared his intention of restoring the powers of the tribunes, his words elicited a murmuring noise of grateful approval from the assembly : but when he observed, in the course of the same speech, that our provinces had been wasted and laid desolate, that our law-courts were behaving scandalously and wickedly, and that he meant to take steps to deal with this evil—then it was with no mere murmur, but with a mighty

clamore, suam populus Romanus significavit voluntatem.

46 XVI. Nunc autem homines in speculis sunt; observant quem ad modum sese unus quisque vestrum gerat in retinenda religione conservandisque legibus. Vident adhuc post legem tribuniciam unum senatorem vel tenuissimum esse damnatum; quod tametsi non reprehendunt, tamen magno opere quod laudent non habent; nulla est enim laus ibi esse integrum ubi nemo est qui aut possit aut conetur 47 corrumpere. Hoc est iudicium in quo vos de reo, populus Romanus de vobis iudicabit. In hoc homine statuetur possitne senatoribus iudicantibus homo nocentissimus pecuniosissimusque damnari. Deinde est eius modi reus in quo homine nihil sit praeter summa peccata maximamque pecuniam; ut, si liberatus sit, nulla alia suspicio nisi ea quae turpissima est residere possit; non gratia, non cognatione, non aliis recte factis, non denique aliquo mediocri vitio, tot tantaque eius vitia sublevata esse videbuntur. 48 Postremo ego causam sic agam, iudices, eius modi res, ita notas, ita testatas, ita magnas, ita manifestas proferam, ut nemo a vobis ut istum absolvatis per gratiam conetur contendere. Habeo autem certam viam atque rationem qua omnes illorum conatus

112

roar, that the people of Rome showed their satisfaction.

XVI. To-day the eyes of the world are upon us, 46 waiting to see how far the conduct of each man among us will be marked by obedience to his conscience and by observance of the law. It is noted that since the passage of the tribunician law a single senator, a man of quite slender means, has been condemned ; an act which, though not censured, nevertheless affords no great room for commendation, for integrity cannot be commendable where no man has either the power or the will to corrupt it. It is the present trial in which, even as you will 47 pass your verdict upon the prisoner, so the people of Rome will pass its verdict upon yourselves. It is this man's case that will determine whether, with a court composed of Senators, the condemnation of a very guilty and very rich man can possibly occur. And further, the prisoner is such that he is distinguished by nothing except his monstrous offences and immense wealth : if, therefore, he is acquitted, it will be impossible to imagine any explanation but the most shameful ; it will not appear that there has been any liking for him, any family bond, any record of other and better actions, no, nor even any moderation in some one vice, that could palliate the number and enormity of his vicious deeds. And 48 lastly, gentlemen, I shall so handle this case, I shall put before you facts of such a kind—so notorious, so well corroborated by evidence, so sweeping, and so convincing—that nobody will seek to urge you to acquit this man as a personal favour. I have a definite plan of procedure by which to unearth and set my hands upon all the intrigues of him and his

investigare et consequi possim; ita res a me agetur
ut in eorum consiliis omnibus non modo aures
hominum,[1] sed etiam oculi populi Romani interesse
videantur.

49 Vos aliquot iam per annos conceptam huic ordini
turpitudinem atque infamiam delere ac tollere
potestis. Constat inter omnes, post haec constituta
iudicia quibus nunc utimur, nullum hoc splendore
atque hac dignitate consilium fuisse. Hic si quid
erit offensum, omnes homines non iam ex eodem
ordine alios magis idoneos, quod fieri non potest, sed
alium omnino ordinem ad res iudicandas quaerendum
50 arbitrabuntur. XVII. Quapropter primum ab dis
immortalibus, quod sperare mihi videor, hoc idem,
iudices, opto, ut in hoc iudicio nemo improbus praeter
eum qui iampridem inventus est reperiatur; deinde,
si plures improbi fuerint, hoc vobis, hoc populo Romano, iudices, confirmo, vitam mehercule mihi prius
quam vim perseverantiamque ad illorum improbitatem persequendam defuturam.

51 Verum quod ego laboribus periculis inimicitiisque
meis tum cum admissum erit dedecus severe me
persecuturum esse polliceor, id ne accidat, tu tua
sapientia, auctoritate, diligentia, M'. Glabrio, potes
providere. Suscipe causam iudiciorum; suscipe
causam severitatis, integritatis, fidei, religionis: suscipe causam senatus, ut is hoc iudicio probatus cum

---

[1] hominum *MSS.*: *Peterson emends to* omnium; *need-
lessly, for* hominum *need not be stressed, nor regarded as
antithetical to* populi Romani; *and improbably—can*
omnium *possibly mean* " all of you " ?

friends; and I shall deal with this business in such a
fashion that all their stratagems will seem to stand
revealed, not merely to men's ears, but to the very
eyes of the people of this country.

You have the power of removing and destroying 49
the dishonour and the disgrace that have for several
years past attached to this our Order.   It is admitted
upon all hands that, since these Courts were first
constituted in their present shape, no body of judges
has assembled of equal eminence and equal distinction.   If this body of judges shall in any way
come to grief, the universal opinion will be, that
for the administration of justice we must seek, not
fitter men from the same Order, for none such could
be found, but some other Order altogether.   XVII. 50
And therefore, gentlemen, in the first place, I pray
Heaven to justify the confidence I feel, that no
man in this Court will be detected in evil-doing,
save that one man whose evil-doing has been long
since discovered ; and in the next place I declare
to you, and, gentlemen, I declare to the people of
Rome, that if other evil-doers there shall be, I will,
so God help me, sooner lose my life than lose the
vigour and the resolution that shall secure their
punishment for the evil they have done.

But indeed this same scandal, for which, when 51
once committed, I thus undertake to secure drastic
punishment at the cost of toil and danger and hostility to myself, you, Manius Glabrio, with the help
of your strength and wisdom and watchfulness, can
prevent from coming to pass at all.   Be the champion
of our courts of law : be the champion of justice
and integrity, of honour and conscience : be the
champion of the Senate, that it may pass the test

115

populo Romano et in laude et in gratia esse possit.
Cogita quo loco sis,[1] quid dare populo Romano, quid
reddere maioribus tuis debeas ; fac tibi paternae
legis Aciliae veniat in mentem, qua lege populus
Romanus de pecuniis repetundis optimis iudiciis
52 severissimisque iudicibus usus est. Circumstant te
summae auctoritates, quae te oblivisci laudis do-
mesticae non sinant, quae te noctes diesque com-
moneant fortissimum tibi patrem, sapientissimum
avum, gravissimum socerum fuisse. Quare si Gla-
brionis patris vim et acrimoniam ceperis ad resisten-
dum hominibus audacissimis, si avi Scaevolae pruden-
tiam ad prospiciendas insidias quae tuae atque horum
famae comparantur, si soceri Scauri constantiam ut
ne quis te de vera et certa possit sententia demovere :
intelleget populus Romanus integerrimo atque
honestissimo praetore delectoque consilio nocenti reo
magnitudinem pecuniae plus habuisse momenti ad
suspicionem criminis quam ad rationem salutis.
53 XVIII. Mihi certum est non committere ut in hac
causa praetor nobis consiliumque mutetur. Non
patiar rem in id tempus adduci ut quos adhuc servi
designatorum consulum non moverunt, cum eos novo
exemplo universos arcesserent, eos tum lictores consulum vocent : ut homines miseri, antea socii atque

---

[1] *Peterson emends the traditional* Cogita qui sis, quo loco
sis : qui sis *is not in the* MSS.

---

[a] This law made the knights judges in such cases.
[b] A Scaevola, probably the great jurist.
[c] Marcus Aemilius Scaurus.
[d] Cicero refers to the incident related in § 27.

116

of this trial, and recover the esteem and favour of the Roman people. Think of the great place you hold, of the duty that you owe to Rome, and the tribute that you owe to your own ancestors. Remember the Acilian Law,[a] your father's work—the law whereby the nation gained efficient courts and strictly honourable judges to deal with extortion claims. You are hedged about with an army of 52 great precedents, forbidding you to forget the high honour your family has won, reminding you night and day of your gallant father, of your wise grandfather,[b] of your noble father-in-law.[c] Show therefore the keen vigour of your father Glabrio, by repelling the assaults of unscrupulous knaves; show the foresight of your grandfather Scaevola, by anticipating the plots now being hatched against your honour and the honour of these gentlemen; show the steadfastness of your father-in-law Scaurus, by letting no man succeed in shaking you out of the truth and certainty of your judgement : and the people of Rome shall see, that when a man of high honour and integrity is presiding over a court of chosen judges, the accused, if he be guilty, will find that his vast fortune has tended rather to heighten belief in his guilt than to furnish him with the means of escaping his doom.

XVIII. I am firmly resolved to prevent our having 53 a change of president or judges for the case before us. I will not allow the decision to be delayed to a time when men who, by a gross innovation, have been collectively summoned before a consul-elect by his servants,[d] and who as yet have refused to go, may be ordered before a consul in office by his constables : to a time when those unhappy persons,

117

amici populi Romani, nunc servi ac supplices, non
modo ius suum fortunasque omnes eorum imperio
amittant, verum etiam deplorandi iuris sui potesta-
54 tem non habeant.   Non sinam profecto, causa a me
perorata, quadraginta diebus interpositis, tum nobis
denique responderi cum accusatio nostra in oblivionem
diuturnitatis adducta sit ; non committam ut tum
res iudicetur cum haec frequentia totius Italiae Roma
discesserit, quae convenit uno tempore undique comitiorum ludorum censendique causa.   Huius iudicii et
laudis fructum et offensionis periculum vestrum,
laborem sollicitudinemque nostram, scientiam quid
agatur, memoriamque quid a quoque dictum sit,
55 omnium puto esse oportere.   Faciam hoc non novum,
sed ab iis qui nunc principes nostrae civitatis sunt
ante factum, ut testibus utar statim : illud a me
novum, iudices, cognoscetis, quod ita testes con-
stituam ut crimen totum explicem ; ubi id inter-
rogando argumentis atque oratione firmavero, tum
testes ad crimen accommodem : ut nihil inter illam
usitatam accusationem atque hanc novam intersit,
nisi quod in illa tum cum omnia dicta sunt testes
dantur, hic in singulas res dabuntur : ut illis quoque

---

[a] By appearing to give evidence against Verres.

who were once the allies and friends of Rome, but
now are slaves and suppliants, will not only be
deprived, through these men's official power, of their
rights and their whole fortunes, but will be denied
even the opportunity of remonstrating ^a about their
loss. Assuredly I will not suffer the reply to our 54
case to be made only when forty days have passed
after I have ended my speech for the prosecution, and the lapse of time has blurred the memory
of the charges we bring. I will not permit the
settlement of this case to be delayed until after the
departure from Rome of these multitudes that have
simultaneously assembled, from all parts of Italy, to
attend the elections, the games, and the census.
As, in this trial, it is for you to reap the reward of
popularity and risk the danger of disapproval, and
for us to face the toil and anxiety involved ; so, I
hold, it is for all men to be admitted to the knowledge of what shall here take place, and to record in
their memories the words that each speaker shall
utter. My calling of my witnesses at once will be 55
no novelty ; that has been done before, and by
men who now hold leading positions in the country.
The novelty that you will note, gentlemen, is this :
I shall so deal with the evidence of my witnesses as
first to state each charge in full, and after supporting
it by questioning, argument, and comment, then to
bring forward my witnesses to that particular charge.
There will thus be no difference between the usual
method of prosecution and this new one of mine,
except that in the former the witnesses are not
called until all the speeches are over, whereas in the
latter they will be called with reference to each
charge in turn : so that, further, our opponents will

eadem interrogandi facultas argumentandi dicendique sit. Si quis erit qui perpetuam orationem accusationemque desideret, altera actione audiet : nunc id quod facimus (ea ratione facimus, ut malitiae illorum consilio nostro occurramus) necessario fieri

56 intellegat. Haec primae actionis erit accusatio. Dicimus C. Verrem, cum multa libidinose, multa crudeliter in cives Romanos atque in socios, multa in deos hominesque nefarie fecerit, tum praeterea quadringentiens sestertium ex Sicilia contra leges abstulisse. Hoc testibus, hoc tabulis privatis publicisque auctoritatibus ita vobis planum faciemus ut hoc statuatis, etiamsi spatium ad dicendum nostro commodo vacuosque dies habuissemus, tamen oratione longa nihil opus fuisse. Dixi.

have the same facilities as ourselves for questions, arguments, and comments. If there is anyone who regrets the absence of the continuous speech for the prosecution, he shall hear it in the second part of the trial : for the moment he must see that our line of action, being directed to thwarting, by rational means, the trickery of our adversaries, is the only one possible. The scope of the prosecution in the 56 first part of the trial will be this. We submit that Gaius Verres has been guilty of many acts of lust and cruelty towards Roman citizens and Roman allies, of many outrageous offences against God and man ; and that he has, moreover, illegally robbed Sicily of four hundred thousand pounds. This fact we will use witnesses, and private records, and official written statements, to make so plain to you that you will conclude that, even had we had days to spare and time to speak at leisure, there would still have been no need to speak at any great length.— I thank you, gentlemen.

ACTIONIS SECUNDAE IN C. VERREM
LIBER PRIMUS

1   I. Neminem vestrum ignorare arbitror, iudices, hunc per hosce dies sermonem vulgi atque hanc opinionem populi Romani fuisse, C. Verrem altera actione responsurum non esse neque ad iudicium adfuturum. Quae fama non idcirco solum emanarat quod iste certe statuerat ac deliberaverat non adesse, verum etiam, quod nemo quemquam tam audacem, tam amentem, tam impudentem fore arbitrabatur qui tam nefariis criminibus, tam multis testibus convictus ora iudicum aspicere aut os suum populo Romano **2** ostendere auderet. Est idem Verres qui fuit semper, ut ad audendum proiectus, sic paratus ad audiendum. Praesto est, respondet, defenditur; ne hoc quidem sibi reliqui facit ut, in rebus turpissimis cum manifesto teneatur, si reticeat et absit, tamen impudentiae suae pudentem exitum quaesisse videatur. Patior, iudices, et non moleste fero me laboris mei, vos virtutis vestrae fructum esse laturos. Nam si iste id fecisset quod prius statuerat, ut non adesset, minus aliquanto quam mihi opus esset cognosceretur quid ego in hac

THE SECOND SPEECH AGAINST
GAIUS VERRES : BOOK I

I. Gentlemen : You are probably none of you un- 1
aware that it has during these last few days been
the common talk, and the belief of this nation, that
Gaius Verres would make no defence at the second
hearing, and would not appear in court. The spread-
ing of this report was not due solely to his own
definite and deliberate intention not to appear, but
also to the universal impression that no man, convicted by so many witnesses of crimes so abominable,
could be so recklessly and insanely impudent as to
venture to look his judges in their faces, or to show his
own face to the people of Rome. But he is still Verres, 2
true to his name as ever, daring the worst without
hesitation, and hearing the worst without reluctance.
He is here before us, he replies to me, his defence
continues : with his vile offences openly brought
home to him, he has not even allowed himself, by
holding his tongue and keeping away, the credit of
some attempt to make, after all, a decent end to his
indecent career. Very well, gentlemen. I am not
sorry that I am to reap the reward of my hard
work, and you the reward of your courage. Had
Verres carried out his original intention of not
appearing, the heavy toil that I have undergone, in
shaping and building up my case as prosecutor,

accusatione comparanda constituendaque elaboras-
sem ; vestra vero laus tenuis plane atque obscura,
3 iudices, esset.   Neque hoc a vobis populus Romanus
exspectat, neque eo potest esse contentus, si condemnatus sit is qui adesse noluerit, et si fortes fueritis
in eo quem nemo sit ausus defendere.   Immo vero
adsit, respondeat ;   summis opibus, summo studio
potentissimorum hominum defendatur ;   certet mea
diligentia cum illorum omnium cupiditate, vestra
integritas cum istius pecunia, testium constantia cum
illius patronorum minis atque potentia.   Tum demum
illa victa videbuntur, cum in contentionem certa-
4 menque venerint.   Absens si iste esset damnatus,
non tam sibi consuluisse quam invidisse vestrae laudi
videretur.

II. Neque enim salus ulla reipublicae maior hoc
tempore reperiri potest quam populum Romanum
intellegere, diligenter reiectis ab accusatore iudicibus,
socios, leges, rempublicam senatorio consilio maxime
posse defendi ; neque tanta fortunis omnium pernicies
potest accedere quam opinione populi Romani
rationem veritatis, integritatis, fidei, religionis ab hoc
5 ordine abiudicari.   Itaque mihi videor magnam et
maxime aegram et prope depositam reipublicae
partem suscepisse ;   neque in eo magis meae quam

would receive somewhat less recognition than my interests demand ; and the credit due to you, gentlemen, would be seriously weakened and obscured. But the Roman people is looking for something **3** better from you than the condemnation of a man who has refused to answer the charge ; nor can it be satisfied that you should display your courage by punishing a man whom nobody has ventured to defend. No, no, let him appear by all means, let him make his reply ; let him be defended by all the wealth, and by all the energy, of the mightiest in the land. Against my exertions let there be arrayed the passionate eagerness of all his great friends ; against your integrity, his money ; against the steady testimony of our witnesses, the threats of his powerful advocates. Never can these hostile forces be openly crushed until they have stood up to fight against us. Had Verres stayed away from his condemnation, it **4** would be felt that he had rather begrudged you your credit than done his best for himself.

II. For indeed, in these days, no surer means of securing our country's welfare can be devised than the assurance of the Roman people that—given the careful challenging of judges by the prosecutor—our allies, our laws, our country can be safely guarded by a court composed of senators ; nor can a greater disaster come upon us all than a conviction, on the part of the Roman people, that the Senatorial Order has cast aside all respect for truth and integrity, for honesty and duty. And I feel in consequence that **5** I have undertaken to rescue an important part of our body politic, a part that is sick unto death and almost beyond recovery ; and that, in so doing, I have worked for your credit and your good name not

vestrae laudi existimationique servisse. Accessi
enim ad invidiam iudiciorum levandam vitupe-
rationemque tollendam ; ut, cum haec res pro
voluntate populi Romani esset iudicata, aliqua ex
parte mea diligentia constituta auctoritas iudiciorum
videretur : postremo, utcumque[1] esset hoc iudicatum,
ut finis aliquando iudiciariae controversiae constituere-
6 tur. Etenim sine dubio, iudices, in hac causa ea res
in discrimen adducitur. Reus est enim nocentissimus ; qui si condemnatur, desinent homines dicere
his iudiciis pecuniam plurimum posse ; sin absolvitur,
desinemus nos de iudiciis transferendis recusare.

Tametsi de absolutione istius neque ipse iam sperat
nec populus Romanus metuit : de impudentia
singulari, quod adest, quod respondet, sunt qui
mirentur. Mihi pro cetera eius audacia atque
amentia ne hoc quidem mirandum videtur. Multa
enim et in deos et in homines impie nefarieque commisit, quorum scelerum poenis agitatur et a mente
7 consilioque deducitur. III. Agunt eum praecipitem
poenae civium Romanorum, quos partim securi
percussit, partim in vinculis necavit, partim implo-
rantes iura libertatis et civitatis in crucem sustulit.
Rapiunt eum ad supplicium di patrii, quod iste inventus
est qui e complexu parentum abreptos filios ad necem
duceret et parentes pretium pro sepultura liberum
posceret. Religiones vero caerimoniaeque omnium

---

[1] postremo ut *MSS.*, perperam si *Peterson. The conjecture in the text gives the required sense.*

less than for my own. For I set about allaying the
unpopularity and eliminating the hostile criticism of
our courts ; intending that, when this case had been
decided as the Roman people would have it decided,
the stronger position thus gained for our courts might
be attributed, in some small measure, to my exertions ; and that, finally, whatever the decision were,
the present controversy about the courts should at
last be terminated. For undoubtedly, gentlemen, 6
the issue in the present case is nothing less than this.
The man accused is a criminal of the worst kind.
If he is found guilty, people will cease to say that
money is the chief power in these courts : but if he
is acquitted, we shall cease to hesitate about putting
the courts into other hands.

Yet his acquittal, after all, is a thing of which he
himself is no longer hopeful, and Rome no longer
afraid. It is his matchless effrontery in appearing
here, in answering his accusers, that some find surprising. To me, remembering the rest of his reckless and insane career, even this is nothing to cause
surprise. The thought of retribution for his evil
deeds, for his sins against heaven and his crimes
against man, is distracting his mind and expelling
good sense and sanity. III. He is being swept into 7
madness by those executions of Roman citizens,
whom he either beheaded, or imprisoned till they
died, or, while they appealed in vain for their rights
as free men and Romans, crucified. The gods of our
fathers are haling him off to punishment, because he
was found capable of tearing sons from their fathers'
arms to be dragged to execution, and of making
parents buy of him the right to bury their children.
And all the shrines and sacred places whose sanctity

sacrorum fanorumque violatae, simulacraque deorum, quae non modo ex suis templis ablata sunt, sed etiam iacent in tenebris ab isto retrusa atque abdita, consistere eius animum sine furore atque amentia non 8 sinunt. Neque iste mihi videtur se ad damnationem solum offerre, neque hoc avaritiae supplicio communi, qui se tot sceleribus obstrinxerit, contentus esse : singularem quandam poenam istius immanis atque importuna natura desiderat. Non id solum quaeritur, ut isto damnato bona restituantur iis quibus erepta sunt, sed et religiones deorum immortalium expiandae et civium Romanorum cruciatus multorumque innocentium sanguis istius supplicio 9 luendus est. Non enim furem sed ereptorem, non adulterum sed expugnatorem pudicitiae, non sacrilegum sed hostem sacrorum religionumque, non sicarium sed crudelissimum carnificem civium sociorumque in vestrum iudicium adduximus ; ut ego hunc unum eius modi reum post hominum memoriam fuisse arbitrer cui damnari expediret.

IV. Nam quis hoc non intellegit, istum absolutum dis hominibusque invitis tamen ex manibus populi Romani eripi nullo modo posse ? Quis hoc non perspicit, praeclare nobiscum actum iri si populus Romanus istius unius supplicio contentus fuerit, ac non sic statuerit, non istum maius in sese scelus conce-

and worship he has defiled, and all the images of the
gods that are not merely removed from their own
temples but stowed away by him in dark neglected
corners, these leave his mind no quietness, no freedom from the ravings of insanity.   I feel, moreover, 8
that he is not presenting himself for a mere verdict
of condemnation ; that, being involved in the guilt
of so many crimes, he cannot be satisfied with that
penalty for greed which other men suffer.   It must
be some unique punishment which this savage and
monstrous creature craves. The demand is not simply
that he should be found guilty, and the property that
he stole be restored to its owners : there must also
be expiation for the violated sanctity of the im-
mortal gods ; his punishment must atone for the
torturing of Roman citizens, for the blood of many
an innocent man that he has shed.   It is no common 9
thief, but a violent robber ; no common adulterer, but
the ravager of all chastity ; no common profaner,
but the grand enemy of all that is sacred and holy ;
no common murderer, but the cruel butcher of our
citizens and our subjects, whom we have haled before
your judgement-seat : so vile, that I conceive him to
be the one man in history who, arraigned as he is
arraigned, could gain, not lose, by a verdict of condemnation.

IV. For who cannot see that, though he were
acquitted in despite of God and man, yet no power
can deliver him from the hands of the people of
Rome ?   Who cannot perceive that we senators shall
be fortunate indeed, if the people of Rome may be
appeased by the punishment of this one man, and
shall not pronounce the heavier judgement, that
plunged deep in evil deeds though Verres is—though

pisse, cum fana spoliarit, cum tot homines innocentes
necarit, cum cives Romanos morte, cruciatu, cruce
affecerit, cum praedonum duces accepta pecunia
dimiserit, quam eos, si qui istum tot, tantis, tam
nefariis sceleribus coopertum iurati sententia sua
10 liberarint? Non est, non est in hoc homine cuiquam
peccandi locus, iudices : non is est reus, non id tempus, non id consilium, (metuo ne quid arrogantius
apud tales viros videar dicere) ne actor quidem est is
cui reus tam nocens, tam perditus, tam convictus aut
occulte surripi aut impune eripi possit. His ego iudicibus non probabo C. Verrem contra leges pecuniam
cepisse? Sustinebunt tales viri se tot senatoribus,
tot equitibus Romanis, tot civitatibus, tot hominibus
honestissimis ex tam illustri provincia, tot populorum
privatorumque litteris non credidisse? Tantae populi
11 Romani voluntati restitisse? Sustineant : reperie-
mus, si istum vivum ad aliud iudicium perducere
poterimus, quibus probemus istum in quaestura pecuniam publicam Cn. Carboni consuli datam avertisse,
quibus persuadeamus istum alieno nomine a quaestoribus urbanis, quod priore actione didicistis,
pecuniam abstulisse ; erunt qui et in eo quoque audaciam eius reprehendant, quod aliquot nominibus de
capite quantum commodum fuerit frumenti decumani
detraxerit ; erunt etiam fortasse, iudices, qui illum
130

he has despoiled sanctuaries, butchered a multitude
of innocent persons, slain and tortured and crucified
citizens of Rome, and taken bribes to let pirate chiefs
go free—yet he is no guiltier than those who, sworn
to vote truly, have voted for the acquittal of this
man loaded with so many monstrous and horrible
crimes ? This man's case offers no liberty for mis- 10
conduct to anyone : no, gentlemen, none : the
accused is such, the times are such, this court is
such, and even—if it will not seem a presumptuous
thing to say to an audience like this—the prosecutor
is such, that neither stealth can effect without detection, nor force effect with impunity, the escape of a
man so guilty, so abandoned, so clearly convicted of
the charges brought against him. Before such a
bench of judges as this, shall I fail to prove that
Gaius Verres has acquired wealth illegally ? Will
such gentlemen as these succeed in disbelieving this
multitude of Senators and Knights, of civic bodies,
of respectable inhabitants of that noble province, of
public and private records ? Will they succeed in
refusing what the people of Rome so strongly desires ? Suppose that they do : if I am able to bring 11
him alive before another court, I shall find others to
convince that in his quaestorship he embezzled public
money assigned to the consul Gnaeus Carbo, others
whom I can make believe what you were told at the
first hearing, that he used another man's name to
embezzle money from the city quaestors : there will
also be some to censure his unscrupulous tampering
with various accounts, whereby he abstracted as much
as he conveniently could from the total of the Sicilian
tithe-corn : there will also, gentlemen, possibly be
some who hold that one of his peculations should

eius peculatum vel acerrime vindicandum putent,
quod iste M. Marcelli et P. Africani monumenta,
quae nomine illorum, re vera populi Romani et erant
et habebantur, ex fanis religiosissimis et ex urbibus
sociorum atque amicorum non dubitarit auferre. V.
12 Emerserit ex peculatus etiam iudicio : meditetur de
ducibus hostium quos accepta pecunia liberavit;
videat quid de illis respondeat quos in eorum locum
subditos domi suae reservavit ; quaerat non solum
quem ad modum nostro crimini, verum etiam quo
pacto suae confessioni, possit mederi ; meminerit se
priore actione, clamore populi Romani infesto atque
inimico excitatum, confessum esse duces praedonum
a se securi non esse percussos, se iam tum esse veritum
ne sibi crimini daretur eos ab se pecunia liberatos ;
fateatur id quod negari non potest, se privatum
hominem praedonum duces vivos atque incolumes
domi suae, posteaquam Romam redierit, usque dum
per me licuerit retinuisse. Hoc in illo maiestatis
iudicio si licuisse sibi ostenderit, ego oportuisse concedam. Ex hoc quoque evaserit : proficiscar eo quo me
13 iampridem vocat populus Romanus ; de iure enim
libertatis et civitatis suum putat esse iudicium, et
recte putat. Confringat iste sane vi sua consilia
senatoria, quaestiones omnium perrumpat, evolet ex
vestra severitate : mihi credite, artioribus apud

be punished quite severely, that of the memorials of
Marcus Marcellus and Publius Africanus, nominally
the gifts of those great men, but really, as all held,
the gifts of the Roman nation ; of which memorials
he did not hesitate to strip the holiest sanctuaries
and the cities of our allies and friends. V. Suppose 12
that he eludes the Embezzlement Court also. Then
let him ponder that matter of the enemy captains
whom he was bribed to set free ; let him consider
his reply when questioned about the men whom he
secretly substituted for those captains and kept shut
up in his house ; let him ask himself not only how
he is to answer the charge we bring, but how he is
to explain away his own admissions ; let him remember how, during the first hearing, terrified by the
angry clamour of the hostile public, he confessed
that he had failed to have those pirate captains
beheaded, and had been afraid at the time that he
would be charged with taking bribes to set them
free ; let him admit what cannot be denied, that
when no longer in office, after his return to Rome,
he kept those pirate chiefs alive and unharmed at
his own house until I interfered to prevent it. Let
him show if he can, before the Treason Court, that
this conduct was even legal, and I will concede that
it was his positive duty. Suppose that he escapes
this danger too. I will then approach that tribunal
to which I have long been invited by the voice of
the Roman nation : for the rights of the free man 13
and the citizen it holds, and justly holds, to be
within its own jurisdiction. Granted that Verres'
violence may break the ranks of senatorial bodies,
force a path through every Criminal Court, and
escape the rigour of your judgement : believe me,

populum Romanum laqueis tenebitur. Credet iis
equitibus Romanis populus Romanus qui ad vos antea
producti testes ipsis inspectantibus ab isto civem
Romanum, qui cognitores homines honestos daret,
14 sublatum esse in crucem dixerunt. Credent omnes
v. et xxx. tribus homini gravissimo atque ornatissimo
M. Annio, qui se praesente civem Romanum securi
percussum esse dixit. Audietur a populo Romano
vir primarius, eques Romanus, L. Flavius, qui suum
familiarem Herennium, negotiatorem ex Africa, cum
eum Syracusis amplius centum cives Romani cognoscerent lacrimantesque defenderent, pro testimonio
dixit securi esse percussum. Probabit fidem et
auctoritatem et religionem suam L. Suettius, homo
omnibus ornamentis praeditus, qui iuratus apud vos
dixit multos cives Romanos in lautumiis istius imperio
crudelissime per vim morte esse multatos. Hanc ego
causam cum agam beneficio populi Romani de loco
superiore, non vereor ne aut istum vis ulla ex populi
Romani suffragiis eripere aut a me ullum munus
aedilitatis amplius aut gratius populo Romano esse
possit.

15 VI. Quapropter omnes in hoc iudicio conentur
omnia ; nihil est iam quod in hac causa peccare quisquam, iudices, nisi vestro periculo possit. Mea quidem ratio cum in praeteritis rebus est cognita, tum

---

^a Witnesses to the fact of his being a Roman citizen.

^b The famous quarries of Syracuse.

^c The offences mentioned in §§ 11-14 are all fully dealt
with later, most of them in Book V.

the cords will bind him more tightly when he stands before the Roman people. The Roman people will believe those Roman knights who, called to give evidence before you, affirmed that a Roman citizen, though he produced respectable men as his guarantors,[a] was crucified before their own eyes. All the 14 thirty-five Tribes will believe a man of so much responsibility and distinction as Marcus Annius, who has stated that, in his presence, a Roman citizen was beheaded. The people of Rome will listen to the words of so important a person as the knight Lucius Flavius, who has given evidence on oath that his acquaintance Herennius, a banker from Africa, was beheaded at Syracuse, although upwards of a hundred Roman citizens identified him there, and pleaded for him with tears in their eyes. Honour, dignity, and conscience will confirm the words of a man so distinguished in all respects as Lucius Suettius, who has testified on oath before you to the cruel and violent death inflicted on many Roman citizens in the stone-quarries [b] by Verres' orders.[c] As I conduct that prosecution from the high place where the favour of the Roman people has set me, I have no fear that violence of any kind will rescue him from the Roman people's verdict, nor that any other spectacle that I offer them as aedile can appear to them more splendid or afford them greater pleasure.

VI. Accordingly, in dealing with this Court, let all 15 the world do its worst : for in this case, gentlemen, no room for misconduct is now left to any of you, save at great risk to yourselves. My own line of action, familiar to you from what has happened already, has been planned and thought out for what

135

in reliquis explorata atque provisa est. Ego meum
studium in rem publicam iam illo tempore ostendi
cum longo intervallo veterem consuetudinem rettuli,
et rogatu sociorum atque amicorum populi Romani,
meorum autem necessariorum, nomen hominis
audacissimi detuli. Quod meum factum lectissimi
viri atque ornatissimi (quo in numero e vobis complures fuerunt) ita probarunt ut ei qui istius quaestor
fuisset, et ab isto laesus inimicitias iustas perse-
queretur, non modo deferendi nominis, sed ne
subscribendi quidem, cum id postularet, facerent
16 potestatem. In Siciliam sum inquirendi causa profectus ; quo in negotio industriam meam celeritas
reditionis, diligentiam multitudo litterarum et testium
declaravit ; pudorem vero ac religionem quod, cum
venissem senator ad socios populi Romani, qui in ea
provincia quaestor fuissem, ad hospites meos ac necessarios causae communis defensor deverti potius
quam ad eos qui a me auxilium petivissent. Nemini
meus adventus labori aut sumptui neque publice neque privatim fuit ; vim in inquirendo tantam habui
quantam mihi lex dabat, non quantam habere pote-
17 ram ipsorum[1] studio, quos iste vexarat. Romam
ut ex Sicilia redii, cum iste atque istius amici, homines lauti et urbani, sermones eius modi dissi-
passent, quo animos testium retardarent, me magna
pecunia a vera accusatione esse deductum ; tametsi
probabatur nemini, quod et ex Sicilia testes erant ii

---

[1] ipsorum *Mueller* : istorum MSS., *retained by Peterson.*

is still to come. I showed my love of my country from the moment when I returned, after a long interval, to my former practice, and at the request of allies and friends of Rome, who were also my own acquaintances, prosecuted this bold miscreant. My action was so cordially approved by persons of high character and distinction, including several of yourselves, that they refused to the man who had been Verres' quaestor, and who had a personal quarrel with Verres justified by the harm Verres had done him, not only the opportunity of prosecuting him, but even, though he asked for it, that of supporting the prosecution. I went off to collect evidence in Sicily : 16 in which matter my energy was indicated by the earliness of my return ; my carefulness, by the crowd of documents and witnesses I secured ; my conscientious regard for propriety, by the way in which, though I was a senator visiting Roman allies in the province where I had been a quaestor, and though I was the champion of the whole community, I nevertheless stayed at the houses of my old hosts and personal acquaintances, rather than with those who had appealed to me for help. Nowhere did my coming cause trouble or expense, official or unofficial, to anyone. I pushed my inquiries with no more advantage than the law allowed me, neglecting that which the enthusiasm of Verres' victims was ready to give me. Upon my return from Sicily to Rome, 17 Verres and his friends, with characteristic good taste and delicacy, tried to discourage my witnesses by circulating stories of my having accepted a heavy bribe to make my prosecution a sham : and although none of the witnesses believed this—those from Sicily being men who had learnt my character

qui quaestorem me in provincia cognoverant, et hinc
homines maxime illustres, qui, ut ipsi noti sunt, sic
nostrum unum quemque optime norunt, tamen
usque eo timui ne quis de mea fide atque integritate
dubitaret donec ad reiciundos iudices venimus.

VII. Sciebam in reiciundis iudicibus nonnullos
memoria nostra pactionis suspicionem non vitasse,
cum in ipsa accusatione eorum industria ac diligentia
18 probaretur. Ita reieci iudices ut hoc constet, post
hunc statum reipublicae quo nunc utimur simili
splendore et dignitate consilium nullum fuisse.
Quam iste laudem communem sibi ait esse mecum ;
qui cum P. Galbam iudicem reiecisset M. Lucretium
retinuit, et cum eius patronus ex eo quaereret cur
suos familiarissimos, Sex. Peducaeum, Q. Con-
sidium, Q. Iunium reici passus esset, respondit quod
eos in iudicando nimium sui iuris sententiaeque
19 cognosset. Itaque iudicibus reiectis sperabam iam
onus meum vobiscum esse commune ; putabam non
solum notis sed etiam ignotis probatam meam fidem
esse et diligentiam. Quod me non fefellit ; nam
comitiis meis, cum iste infinita largitione contra me
uteretur, populus Romanus iudicavit istius pecuniam,
quae apud me contra fidem meam nihil potuisset, apud
se contra honorem meum nihil posse debere. Quo

---

* Sulla's constitution, now ten years old.

when I was quaestor in the province, and those from
Rome men of shining reputation, to whom my
character, and that of each of my supporters, is as
familiar as their own is familiar to the world—none
the less I did feel misgivings lest my honour and
integrity should be distrusted, until we came to the
challenging of the judges.

VII. In the challenging of judges, I well knew
that in our time there had been those who had not
escaped the suspicion of underhand dealing, active
and strenuous as they had proved themselves in their
conduct of the prosecution itself. As the result of 18
my own challenging, it is agreed that never, since
the present form of government [a] was established,
has a court of such illustrious and acknowledged
merit assembled. The credit for this Verres claims
to share with me : Verres, who rejected Publius
Galba as a judge, and kept in Marcus Lucretius,
and when his advocate asked him why he had allowed
his intimate friends Sextus Peducaeus, Quintus
Considius, and Quintus Junius to be rejected, replied
that it was because he knew they were too independent in the way they thought and voted ! Well 19
then, the challenging of the judges being over, I
began to hope that part of my burden was now resting
upon you, and to feel that my honesty and watchfulness had been approved by those whom I did not
know as well as by those whom I did. Nor was I
mistaken ; for at my election, in spite of the vast
sums of money that Verres lavished to secure my
defeat, the Roman people expressed their judgement
that, since the man's money had not so prevailed
with me as to damage my honour, it must not so
prevail with them as to damage my success. And

139

quidem die primum, iudices, citati in hunc reum consedistis, quis tam iniquus huic ordini fuit, quis tam novarum rerum iudiciorum iudicumque cupidus, qui non aspectu consessuque vestro commoveretur?

20 Cum in eo vestra dignitas mihi fructum diligentiae referret, id sum assecutus, ut una hora qua coepi dicere reo audaci, pecunioso, profuso, perdito spem iudicii corrumpendi praeciderem; ut primo die testium tanto numero citato populus Romanus iudicaret isto absoluto rempublicam stare non posse; ut alter dies amicis istius ac defensoribus non modo spem victoriae sed etiam voluntatem defensionis auferret; ut tertius dies sic hominem prosterneret ut, morbo simulato, non quid responderet, sed quem ad modum non responderet deliberaret. Deinde reliquis diebus his criminibus, his testibus, et urbanis et provincialibus, sic obrutus atque oppressus est ut his ludorum diebus interpositis nemo istum comperendinatum sed condemnatum iudicaret.

21 VIII. Quapropter ego, quod ad me attinet, iudices, vici: non enim spolia C. Verris sed existimationem populi Romani concupivi. Meum fuit cum causa accedere ad accusandum: quae causa fuit honestior quam a tam illustri provincia defensorem constitui et

---

^a This account of the proceedings at the first hearing is, of course, at least partly fictitious. Compare §§ 1-2, and see the last paragraph of the Introduction, p. xix. We do not know how many days the trial lasted before the defence was abandoned.

indeed, gentlemen, on the day when you were first
called together, and took your seats to try this man,
was there anyone so hostile to the Senatorial Order,
anyone so eager for new arrangements, new courts,
and new judges, as not to be deeply impressed by
the sight of you thus assembled ? The very fact of 20
this noble spectacle was a reward to me for my
patient endeavours ; but I gained more than this.
Before my first speech had lasted for an hour, I had
cut short, in the mind of this wealthy scoundrel and
immoral spendthrift, his hopes of bribing the judges
who were to try him. On the first day of the trial,
when that great multitude of witnesses was called
into court, it became clear to the people of Rome
that if Verres were acquitted the country was lost.
The following day took from his friends and defenders
not merely all hope of success, but all disposition to
continue the defence. The third day prostrated the
man so completely that he feigned illness, and began
to think, not about what reply to make, but how to
avoid replying at all. The charges brought on the
rest of the days that followed, and the evidence
produced from both Rome and Sicily, crushed and
overwhelmed him so thoroughly that during this
interval for the Games everyone regarded his
case not as adjourned but as already settled
against him.[a]

VIII. The result is, gentlemen, that so far as I 21
am concerned my case is won ; for it is not a triumph
over Gaius Verres, but the vindication of the honour
of Rome, on which my heart has been set. My duty
has been to have good reason for undertaking the
prosecution ; and what reason could be more honourable than to be selected and appointed by so famous

deligi ? rei publicae consulere : quid tam e re publica
quam in tanta invidia iudiciorum adducere hominem
cuius damnatione totus ordo cum populo Romano et
in laude et in gratia possit esse ? ostendere ac
persuadere hominem nocentem adductum esse : quis
est in populo Romano qui hoc non ex priore actione
abstulerit, omnium ante damnatorum scelera, furta,
flagitia, si unum in locum conferantur, vix cum huius
22 parva parte aequari conferrique posse ? Vos, quod
ad vestram famam existimationem salutemque communem pertinet, iudices, prospicite atque consulite.
Splendor vester facit ut peccare sine summo rei
publicae detrimento ac periculo non possitis. Non
enim potest sperare populus Romanus esse alios in
senatu qui recte possint iudicare, vos si non potueritis ;
necesse est, cum de toto ordine desperarit, aliud
genus hominum atque aliam rationem iudiciorum
requirat. Hoc si vobis ideo levius videtur quod
putatis onus esse grave et incommodum iudicare,
intellegere debetis primum interesse utrum id onus
vosmet ipsi reieceritis, an, quod probare populo
Romano fidem vestram et religionem non potueritis,
eo vobis iudicandi potestas erepta sit ; deinde etiam
illud cogitare, quanto periculo venturi simus ad eos
iudices quos propter odium nostri populus Romanus

a province to defend it ?   My duty has been to think
of our country ; and what could help our country
better than meeting the unpopularity of our courts
by bringing a man to trial whose condemnation
would be enough to secure, for our whole Order, the
approval and favour of the Roman people ?   My
duty has been to prove, and to make it believed,
that the man thus brought to trial is guilty ; and is
there one single Roman who has not come away
from the first hearing convinced of this, that if we
could gather together in one the crimes and robberies
and wicked deeds of every man found guilty in the
past, they could hardly be held equal, or comparable,
to the tithe of what this man has done ?   You, 22
gentlemen, you must take thought and make provision for what concerns the credit, the good name,
the safe existence of you all.   Your eminent merit
makes misconduct impossible for you, save at the
cost of extreme injury and danger to the state.   For
the Roman people cannot hope that, if you cannot
give a righteous verdict, there may be other members of the Senate who can : it can only despair of
the whole Senatorial Order, and therefore look round
for some other type of man, and some other method
of administering justice.   If you think this no great
matter, because you regard your judicial duties as a
heavy and irksome burden, you must in the first
place remember that it is one thing to cast this
burden off of your own accord, and another thing,
through inability to prove yourselves honest and
conscientious in the eyes of Rome, to have your
judicial powers taken from you ; and then you must
further consider the grave risks we shall run when
we appear before those men whom, through hatred of

23 de nobis voluerit iudicare. Verum vobis dicam id quod intellexi, iudices. Homines scitote esse quosdam quos tantum odium nostri ordinis teneat ut hoc palam iam dictitent, se istum, quem sciant esse hominem improbissimum, hoc uno nomine absolvi velle, ut ab senatu iudicia per ignominiam turpitudinemque auferantur. Haec me pluribus verbis, iudices, vobiscum agere coegit non timor meus de vestra fide, sed spes illorum nova, quae cum Verrem a porta subito ad iudicium retraxisset, nonnulli suspicati sunt non sine causa illius consilium tam repente esse mutatum.

24 IX. Nunc, ne novo querimoniae genere uti possit Hortensius et ea dicere, opprimi reum de quo nihil dicat accusator, nihil esse tam periculosum fortunis innocentium quam tacere adversarios ; et ne aliter quam ego velim meum laudet ingenium cum dicat me, si multa dixissem, sublevaturum fuisse eum quem contra dicerem, quia non dixerim, perdidisse : morem illi geram, utar oratione perpetua ; non quoniam hoc sit necesse, verum ut experiar utrum ille ferat molestius me tunc tacuisse an nunc dicere.

25 Hic tu fortasse eris diligens, ne quam ego horam de meis legitimis horis remittam ; nisi omni tempore quod mihi lege concessum est abusus ero, querere,

us, the Roman people will desire to set up as judges
of our conduct. Yes, and I will tell you one thing, **23**
gentlemen, that I have discovered. You must know
that there are certain persons possessed by such
hatred of our Order that they are already saying,
openly and often, that they wish for the acquittal of
Verres, thorough scoundrel as they know him to be,
simply for the sake of having the Senate deprived,
with ignominy and shame, of its judicial rights. I
have felt bound to enlarge on this topic to you,
gentlemen, not through any fear of mine that you
cannot be trusted, but because of the new-born
hopes of Verres and his friends, which have suddenly
dragged him back to this court-house from the city
gate, and thus led some people to suspect that he
had some good reason for so hasty a change in his
plans.

IX. I have now to see to it that Hortensius has **24**
no ground for a new form of protest, for saying that
any man's case is ruined by his prosecutor's refusing
to make a speech, and that nothing endangers the
happiness of innocent persons so gravely as the
silence of their assailants ; no ground for offering an
unwelcome commendation of my ability, by saying
that, if I had made a long attack, I should have
helped the man I was attacking, and that I have
ruined him by not making one ; and I will therefore
oblige him by delivering a continuous speech, not
because it is needed, but because I would learn
whether he objects more strongly to my silence then
or to my speaking now. You, Hortensius, will now **25**
be watching carefully, I daresay, to see that I do not
forgo one hour of the time that the law allows me.
Unless I use every minute of my full legal time, you

deum atque hominum fidem implorabis, circumveniri
C. Verrem quod accusator nolit tam diu quam diu
liceat dicere. Quod mihi lex mea causa dedit, eo
mihi non uti non licebit? Nam accusandi mihi
tempus mea causa datum est, ut possem oratione mea
crimina causamque explicare ; hoc si non utor, non
tibi iniuriam facio, sed de meo iure aliquid et commodo detraho. "Causam enim" inquit "cognosci
oportet." Ea re quidem, quod aliter condemnari
reus, quamvis sit nocens, non potest. Id igitur tu
moleste tulisti, a me aliquid factum esse quo minus
iste condemnari posset? Nam causa cognita multi
possunt absolvi, incognita quidem condemnari nemo
26 potest. Adimo enim comperendinatum? Quod
habet lex in se molestissimum, bis ut causa dicatur,
id aut mea causa potius est constitutum quam tua,
aut nihilo tua potius quam mea. Nam si bis dicere
est commodum, certe utriusque commune est ; si
eum qui posterius dixit opus est redargui, accusatoris
causa ut bis ageretur constitutum est. Verum, ut
opinor, Glaucia primus tulit ut comperendinaretur
reus ; antea vel iudicari primo poterat vel amplius
pronuntiari. Utram igitur putas legem molliorem?
opinor illam veterem, qua vel cito absolvi vel tarde

---

[a] *i.e.*, postponement was (i.) optional, (ii.) shorter or
longer, as the court might decide, than the precise period
prescribed by Glaucia's law—the Lex Servilia of about
106 B.C.

will be protesting, and calling heaven and earth to
witness, that Gaius Verres is being treated unfairly
because the prosecutor refuses to go on speaking as
long as he lawfully may. May I, then, not lawfully
decline a privilege that the law has conferred on me
for my own benefit? It certainly is for my own
benefit that a certain amount of time was allowed me
as prosecutor, enough to set forth my charges and
expound my case. If I fail to use it, I do you no
wrong; I merely detract, to some extent, from my
own rights and my own advantage. "Yes," you
say, "but the case ought to be properly investigated." To be sure; and why? Because otherwise, however guilty the accused may be, he cannot
be convicted. Is this your grievance, then, that I
have done something to make his conviction more
difficult? People may often be acquitted when their
cases have been investigated: when they have not,
it is impossible to convict. Ah, you say, but I am 26
doing away with the object of the second hearing.
Yes, with the most troublesome provision of the law,
this compulsory double pleading—an arrangement
devised either for my benefit more than for yours,
or at least quite as much for mine as for yours; for
if it is an advantage to speak twice, the advantage
is certainly shared by both sides; and if the great
thing is to refute the arguments of the last speaker,
this arrangement of a second pleading is for the
benefit of the prosecutor. After all, if I am not
mistaken, it was Glaucia's law that first provided for
the adjourned hearing: before that time, the case
could either be settled at once or postponed for
further inquiry.[a] Well now, which provision do you
consider the milder? Surely the old one, which

condemnari licebat. Ego tibi illam Aciliam legem
restituo, qua lege multi semel accusati, semel dicta
causa, semel auditis testibus condemnati sunt, nequaquam tam manifestis neque tantis criminibus quantis
tu convinceris. Puta te non hac tam atroci, sed illa
lege mitissima causam dicere. Accusabo ; respon-
debis ; testibus editis, ita mittam in consilium ut,
etiamsi lex ampliandi faciat potestatem, tamen isti
turpe sibi existiment non primo iudicare.

27 X. Verum si causam cognosci opus est, parumne
cognita est ? Dissimulamus, Hortensi, quod saepe
experti in dicendo sumus. Quis nos magno opere
attendit umquam, in hoc quidem genere causarum,
ubi aliquid ereptum aut ablatum a quopiam dicitur ?
nonne aut in tabulis aut in testibus omnis exspectatio
iudicum est ? Dixi prima actione me planum esse
facturum C. Verrem HS quadringentiens contra legem
abstulisse. Quid ? hoc planius egissem si ita nar-
rassem ? " Dio quidam fuit Halaesinus, qui, cum
eius filio, praetore Sacerdote, hereditas a propinquo
permagna venisset, nihil habuit tum neque negotii
neque controversiae. Verres, simul ac tetigit provinciam, statim Messana litteras dedit, Dionem evo-

---

^a *i.e.*, your client Verres.

might either hasten an acquittal or delay a conviction. It is this, the old Acilian law, that I am reviving for your benefit—a law under which many a man, after a single prosecution, a single pleading of his case, a single hearing of evidence, has been found guilty of offences not nearly so plainly proved, not nearly so grave, as these of which you *a* are now being convicted. Imagine yourself pleading, not under the existing rigorous law, but under the older and more indulgent. I will prosecute, you will reply, the witnesses will be called; and I will submit such an issue for the verdict of the Court that, however much postponement the law might allow, these gentlemen would be ashamed not to give their verdict forthwith.

X. And after all, granted that the case must be 27 tried, has it not been fully tried already? We are pretending ignorance, Hortensius, of what our experience at the Bar has repeatedly shown to us. In cases of this type, where anyone is alleged to have stolen or appropriated anything, who cares much what we pleaders say? Is not the judges' whole concern with the evidence of the witnesses and written records? I stated, at the first hearing, that I would prove that Gaius Verres had illegally appropriated four hundred thousand pounds. Well, should I have proved it any more clearly by a narrative of the following kind? "There was a man of Halaesa named Dio, whose son inherited a large property from a relative during the praetorship of Gaius Sacerdos; the fact was not disputed at the time, and caused Dio no trouble. Verres had no sooner touched the soil of Sicily, than he promptly wrote from Messana summoning Dio, set up some

149

cavit, calumniatores ex sinu suo apposuit qui illam
hereditatem Veneri Erycinae commissam esse, dicerent, hac de re ostendit se ipsum cogniturum."
28 Possum deinceps totam rem explicare, deinde ad
extremum id, quod accidit, dicere : Dionem HS
deciens centena millia numerasse, ut causam certissimam obtineret : praeterea greges equarum eius
istum abigendos curasse, argenti, vestis stragulae
quod fuerit curasse auferendum. Haec neque cum
ego dicerem neque cum tu negares magni momenti
nostra esset oratio. Quo tempore igitur aures iudex
erigeret animumque attenderet ? Cum Dio ipse
prodiret, cum ceteri qui tum in Sicilia negotiis Dionis
interfuissent, cum per eos ipsos dies per quos causam
Dio diceret reperiretur pecunias sumpsisse mutuas,
nomina sua exegisse, praedia vendidisse, cum tabulae
virorum bonorum proferrentur, cum qui pecuniam
Dioni dederunt dicerent se iam tum audisse eos
nummos sumi ut Verri darentur, cum amici, hospites,
patroni Dionis, homines honestissimi, haec eadem se
29 audisse dicerent. Opinor, cum haec fierent, tum
vos audiretis, sicut audistis ; tum causa agi vere
videretur. Sic a me sunt acta omnia priore actione
ut in criminibus omnibus nullum esset in quo quisquam vestrum perpetuam accusationem requireret.
Nego esse quicquam a testibus dictum quod aut

of his own gang to allege, what they knew to be
false, that the property in question was forfeited to
Venus of Eryx, and announced that he would try
the case himself." I might go on to give a full 28
account of the whole affair, and then finally state,
what actually happened, that Dio paid up ten thousand pounds to secure his unquestionable rights, and
that, besides this, Verres had his stables emptied of
his studs of mares, and his house stripped of all the
plate and tapestry it contained. I might state these
facts, and you might deny them ; but our speeches
would matter very little. What would be the time,
then, for a judge to prick up his ears and arouse
his attention ? Why, it would be when Dio himself
came forward, and likewise all those persons who
had dealings with Dio in Sicily at the time when,
during the actual course of his case, it was found
that he had borrowed money, called in his debts,
and sold his land ; it would be when the accounts
of those honest gentlemen were produced in court ;
when those who lent Dio money testified to having
heard at the time that he was borrowing it to
pay over to Verres ; when the excellent men who
were Dio's friends, hosts and protectors, testified to
having heard exactly the same thing. It was while 29
all this was happening, I take it, that you, gentlemen, would be listening, as indeed you were ; it
was then that you would feel the real trial was
taking place. At the first hearing I conducted the
whole of my case in such a fashion that, out of the
whole body of charges, there was no single one for
which any of you felt the need of a continuous
speech from the prosecutor. I maintain that no
detail of the witnesses' evidence was unintelligible

151

vestrum cuipiam esset obscurum aut cuiusquam
oratoris eloquentiam quaereret. XI. Etenim sic me
ipsum egisse memoria tenetis ut in testibus interro-
gandis omnia crimina proponerem et explicarem, ut
cum rem totam in medio proposuissem, tum denique
testem interrogarem. Itaque non modo vos, quibus
est iudicandum, nostra crimina tenetis, sed etiam
populus Romanus totam accusationem causamque
cognovit.

Tametsi ita de meo facto loquor quasi ego illud
mea voluntate potius quam vestra iniuria adductus
30 fecerim ? Interposuistis accusatorem qui, cum ego
mihi c. et x. dies solos in Siciliam postulassem, c. et
VIII. sibi in Achaiam postularet. Menses mihi tres
cum eripuissetis ad agendum maxime appositos,
reliquum omne tempus huius anni me vobis remis-
surum putastis ; ut, cum horis nostris nos essemus
usi, tu, binis ludis interpositis, quadragesimo post die
responderes, deinde ita tempus duceretur ut a M'.
Glabrione praetore et a magna parte horum iudicum
ad praetorem alium iudicesque alios veniremus.
31 Hoc si ego non vidissem, si me non omnes noti
ignotique monuissent id agi, id cogitari, in eo elabo-
rari, ut res in illud tempus reiiceretur, credo, si meis

---

[a] See *Actio Prima*, § 6.

[b] See Introduction, p. xvi.

[c] *Sc.* " as I well might have felt (since it is the regular
procedure) but for the discovery of the plot."

to any of you, or required the addition of any
pleader's eloquence. XI. And indeed you will remember that my own procedure in examining my
witnesses was first to introduce and expound each
of the various charges, so that I never examined a
witness until I had clearly stated the whole facts of
the charge concerned. The result is, not only that
the charges we brought are grasped clearly by yourselves, who have to pronounce the verdict, but also
that the Roman people have become familiar with
the entire case for the prosecution.

Yet why should I speak of my conduct as though
I had been led to it by my own inclination, and
not by the unfairness of you and your friends,
Hortensius ? Upon my asking for no more than 30
110 days to collect evidence in Sicily, you tried to
block my way with a prosecutor who asked for two
days less to do the same in Achaia.[a] After robbing
me of three months particularly well fitted for judicial
proceedings,[b] you reckoned on my leaving all the
rest of the year free for you ; you intended us to
take up all the time allowed us, and then, forty
days later, after the interval for the two sets of
Games, you would begin your speech ; and after
that the time was to be spun out till we no longer
had Manius Glabrio as president, nor the majority
of these gentlemen as members of the Court, but
had to appear before a new president and new
judges. Had I not discovered all this—had not 31
everyone, friend and stranger alike, pointed out to
me that the object of your plots and your schemes
and your intrigues was to push back the proceedings
to that later date—it is likely indeed that, if I had
felt inclined [c] to spend my full time over my speech

153

horis in accusando uti voluissem, vererer ne mihi
crimina non suppeterent, ne oratio deesset, ne vox
viresque deficerent, ne, quem nemo prima actione
defendere ausus esset, eum ego bis accusare non
possem. Ego meum consilium cum iudicibus tum
populo Romano probavi ; nemo est qui alia ratione
istorum iniuriae atque impudentiae potuisse obsisti
arbitretur. Etenim qua stultitia fuissem, si, quam
diem qui istum eripiendum redemerunt in cautione
viderunt, cum ita caverent, " si post Kalendas
Ianuarias in consilium iretur," in eam diem ego,
cum potuissem vitare, incidissem ?

32   Nunc mihi temporis eius quod mihi ad dicendum
datur, quoniam in animo est causam omnem exponere, habenda ratio est diligenter. XII. Itaque
primum illum actum istius vitae turpissimum et
flagitiosissimum praetermittam. Nihil a me de
pueritiae suae flagitiis audiet, nihil ex illa impura
adulescentia sua, quae qualis fuerit aut meministis
aut ex eo quem sui simillimum produxit recognoscere
potestis. Omnia praeteribo quae mihi turpia dictu
videbuntur, neque solum quid istum audire, verum
etiam quid me deceat dicere, considerabo. Vos,
quaeso, date hoc et concedite pudori meo ut aliquam
33 partem de istius impudentia reticere possim. Omne
illud tempus quod fuit antequam iste ad magistratus
remque publicam accessit habeat per me solutum ac

ᵃ Bribery-agents and the like, who agreed for a lump
sum to secure Verres' acquittal: compare *Actio Prima*, § 23,
for a somewhat similar contract.
154

for the prosecution, I should have been deterred by
the fear that I should run short of charges to bring ;
that my eloquence would fail me ; that my voice or
my strength would give way ; that I should be unable
to attack a second time the man whom nobody had
ventured to defend at the first hearing ! I have
justified, to the Court and to the people of Rome,
the plan I adopted ; there is no one who supposes
that the shameless unfairness of my opponents could
possibly have been thwarted otherwise. What a
fool I should have been, indeed, if I had wilfully
fallen into the trap of waiting for the very day on
which the contractors for Verres' escape [a] had their
eyes fixed, when they inserted in their contract the
caveat " provided that the case shall come on after
the 1st of January."

But I must now take careful account of the time 32
allowed me for my speech, since I intend to set
forth the case in full. XII. I shall therefore pass
over the notoriously vile and immoral " first act " of
Verres' career. He shall hear nothing from me of
the sins of his boyhood, no tales of his unclean
youth—what that was like you either remember or
can infer from the faithful copy of himself that he
has brought into the world.[b] I will pass over all
that I cannot refer to without indecency, and will
take into account what it is proper for me to tell,
as well as what it is proper for him to be told.
Please indulge my sense of modesty so far as to
allow me the liberty of holding my tongue about
some small part of his shameless career. All those 33
earlier years, up to the time when he entered upon
public office and political life, may remain free and

[b] *Produxit* may mean " has brought into court."

liberum. Sileatur de nocturnis eius bacchationibus
ac vigiliis ; lenonum, aleatorum, perductorum nulla
mentio fiat ; damna, dedecora, quae res patris eius,
aetas ipsius pertulit, praetereantur ; lucretur indicia
veteris infamiae ; patiatur eius vita reliqua me hanc
34 tantam iacturam criminum facere. Quaestor Cn.
Papirio consuli fuisti abhinc annos quattuordecim :
ex ea die ad hanc diem quae fecisti in iudicium voco.
Hora nulla vacua a furto, scelere, crudelitate, flagitio
reperietur. Hi sunt anni consumpti in quaestura et
legatione Asiatica et praetura urbana et praetura
Siciliensi. Quare haec eadem erit quadripertita
distributio totius accusationis meae.

XIII. Quaestor ex senatus consulto provinciam
sortitus es ; obtigit tibi consularis, ut cum consule
Cn. Carbone esses eamque provinciam obtineres.
Erat tum dissensio civium ; de qua nihil sum dicturus
quid sentire debueris ; unum hoc dico, in eius modi
tempore ac sorte statuere te debuisse utrum malles
sentire atque defendere. Carbo graviter ferebat
sibi quaestorem obtigisse hominem singulari luxuria
atque inertia ; verum tamen ornabat eum beneficiis
officiisque omnibus. Ne diutius teneam, pecunia at-
tributa, numerata est ; profectus est quaestor in

ᵃ Gnaeus Papirius Carbo, one of the four Democrat
leaders who seized Rome when Sulla left for the east in 87 :
the other three were Marius, Sertorius, and Cinna.

ᵇ The usual method : but the Senate might, in any year,
assign particular spheres of duty to some or all of the
quaestors.

ᶜ Really " proconsul " : *consul* often means this. Carbo
was consul during 84. In 83 he went as proconsul to

clear for him, so far as I am concerned. Let nothing be said about the drunken orgies that lasted all night ; let there be no mention of pimps and gamblers and seducers ; let his inroads on his father's purse and his defilements of his own manhood, be passed by without a word ; let him score, so far as the evidence for his earlier infamy goes ; let us consider that the rest of his life enables me to sacrifice all this material for prosecution. Fourteen years ago, Verres, you 34 became quaestor to the consul Gnaeus Papirius.ᵃ I call you to account for all you have done from that day to this. Not one hour, it will be found, has been free from robbery and crime, from cruelty and wickedness. These years you spent as quaestor, as adjutant in Asia, as city praetor, and as praetor of Sicily ; and I shall therefore distribute my speech for the prosecution into four corresponding parts.

XIII. In accordance with a decree of the Senate, your sphere of duty as quaestor was determined by lot.ᵇ A consular department fell to you ; you were to accompany the consul ᶜ Gnaeus Carbo and be his quaestor. At that time, civil strife prevailed : I am not going to say anything about the side you ought to have taken ; but one thing I do say, that at such a crisis, and the lot having fallen as it did, you ought to have made up your mind which side you did mean to take and to support. Carbo was annoyed that the lot had given him as quaestor a particularly lazy and self-indulgent man ; none the less, he loaded him with every sort of kindness and attention. To cut the story short : funds were allotted and paid over to the quaestor ; he left for his province, and

Cisalpine Gaul, to raise troops and secure that region, in view of Sulla's expected return : Verres went with him.

provinciam ; venit exspectatus in Galliam ad exercitum consularem cum pecunia. Simul ac primum ei
occasio visa est (cognoscite hominis principium
magistratuum gerendorum et rei publicae admini-
strandae) aversa pecunia publica quaestor consulem,
35 exercitum, sortem provinciamque deseruit. Video
quid egerim : erigit se, sperat sibi auram posse
aliquam adflari in hoc crimine voluntatis assensionis-
que eorum quibus Cn. Carbonis mortui nomen odio
sit, quibus illam relictionem proditionemque consulis
sui gratam sperat fore. Quasi vero id cupiditate
defendendae nobilitatis aut studio partium fecerit,
ac non apertissime consulem, exercitum provinciamque compilarit et propter impudentissimum furtum
aufugerit. Est enim obscurum et eius modi factum
eius, ut possit aliquis suspicari C. Verrem quod ferre
novos homines non potuerit ad nobilitatem, hoc est
ad suos, transisse, nihil fecisse propter pecuniam.

36 Videamus rationes quem ad modum rettulerit ;
iam ipse ostendet quam ob rem Cn. Carbonem re-
liquerit, iam se ipse indicabit. XIV. Primum brevi-
tatem cognoscite. ACCEPI, inquit, VICIENS DUCENTA
TRIGINTA QUINQUE MILIA QUADRINGENTOS X. ET VII.
NUMMOS. DEDI STIPENDIO, FRUMENTO, LEGATIS, PRO
QUAESTORE, COHORTI PRAETORIAE, HS MILLE SESCENTA
TRIGINTA QUINQUE MILIA QUADRINGENTOS XVII. NUMMOS.
RELIQUI ARIMINI HS SESCENTA MILIA. Hoc est rationes
referre ? hoc modo aut ego aut tu, Hortensi, aut

ᵃ Literally, " the lot and his sphere of duty." The lot
was held to declare heaven's will, and to impose very sacred
obligations on the person chosen by it.
ᵇ The sesterce may fairly be reckoned as $\frac{1}{100}$ of the £
sterling.

joined the consular army in Gaul with his welcome
supply of money. The moment he saw his chance—
note the man's first step as a public official and
administrator—this precious quaestor embezzled the
public money, and deserted his consul, his consul's
army, and his sacred duty.[a] Ah, I see what I have 35
done. He is lifting up his head, and hoping that
some flimsy defence can be patched up for him, on
this charge, through the goodwill of those who hold
the late Gnaeus Carbo's memory in abhorrence ; he
hopes that such persons will be pleased by this
desertion and betrayal of his consul. As though his
action were inspired by eagerness to support the
aristocracy, and by zeal for their cause ! As though
he did anything but openly fleece consul, army, and
province, and then take to his heels in consequence
of this impudent robbery ! An unintelligible act
indeed ! and likely to suggest that Gaius Verres
deserted to the aristocracy—his own party, of course !
—because he could not bear political upstarts, and
that he was quite uninfluenced by financial motives !

Let us see how he presented his accounts : he 36
will prove to us himself why he ran away from
Carbo ; he will give evidence against himself.
XIV Note first their conciseness :

Received	2,235,417 sesterces [b]
Expended : soldiers' pay, corn, adjutants, deputy-quaestor, commander's private staff . . .	1,635,417 ,,
Balance left at Ariminum	600,000 sesterces

Is that the way to present accounts ? Have you or I,
Hortensius, has anyone in the world, ever presented

quisquam hominum rettulit ? Quid hoc est ? quae
impudentia ? quae audacia ? quod exemplum ex tot
hominum rationibus relatis huiusce modi est ? Illa
tamen HS sescenta milia, quae ne falso quidem
potuit quibus data essent describere, quae se Arimini
scribit reliquisse, quae ipsa HS sescenta milia reliqua
facta sunt, neque Carbo attigit neque Sulla vidit,
neque in aerarium relata sunt. Oppidum sibi elegit
Ariminum quod tum, cum iste rationes referebat,
oppressum direptumque erat ; non suspicabatur id
quod nunc sentiet, satis multos ex illa calamitate
Ariminensium testes nobis in hanc rem reliquos esse.

37 Recita denuo. P. LENTULO L. TRIARIO QUAESTORIBUS
URBANIS RES RATIONUM RELATARUM. Recita. Ex
SENATUS CONSULTO. . . . Ut hoc pacto rationem
referre liceret, eo Sullanus repente factus est, non
ut honos et dignitas nobilitati restitueretur.

Quodsi illinc inanis profugisses, tamen ista tua
fuga nefaria proditio consulis tui conscelerata iudi-
caretur. "Malus civis, improbus consul, seditiosus
homo Cn. Carbo fuit." Fuerit aliis : tibi quando esse
coepit ? Posteaquam tibi pecuniam, rem frumen-
tariam, rationes omnes suas exercitumque commisit.
Nam si tibi antea displicuisset, idem fecisses quod
anno post M. Piso : quaestor cum L. Scipioni
consuli obtigisset, non attigit pecuniam, non ad
exercitum profectus est ; quod de republica sensit ita

<a>a</a> Lit. " 600,000 sesterces."
b The first words of some piece of written evidence,
possibly by the Ariminum witnesses.

them like that? Confound the man's unscrupulous
impudence! What does this mean? Among all the
thousands of accounts that have been presented, is
there any parallel for this style of thing? Even so,
that six thousand pounds,*a* which he could not set
down, even untruly, as paid to anyone, which he
enters as left at Ariminum, the six thousand that
really was left over, was never handled by Carbo or
seen by Sulla or paid back to the Treasury. He
chose Ariminum for his purpose, because, at the date
when he made his return, this town had been taken
and plundered: not suspecting, what he will now
learn to his cost, that enough people of the town
had survived the disaster to give evidence for us
about this matter. Read the documents again. 37
*Statement of accounts rendered to the City Quaestors,
Publius Lentulus and Lucius Triarius.* Read this. " *In
accordance with the decree of the Senate . . .*" *b* It was
to have the chance of rendering his accounts like
this that he joined the Sullan party so suddenly,
not to restore the power and dignity of the aristocracy.

But had you run off empty-handed, even so your
abominable flight would be reckoned a criminal act
of treachery to your consul. Oh, you say, Carbo
was a bad consul, a traitor and a rebel. Others
thought so, perhaps; but when did you begin to
think so? Not till after he had trusted you with
his money, his supply of corn, the whole of his
account-books, and his army. Had you objected to
him before that, you would have done what Marcus
Piso did the year after. The lot had assigned him
as quaestor to the consul Lucius Scipio, but he
neither took charge of any money nor went to join
Scipio's army; he managed to hold his political

sensit ut nec fidem suam nec morem maiorum nec
38 necessitudinem sortis laederet. XV. Etenim si haec
perturbare omnia et permiscere volumus, totam vitam
periculosam, insidiosam infestamque reddemus—si
nullam religionem sors habebit, nullam societatem
coniunctio secundae dubiaeque fortunae, nullam
auctoritatem mores atque instituta maiorum. Omnium est communis inimicus qui fuit hostis suorum.
Nemo umquam sapiens proditori credendum putavit.
Ipse Sulla, cui adventus istius gratissimus esse debuit,
ab se hominem atque ab exercitu suo removit:
Beneventi esse iussit, apud eos quos suis partibus
amicissimos esse intellegebat, ubi iste summae rei
causaeque nocere nihil posset. Ei postea praemia
tamen liberaliter tribuit, bona quaedam proscrip-
torum in agro Beneventano diripienda concessit;
habuit honorem ut proditori, non ut amico fidem.
39 Nunc quamvis sint homines qui mortuum Cn. Carbonem oderint, tamen hi debent non quid illi accidere
voluerint, sed quid ipsis in tali re metuendum sit,
cogitare. Commune est hoc malum, communis metus,
commune periculum. Nullae sunt occultiores insidiae quam eae quae latent in simulatione officii aut
in aliquo necessitudinis nomine. Nam eum qui palam
est adversarius facile cavendo vitare possis : hoc vero
occultum, intestinum ac domesticum malum non

---

a In tali re perhaps means " in similar circumstances."

views without violating either his personal honour, or the traditions of Rome, or the loyalty imposed by the lot. XV. The fact is that if we are prepared 38 to reduce all these principles to chaos and confusion, we shall fill life with danger and resentment and hostility at every turn—if the decisions of the lot are to lose all their sanctity, if men are not to feel bound to one another by sharing in good or bad fortune, if we are not to respect the customs and traditions of our fathers. That man must be every-one's personal enemy who has behaved like a public enemy to his own friends. No wise man ever felt that a traitor ought to be trusted. Sulla himself, who might have been expected to welcome the man, detached him from his person and from his army, stationing him at Beneventum, among people who he knew were thoroughly on his own side, in a place where the fellow would be able to do no harm to the main interests of the Sullan cause. Later on, to be sure, he treated him liberally, and let him have the properties of certain proscribed persons in the district of Beneventum to plunder ; he gave him, not the trust due to a friend, but the fee due to a traitor. There may be those who detest the memory of 39 Carbo : but what such persons have now to consider is not the fate they desired should befall him, but the danger to themselves suggested by behaviour like that of Verres.[a] All of us must be injured by it, all of us alarmed, all of us endangered. No acts of treachery are harder to detect than those which lurk under the false show of loyal service, or some nominal fidelity to a personal obligation. With an open enemy, it is easy to be on your guard and escape him ; but this hidden peril, in your own circle and

modo non exsistit, verum etiam opprimit antequam
4) prospicere atque explorare potueris. Itane vero?
Tu, cum quaestor ad exercitum missus sis, custos non
solum pecuniae sed etiam consulis, particeps omnium
rerum consiliorumque fueris, habitus sis in liberum
loco, sicut mos maiorum ferebat, repente relinquas,
deseras, ad adversarios transeas? O scelus! o por-
tentum in ultimas terras exportandum! Non enim
potest ea natura quae tantum facinus commiserit hoc
uno scelere esse contenta; necesse est semper
aliquid eius modi moliatur, necesse est in simili
audacia perfidiaque versetur.

41   Itaque idem iste, quem Cn. Dolabella postea, C.
Malleolo occiso, pro quaestore habuit—haud scio
an maior etiam haec necessitudo fuerit quam illa
Carbonis, ac plus iudicium voluntatis valere quam
sortis debeat—idem in Cn. Dolabellam qui in Cn.
Carbonem fuit. Nam quae in ipsum valebant crimina
contulit in illum, causamque illius omnem ad inimicos
accusatoresque detulit; ipse in eum cui legatus, cui
pro quaestore fuerat, inimicissimum atque improbissimum testimonium dixit. Ille miser cum esset Cn.
Dolabella cum proditione istius nefaria, tum improbo
et falso eiusdem testimonio—tum multo ex maxima
parte istius furtorum ac flagitiorum invidia conflagra-

under your own roof, not only does not reveal itself, but overwhelms you before you have time to think how to deal with it. Can such things be ? You **40** were sent as quaestor to join the army ; not only the money but the consul's person, was entrusted to you ; you were admitted to a share in all his actions and secrets ; you were treated like his son in the old Roman way : and in a moment you can forsake and desert him and join his enemies ? Unnatural prodigy of crime, deserving to be banished to the furthest corners of the earth ! For a being that has wrought a thing like this cannot rest content with this single wickedness : it must for ever be seeking to compass some such purpose, for ever be busy with some such piece of unscrupulous treachery.

And we find him accordingly, when appointed **41** acting quaestor by Gnaeus Dolabella after Gaius Malleolus was killed—and I am not sure that the personal tie here was not closer even than that with Carbo, or that the lot's decision should be accounted more binding than a decision freely taken—we find him behaving to Dolabella just as he behaved to Carbo. Charges that really applied to himself he transferred to Dolabella, and furnished a full account of the case against him to the personal enemies who were prosecuting him ; and he showed himself his bitter enemy, and a thorough scoundrel, by himself giving evidence against the man whose adjutant and acting quaestor he had been. Poor Dolabella had enough to make him unhappy in his abominable betrayal by Verres, and in the villainous and lying evidence Verres had given against him : but much the greatest part of his sufferings arose from the dislike of himself excited by the thefts and outrages

42 vit. XVI. Quid hoc homine faciatis ? aut ad quam spem tam perfidiosum, tam importunum animal reservetis ? qui in Cn. Carbone sortem, in Cn. Dolabella voluntatem neglexerit ac violarit, eosque ambos non solum deseruerit sed etiam prodiderit atque oppugnarit. Nolite, quaeso, iudices, brevitate orationis meae potius quam rerum ipsarum magnitudine crimina ponderare ; mihi enim properandum necessario est, ut omnia vobis quae mihi constituta sunt
43 possim exponere. Quam ob rem, quaestura istius demonstrata, primique magistratus et furto et scelere perspecto, reliqua attendite. In quibus illud tempus Sullanarum proscriptionum ac rapinarum praetermittam ; neque ego istum sibi ex communi calamitate defensionem ullam sinam sumere ; suis eum certis propriisque criminibus accusabo. Quam ob rem hoc omni tempore Sullano ex accusatione circumscripto legationem eius praeclaram cognoscite.
44 XVII. Posteaquam Cn. Dolabellae provincia Cilicia constituta est, o di immortales ! quanta iste cupiditate, quibus allegationibus illam sibi legationem expugnavit ! id quod Cn. Dolabellae principium maximae calamitatis fuit. Nam ut est profectus, quacumque iter fecit, eius modi fuit, non ut legatus populi Romani, sed ut quaedam calamitas pervadere

that Verres had committed. XVI. What shall be 42
done with a man like this ? For what possible use
should you keep so treacherous and savage a creature?
He has shown no more respect, no more fidelity, to
Dolabella who chose him than to Carbo to whom
the lot assigned him ; both Carbo and Dolabella he
has not only failed but deliberately betrayed and
assaulted. I would ask you, gentlemen, to judge
the gravity of those charges not so much by the
length of time I devote to them as by the seriousness
of the facts themselves ; for I must hasten on, if I
am to be able to carry out my plan of putting
the whole case fully before you. Having therefore 43
described the man's performances as quaestor, and
brought out clearly his dishonesty and criminal conduct during his first tenure of office, I ask your attention for the rest of the story. That part of it which
belongs to the time of the Sullan proscriptions, with
its acts of pillage, I shall omit ; I will not allow
Verres to extract from our national misfortunes any
arguments in his support ; I will prosecute him only
for offences that are definitely and exclusively his
own. I will therefore rule out all charges against
him that would belong to this period of Sulla's
power ; let us now examine his splendid record as
assistant governor.

XVII. Upon the allotment of Cilicia to Gnaeus 44
Dolabella as his province, merciful Heaven! with
what greed, what importunities Verres extorted from
him that assistant governorship ! And indeed this
proved for Dolabella the first step to the worst of
his disasters. Rome once left behind, the behaviour
of Verres, at every stage of his journey, made him
seem less like a Roman governor than a kind of human

167

videretur. In Achaia (praetermittam minora omnia, quorum simile forsitan alius quoque aliquid aliquando fecerit ; nihil dicam, nisi singulare, nisi quod, si in alium reum diceretur, incredibile videretur) magistratum Sicyonium nummos poposcit. Ne sit hoc crimen in Verrem ; fecerunt alii. Cum ille non daret, animadvertit. Improbum, sed non inauditum.

45 Genus animadversionis videte : quaeretis ex quo genere hominum istum iudicetis. Ignem ex lignis viridibus atque humidis in loco angusto fieri iussit ; ibi hominem ingenuum, domi nobilem, populi Romani socium atque amicum, fumo excruciatum semivivum reliquit. Iam quae iste signa, quas tabulas pictas ex Achaia sustulerit, non dicam hoc loco ; est alius mihi locus ad hanc eius cupiditatem demonstrandam separatus. Athenis audistis ex aede Minervae grande auri pondus ablatum ; dictum hoc est in Cn. Dolabellae iudicio ; dictum ? etiam aestimatum. Huius consilii non modo participem C. Verrem, sed principem fuisse reperietis.

46 Delum venit. Ibi ex fano Apollinis religiosissimo noctu clam sustulit signa pulcherrima atque antiquissima, eaque in onerariam navem suam conicienda curavit. Postridie cum fanum spoliatum viderent ii qui Delum incolebant, graviter ferebant ; est enim tanta apud eos eius fani religio atque antiquitas ut in

---

pestilence In Achaia—I pass over all minor misdeeds, some of which may possibly have occasional
parallels in what other men have done ; I will mention only what is unique, only what would seem incredible in anyone else who was charged with it—
he demanded a sum of money from the chief magistrate of Sicyon. But let us not accuse Verres of
that ; others have done the same. The magistrate
refusing, Verres punished him. Wrong, to be sure,
but not without precedent. But note the method of 45
punishment, and you will wonder to what species of
human being you are to assign him. He ordered a
fire of moist green wood to be made in a confined
spot : and there this free-born man, a man of high
rank in his own town, one of the allies and friends
of Rome, was put through the agonies of suffoca-
tion, and left there more dead than alive. What
statues and pictures he carried off from Achaia I
will not state here ; there is another part *a* of my
speech reserved for dealing with this side of his
greedy character. You have been told that at
Athens a large amount of gold was carried away
from the temple of Minerva. The fact was stated
at Dolabella's trial : stated ? the very weight was
given. In this enterprise, you will find, Verres did
not simply take part : he took command.

He reached Delos. There one night he secretly 46
carried off, from the much-revered sanctuary of
Apollo, several ancient and beautiful statues, and
had them put on board his own transport. Next
day, when the inhabitants of Delos saw their sanctuary stripped of its treasures, they were much
distressed ; for, to show how ancient, and how much
venerated by them, that sanctuary is, they believe

eo loco ipsum Apollinem natum esse arbitrentur.
Verbum tamen facere non audebant, ne forte ea res ad
Dolabellam ipsum pertineret. XVIII. Tum subito
tempestates coortae sunt maximae, iudices, ut non
modo proficisci cum cuperet Dolabella non posset, sed
vix in oppido consisteret ; ita magni fluctus eicie-
bantur. Hic navis illa praedonis istius, onusta signis
religiosis, expulsa atque eiecta fluctu frangitur. In
litore signa illa Apollinis reperiuntur ; iussu Dolabellae reponuntur ; tempestas sedatur ; Dolabella
Delo proficiscitur.

47   Non dubito quin, tametsi nullus in te sensus
humanitatis, nulla ratio umquam fuit religionis, nunc
tamen in metu periculoque tuo tuorum tibi scelerum
veniat in mentem. Potestne tibi ulla spes salutis
commoda ostendi, cum recordaris in deos immortales
quam impius, quam sceleratus, quam nefarius fueris ?
Apollinemne tu Delium spoliare ausus es ? Illine
tu templo tam antiquo, tam sancto, tam religioso
manus impias ac sacrilegas adferre conatus es ? Si in
pueritia non his artibus ac disciplinis institutus eras ut
ea quae litteris mandata sunt disceres atque cogno-
sceres, ne postea quidem, cum in ea ipsa loca venisti,
potuisti accipere id quod est proditum memoriae ac
48 litteris, Latonam ex longo errore et fuga, gravidam
et iam ad pariendum temporibus exactis, confugisse
Delum atque ibi Apollinem Dianamque peperisse ?
qua ex opinione hominum illa insula eorum deorum

170

it to be the birthplace of Apollo himself. However, they dared not say a word, fearing that Dolabella himself might be concerned in the outrage. XVIII. Then so tremendous a storm suddenly came on, gentlemen, that Dolabella was prevented from starting when he intended, and almost from staying in the town, it was being lashed by such huge waves. In that storm this pirate's ship, with its load of sacred statues, was driven ashore by the waves and went to pieces. The statues of Apollo were found lying on the beach : by Dolabella's order, they were put back where they came from ; the storm abated, and Dolabella left Delos.

I have no doubt, Verres, that destitute as you 47 have always been of human feelings and religious principle, yet now, in your hour of anxiety and danger, the thought of your crimes recurs to you. Is it possible that any agreeable hope of escaping can present itself to you, when you remember how impious and criminal and wicked your behaviour has been towards the gods in heaven ? You dared to rob Apollo—Apollo of Delos ? Upon that temple, so ancient, so holy, so profoundly venerated, you sought to lay your impious and sacrilegious hands ? Even though as a boy you did not receive the kind of education and training that would enable you to learn or understand the records of literature, could you not even take in later, when you came to the actual spot, the story of which both tradition and literature inform us : how after long wanderings the 48 fugitive Latona, being pregnant, and the time of her delivery now fully come, found refuge in Delos, and there brought forth Apollo and Diana ? Because men believe this story, they hold the island sacred

171

sacra putatur ; tantaque eius auctoritas religionis et
est et semper fuit ut ne Persae quidem, cum bellum
toti Graeciae dis hominibusque indixissent et mille
numero navium classem ad Delum appulissent, quicquam conarentur aut violare aut attingere. Hoc tu
fanum depopulari, homo improbissime atque amentissime, audebas ? Fuit ulla cupiditas tanta quae
tantam exstingueret religionem ? Et si tum haec
non cogitabas, ne nunc quidem recordaris nullum
esse tantum malum quod non tibi pro sceleribus tuis
iam diu debeatur ?

49   XIX. In Asiam vero postquam venit, quid ego
adventus istius prandia, cenas, equos muneraque
commemorem ? Nihil cum Verre de cotidianis
criminibus acturus sum. Chio per vim signa pulcherrima dico abstulisse, item Erythris et Halicar-
nasso. Tenedo (praetereo pecuniam quam eripuit)
Tenem ipsum, qui apud Tenedios sanctissimus deus
habetur, qui urbem illam dicitur condidisse, cuius ex
nomine Tenedus nominatur, hunc ipsum, inquam,
Tenem, pulcherrime factum, quem quondam in
comitio vidistis, abstulit magno cum gemitu civitatis.

50 Illa vero expugnatio fani antiquissimi et nobilissimi
Iunonis Samiae quam luctuosa Samiis fuit, quam
acerba toti Asiae, quam clara apud omnes, quam
nemini vestrum inaudita ! De qua expugnatione
cum legati ad C. Neronem in Asiam Samo venissent,

---

^a These were all extracted from the inhabitants.
    ^b Part of the Forum, where the old assembly of the
curiae met.   Verres had lent the aediles this statue to form
part of the decorations for some festival show.

to those deities ; and the reverence felt for it is,
and has always been, so strong, that not even the
Persians—though they had declared war upon all
Greece, gods and men alike, and their fleet, to the
number of a thousand ships, had put in at Delos—yet
not even they sought to profane, or to lay a finger
upon, anything therein. Was this the sanctuary
that you in your utter folly and wickedness dared to
devastate ? Was ever such devouring greed known
before, greed capable of such destruction of what
is high and holy ? And if at the time you did not
think of this, can you not even now reflect that
there is no retribution too terrible to be due, and
overdue, for the evil that you have done ?

XIX. Once he had reached Asia, what need to go 49
through the list of his dinner and supper parties, the
horses and other presents made to him ?ᵃ I am
not going to attack a man like Verres for every-day
offences. But I do assert that he carried off statues
of great beauty from Chios, and also from Erythrae
and Halicarnassus. From Tenedos—I make no reference to the money he seized—Tenes himself, the
god for whom the people of Tenedos feel special
reverence, who is said to have founded the city, and
after whom Tenedos is named—this very Tenes himself, I say, a beautiful work of art, which you have,
on one occasion, seen in the Comitium,ᵇ—this he
carried off, amid the loud lamentations of the citizens.
And then mark how he stormed and sacked the 50
ancient and glorious temple of Juno of Samos : how
it plunged the Samians in grief, and distressed all
Asia ! how the story spread through the world, so
that not one of you has not heard it ! A deputation
from Samos went to Asia to complain to Gaius Nero

responsum tulerunt eius modi querimonias, quae ad
legatum populi Romani pertinerent, non ad praetorem sed Romam deferri oportere. Quas iste
tabulas illinc, quae signa sustulit! quae cognovi
egomet apud istum in aedibus nuper, cum obsignandi
51 gratia venissem. Quae signa nunc, Verres, ubi sunt?
illa quaero quae apud te nuper ad omnes columnas,
omnibus etiam intercolumniis, in silva denique dis-
posita sub divo vidimus. Cur ea, quam diu alium
praetorem cum iis iudicibus quos in horum locum
subsortitus es de te in consilium iturum putasti, tam
diu domi fuerunt: posteaquam nostris testibus nos
quam horis tuis uti malle vidisti, nullum signum
domi reliquisti, praeter duo quae in mediis aedibus
sunt—quae ipsa Samo sublata sunt? Non putasti
me tuis familiarissimis in hanc rem testimonia denun-
tiaturum, qui tuae domi saepe fuissent, ex quibus
quaererem signa scirentne fuisse quae non essent?
52 XX. Quid tum hos de te iudicaturos arbitratus es,
cum viderent te iam non contra accusatorem tuum
sed contra quaestorem sectoremque pugnare? Qua
de re Charidemum Chium testimonium priore actione

---

^a Nero had no power to punish the *legatus* of the governor
of another province. Cicero is not blaming him: but
pointing out the seriousness of Verres' offence, and hinting,
perhaps, that he is doing something to carry out Nero's
suggestion to the Samians.

^b Evidently to seal up, and secure against removal, objects
that might be required as evidence at the trial.

^c Ironically for " had expected to ballot for."

^d The reference is to the plot described in *Actio Prima*,
§§ 26-31, and to Cicero's plan to frustrate it, § 55. The
"time that suited you" is the time that Cicero did *not*
waste, at the first hearing, on a long continuous speech.

about this outrage, and they were told that grievances
of this kind, having reference to imperial assistant-
governors, must be submitted not to the local governor, but at Rome.[a] The pictures, the statues
he robbed that island of! I recognized the statues
myself the other day in his house, on going there
to do my sealing.[b] Where are those statues now, 51
Verres? I mean those we saw in your house the
other day, standing by all the pillars, and in all the
spaces between the pillars too, yes, and even set
about your shrubbery in the open air. Why did
they stay there in your house as long as you expected to be tried by a fresh president, and by the
judges you had balloted for [c] to take these gentlemen's places, and then, later on, when you found
that we on this side meant to employ the witnesses
that suited us, and not the time that suited you,[d]
did you leave not one statue in your house, except
the two in the middle of it—and they too were
carried off from Samos? Did it never occur to you
that on this point I was likely to subpoena your
special friends who had continually been at your
house, and make them say whether they knew of
the previous existence of statues not now there?
XX. What conclusion did you expect these gentle- 52
men to draw about you, when they found you now
trying to frustrate, not the prosecutor, but the
quaestor and the dealer [e]? The Court has heard,
at the first hearing, the evidence given on this matter
by Charidemus of Chios: how, being in command

[e] The city quaestors confiscated and sold the property of
condemned persons: the *sector* speculated in the purchase
of it. Verres, expecting bankruptcy, was trying, illegally,
to save what he could from the wreck.

dicere audistis, sese, cum esset trierarchus, et Verrem
ex Asia decedentem prosequeretur iussu Dolabellae,
fuisse una cum isto Sami ; seseque tum scire spoliatum esse fanum Iunonis et oppidum Samum :
posteaque se causam apud Chios, cives suos, Samiis
accusantibus, publice dixisse, eoque se esse absolutum
quod planum fecisset ea quae legati Samiorum
dicerent ad Verrem, non ad se, pertinere.

53   Aspendum vetus oppidum et nobile in Pamphylia
scitis esse, plenissimum signorum optimorum. Non
dicam illinc hoc signum ablatum esse et illud : hoc
dico, nullum te Aspendi signum, Verres, reliquisse,
omnia ex fanis, ex locis publicis, palam, spectantibus
omnibus, plaustris evecta exportataque esse. Atque
etiam illum Aspendium citharistam, de quo saepe
audistis id quod est Graecis hominibus in proverbio,
quem omnia intus canere dicebant, sustulit et in
intimis suis aedibus posuit, ut etiam illum ipsum
54 suo artificio superasse videatur. Pergae fanum anti-
quissimum et sanctissimum Dianae scimus esse ; id
quoque a te nudatum ac spoliatum esse, ex ipsa
Diana quod habebat auri detractum atque ablatum
esse dico.

    Quae, malum, est ista tanta audacia atque amentia ?
Quas enim sociorum atque amicorum urbes adisti
legationis iure et nomine, si in eas vi cum exercitu

---

    [a] The proverb was applied to those who do things for
their own pleasure and not that of others. The lifelike
figure appeared to be enjoying his own music, inaudible to
everyone else.

    [b] Verres knew still better (as Long suggests) how to
" play for himself alone."

of a warship, by Dolabella's orders he acted as escort
when Verres was leaving Asia, was with Verres at
Samos, and knew at the time about the pillaging of
the sanctuary of Juno and the city of Samos ; and
how later he was officially prosecuted, before his
own countrymen in Chios, by Samian representatives,
and was acquitted on the ground that he had clearly
proved the actions complained of by the Samian
representatives to be the work of Verres and not
his own.

You are aware, gentlemen, that Aspendus is an old 53
and famous town in Pamphylia, full of fine statuary.
I shall not allege that from this town this or that
particular statue was removed. My charge is that
Verres did not leave one single statue behind ; that
from temples and public places alike, with the whole
of Aspendus looking on, they were all openly loaded
on wagons and carted away. Yes, even the famous
Harper of Aspendus, about whom you have often
heard the saying that is proverbial among the
Greeks, of whom it was said that he made " all his
music inside " [a]—him too Verres carried off and put
right inside his own house, so as to get the reputation of having beaten the Harper himself at his own
game.[b] At Perga there is, as we know, a very 54
ancient and much revered sanctuary of Diana : I
assert that this too has been stripped and plundered
by him, and that all the gold from the figure of
Diana herself has been pulled off and taken away.

You villain, you knave, and you fool, what is the
meaning of this ? You visited these allied and
friendly cities with the rights and the rank of
assistant governor ; but had you forcibly invaded
them as a general at the head of an army, even

imperioque invasisses, tamen, opinor, quae signa
atque ornamenta ex iis urbibus sustulisses, haec non
in tuam domum neque in suburbana amicorum sed
55 Romam in publicum deportasses. XXI. Quid ego de
M. Marcello loquar, qui Syracusas urbem ornatissimam cepit? quid de L. Scipione, qui bellum in Asia
gessit Antiochumque regem potentissimum vicit?
quid de Flaminino, qui regem Philippum et Macedo-
niam subegit? quid de L. Paulo, qui regem Persen vi
ac virtute superavit? quid de L. Mummio, qui urbem
pulcherrimam atque ornatissimam Corinthum, plenis-
simam rerum omnium, sustulit, urbesque Achaiae
Boeotiaeque multas sub imperium populi Romani
dictionemque subiunxit? Quorum domus, cum honore
et virtute florerent, signis et tabulis pictis erant
vacuae; at vero urbem totam templaque deorum
omnesque Italiae partes illorum donis ac monumentis
56 exornatas videmus. Vereor ne haec forte cuiquam
nimis antiqua et iam obsoleta videantur; ita enim
tum aequabiliter omnes erant eius modi ut haec laus
eximiae virtutis et innocentiae non solum hominum
verum etiam temporum illorum esse videatur. P.
Servilius, vir clarissimus maximis rebus gestis, adest
de te sententiam laturus: Olympum vi, copiis, consilio, virtute cepit, urbem antiquam et omnibus rebus
auctam et ornatam. Recens exemplum fortissimi viri
profero; nam postea Servilius imperator populi
Romani Olympum urbem hostium cepit quam tu
in iisdem locis legatus quaestorius oppida pacata

---

[a] The innuendo is that of § 51.

[b] And therefore entitled to outward splendours.

[c] Lit. " who by force, with his troops, by his skill, by his valour, took . . ."

[d] A pirate city on the coast of Lycia.   [e] In the year 77.

so, any statuary or works of art that you might take away from them you were surely bound to transport, not to your own town house or [a] the suburban estates of your friends, but to Rome for the benefit of the nation. XXI. Need I quote the example of 55 Marcus Marcellus, who captured Syracuse, that treasury of art ? Of Lucius Scipio, who conducted the war in Asia and overthrew that mighty monarch Antiochus ? Of Flamininus, who conquered King Philip and Macedonia ? Of Lucius Paulus, whose energy and bravery overcame King Perseus ? Of Lucius Mummius, who took the beautiful city of Corinth, full of art treasures of every kind, and brought so many cities of Achaia and Boeotia under the empire and sovranty of Rome ? These were men of high rank and eminent character,[b] but their houses were empty of statues and pictures ; while we still see the whole city, and the temples of the gods, and every part of Italy, adorned with the gifts and memorials that they brought us. But there are 56 some, I fear, to whom these instances may seem old-fashioned and already out of date ; for so universal, in those days, were these fine qualities of virtue and integrity, that my praise of them must be felt to extend beyond the great men themselves to the age in which they lived. Well, here among your judges sits Publius Servilius, the hero of very great deeds, through whose skill and valour our troops forcibly captured [c] the ancient city of Olympus,[d] a place full of riches and works of art. This I quote as a modern example of how a brave man should behave ; for this enemy city of Olympus has been captured by Servilius as a general in the Roman army since [e] the time when you, Verres, as quaestor-governor in that

179

sociorum atque amicorum diripienda ac vexanda
57 curasti. Tu quae ex fanis religiosissimis per scelus
et latrocinium abstulisti, ea nos videre nisi in tuis
amicorumque tuorum tectis non possumus : P.
Servilius, quae signa atque ornamenta ex urbe
hostium, vi et virtute capta, belli lege atque impera-
torio iure sustulit, ea populo Romano apportavit, per
triumphum vexit, in tabulas publicas ad aerarium
perscribenda curavit. Cognoscite ex litteris publicis
hominis amplissimi diligentiam. Recita. RATIONES
RELATAE P. SERVILII. Non solum numerum signorum
sed etiam unius cuiusque magnitudinem, figuram,
statum litteris definiri vides. Certe maior est virtutis
victoriaeque iucunditas quam ista voluptas quae
percipitur ex libidine et cupiditate. Multo diligentius habere dico Servilium praedam populi Romani
quam te tua furta notata atque perscripta.

58 XXII. Dices tua quoque signa et tabulas pictas
ornamento urbi foroque populi Romani fuisse. Me-
mini ; vidi simul cum populo Romano forum comitium-
que adornatum, ad speciem magnifico ornatu, ad
sensum cogitationemque acerbo et lugubri ; vidi
collucere omnia furtis tuis, praeda provinciarum,
spoliis sociorum atque amicorum. Quo quidem
tempore, iudices, iste spem maximam reliquorum
quoque peccatorum nactus est ; vidit enim eos qui
180

same part of the world, had the towns of allies and
friends at peace with us plundered and devastated.
What you criminally and piratically stole from ven- 57
erated sanctuaries we can see only in the private
houses of you and your friends ; the statues and
objects of art, which, in accordance with the rights
of war and his powers as general, Servilius removed
from the enemy city that his strength and valour
had captured, he brought home to his countrymen,
displayed them in his triumphal procession, and had
them entered in full in the official catalogue of the
public Treasury. Let the national records inform us
of the scrupulous care shown by this eminent man.
Read them, please. *Statement of accounts submitted
by Publius Servilius.* You see carefully stated in
these records, not simply the number of the statues,
but the size, shape, and attitude of each one of
them. How surely the satisfaction of a gallant con-
queror surpasses the pleasure derived from self-
indulgence and from greed ! I declare that Servilius
had this captured treasure, the property of the
nation, far more carefully identified and catalogued
than you, Verres, ever had what you stole for yourself.

XXII. You will plead that your statues and pictures, 58
like his, have adorned the city and forum of the
people of Rome. Yes : I remember standing among
the people of Rome, and looking at the decorated
Forum and Comitium ; a decoration splendid to the
eye, but painful and melancholy to the heart and
mind : I looked at the brilliant show that was made
by your thefts, by the robbing of our provinces, by
the spoliation of our friends and allies. Note that
it was then, gentlemen, that Verres received his chief
encouragement to continue his misdeeds : he saw

iudiciorum dominos se dici volebant harum cupidi-
59 tatum esse servos. Socii vero nationesque exterae
spem omnium tum primum abiecere rerum ac
fortunarum suarum, propterea quod casu legati ex
Asia atque Achaia plurimi Romae tunc fuerunt, qui
deorum simulacra ex suis fanis sublata in foro
venerabantur, itemque cetera signa et ornamenta
cum cognoscerent, alia alio in loco lacrimantes
intuebantur. Quorum omnium hunc sermonem tum
esse audiebamus, nihil esse quod quisquam dubitaret
de exitio sociorum atque amicorum, cum quidem
viderent in foro populi Romani, quo in loco antea qui
sociis iniurias fecerant accusari et condemnari solebant, ibi esse palam posita ea quae ab sociis per scelus
ablata ereptaque essent.

60   Hic ego non arbitror illum negaturum signa se
plurima, tabulas pictas innumerabiles habere ; sed,
ut opinor, solet haec quae rapuit et furatus est non
numquam dicere se emisse, quoniam quidem in
Achaiam, Asiam, Pamphyliam sumptu publico et
legationis nomine mercator signorum tabularumque
pictarum missus est. XXIII. Habeo et istius et patris
eius[1] tabulas omnes, quas diligentissime legi atque
digessi, patris quoad vixit, tuas quoad ais te confecisse

---

[1] *The MSS. have* accepi *after* eius : *Peterson retains it and
omits* Habeo.
182

that the men who aimed at being called the masters
of the courts were the servants of desire for such
things as these. And it was then, on the other 59
hand, and only then, that the allied and foreign
peoples abandoned their last hope of prosperity and
happiness ; for a large number of persons from Asia
and Achaia, who happened at the time to be in
Rome serving on deputations, beheld in our Forum
the revered images of their gods that had been
carried away from their own sanctuaries, and re-
cognizing as well the other statues and works of art,
some here and some there, would stand gazing at
them with weeping eyes. What we then heard these
people saying was always this, that the ruin of our
allies and friends was certain beyond all question ;
for there in the Forum of Rome, in the place where
once those who had wronged our allies used to be
prosecuted and found guilty, now stood, openly
exposed to view, the objects reft from those allies by
criminals and robbers.

Now I do not suppose that Verres will at this 60
point deny that he has numerous statues, and more
pictures than he can count, in his possession. But
I understand it to be his habit now and then to
assert that these objects, which he has stolen by
force or fraud, have really been bought. It would
appear that he was sent out to Achaia and Asia and
Pamphylia, at the national expense and with the
title of assistant governor, in order to engage in the
statue and picture trade. XXIII. Both his own
accounts and his father's have come into my hands ;
I have read and studied them carefully ; the father's
up to the day of his death, his own for the period
during which he claims to have kept them. For

183

Nam in isto, iudices, hoc novum reperietis.   Audimus
aliquem tabulas numquam confecisse : quae est opinio
hominum de Antonio, falsa, nam fecit diligentissime :
verum sit hoc genus aliquod, minime probandum.
Audimus alium non ab initio fecisse, sed ex tempore
aliquo confecisse : est aliqua etiam eiusce rei ratio.
Hoc vero novum et ridiculum est quod hic nobis
respondit cum ab eo tabulas postularemus, usque ad
M. Terentium et C. Cassium consules confecisse,
61 postea destitisse.   Alio loco hoc cuius modi sit
considerabimus ; nunc nihil ad me attinet, horum enim
temporum in quibus nunc versor habeo tabulas et
tuas et patris.   Plurima signa pulcherrima, plurimas
tabulas optimas deportasse te negare non potes ;
atque utinam neges !   Unum ostende in tabulis aut
tuis aut patris tui emptum esse : vicisti. Ne haec
quidem duo signa pulcherrima quae nunc ad impluvium tuum stant, quae multos annos ad valvas
Iunonis Samiae steterunt, habes quo modo emeris ;
haec, inquam, duo, quae in aedibus tuis sola iam
sunt, quae sectorem exspectant, relicta ac destituta a
ceteris signis.
62   XXIV. At, credo, in hisce solis rebus indomitas
cupiditates atque effrenatas habebat : ceterae libidines eius ratione aliqua aut modo continebantur.

---

[a] It is doubtful who is meant.
[b] 73 B.C.   [c] See § 51.
184

you will find this novelty in Verres' case, gentlemen.
We have heard of a man's never keeping any
accounts ; that is what is widely believed about
Antonius,[a] though incorrectly, for he kept very careful accounts ; still we may admit that this sort of
thing occurs, and it is far from satisfactory. We
have also heard of a man's not keeping accounts to
begin with, but doing so from a certain date onwards ;
and that too one can to some extent understand.
But what we have here is a ridiculous novelty : I
demanded his accounts, and he told me that he had
kept them duly up to the consulship of Marcus
Terentius and Gaius Cassius,[b] but stopped keeping
them after that. We will consider the significance 61
of this elsewhere ; for the moment I am not concerned with it, as I have both your own accounts,
Verres, and your father's, for the period with which
I am now dealing. You cannot deny that you
brought away a large number of beautiful statues
and a large number of fine paintings. I only wish
you would deny it ! Show me the record, either in
your own accounts or your father's, of your buying a
single one of these things, and I surrender. You
cannot show that you have bought even those two
beautiful statues which are standing now beside the
rainpool in your hall, and stood for many long years
before the doors of Juno in Samos—those two, I
mean, that are now left lonely in your house, waiting
for the dealer,[c] deserted and abandoned by all the
others.

XXIV. But we are no doubt to understand that 62
it is in these directions only that the man's greedy
desires were free from all restraint or control, and
that there was some limit or check imposed upon

Quam multis istum ingenuis, quam multis matribus familias in illa taetra atque impura legatione vim attulisse existimatis ? Ecquo in oppido pedem posuit ubi non plura stuprorum flagitiorumque suorum quam adventus sui vestigia reliquerit ? Sed ego omnia quae negari poterunt praetermittam ; etiam haec quae certissima sunt et clarissima relinquam ; unum aliquod de nefariis istius factis eligam, quo facilius ad Siciliam possim aliquando, quae mihi hoc oneris negotiique imposuit, pervenire.

63 Oppidum est in Hellesponto Lampsacum, iudices, in primis Asiae provinciae clarum et nobile ; homines autem ipsi Lampsaceni tum summe in omnes cives Romanos officiosi, tum praeterea maxime sedati et quieti, prope praeter ceteros ad summum Graecorum otium potius quam ad ullam vim aut tumultum accommodati. Accidit, cum iste a Cn. Dolabella efflagitasset ut se ad regem Nicomedem regemque Sadalam mitteret, cumque iter hoc sibi magis ad quaestum suum quam ad rei publicae tempus accommodatum depoposcisset, ut illo itinere veniret Lampsacum, cum magna calamitate et prope pernicie civitatis. Deducitur iste ad Ianitorem quendam hospitem, comitesque eius item apud ceteros hospites collocantur. Ut mos erat istius atque ut eum suae libidines flagitiose facere admonebant, statim negotium dat illis suis comitibus, nequissimis turpissimisque hominibus, uti videant et investigent ecqua virgo

his other passions. Are you aware of the number of free-born persons, of respectable married women, to whom he offered violence during his foul and disgusting career as assistant governor? Is there one town in which he set foot where the traces left by his arriving feet are not outnumbered by those of his adulteries and criminal assaults? I will, however, pass over all the outrages whose commission might be denied; I will even omit those that are wholly undeniable and notorious, selecting only a single one of his wicked deeds, that I may the sooner get at last to Sicily, the country that has laid this burdensome duty upon my shoulders.

There is on the shores of the Hellespont, gentle- 63 men, a town called Lampsacum, one of the most famous and illustrious in the province of Asia. The inhabitants are particularly ready to oblige all Roman citizens, and besides that are extremely quiet and well-behaved, almost more inclined than other Greeks are to taking things very easily, and not to any form of violence or turbulence. Verres, having pestered Dolabella to send him on a mission to King Nicomedes and King Sadala, and insisted on a journey more likely to add to his own gains than to forward the interests of Rome, happened in the course of his journey to arrive at Lampsacum, with terrible and almost ruinous consequences to that community. He was received as a guest in the house of a man called Ianitor, and his staff found quarters and hospitality among the rest of the inhabitants. In accordance with his custom and the promptings of his wicked passions, he forthwith instructed the worthless and degraded men who composed his staff to make investigations, and discover whether there was any

187

sit aut mulier digna quam ob rem ipse Lampsaci
64 diutius commoraretur.   XXV. Erat comes eius
Rubrius quidam, homo factus ad istius libidines, qui
miro artificio, quocumque venerat, haec investigare
omnia solebat.   Is ad eum rem istam defert, Philodamum esse quendam, genere, honore, copiis, existimatione facile principem Lampsacenorum ; eius
esse filiam, quae cum patre habitaret, propterea quod
virum non haberet, mulierem eximia pulchritudine ;
sed eam summa integritate pudicitiaque existimari.
Homo, ut haec audivit, sic exarsit ad id quod non
modo ipse numquam viderat sed ne audierat quidem
ab eo qui ipse vidisset, ut statim ad Philodamum
migrare se diceret velle.   Hospes Ianitor, qui nihil
suspicaretur, veritus ne quid in ipso se offenderetur,
hominem summa vi retinere coepit.   Iste, qui hospitis relinquendi causam reperire non posset, alia sibi
ratione viam munire ad stuprum coepit ; Rubrium,
delicias suas, in omnibus eius modi rebus adiutorem
suum et conscium, parum laute deversari dicit, ad
65 Philodamum deduci iubet.   Quod ubi est Philodamo
nuntiatum, tametsi erat ignarus quantum sibi ac
liberis suis iam tum mali constitueretur, tamen ad
istum venit ; ostendit munus illud suum non esse :
se, cum suae partes essent hospitum recipiendorum,
tum ipsos tamen praetores et consules, non legato-
188

girl or woman there on whose account it would be
worth his while to prolong his stay at Lampsacum.
XXV. There was a man on his staff called Rubrius, 64
just the sort of creature for the service of his lusts,
who used to show remarkable ingenuity, wherever
they went, in investigating matters of this sort.
Rubrius reported to him that there was a man called
Philodamus, whose birth, official position, wealth, and
high reputation made him easily the first man in
Lampsacum ; and that he had a daughter, who,
being unmarried, was living at home ; a woman of
exceptional beauty, but accounted entirely chaste
and modest. On hearing this, the scoundrel was so
inflamed by the thought of what he had not only
never himself seen but not even heard of from anyone
who had, that he immediately announced his wish
to move to the house of Philodamus. His host Ianitor,
having no suspicion of the truth, and being afraid
that he was himself failing in some way to give
satisfaction, began most urgently to dissuade him
from going. Unable to hit upon an excuse for
deserting his host, Verres proceeded with a new
scheme for achieving his licentious purpose : he complained of the shabby accommodation allotted to his
favourite Rubrius, his helper and confidant in all
matters of this kind, and ordered him to be transferred to the house of Philodamus. On being told 65
of this, Philodamus, though unaware how great an
injury was already being planned against himself and
his family, went nevertheless to see Verres, and urged
that it was not fair to expect this of him ; that
while he had his own share of hospitable duties to
perform, it was his custom to invite praetors and
consuls to be his guests, and not their assistants'

rum adseculas, recipere solere.   Iste, qui una cupiditate raperetur, totum illius postulatum causamque
neglexit ; per vim ad eum, qui recipere non debebat,
Rubrium deduci imperavit.   XXVI. Hic Philodamus,
posteaquam ius suum obtinere non potuit, ut huma-
nitatem consuetudinemque suam retineret laborabat.
Homo, qui semper hospitalissimus amicissimusque
nostrorum hominum existimatus esset, noluit videri
ipsum illum Rubrium invitus domum suam recepisse :
magnifice et ornate, ut erat in primis inter suos
copiosus, convivium comparat ; rogat Rubrium ut
quos ei commodum sit invitet ; locum sibi soli, si
videatur, relinquat ; etiam filium suum, lectissimum
adulescentem, foras ad propinquum suum quendam
66 mittit ad cenam.   Rubrius istius comites invitat :
eos omnes Verres certiores facit quid opus esset.
Mature veniunt ; discumbitur.   Fit sermo inter eos,
et invitatio ut Graeco more biberetur.   Hortatur
hospes ;   poscunt   maioribus   poculis ;   celebratur
omnium sermone laetitiaque convivium.   Posteaquam satis calere res Rubrio visa est, " Quaeso "
inquit, " Philodame, cur ad nos filiam tuam non intro
vocari iubes ? "   Homo, qui et summa gravitate et
iam id aetatis et parens esset, obstupuit hominis
improbi dicto.   Instare Rubrius ; tum ille, ut aliquid
responderet, negavit moris esse Graecorum ut in
convivio virorum accumberent mulieres.   Hic tum
alius ex alia parte " enim vero ferendum hoc quidem
non est ;   vocetur   mulier ! "   et   simul   servis   suis

---

a *i.e.*, (probably) προπίνειν, to " take wine with " their
host : a touch of special courtesy.
190

attendants. Verres, carried away by his one over-
mastering desire, paid no attention to this request or
to its justice, and ordered Rubrius to be forcibly
installed in the house of a man to whose hospitality
he had no claim. XXVI. Unable to maintain his
rights, Philodamus now did his best to maintain his
accustomed courtesy. He had always been considered most hospitable and cordial towards our
people, and he did not wish to give the impression
that he was receiving even a man like Rubrius into
his house unwillingly. He arranged a dinner-party
with the lavish splendour appropriate to one of the
most well-to-do men in the place ; asked Rubrius to
invite to it anyone he wanted, and to be kind enough
to reserve a place for himself only ; even his son, an
extremely nice boy, he sent out to supper with a
relative. Rubrius invited Verres' staff, and Verres 66
gave them instructions what to do. The guests
assembled in good time, and took their places.
Conversation began ; they were invited to drink in
the Greek fashion ^a; their host urged them to
drink ; they asked for bumpers, and the party
became a general buzz of talk and merriment. As
soon as Rubrius thought the ice was sufficiently
broken, he said, " Tell me, Philodamus, why not
send for your daughter to come in and see us ? "
The respectable and already elderly father received
the rascal's suggestion with astonished silence. As
Rubrius persisted, he replied, in order to say something, that it was not the Greek custom for women
to be present at a men's dinner-party. At this
someone in another part of the room called out,
" But really, this is intolerable : let the woman be
sent for ! " At the same moment, Rubrius told his

191

Rubrius ut ianuam clauderent et ipsi ad fores adsiste-
67 rent imperat. Quod ubi ille intellexit, id agi atque
id parari ut filiae suae vis afferretur, servos suos ad
se vocat; his imperat ut se ipsum neglegant, filiam
defendant; excurrat aliquis qui hoc tantum domestici
mali filio suo nuntiet. Clamor interea fit tota domo;
inter servos Rubrii atque hospitis iactatur domi suae
vir primarius et homo honestissimus; pro se quisque
manus affert; aqua denique ferventi a Rubrio ipso
Philodamus perfunditur. Haec ubi filio nuntiata
sunt, statim exanimatus ad aedes contendit, ut et
vitae patris et pudicitiae sororis succurreret. Omnes
eodem animo Lampsaceni, simul ut hoc audiverunt,
quod eos cum Philodami dignitas tum iniuriae magnitudo movebat, ad aedes noctu convenerunt. Hic
lictor istius Cornelius, qui cum eius servis erat a
Rubrio quasi in praesidio ad auferendam mulierem
collocatus, occiditur; servi nonnulli vulnerantur,
ipse Rubrius in turba sauciatur. Iste, qui sua
cupiditate tantos tumultus concitatos videret, cupere
68 aliqua evolare, si posset. XXVII. Postridie homines
mane in contionem veniunt; quaerunt quid optimum
factu sit; pro se quisque, ut in quoque erat auctoritatis
plurimum, ad populum loquebatur; inventus est
nemo cuius non haec et sententia esset et oratio,
non esse metuendum, si istius nefarium scelus
Lampsaceni ulti vi manuque essent, ne senatus
populusque Romanus in eam civitatem animadverten-

slaves to shut the front door and stand on guard at
the entrance. Philodamus, seeing that their pur- 67
pose and intention was the violation of his daughter,
called to his slaves, and told them not to trouble
about himself, but to save his daughter ; one of
them had better rush off to his son with the news
of this trouble at home. Before long the whole
house was in an uproar, and its most respectable
and worthy owner was being knocked about under
his own roof in the struggle between his own slaves
and those of Rubrius, everyone trying to lay hands
upon him ; he was even drenched with a jug of boiling
water by Rubrius himself. His son, on receiving
the news, was terrified, and at once dashed off home
to save his father's life and his sister's honour : and
with one accord the people of Lampsacum, when
they heard about it, shocked by this gross outrage on
a gentleman they respected, gathered in a crowd
before his house that night. In the sequel, Cornelius,
a lictor of Verres, who with some of Verres' slaves
had been posted by Rubrius at the strategic point
for abducting the woman, lost his life ; several slaves
were wounded, and Rubrius himself was hurt in the
struggle. Verres, seeing the fearful uproar to which
his licentious passions had led, began to feel anxious
to escape somehow if he could. XXVII. The follow- 68
ing morning there was a mass meeting of the inhabitants to consider what it was best to do. Those
whose opinions carried most weight made speeches
to the gathering, each putting his own view ; and
not a man among them but thought, and said,
that they ought not to be afraid that if the people
of Lampsacum avenged that wicked outrage by main
force, the Senate and People of Rome would regard

dum putaret; quodsi hoc iure legati populi Romani
in socios nationesque exteras uterentur, ut pudicitiam liberorum servare ab eorum libidine tutam non
liceret, quidvis esse perpeti satius quam in tanta vi
atque acerbitate versari.   Haec cum omnes sentirent,
et cum in eam rationem pro suo quisque sensu ac
dolore loqueretur, omnes ad eam domum in qua iste
deversabatur profecti sunt; caedere ianuam saxis,
instare ferro, ligna et sarmenta circumdare ignemque
subicere coeperunt.   Tum cives Romani, qui Lampsaci negotiabantur, concurrunt; orant Lampsacenos ut gravius apud eos nomen legationis quam
iniuria legati putaretur; sese intellegere hominem
illum esse impurum ac nefarium; sed quoniam nec
perfecisset quod conatus esset neque futurus esset
Lampsaci postea, levius eorum peccatum fore si
homini scelerato pepercissent quam si legato non
pepercissent.

70   Sic iste, multo sceleratior et nequior quam ille
Hadrianus, aliquanto etiam felicior fuit.   Ille, quod
eius avaritiam cives Romani ferre non potuerant,
Uticae domi suae vivus exustus est; idque ita illi
merito accidisse existimatum est ut laetarentur
omnes neque ulla animadversio constitueretur: hic
sociorum ambustus incendio tamen ex illa flamma
periculoque evolavit, neque adhuc causam ullam

---

[a] Governor of the province of Africa a few years earlier.
[b] It is implied that Roman citizens would be less likely
than *socii* to resort to lynch-law.
194

the town as deserving punishment for doing so ; for
if the rights of a Roman assistant governor over
members of allied and foreign nations were going to
preclude them from successfully protecting their
children against his lust, any fate would be more
endurable than living in such circumstances of
violence and wretchedness. This view commanded 69
universal support, man after man expressing, to the
same effect, his feelings of indignation. There was
a general move to the house in which Verres was
staying. They set to work battering the front door
with stones and iron implements, and made a pile
of logs and brushwood round it which they set on
fire. At this point a number of Roman citizens
carrying on business in Lampsacum collected hastily
on the spot, and began to urge the people of the
town to let their respect for Verres' official position
outweigh their resentment of his outrageous conduct, admitting that the man was a dirty villain, but
urging that, since he had failed in his attempt and
would never be at Lampsacum again, they would
make a smaller mistake in sparing the life of a
criminal than in taking the life of a governor.

The result was that Verres, though a much worse 70
criminal than the notorious Hadrianus,[a] had considerably better luck. Hadrianus was burnt alive in
his house at Utica because his avarice had become
intolerable to Roman citizens,[b] and was held so
thoroughly to have deserved his fate that everyone
was pleased that no steps were taken to punish the
doers. But Verres, though the fire was lit by allied [b]
hands, and scorched him badly, escaped that dangerous conflagration. Why indeed he allowed himself, or what happened to allow him, to run into so

excogitare potuit quam ob rem commiserit, aut quid
evenerit, ut in tantum periculum veniret. Non enim
potest dicere "cum seditionem sedare vellem, cum
frumentum imperarem, cum stipendium cogerem,
cum aliquid denique rei publicae causa gererem, quod
acrius imperavi, quod animadverti, quod minatus
sum." Quae si diceret, tamen ignosci non oporteret,
si nimis atrociter imperando sociis in tantum adductus
71 periculum videretur. XXVIII. Nunc cum ipse causam illius tumultus neque veram dicere neque falsam
confingere audeat, homo autem ordinis sui frugalissimus, qui tum accensus C. Neroni fuit, P. Tettius,
haec eadem se Lampsaci cognosse dixerit, vir omnibus rebus ornatissimus C. Varro, qui tum in Asia
militum tribunus fuit, haec eadem ipsa se ex Philodamo audisse dicat, potestis dubitare quin istum
fortuna non tam ex illo periculo eripere voluerit
quam ad vestrum iudicium reservare ? Nisi vero
illud dicet quod et in testimonio Tettii priore actione
interpellavit Hortensius (quo tempore quidem signi
satis dedit, si quid esset quod posset dicere, se tacere
non posse, ut quamdiu tacuit in ceteris testibus scire
omnes possemus nihil habuisse quod diceret)—hoc
tum dixit, Philodamum et eius filium a C. Nerone
72 esse damnatos. De quo ne multa disseram, tantum
dico, secutum id esse Neronem et eius consilium :
quod Cornelium lictorem occisum esse constaret,

serious a danger at all, is more than he has, from
that day to this, been able to explain. For he cannot
allege that it was because he wanted to suppress a
revolt, requisition corn, exact a tax, or perform, at
any rate, some imperial duty : that it was because of
any harsh order, any inflicted or threatened punishment. Even did he allege such a cause, he would
still deserve censure, did it appear that the reason of
his incurring a danger so grave was the brutality of
his orders to our allies. XXVIII. As things are, he 71
dare not himself either confess the true explanation
of that riot or concoct a false one ; and inasmuch as
Publius Tettius, who was at that time a police officer
under Gaius Nero and a most respectable member of
that profession, has told us how he learnt the same
story in Lampsacum, while a man of so much distinction as Gaius Varro, who was at that time an
army captain in Asia, tells us that he has himself
heard exactly the same story from Philodamus, can
you doubt that Fortune's purpose was not so much
to rescue Verres from that danger as to keep him to
be sentenced by yourselves ? Perhaps, however, he
will argue as Hortensius did when cross-examining
Tettius during the first part of the trial—and by the
way, Hortensius then showed clearly enough that
where there was anything he could say he could not
help saying it, so that all the time when the other
witnesses were being examined, and he kept silence,
we could all be sure that he had nothing to say :—
well, he then argued that Philodamus and his son
had been tried and sentenced by Gaius Nero. I will 72
not discuss this subject at length, only observing
that the principle on which Nero and his court went
was this, that the killing of the lictor Cornelius being

putasse non oportere esse cuiquam, ne in ulciscenda quidem iniuria, hominis occidendi potestatem. In quo video Neronis iudicio non te absolutum esse improbitatis, sed illos damnatos esse caedis.

Verum ista damnatio tamen cuius modi fuit? Audite, quaeso, iudices, et aliquando miseremini sociorum, et ostendite aliquid iis in vestra fide praesidii esse oportere. XXIX. Quod toti Asiae iure occisus videbatur istius ille verbo lictor, re vera minister improbissimae cupiditatis, pertimuit iste ne Philodamus Neronis iudicio liberaretur. Rogat et orat Dolabellam ut de sua provincia decedat, ad Neronem proficiscatur ; se demonstrat incolumem esse non posse si Philodamo vivere atque aliquando

73 Romam venire licuisset. Commotus est Dolabella ; fecit id quod multi reprehenderunt, ut exercitum, provinciam, bellum relinqueret, et in Asiam hominis nequissimi causa in alienam provinciam proficisceretur. Posteaquam ad Neronem venit, contendit ab eo ut Philodami causam cognosceret. Venerat ipse qui esset in consilio et primus sententiam diceret ; adduxerat etiam praefectos et tribunos militares suos, quos Nero omnes in consilium vocavit ; erat in consilio etiam aequissimus iudex ipse Verres ; erant nonnulli togati creditores Graecorum, quibus ad exigendas pecunias improbissimi cuiusque legati

74 plurimum prodest gratia. Ille miser defensorem

established, they were bound to hold that homicide was not justifiable for any man, even in order to avenge a wrong. It is clear to me that this decision of Nero's merely finds those two guilty of homicide, and does not acquit Verres of gross misconduct.

And yet, after all, how was this precious verdict of homicide arrived at? Let me tell you the story, gentlemen; let your hearts at last feel some pity for our allies, and let them see that they may fairly trust your honour to grant them some measure of protection. XXIX. Since the whole of Asia regarded the slaying of that man—nominally Verres' lictor, really the instrument of his foul passions—as a just act, Verres was much afraid that Philodamus would be acquitted by Nero's court. He begged and implored Dolabella to leave his province and pay a visit to Nero, pointing out that he was himself a lost man if Philodamus were allowed to live and later on to come to Rome. Dolabella was moved by this appeal, **73** and allowed himself to take the step, which has been widely censured, of leaving his army, his province, and the war he was conducting, and proceeding to Asia, another man's province, for the sake of a wholly worthless man. Upon reaching Nero, he pressed him strongly to try Philodamus. He had come there himself to be one of the court and give his verdict first; he had brought along with him his own civil and military officers, all of whom Nero invited to be members of the court; Verres, most impartial of judges, was himself a member; and there were also a number of Roman citizens to whom the Greeks owed money, for the recovery of which the favour of an unscrupulous assistant-governor is highly useful. The unhappy Philodamus could find nobody **7**

reperire neminem poterat ; quis enim esset aut
togatus, qui Dolabellae gratia, aut Graecus, qui
eiusdem vi et imperio non moveretur ? Accusator
autem opponitur civis Romanus de creditoribus
Lampsacenorum : qui si dixisset quod iste iussisset,
per eiusdem istius lictores a populo pecuniam posset
exigere. Cum haec omnia tanta contentione, tantis
copiis agerentur ; cum illum miserum multi accusa-
rent, nemo defenderet ; cumque Dolabella cum suis
praefectis pugnaret in consilio, Verres fortunas agi
suas diceret, idem testimonium diceret, idem esset
in consilio, idem accusatorem parasset ; haec cum
omnia fierent, et cum hominem constaret occisum :
tamen tanta vis istius iniuriae, tanta in isto improbitas putabatur, ut de Philodamo " amplius " pro-
75 nuntiaretur. XXX. Quid ego nunc in altera actione
Cn. Dolabellae spiritus, quid huius lacrimas et con-
cursationes proferam, quid C. Neronis, viri optimi
atque innocentissimi, non nullis in rebus animum
nimis timidum atque demissum ? qui in illa re quid
facere potuerit non habebat, nisi forte, id quod omnes
tum desiderabant, ut ageret eam rem sine Verre et
sine Dolabella : quicquid esset sine his actum omnes
probarent ; tum vero quod pronuntiatum est non
per Neronem iudicatum, sed per Dolabellam ereptum
existimabatur. Condemnatur enim perpaucis sen-

to defend him : for what Roman citizen could avoid
being influenced by the desire of pleasing Dolabella,
and what Greek could help fearing the strong arm
of Dolabella's authority ? The man selected as prosecutor was a Roman citizen, one of the Lampsacum
money-lenders, who might expect the help of
Dolabella's lictors in extorting his money from his
debtors, provided he said what Dolabella ordered
him to say. Yet though the campaign was pressed
so vigorously, and forces so large employed ; though
the poor victim had many prosecutors and not one
defender ; though Dolabella and his officials fought
hard as members of the court, and Verres declared
that his fate was at stake ; though Verres was at
once a witness, a member of the court, and the
organizer of the prosecution ; in spite of all this,
and in spite of the admitted fact of the homicide :
nevertheless the wrong that Verres did was held to
be so serious, and his own character so bad, that the
verdict on Philodamus was " Further trial required."
XXX. No need for me to tell here how, at this second 75
hearing, Dolabella breathed fire and slaughter ; how
Verres ran appealing to this person and that with
tears in his eyes ; how a man with so good and
clean a record as Nero could in some respects prove
timid and over-submissive ; though in this case he
could not do other than he did, except perhaps
what everyone at the time regretted his not doing,
try the case without the help of Verres or Dolabella ; everyone would approve a result reached
without them, whatever it were, whereas the sentence actually pronounced was considered due more
to Dolabella's intrigues than to Nero's judgement.
Philodamus and his son by a very small majority

tentiis Philodamus et eius filius. Adest, instat, urget
Dolabella ut quam primum securi feriantur, quo quam
minime multi ex illis de istius nefario scelere audire
76 possent. Constituitur in foro Laodiceae specta-
culum acerbum et miserum et grave toti Asiae
provinciae, grandis natu parens adductus ad supplicium, ex altera parte filius : ille quod pudicitiam
liberorum, hic quod vitam patris famamque sororis
defenderat. Flebat uterque non de suo supplicio,
sed pater de filii morte, de patris filius. Quid lacri-
marum ipsum Neronem putatis profudisse ? quem
fletum totius Asiae fuisse ? quem luctum et gemitum
Lampsacenorum ? securi esse percussos homines
innocentes, nobiles, socios populi Romani atque
amicos, propter hominis flagitiosissimi singularem
nequitiam atque improbissimam cupiditatem !

77 Iam iam, Dolabella, neque me tui neque tuorum
liberum, quos tu miseros in egestate atque in soli-
tudine reliquisti, misereri potest. Verresne tibi
tanti fuit ut eius libidinem hominum innocentium
sanguine lui velles ? Idcircone exercitum atque
hostem relinquebas, ut tua vi et crudelitate istius
hominis improbissimi pericula sublevares ? Quod
enim eum tibi quaestoris in loco constitueras, idcirco
tibi amicum in perpetuum fore putasti ? Nesciebas,
ab eo Cn. Carbonem consulem, cuius re vera quaestor
fuerat, non modo relictum sed etiam spoliatum
auxiliis, pecunia, nefarie oppugnatum et proditum ?

were found guilty of murder. Dolabella pressed
and clamoured and appealed for their heads to be
cut off at the first possible moment, so that the
fewest possible people might have the chance of
hearing, from the victims' own lips, the tale of
Verres' nefarious wickedness. In the forum of 76
Laodicea a cruel scene was enacted, which caused
all the province of Asia profound unhappiness and
distress : here the aged father led forth to execution, and there his son : the one for defending the
purity of his children, the other for saving his father's
life and sister's honour. Both wept, but neither for
his own doom : the father for his son's fate, the son
for his father's. Imagine the tears that Nero himself must have shed, the sorrow of all Asia, the grief
and loud lamentations of the people of Lampsacum,
for these innocent and high-born citizens of a state
in friendly alliance with the Roman people, brought
to the block by the rascality and lecherous passions
of an unparalleled blackguard.

After this, Dolabella, I can feel no pity for you ; 77
nor, after this, for the unhappy children you have
left behind you in poverty and loneliness. Was
Verres so precious to you that you could desire the
marks of his lust to be washed out with innocent
blood ? Could you desert your troops as they faced
the enemy, merely to lessen, by violent and cruel
means, the risks to a scoundrel like that ? Did you
think that your having given him the position of
your acting quaestor would keep him your friend
for ever ? Did you not know that the consul Gnaeus
Carbo, whose quaestor he really was, was not merely
forsaken by him, but robbed by him of supplies and
money, most vilely attacked and betrayed by him ?

Expertus igitur es istius perfidiam tum cum se ad
inimicos tuos contulit, cum in te homo ipse nocens
acerrimum testimonium dixit, cum rationes ad
aerarium nisi damnato te referre noluit.

78 XXXI. Tantaene tuae, Verres, libidines erunt ut
eas capere ac sustinere non provinciae populi Romani,
non nationes exterae possint ? Tune quod videris,
quod audieris, quod concupieris, quod cogitaris, nisi
id ad nutum tuum praesto fuerit, nisi libidini tuae
cupiditatique paruerit, immittentur homines, expug-
nabuntur domus, civitates non modo pacatae, verum
etiam sociorum atque amicorum, ad vim atque ad
arma confugient, ut ab se atque a liberis suis legati
populi Romani scelus ac libidinem propulsare possint ?
Nam quaero abs te circumsessusne sis Lampsaci,
coeperitne domum in qua deversabare illa multitudo
incendere, voluerintne legatum populi Romani
comburere vivum Lampsaceni ? Negare non potes ;
habeo enim testimonium tuum quod apud Neronem
dixisti, habeo quas ad eundem litteras misisti. Recita
79 hunc ipsum locum de testimonio. TESTIMONIUM C.
VERRIS IN ARTEMIDORUM. NON MULTO POST IN DOMUM.
. . . Bellumne populo Romano Lampsacena civitas
facere conabatur ? deficere ab imperio ac nomine
nostro volebat ? Video enim et ex iis quae legi et
audivi intellego, in qua civitate non modo legatus
populi Romani circumsessus, non modo igni, ferro,
manu, copiis oppugnatus, sed aliqua ex parte violatus
sit, nisi publice satis factum sit, ei civitati bellum in-

---

a So that Dolabella, being in exile, could not be present
to contradict any of Verres' false returns.

b Probably the son of Philodamus.

Well, you learnt how little he could be trusted, on the day when he joined the ranks of your enemies, when—guilty himself—he gave his savage evidence against you, and determined to secure your conviction before his accounts were audited by the Treasury.[a]

XXXI. Now shall your licentiousness, Verres, grow 78 and multiply till it overflows the limits and overtaxes the strength of the Roman and foreign world alike? Must you but see an object, or hear of it, or conceive the desire or even the thought of it, and then, unless it is on the spot at a sign from you, unless it complies with your lust and cupidity, shall assaults be made and houses taken by storm, shall the towns, not merely of conquered enemies, but of our allies and friends, resort to armed violence, as their only means of averting, from themselves and their children, the wicked passions of a Roman assistant-governor? Do you deny the facts? That you were besieged at Lampsacum, that the crowd there began to set fire to the house where you were staying, that the people of Lampsacum intended to burn a Roman governor alive? No, that you cannot: for the evidence you gave before Nero, the letter you wrote to Nero, are in my possession. Kindly read the actual passage from his evidence. *Evidence of Gaius Verres against* 79 *Artemidorus.*[b] " *Into the house, soon afterwards . . .*" Was the town of Lampsacum aiming at making war upon Rome? Did it mean to revolt from its allegiance to our rule? For I observe, and gather from what I have read and heard, that a town where a Roman representative is, I do not say blockaded, I do not say physically attacked on a large scale with fire and sword, but subjected to the least infraction of his dignity, if it fails officially to make amends, usually

80 dici atque inferri solere.   Quae fuit igitur causa, cur
cuncta civitas Lampsacenorum de contione, quem ad
modum tute scribis, domum tuam concurrerit ?   Tu
enim neque in litteris quas Neroni mittis neque in
testimonio causam tanti tumultus ostendis ullam.
Obsessum te dicis, ignem allatum, sarmenta circum-
data, lictorem tuum occisum esse dicis, prodeundi
tibi in publicum potestatem factam negas : causam
huius tanti terroris occultas.   Nam si quam Rubrius
iniuriam suo nomine ac non impulsu tuo et tua cupiditate fecisset, de tui comitis iniuria questum ad te
potius quam te oppugnatum venirent.   Cum igitur
quae causa illius tumultus fuerit testes a nobis producti dixerint, ipse celarit, nonne causam hanc quam
nos proposuimus cum illorum testimonia tum istius
taciturnitas perpetua confirmat ?

81   XXXII. Huic homini parcetis igitur, iudices, cuius
tanta peccata sunt ut ii quibus iniurias fecerit neque
legitimum tempus exspectare ad ulciscendum neque
vim tantam doloris in posterum differre potuerint ?
Circumsessus es.   A quibus ?   A Lampsacenis.   Bar-
baris hominibus, credo, aut iis qui populi Romani
nomen contemnerent ?   Immo vero ab hominibus
et natura et consuetudine et disciplina lenissimis ;
porro autem populi Romani condicione sociis, fortuna
servis, voluntate supplicibus : ut perspicuum sit
omnibus, nisi tanta acerbitas iniuriae, tanta vis

has war declared, and made, upon it. What then 80
made the whole community of Lampsacum, when
their meeting broke up, gather together, as you say
yourself in your letter, to attack your house? For
neither in the letter you send Nero, nor in your
evidence, do you suggest any reason for such an
upheaval. You say that you were besieged, that
fire was applied and brushwood heaped up round the
door, that your lictor was killed, and that you were
prohibited from going out into the street; but the
cause of this alarming occurrence you suppress. For
had Rubrius committed an outrage on his own
account, and not at your instigation and to gratify
your passions, they would have come before you to
complain of the injury done by a member of your
staff, and not to attack yourself. Since, therefore,
the witnesses I have brought forward have told us
the cause of that upheaval, and Verres has suppressed it, is not the case as I state it confirmed both
by their evidence and by his continued silence?

XXXII. Will you then, gentlemen, have any mercy 81
on a man like this, who has committed wrongs so
horrible that his victims could not wait for the legal
hour of vengeance, nor postpone the satisfaction of
resentment so overpowering? You were besieged,
Verres; and by whom? By the people of Lampsacum.
Savages, no doubt? Men who would feel no dread of
the name of Rome? Far from it: by those whose
nature, habits, and training made them the gentlest
of human beings; by their status the allies, by their
condition the slaves, by their disposition the humble
suppliants, of the Roman nation: so that it must be
obvious to everyone that, had not the wrong been so
galling, the outrage so overpowering, as to make

sceleris fuisset ut Lampsaceni moriendum sibi potius
quam perpetiendum putarent, numquam illos in eum
locum progressuros fuisse ut vehementius odio libidinis
82 tuae quam legationis metu moverentur.   Nolite, per
deos immortales, cogere socios atque exteras nationes
hoc uti perfugio, quo, nisi vos vindicatis, utentur
necessario.   Lampsacenos in istum numquam ulla
res mitigasset nisi eum poenas Romae daturum credi-
dissent.   Etsi talem acceperant iniuriam quam nulla
lege satis digne persequi possent, tamen incommoda
sua nostris committere legibus et iudiciis quam dolori
suo permittere maluerunt.   Tu mihi, cum circumsessus a tam illustri civitate sis propter tuum scelus
atque flagitium ; cum coegeris homines miseros et
calamitosos, quasi desperatis nostris legibus et iudiciis, ad vim, ad manus, ad arma confugere ; cum te in
oppidis et civitatibus amicorum non legatum populi
Romani, sed tyrannum libidinosum crudelemque prae-
bueris ; cum apud exteras nationes imperii nominisque nostri famam tuis probris flagitiisque violaris ;
cum te ex ferro amicorum populi Romani eripueris
atque ex flamma sociorum evolaris : hic tibi perfugium speras futurum ?   Erras.   Ut huc incideres,
non ut hic conquiesceres, illi te vivum exire passi sunt.
83   XXXIII. Et ais iudicium esse factum te iniuria
circumsessum esse Lampsaci, quod Philodamus cum

these people feel death better than continued endurance, they would never have reached the point of being more influenced by loathing for your lewdness than by fear of your power as governor. In God's 82 name, gentlemen, do not force the nations, without or within our empire, to resort to such extremities, as they must do, if you will not be their champions ! Nothing would have stayed the fury of the people of Lampsacum against that man but the belief that he would be punished at Rome. Though they had suffered a wrong for which no legal process could give them adequate redress, yet even so they resolved to let our laws and judges do what they should, and not their resentment do what it would, to assuage their misery. Tell me this, Verres. Seeing that you were beset by the people of that reputable town through your own criminal and wicked act ; that you forced those unhappy and unfortunate beings, as if there were no hope for them in our laws and law-courts, to fall back upon force and armed violence ; that you have behaved, in the towns and territories of friendly states, not like a Roman governor but like a lustful and cruel despot ; that by your vile and wicked conduct you have defiled the fair name of Roman government in the eyes of all foreign nations ; that you have eluded the sword Rome's friends raised to strike you, and escaped the flames Rome's allies kindled to consume you : do you think to find yourself a place of safety *here* ? Not so. They meant this place to be a trap for you, and not a harbour of refuge, or they would never have let you get away alive.

XXXIII. The verdict against Philodamus and his 83 son implies, according to you, a verdict that the beleaguering of the house at Lampsacum was a

filio condemnatus sit. Quid si doceo, si planum facio
teste homine nequam, verum ad hanc rem tamen
idoneo—te ipso, inquam, teste docebo te huius circum-
sessionis tuae causam et culpam in alios transtulisse,
neque in eos quos tu insimularas esse animadversum.
Iam nihil te iudicium Neronis adiuvat. Recita quas
ad Neronem litteras misit. EPISTOLA C. VERRIS AD
NERONEM. THEMISTAGORAS ET THESSALUS. . . . The-
mistagoram et Thessalum scribis populum concitasse.
Quem populum ? qui te circumsedit, qui te vivum
comburere conatus est. Ubi hos persequeris, ubi
84 accusas, ubi defendis ius nomenque legati ? In Philodami iudicio dices id actum ? Cedo mihi ipsius Verris
testimonium ; videamus quid idem iste iuratus
dixerit. Recita. AB ACCUSATORE ROGATUS RESPONDIT
IN HOC IUDICIO NON PERSEQUI : SIBI IN ANIMO ESSE ALIO
TEMPORE PERSEQUI. Quid igitur te iuvat Neronis
iudicium, quid Philodami damnatio ? Legatus cum
esses circumsessus, cumque, quem ad modum tute ad
Neronem scripsisti, populo Romano communique
causae legatorum facta esset insignis iniuria, non es
persecutus. Dicis tibi in animo esse alio tempore
persequi. Quod fuit id tempus ? quando es persecutus ? Cur imminuisti ius legationis ? cur causam

wrong done to yourself. What if I prove, what if I
establish clearly, on the evidence of a worthless person indeed, but still a useful one for my purpose—
on your own evidence, I say, I will prove that you
transferred to quite different persons the responsibility and blame for this beleaguering of you, and
nevertheless took no steps to punish those whom
you alleged to be guilty. The verdict of Nero's
court does you no good now. Read the letter he
wrote to Nero. *Letter of Gaius Verres to Nero.*
" *Themistagoras and Thessalus . . .*" You here write
that it was Themistagoras and Thessalus who instigated the populace. Instigated it to what ? To
beleaguer your house, and try to burn you alive.
Where do we then find you proceeding against these
persons, or prosecuting them, or maintaining the
rights and prestige of the assistant-governorship ?
Will you pretend that this was done at the trial of **84**
Philodamus ? Let us have the evidence there given
by Verres himself : let us see what this same gentleman said as a sworn witness. Read the passage.
" *In answer to the prosecutor he said that he was not
taking proceedings in connexion with this case : that he
intended to do so on some other occasion.*" Now then,
how are you helped by the verdict of Nero's court,
or by the condemnation of Philodamus ? Although
you, an assistant-governor, were beleaguered in your
house, and although, as you wrote to Nero yourself,
a signal wrong was done to the Roman nation and to
the interests of all assistant-governors, yet you took
no proceedings. You assert that you intend to do
so on some other occasion. When was this occasion ?
When did you take proceedings ? Why did you in-
fringe the privileges of assistant-governors ? Why did

populi Romani deseruisti ac prodidisti ? cur iniurias
tuas coniunctas cum publicis reliquisti ? Non te ad
senatum causam deferre, non de tam atrocibus iniuriis
conqueri, non eos homines qui populum concitarant
85 consulum litteris evocandos curare oportuit ? Nuper
M. Aurelio Scauro postulante, quod is Ephesi se
quaestorem vi prohibitum esse dicebat quo minus e
fano Dianae servum suum, qui in illud asylum con-
fugisset, abduceret, Pericles Ephesius, homo nobilis-
simus, Romam evocatus est, quod auctor illius
iniuriae fuisse arguebatur : tu, si te legatum ita
Lampsaci tractatum esse senatum docuisses ut tui
comites vulnerarentur, lictor occideretur, ipse circumsessus paene incenderere, eius autem rei duces
et auctores principes fuisse, quos scribis, Themista-
goram et Thessalum, quis non commoveretur ? quis
non ex iniuria quae tibi esset facta sibi provideret ?
quis non in ea re causam tuam, periculum commune
agi arbitraretur ? Etenim nomen legati eius modi
esse debet quod non modo inter sociorum iura sed
etiam inter hostium tela incolume versetur.

86   XXXIV. Magnum hoc Lampsacenum crimen est
libidinis atque improbissimae cupiditatis : accipite
nunc avaritiae prope modum in suo genere non levius.

---

^a This rather thin sophistry depends on the accident that
an envoy under a flag of truce has the same title as an
assistant-governor : both are *legati*, " representatives."

you fail to be loyal and faithful to Rome? Why did
you fail to right the public wrongs that were thus
bound up with your own? Was it not your duty to
bring up the case before the Senate? To protest
against these grave outrages? To have the persons
who instigated the populace summoned for trial to
Rome by consular warrant? Not long ago Marcus 85
Aurelius Scaurus asserted that, while serving as
quaestor at Ephesus, he was forcibly prevented from
removing from the temple of Diana his own slave
who had there taken sanctuary: and on his application an Ephesian of the highest rank named Pericles
was summoned for trial to Rome, on the ground that
he had been responsible for this act of injustice. If
you had informed the Senate how you, an assistant-
governor, had been treated by the people of Lampsacum—members of your staff wounded, your lictor
killed, you yourself surrounded and almost burnt
alive—and that the ringleaders and chief promoters
had been the men you mention in your letter,
Themistagoras and Thessalus: who would not have
felt indignation? Who would not have reflected on
the risk to himself implied in the wrong done to you?
Who would not have held that, while the matter concerned yourself directly, the interests of everyone
were endangered? And indeed the very name
legatus[a] should inspire such respect that its bearer
should be able to move unharmed not only among
allies, who acknowledge our rights, but among
enemies, whose swords are drawn against us.

XXXIV. Grave as this Lampsacene crime of lust 86
and evil passion must appear, you are now to listen
to a charge of avaricious greed that in its own class

Milesios navem poposcit quae eum praesidii causa Myndum prosequeretur. Illi statim myoparonem egregium de sua classe ornatum atque armatum dederunt; hoc praesidio Myndum profectus est. Nam quid a Milesiis lanae publice abstulerit, item de sumptu in adventum, de contumeliis et iniuriis in magistratum Milesium, tametsi dici cum vere tum graviter et vehementer potest, tamen dicere praetermittam, eaque omnia testibus integra reservabo : illud, quod neque taceri ullo modo neque dici pro 87 dignitate potest, cognoscite. Milites remigesque Miletum Myndo pedibus reverti iubet: ipse myoparonem pulcherrimum, de decem Milesiorum navibus electum, L. Magio et L. Fannio, qui Myndi habitabant, vendidit. Hi sunt homines quos nuper senatus in hostium numero habendos censuit ; hoc illi navigio ad omnes populi Romani hostes, usque ab Dianio ad Sinopen navigaverunt.

O di immortales, incredibilem avaritiam singularemque audaciam ! Navem tu de classe populi Romani, quam tibi Milesia civitas ut te prosequeretur dedisset, ausus es vendere ? Si te magnitudo maleficii, si te hominum existimatio non movebat, ne illud quidem cogitabas, huius improbissimi furti, sive adeo nefariae praedae, tam illustrem ac tam nobilem civitatem 88 testem futuram ? An quia tum Cn. Dolabella in

---

^a Some fifty miles, as against about thirty by sea.
^b On the E. coast of Spain. The Sertorians there were in touch with Mithridates in Pontus.

is hardly less serious. Verres demanded from the
people of Miletus a ship to accompany and protect
him as far as Myndus. They promptly supplied him
from their fleet with an excellent cruiser, fully furnished and equipped ; and with this escort he set
sail for Myndus. The story of the wool that he stole
from the Milesians in the name of the state, of the
expense, moreover, that his visit caused, and of his
insolent and unjust behaviour towards the chief
magistrate of the city—though this true story might
be told in stern and emphatic language, I shall
nevertheless forbear to tell it, keeping the whole of
it for my witnesses. But I will ask you to listen to
another story, which can neither by any means be
suppressed nor be told as it deserves to be told.
Verres ordered the marines and rowers to return **87**
from Myndus to Miletus on foot ; [a] he himself took
that handsome cruiser, the pick of the ten Milesian
ships, and sold it to two residents of Miletus, Lucius
Magius and Lucius Fannius. These are men whom
the Senate recently declared public enemies, and
this is the vessel in which they have made voyages,
carrying messages between all the enemies of this
country from Dianium [b] to Sinope.

God help us, what incredible greed, what matchless
impudence ! Here was a ship belonging to the
Roman navy, given you by the city of Miletus as an
escort, and you dared to sell it ! Even though you
were indifferent to the grossness of the offence, and
to the discredit that it brought you, did it not even
occur to you that this immoral theft—or rather, this
nefarious act of piracy—would be established by the
evidence of that reputable and famous city ? Or if **88**
Dolabella, in deference to you, took steps at the

eum qui ei myoparoni praefuerat Milesiisque rem
gestam renuntiarat animadvertere tuo rogatu conatus
est, renuntiationemque eius, quae erat in publicas
litteras relata illorum legibus, tolli iusserat, idcirco te
ex hoc crimine elapsum esse arbitrabare ?   XXXV.
Multum te ista fefellit opinio, et quidem multis in
locis.   Semper enim existimasti, et maxime in Sicilia,
satis cautum tibi ad defensionem fore, si aut referri
aliquid in litteras publicas vetuisses, aut quod relatum
esset tolli coegisses.   Hoc quam nihil sit, tametsi ex
multis Siciliae civitatibus priore actione didicisti,
tamen etiam in hac ipsa civitate cognosce.   Sunt illi
quidem dicto audientes quam diu adsunt ii qui
imperant :   simulac discesserunt, non solum illud
perscribunt quod tum prohibiti sunt, sed etiam
causam ascribunt cur non tum in litteras relatum sit.
89 Manent istae litterae Mileti, manent, et dum erit illa
civitas manebunt.   Decem enim naves iussu L.
Murenae populus Milesius ex pecunia vectigali populi
Romani fecerat, sicut pro sua quaeque parte Asiae
ceterae civitates.   Quam ob rem unam ex decem, non
praedonum repentino adventu sed legati latrocinio,
non vi tempestatis sed hac horribili tempestate
sociorum amissam, in litteras publicas rettulerunt.
90 Sunt Romae legati Milesii, homines nobilissimi ac
principes civitatis, qui tametsi mensem Februarium
et consulum designatorum nomen exspectant, tamen

ᵃ Left in charge of the legions in Asia by Sulla at the
end of 83.

ᵇ The usual month for receiving deputations from allied
and foreign states.

ᶜ And therefore fearing for the success of their mission,
if they offended these supporters of Verres in this trial.
216

time to punish the cruiser's captain, who had reported the occurrence to the Milesians ; or if he ordered this report, which, as required by Milesian law, had been entered in their public records, to be removed therefrom : did that make you think you had escaped this charge ? XXXV. That notion has played you very false, and done so very often too. You have always reckoned, and in Sicily more than anywhere, that you would find yourself adequately secured against attack, if you either forbade a fact to be entered in the public records, or compelled its removal if entered already. How futile this belief is you learnt, to be sure, at the first hearing, from not a few of the states of Sicily, but you may learn it a little better from this same state Miletus. They certainly obeyed the order given them so long as the man who gave it was on the spot ; but the moment he went away, they not only made the prohibited entry, but added the reason why it was not made at the time. There that record of you is at Miletus : 89 there it is, and so long as Miletus endures, there it will be. By the orders of Lucius Murena,[a] the people of Miletus built ten ships as part of their imperial tribute, as the other cities of Asia likewise did, each in proportion to its means : and this is why the loss of one of their ten—not through a sudden descent of pirates but through open robbery on the part of a governor, not in a hurricane at sea but in this appalling human hurricane that shipwrecks our allies—was entered in their public records. Envoys 90 from Miletus are now in Rome, men of high rank and political importance in their own community. These await with misgiving the month of February,[b] knowing as they do the names of the consuls-elect[c] ;

hoc tantum facinus non modo negare interrogati sed
ne producti quidem reticere poterunt : dicent, inquam,
et religione adducti et domesticarum legum metu,
quid illo myoparone factum sit ; ostendent C.
Verrem, in ea classe quae contra piratas aedificata sit,
piratam ipsum consceleratum fuisse.

XXXVI. C. Malleolo quaestore Cn. Dolabellae
occiso, duas sibi hereditates venisse arbitratus est ;
unam quaestoriae procurationis, nam a Dolabella
statim pro quaestore iussus est esse : alteram tutelae,
nam, cum pupilli Malleoli tutor esset, in bona eius
91 impetum fecit. Nam Malleolus in provinciam sic
copiose profectus erat ut domi prorsus nihil relinqueret ; praeterea pecunias occuparat apud populos
et syngraphas fecerat ; argenti optimi caelati grande
pondus secum tulerat (nam ille quoque sodalis istius
erat in hoc morbo et cupiditate) ; grande pondus argenti, familiam magnam, multos artifices, multos formosos homines reliquerat.   Iste quod argenti placuit
invasit ; quae mancipia voluit abduxit ; vina cetera-
que quae in Asia facillime comparantur, quae ille
reliquerat, asportavit ; reliqua vendidit, pecuniam
92 exegit. Cum ad HS viciens quinquiens redegisse
constaret, ut Romam rediit nullam litteram pupillo,
nullam matri eius, nullam tutoribus reddidit ; servos

none the less, they will not be able to deny, when cross-examined, their knowledge of this monstrous action, nor even to refrain from speaking of it as soon as they are in the witness-box. They will tell us, I repeat—conscience, and respect for their own law, will make them tell us—what happened to that cruiser; they will prove that Gaius Verres acted, towards the fleet that was built to fight the pirates, like a pirate of the guiltiest description.

XXXVI. When Gaius Malleolus, Dolabella's quaestor, was killed, Verres reckoned that two inheritances had come to him; one was that of the quaestorial functions, for he was at once instructed to act as quaestor by Dolabella; the other that of a guardianship, for the young Malleolus being his ward he launched an attack upon his property. Malleolus 91 had gone off to his province so amply provided that he had left nothing at all at home behind him; he had, moreover, invested money locally, and lent sums on note of hand. He had brought with him a great mass of fine silver plate, his morbid passion for which was a bond of union between himself and Verres. At his death he left this great mass of plate, and a large household of slaves, including a number of skilled workmen and a number of handsome attendants. Verres seized all the plate that took his fancy; took away all the slaves he wanted; shipped off what wine and other things easily procurable in Asia Malleolus had left; sold everything else, and got the money from the buyers. Though it was clearly 92 understood that he had received not less than £25,000, he sent not a word of acknowledgement to his ward when he got back to Rome, not a word to the mother or to the other guardians. Keeping those

artifices pupilli cum haberet domi, circum pedes
autem homines formosos et litteratos, suos esse dicebat, se emisse. Cum saepius mater et avia pueri
postularent uti, si non redderet pecuniam nec
rationem daret, diceret saltem quantum pecuniae
Malleoli deportasset, a multis efflagitatus aliquando
dixit HS deciens; deinde in codicis extrema cera
nomen infimum in flagitiosa litura fecit : expensa
Chrysogono servo HS sescenta milia, accepta pupillo
Malleolo rettulit. Quo modo ex deciens HS sescenta
sint facta, quo modo DC. eodem modo quadrarint ut
illa de Cn. Carbonis pecunia reliqua HS sescenta facta
sint, quo modo Chrysogono expensa lata sint, cur id
nomen infimum in lituraque sit, vos existimabitis.
93 Tamen HS sescenta milia cum accepta rettulisset,
HS quinquaginta milia soluta non sunt ; homines,
posteaquam reus factus est, alii redditi, alii etiam
nunc retinentur, peculia omnium vicariique retinentur.

XXXVII. Haec est istius praeclara tutela. En cui
tuos liberos committas, en memoriam mortui sodalis, en metum vivorum existimationis. Cum tibi se
tota Asia spoliandam ac vexandam tradidisset, cum
tibi exposita esset omnis ad praedandum Pamphylia,
contentus his tam opimis rebus non fuisti ? manus a

---

a That of the Malleolus estate.

b i.e., with instructions to refund it to young Malleolus.
Or, perhaps, Chrysogonus was the slave of Malleolus.

c See § 36. Verres has a tendency to invent fictitious
sums of £6000.

d Or perhaps " £500 of this was not paid back " ; but
non soluta sunt would be more natural Latin in that case.

of his ward's slaves who were skilled workmen in
his house, and those who were good-looking and well-
educated in attendance upon himself, he gave out
that they were his own, that he had bought them.
The boy's mother and grandmother asked him repeatedly to tell them at least how much money
belonging to Malleolus he had brought away with
him, even if he would not hand it over or furnish a
statement of account ; and appeals from many
quarters at last made him own up to £10,000. After
this, on the last leaf of the account-book,[a] he inserted a final entry over a disgraceful erasure, showing £6000 as received from his ward Malleolus and
paid over to his slave Chrysogonus.[b] How that
£10,000 has become £6000 ; how that £6000
works out so exactly in the same way that it
becomes the same total as the £6000 balance in the
Carbo account ;[c] how that money came to be
entered as paid to Chrysogonus ; and why that
item is at the foot of the page and written over an
erasure : all this you, gentlemen, will judge for
yourselves. Even so, though he had entered £6000 93
as received from Malleolus, not £500 was paid back [d] ;
some of the slaves were handed over, after this case
against him began, but others are being withheld
even now, and their private possessions and their
own slaves are also all being withheld.

XXXVII. This is the edifying story of his guardianship. Here is the man to whom to entrust your
children ! Here is loyalty to the memory of a dead
friend, and respect for the opinion of the living !
With all Asia offered you to harry and plunder,
Verres, and all Pamphylia at the mercy of your
piratical raids, did such riches as that not satisfy

tutela, manus a pupillo, manus a sodalis filio abstinere
non potuisti ? Iam te non Siculi, non aratores, ut
dictitas, circumveniunt, non hi qui decretis edictis-
que tuis in te concitati infestique sunt : Malleolus
a me productus est et mater eius atque avia, quae
miserae flentes eversum a te puerum patriis bonis
94 esse dixerunt. Quid exspectas ? an dum ab in-
feris ipse Malleolus exsistat atque abs te officia tutelae, sodalitatis familiaritatisque flagitet ? Ipsum
putato adesse. Homo avarissime et spurcissime,
redde bona sodalis filio, si non quae abstulisti, at quae
confessus es ! Cur cogis sodalis filium hanc primam
in foro vocem cum dolore et querimonia emittere ?
cur sodalis uxorem, sodalis socrum, domum denique
totam sodalis mortui contra te testimonium dicere ?
cur pudentissimas lectissimasque feminas in tantum
virorum conventum insolitas invitasque prodire cogis ?
Recita omnium testimonia. TESTIMONIUM MATRIS ET
AVIAE.

95 XXXVIII. Pro quaestore vero quo modo iste
commune Milyadum vexarit, quo modo Lyciam, Pamphyliam, Pisidiam Phrygiamque totam frumento imperando, aestimando, hac sua, quam tum primum
excogitavit, Siciliensi aestimatione afflixerit, non est
necesse demonstrare verbis. Hoc scitote, cum iste civi-

ª Milyas was in Pisidia.
ᵇ The province of Cilicia at this date covered a wide area.
Part of Phrygia was in Asia : but Cilicia also included
Lycaonia and Cyprus.

you ? Could you not keep your hands from outraging your guardian's duty, your ward, your friend's son ? In *this* matter it is not the Sicilians, not the farmers, who (as you keep asserting) are trying to circumvent you, not those whose hatred of you has been aroused by your decisions and regulations : it is young Malleolus whom I have brought into court, it is his mother and grandmother, who testify with tears in their eyes, poor creatures, that you have cheated the boy out of his patrimony. What more would 94 you have ? Shall Malleolus himself rise up from the world of shades, and demand of you the performance of your duties towards him as guardian and companion and friend ? Imagine him here in person. Greedy and unclean wretch, restore the property of your friend's son ; if not all that you stole, at least all that you admitted to stealing. Why do you force the first words that your friend's son utters in our Forum to be a cry of pain and protest ? Why do you force your friend's wife, and the mother of your friend's wife, the whole household of your dead friend, to testify thus against you ? See these modest and virtuous ladies, unwillingly facing the unaccustomed sight of this great gathering of men—why do you force them to do it ?—Read the evidence given by all of them. *Evidence of the mother and the grandmother.*

XXXVIII. How, as acting quaestor, he harried the 95 Milyad [a] community, and the injuries he inflicted throughout Lycia and Pamphylia, Pisidia and Phrygia,[b] by demanding corn and making them pay money instead, on his own Sicilian system which he first invented during this period—this I need not expound in detail. But you should note this result

tatibus frumentum, coria, cilicia, saccos imperaret,
neque ea sumeret, proque his rebus pecuniam exigeret,
his nominibus solis Cn. Dolabellae HS ad triciens litem
esse aestimatam ; quae omnia, etiamsi voluntate
Dolabellae fiebant, per istum tamen omnia gere-
96 bantur. Consistam in uno nomine : multa enim sunt
ex eodem genere. Recita. DE LITIBUS AESTIMATIS
CN. DOLABELLAE PR. PECUNIAE REDACTAE. QUOD A COM-
MUNI MILYADUM . . . Te haec coegisse, te aesti-
masse, tibi pecuniam numeratam esse dico ; eadem-
que vi et iniuria, cum pecunias maximas cogeres, per
omnes partes provinciae te tamquam aliquam cala-
mitosam tempestatem pestemque pervasisse de-
97 monstro. Itaque M. Scaurus, qui Cn. Dolabellam
accusavit, istum in sua potestate ac dicione tenuit.
Homo adulescens cum istius in inquirendo multa furta
ac flagitia cognosceret, fecit perite et callide :
volumen eius rerum gestarum maximum isti ostendit ;
ab homine quae voluit in Dolabellam abstulit ; istum
testem produxit ; dixit iste quae velle accusatorem
putavit. Quo ex genere mihi testium, qui cum isto
furati sunt, si uti voluissem, magna copia fuisset ; qui
ut se periculo litium, coniunctione criminum liberarent,

---

[a] He threatened to prosecute Verres, on the strength of
what he knew against him, unless Verres would help him
against Dolabella.

224

of his practice of demanding corn, hides, Cilician rugs and sacks from the various cities, refusing to accept them, and exacting their money value instead—that under these heads alone the damages assessed against Gnaeus Dolabella amounted to thirty thousand pounds : and though it all took place with Dolabella's approval, it was all carried out under Verres' personal direction. I will pause 96 to consider a single item ; there are plenty of others like it. Read this, please. *The assessment of damages against the praetor Gnaeus Dolabella on account of money illegally exacted by the state. " Inasmuch as from the Milyad community . . ."* It was you, Verres, I assert, who made these requisitions, you who fixed their value in money, you to whom the money was paid ; and I am prepared to show how, amassing huge sums of money with equal violence and injustice, you swept like some destroying hurricane or pestilence through every district in the province. And that, gentlemen, is why Marcus Scaurus, the 97 prosecutor of Dolabella, kept Verres in his power and under his control. Having in the course of his inquiries discovered the man's numerous thefts and evil deeds, the young fellow took an ingenious and skilful line with him. He showed him a large book full of his exploits,[a] extracted from him the information he needed against Dolabella, and called him as a witness ; whereupon the rascal said what he supposed the prosecutor wished him to say. (I myself could have found any number of witnesses of this type, Verres' accomplices in robbery, if I had cared to make use of them : men who, to secure themselves against the risk of being fined or prosecuted in conjunction with him, were ready to sink to any depth

98 quo ego vellem descensuros pollicebantur. Eorum
ego voluntatem omnium repudiavi; non modo
proditori sed ne perfugae quidem locus in meis castris
cuiquam fuit. Forsitan meliores illi accusatores
habendi sint, qui haec omnia fecerunt. Ita est; sed
ego defensorem in mea persona, non accusatorem,
maxime laudari volo. Rationes ad aerarium antequam Dolabella condemnatus est non audet referre;
impetrat a senatu ut dies sibi prorogaretur, quod
tabulas suas ab accusatoribus Dolabellae obsignatas
diceret, proinde quasi exscribendi potestatem non
haberet. Solus est hic qui numquam rationes ad
aerarium referat.[a]

XXXIX. Audistis quaestoriam rationem, tribus
versiculis relatam; legationis, non nisi condemnato
et eiecto eo qui posset reprehendere: nunc denique
praeturae, quam ex senatus consulto statim referre
99 debuit, usque ad hoc tempus non rettulit. Quaestorem se in senatu exspectare dixit: proinde quasi
non, ut quaestor sine praetore possit rationem referre
(ut tu, Hortensi, ut omnes), eodem modo sine quaestore praetor. Dixit idem Dolabellam impetrasse.
Omen magis patribus conscriptis quam causa placuit;
probaverunt. Verum quaestores quoque iampridem
venerunt: cur non rettulisti? Illarum rationum ex

---

[a] *i.e.*, never does it properly, and always tries to avoid
doing it at all.

I might choose to order. I rejected the advances of **98**
all such persons : no room has been found in my
camp for traitors, nor even for simple deserters. It
may be that those who have adopted all such methods
are to be accounted better prosecutors than I am.
Very good. But it is the defender's part, and not
the prosecutor's, which I am most ambitious to play
with applause.) Well, Verres dared not submit his
accounts to the Treasury till after Dolabella's condemnation. He obtained leave from the Senate for
an extension of time, on the ground that his account-
books had been taken into custody by Dolabella's
prosecutors ; as if he were not at liberty to make
copies of them ! He is the one man who will *never*
submit his accounts *a* to the Treasury.

XXXIX. You have heard read the accounts relating to his quaestorship, three lines long ; and
those relating to his assistant-governorship, submitted only after the man who might have exposed
them was condemned and banished ; and now, lastly,
there are those of his praetorship, which he was
bound, by decree of the Senate, to submit without
delay, and to this very day has not submitted at
all. He told the Senate that he was waiting for **99**
his quaestor : ridiculous ! a quaestor can submit
accounts in his praetor's absence—as you did yourself, Hortensius, and everyone else ; and of course
a praetor can equally well do so in his quaestor's
absence. He said that Dolabella had been granted
the same concession : the House found the argument weak but the parallel suggestive, and agreed.
But the quaestors too arrived long ago : why are the
accounts not yet submitted ? Of the former accounts
belonging to your disgusting administration as

ea faece legationis quaestoriaeque tuae procurationis illa sunt nomina, quae Dolabellae necessario sunt aestimata. EX LITIBUS AESTIMATIS DOLABELLAE PR. ET 100 PRO PR. Quod minus Dolabella Verri acceptum rettulit quam Verres illi expensum tulerit, HS quingenta triginta quinque milia ; et quod plus fecit Dolabella Verrem accepisse quam iste in suis tabulis habuit, HS ducenta triginta duo milia ; et quod plus frumenti fecit accepisse istum, HS deciens et octingenta milia—quod tu, homo castissimus, aliud in tabulis habebas. Hinc illae extraordinariae pecuniae, quas nullo duce tamen aliqua ex particula investigamus, redundarunt ; hinc ratio cum Q. et Cn. Postumis Curtiis, multis nominibus, quorum in tabulis iste habet nullum ; hinc HS quater deciens P. Tadio numeratum Athenis testibus planum faciam ; hinc empta apertissime praetura—nisi forte id etiam 101 dubium est, quo modo iste praetor factus sit. Homo scilicet aut industria aut opera probata aut frugalitatis existimatione praeclara aut denique, id quod levissimum est, assiduitate, qui ante quaesturam cum meretricibus lenonibusque vixisset, quaesturam ita gessisset quem ad modum cognovistis, Romae post quaesturam illam nefariam vix triduum constitisset, absens non in oblivione iacuisset sed in assidua commemoratione omnibus omnium flagitiorum fuisset :

---

a *i.e.*, the false entries that, being accepted as true, led to Dolabella's being condemned to pay the discrepancies between them and his own entries.

b † . . . † These words are perhaps a verbal quotation from the assessment.

c *i.e.*, as the result of such deliberate falsifications as that just mentioned.

228

assistant-governor and quaestor, here are the items
that necessarily came into the damages assessed
against your friend Dolabella.[a] *Extract from the
schedule of damages assessed against the praetor and
propraetor Dolabella.* †Amount entered by Verres 100
as paid to Dolabella, less amount returned by
Dolabella as received from Verres, £5350 : amount
shown by Dolabella as paid to Verres, in excess of
what was shown in Verres' account, £2320 : corn
shown by Dolabella as received by Verres, in excess of
amount actually received, £18,000† [b]—this because
a man of your spotless honesty, Verres, entered the
amount otherwise. Hence [c] the abundance of those
unrecorded sums of money which—though without
assistance—I have to some small extent tracked
down : hence the account Verres kept [d] with the
Postumi Curtii, Quintus and Gnaeus, containing a
great many entries, not one of which appears in his
books : hence the £40,000 which I will bring evidence
to prove was paid at Athens to Publius Tadius : hence
the bare-faced purchase of his praetorship—or is
there some doubt even about the way in which he
made himself praetor ? As if he were a man who 101
had toiled hard, or done good work, or had a high
character for uprightness, or even, to go no higher,
taken trouble about anything ! This man, who before
he was quaestor spent his time with courtesans and
their keepers, discharged his quaestor's duties in the
way you have heard related, hardly stayed three days
together in Rome after that nefarious quaestorship
was over, and did not rest forgotten in his absence,
but had everyone perpetually talking about all his

[d] Cicero had got hold of the books kept by the Curtii
showing their account with Verres ; see § 102.

is repente, ut Romam venit, gratis praetor factus est ?
Alia porro pecunia ne accusaretur data. Cui sit data,
nihil ad me, nihil ad rem pertinere arbitror : datam
quidem esse tum inter omnes recenti negotio facile
102 constabat.   Homo stultissime et amentissime, tabulas
cum conficeres et cum extraordinariae pecuniae
crimen subterfugere velles, satis te elapsurum omni
suspicione arbitrabare, si quibus pecuniam credebas
iis expensum non ferres, neque in tuas tabulas ullum
nomen referres, cum tot tibi nominibus acceptum
Curtii referrent ?   Quid proderat tibi te expensum
illis non tulisse ?   An tuis solis tabulis te causam
dicturum existimasti ?

103   XL. Verum ad illam iam veniamus praeclaram
praeturam, criminaque ea quae notiora sunt his qui
adsunt quam nobis qui meditati ad dicendum parati-
que venimus ; in quibus non dubito quin offensionem
neglegentiae vitare atque effugere non possim.   Multi
enim ita dicent : " De illo nihil dixit in quo ego interfui : illam iniuriam non attigit quae mihi aut quae
amico meo facta est, quibus ego in rebus interfui."
His omnibus qui istius iniurias norunt, hoc est populo
Romano universo, me vehementer excusatum volo,

wicked actions—it is likely indeed that the moment
he came to Rome he was made praetor free of
charge. More money still was paid to hinder his
prosecution. To whom it was paid is a question that,
I take it, concerns neither me nor the matter in
hand : that paid it was, nobody at the time doubted
for one moment, when the business was fresh. Oh 102
you consummate fool and madman, when you were
making up your books and scheming to escape being
charged in connexion with those unrecorded sums
of money, did you fancy that you could quite evade
all suspicion simply by not recording the payment
of money to those who took charge of it for you,
or by showing your books with no such entries at
all, when the accounts of the Curtii recorded all
these sums received from you ? How did it help
you to make no entry of what you paid to them ?
Or did you imagine that your case would be tried
on the evidence of no one's accounts but your own ?

XL. But now let us come to his illustrious career 103
as praetor. Let us proceed to offences that are
more familiar to this audience than to us who have
thought out and prepared the case we have come
here to conduct. In dealing with these I shall
doubtless not succeed in escaping criticism for want
of thoroughness. Complaints like this will be common : " He has not referred to such-and-such an
instance, with which I was concerned ; he has not
touched on such-and-such an act of injustice done to
me, or done to my friend, things with which I was
concerned " To all those who are acquainted with
the man's perversions of justice—which is as much
as to say, to the entire Roman nation—I wish to
offer this emphatic defence of myself. It is not any

231

non neglegentia mea fore ut multa praeteream, sed quod alia testibus integra reservari velim, multa autem propter rationem brevitatis ac temporis praetermittenda existimem. Fatebor etiam illud invitus, me prorsus, cum iste punctum temporis nullum vacuum peccato praeterire passus sit, omnia quae ab isto commissa sunt non potuisse cognoscere. Quapropter ita me de praeturae criminibus auditote ut ex utroque genere, et iuris dicendi et sartorum tectorum exigendorum, ea postuletis quae maxime digna sint eo reo cui parvum aut mediocre obici nihil 104 oporteat. Nam ut praetor factus est, qui auspicato a Chelidone surrexisset, sortem nactus est urbanae provinciae magis ex sua Chelidonisque, quam ex populi Romani voluntate. Qui principio qualis in edicto constituendo fuerit cognoscite.

XLI. P. Annius Asellus mortuus est C. Sacerdote praetore. Is cum haberet unicam filiam neque census esset, quod eum natura hortabatur, lex nulla prohibebat, fecit, ut filiam bonis suis heredem

---

[a] Instead of his going to the temple to take his auspices, as praetor-elect, before the drawing of lots, he bade the augur attend him in the chamber where he and his mistress were lying : an irreligious proceeding that unfortunately, though appropriately, was followed by his securing the sphere of duty in which he could do most harm. (Or the meaning may be that he took no auspices, but substituted the embraces of his mistress.)

[b] The *edictum perpetuum*, or code of regulations regarding all matters that came within the praetor's jurisdiction, revised by each praetor (usually with close respect to the principles followed by his predecessors) at the beginning of his tenure of office, and supposed to be binding on him throughout his tenure. It was meant to interpret, to supplement, and to define the application of existing statute law (*leges*).

want of thoroughness that will cause me to pass over a great deal ; but there are some things I wish to reserve untouched for my witnesses' evidence ; and there are many that considerations of brevity and economy of time I feel make it necessary to leave out. I must also confess with regret that, since Verres never let one minute go by without doing something wrong, I have simply been unable to acquaint myself with every villainy he has perpetrated. In listening to me, therefore, as I deal with the crimes of his praetorship, I would have you look under both heads, those namely of judicial decisions and the maintenance of public buildings, for mention of such crimes only as most befit the dignity of a man who can never be fitly charged with anything trifling or even moderately serious. For as soon as 104 he became praetor he rose, after taking his auspices, from the embraces of Chelidon, to receive the city praetorship as his department, a result of the lot that was more gratifying to him and Chelidon than it was to the Roman nation.[a] And first let us see the light in which the composition of his edict [b] displays him.

XLI. During the praetorship of Gaius Sacerdos,[c] there died one Publius Annius Asellus. He, being the father of an only child, a daughter, and not having been registered,[d] had taken the step, which his natural feelings prompted and there was no law to forbid, of making his daughter his heir : and she

[c] The preceding year 75. He preceded Verres both as city praetor and as propraetor of Sicily.
[d] The Lex Voconia apparently forbade a man to make a woman his heir. But it seems that any man who had not been registered at the last *census* was not subject to this law.

institueret : heres erat filia.   Faciebant omnia cum
pupilla, legis aequitas, voluntas patris, edicta praetorum, consuetudo iuris eius quod erat tum cum
105 Asellus est mortuus.   Iste praetor designatus (utrum
admonitus, an temptatus, an, qua est ipse sagacitate
in his rebus, sine duce ullo, sine indice, pervenerit ad
hanc improbitatem, nescio : vos tantum hominis
audaciam amentiamque cognoscite) appellat heredem L. Annium, qui erat institutus secundum filiam
(non enim mihi persuadetur istum ab illo prius appel-
latum) ; dicit se posse ei condonare edicto hereditatem ; docet hominem quid possit fieri.   Illi bona
res, huic vendibilis videbatur.   Iste, tametsi singulari
est audacia, tamen ad pupillae matrem summittebat ;
malebat pecuniam accipere ne quid novi ediceret,
quam ut hoc edictum tam improbum et tam in-
106 humanum interponeret.   Tutores pecuniam praetori
si pupillae nomine dedissent, grandem praesertim,
quem ad modum in rationem inducerent, quem ad
modum sine periculo suo dare possent, non videbant ;
simul et istum fore tam improbum non arbitrabantur :
saepe appellati pernegaverunt.   Iste ad arbitrium
eius cui condonarat hereditatem ereptam a liberis
quam aequum edictum scripserit, quaeso, cognoscite.
CUM INTELLEGAM LEGEM VOCONIAM . . . Quis umquam
crederet mulierum adversarium Verrem futurum ? an
ideo aliquid contra mulieres fecit ne totum edictum ad

was so accordingly. All the arguments were in the
child's favour—equity, the father's wishes, the edicts
of past praetors, and the legal usage existing at the
date of Asellus's death. Verres after his election— 105
whether somebody advised him of the facts or set
him on, or his own natural acuteness in these matters
led him without guidance or information to such an
immoral proceeding, is more than I can say; I
merely tell you the reckless and unscrupulous thing
he did—Verres called on Lucius Annius, the reversionary heir (for I cannot believe the suggestion that
Annius called on him first); told him that he could,
by means of his edict, get him the inheritance; and
showed him what could be done about it. Annius
was disposed to do business, and Verres reckoned on
getting his price for it. But in spite of his extreme
audacity he nevertheless made secret proposals to
the girl's mother; to be bribed not to make an
innovation in his edict suited him better than to
bring into play a clause so immoral and brutal. The 106
child's guardians did not like the idea of paying
him money, and that a large sum, on their ward's
behalf, not seeing how they could enter it in their
accounts, nor how they could pay it without risk to
themselves. Nor did they suppose him capable of
such villainy; and though often pressed, they refused their consent. Listen, if you please, to the
equitable clause in his edict composed to suit the
person for whom he was getting this inheritance at
the cost of its owner's child. "*Since I understand
that the Voconian Law . . .*" Now who would ever
suspect that Verres would be the enemy of women?
Has he, I wonder, done a little to hurt them in order

Chelidonis arbitrium scriptum videretur ? Cupiditati hominum ait se obviam ire. Quis potius, non modo his temporibus sed etiam apud maiores nostros ? quis tam remotus fuit a cupiditate ? Dic, quaeso, cetera ; delectat enim me hominis gravitas, scientia iuris, auctoritas. QUI AB A. POSTUMIO, Q. FULVIO CENSORIBUS,

107 POSTVE EA . . . . . . FECIT FECERIT. Fecit fecerit ? quis umquam edixit isto modo ? quis umquam eius rei fraudem aut periculum proposuit edicto quae neque post edictum reprehendi neque ante edictum provideri potuit ? XLII. Iure, legibus, auctoritate omnium qui consulebantur, testamentum P. Annius fecerat non improbum, non inofficiosum, non inhumanum ; quodsi ita fecisset, tamen post illius mortem nihil de testamento illius novi iuris constitui oporteret. Voconia lex te videlicet delectabat. Imitatus esses ipsum illum Q. Voconium, qui lege sua hereditatem ademit nulli neque virgini neque mulieri : sanxit in posterum, qui post eos censores census esset, ne quis heredem virginem neve mulierem faceret.

108 In lege Voconia non est FECIT FECERIT ; neque in ulla praeteritum tempus reprehenditur, nisi eius rei quae sua sponte scelerata ac nefaria est, ut, etiamsi lex

---

^a *i.e.*, there was no reason for anyone to avoid it, since it was neither wrong *nor* illegal then.

to avoid the impression that the whole of his edict
was composed to suit Chelidon's tastes ? He tells
us that he is taking measures against greed : and
who more fit to do so, in our own time, or at any
time in our history ? Was ever man so untouched
by greed as he is ? Pray let us hear the rest ; it
is really delightful to see the man's high moral
tone, and his knowledge of law, and his impressive
personality ; read, please. *" Any man who, since the
censorship of Aulus Postumius and Quintus Fulvius or
any following year . . . has done or shall do so."*
" Has done or shall do " ? Did ever such an ex- 107
pression occur in an edict before ? Did an edict ever
before attach illegality, or liability to punishment,
to an act that cannot be attacked as wrong after the
edict was issued, and could not be avoided *ᵃ* before
it was issued ? XLII. The law, the statute-book,
and all the experts consulted, declared that Publius
Annius had made a will that was neither wrong nor
neglectful nor unfeeling. But had it been so, there
was still no justification, after his death, for making
any legal innovation applicable to his will. It appears that the Voconian law enjoyed your approval.
You might well have followed the example of Quintus
Voconius himself, then : for his law did not deprive
any girl or woman of her position of heiress if she
had it already ; it merely enjoined that no one,
registered after the year of the censors named,
should make a girl or woman his heiress in future.
In the Voconian Law we do not find " Has done or 108
shall do " ; nor in any law is a past action made
subject to censure, except such as of their own
nature are criminal and vile, so that they ought to
have been avoided at all costs even if no law for-

non esset, magno opere vitanda fuerit. Atque in his
ipsis rebus multa videmus ita sancta esse legibus ut
ante facta in iudicium non vocentur : Cornelia testa-
mentaria, nummaria, ceterae complures, in quibus
non ius aliquod novum populo constituitur, sed san-
citur ut, quod semper malum facinus fuerit, eius
quaestio ad populum pertineat ex certo tempore.
109 De iure vero civili si quis novi quid instituerit, is non
omnia quae ante acta sunt rata esse patietur ? Cedo
mihi leges Atinias, Furias, Fusias, ipsam, ut dixi,
Voconiam, omnes praeterea de iure civili ; hoc
reperies in omnibus statui ius quo post eam legem
populus utatur. Qui plurimum tribuunt edicto praetoris edictum legem annuam dicunt esse : tu edicto
plus complecteris quam lege. Si finem edicto praetoris afferunt Kalendae Ianuariae, cur non initium
quoque edicti nascitur a Kalendis Ianuariis ? An in
eum annum progredi nemo poterit edicto quo praetor
alius futurus est, in illum quo alius praetor fuit re-
110 gredietur ? Ac si hoc iuris, non unius hominis causa
edixisses, cautius composuisses. XLIII. Scribis SI QUIS
HEREDEM FECIT FECERIT. Quid si plus legarit quam
ad heredem heredesve perveniat, quod per legem
Voconiam ei qui census non sit licet : cur hoc, cum in

---

[a] Because retrospectively.
[b] *i.e.*, more than half the whole estate.

bade them. And even so we often find that a law
prohibiting such actions precludes prosecution of
those who have already committed them : the
Cornelian laws against forgery of wills, for instance,
and coining, and a number of others, in which no
new legal principle is set up for the community, but
it is provided that what has always in fact been an
immoral action shall become subject to criminal proceedings before the community after a fixed date.
But where a man makes some innovation in *civil* law, 109
he must surely allow all acts previously committed
to be legally valid. Look at the Atinian Law, the
Furian, the Fusian, the Voconian Law itself, as I
have said, and all the others that are concerned with
civil rights : in all of them you will find the same
thing, provisions that are to be binding on the community *after* the law comes into force. Even those
who attach most weight to the praetor's edict say
that an edict is a law valid for twelve months : you
make your edict operate more widely [a] than a law
can. If the validity of a praetor's edict ends on the
1st of January, why does its validity not also begin
from the 1st of January ? Nobody can use his edict
to make a forward encroachment on the year in
which another man will be praetor : is he to make
a backward encroachment on the year in which
another man has been praetor ? Moreover, had you 110
framed this clause to improve the law and not the
prospects of an individual, you would have done it
more carefully. XLIII. You write " Any person
who has made or shall make his heir . . ." What
of his bequeathing away more than comes to the
heir or heirs ? [b] That by the Voconian law is legal
for a person not registered at a census : why do you

eodem genere sit, non caves ? Quia non generis sed
hominis causam verbis amplecteris ; ut facile appareat
te pretio, non iure, esse commotum. Atque hoc si
in posterum edixisses, minus esset nefarium ; tamen
esset improbum ; sed tum vituperari posset, in
crimen[1] venire non posset, nemo enim committeret.
Nunc est eius modi edictum ut quivis intellegat non
populo esse scriptum sed P. Annii secundis here-
111 dibus. Itaque cum abs te caput illud tam multis
verbis mercennarioque prooemio esset ornatum, ecquis
est inventus postea praetor, qui idem illud ediceret ?
Non modo nemo edixit, sed ne metuit quidem
quisquam ne quis ediceret. Nam post te praetorem
multi testamenta eodem modo fecerunt[2] : in his
nuper Annaea de multorum propinquorum sententia,
pecuniosa mulier, quod censa non erat, testamento
fecit heredem filiam. Itaque hoc magnum iudicium
hominum de istius singulari improbitate, quod C.
Verres sua sponte instituisset, id neminem metuisse,
ne quis reperiretur qui istius institutum sequi vellet.
Solus enim tu inventus es cui non satis fuerit corrigere
voluntates vivorum nisi etiam rescinderes mortuorum.
112 Tu ipse ex Siciliensi edicto hoc sustulisti ; voluisti, ex
improviso si quae res nata esset, ex urbano edicto
decernere. Quam postea tu tibi defensionem relin-

[1] in discrimen, *the reading of the Vatican palimpsest, is
adopted by Peterson, Mueller, etc.*: in dubium *is the old
reading, being that of the other MSS.*: in crimen *is my
conjecture.*
[2] *Many editors, following the Vatican palimpsest, read*
multi in isdem causis fuerunt.

[a] Text uncertain here : the true original has possibly the
sense " who have been in the same position."

not guard against this action, since it belongs to the
same class ? Because your wording is not meant to
apply to a class, but to an individual : which shows
at once that your motives have not been legal, but
financial. Had your edict been made to apply to
the future only, it would have been less abominable ;
it would still have been wrong ; but in that case,
while it might have been censured, it could not have
been attacked as criminal, for nobody would have
transgressed it. As the matter stands, the character
of the clause would show anyone that it was put in
to benefit not the community but the reversionary
heir of Publius Annius. That is why, after all the 111
verbiage and the profit-hunting preamble with which
you adorned the clause, no subsequent praetor,
you will find, has reproduced it in his edict. Not
only so, but nobody has even been afraid of this
being done. Since your praetorship there are many
who have made their wills in the same fashion[a]:
among these is a wealthy woman named Annaea,
who, not having been registered, with the approval
of many of her family made her daughter her heir.
Now is not this a really emphatic condemnation of
the man's immoral conduct ? Gaius Verres devises a
regulation of his own, and nobody has been afraid
of finding any praetor inclined to carry that regulation on ! You, Verres, are indeed the one known
case of a man who has not been content with im-
proving the wills of the living, but must also annul
the wills of the dead. You yourself removed the 112
clause from your Sicilian edict, merely expressing
your intention to apply the principles of your city
edict to meet any unforeseen contingencies. What
you meant to be a reserve line of defence in future

241

quebas, in ea maxime offendisti, cum tuam auctoritatem tute ipse edicto provinciali repudiabas.

XLIV. Atque ego non dubito quin, ut mihi, cui mea filia maxime cordi est, res haec acerba videtur atque indigna, sic uni cuique vestrum, qui simili sensu atque indulgentia filiarum commovemini. Quid enim natura nobis iucundius, quid carius esse voluit ? quid est dignius in quo omnis nostra diligentia indul-
113 gentiaque consumatur ? Homo importunissime, cur tantam iniuriam P. Annio mortuo fecisti ? cur hunc dolorem cineri eius atque ossibus inussisti, ut liberis eius bona patria, voluntate patris, iure, legibus tradita, eriperes et cui tibi esset commodum condonares ? Quibuscum vivi bona nostra partimur, iis praetor adimere nobis mortuis bona fortunasque poterit ? NEC PETITIONEM, inquit, NEC POSSESSIONEM DABO. Eripies igitur pupillae togam praetextam, detrahes ornamenta non solum fortunae sed etiam ingenuitatis ? Miramur ad arma contra istum hominem Lampsacenos isse ? Miramur istum de provincia decedentem clam Syracusis profugisse ? Nos si alienam vicem pro nostra iniuria doleremus, vestigium istius in foro non esset

---

^a *i.e.*, the general proviso that the city edict might be applied was intended to enable Verres to apply it where convenient, and it was meant of course to refer to the clause of that edict now in question as well as to the rest : but this, Cicero argues, does not make up for the damaging effect of omitting the clause from the Sicilian edict.

^b Part of the clause in the *edictum*. The praetor would not allow the woman even to bring an action seeking to establish her claim to the property : nor would he allow her to have, or to remain in, provisional occupation of the property pending its final assignment.

^c The right of bringing a civil action before the city praetor was a privilege of the citizen ; and the *toga praetexta* was the dress of the child of free citizen parents.

has proved your chief stumbling-block[a]: by your own act, in your provincial edict, you denied that any weight was to be attached to your own judgement.

XLIV. Now I have no doubt that, just as this affair causes distress and resentment to me, in whose heart my daughter holds a chief place, so it is with each one of you, who are stirred by a like affection and tenderness for your own daughters : for indeed it is our daughters that nature bids us make the great source of our happiness and object of our devotion, nor can any other thing better deserve to have lavished on it all our care and tenderness. Cruel savage ! why have you done this foul wrong 113 to dead Publius Annius ? Why have you tortured his very bones and ashes with the agony of knowing how you tore away from his child the possessions that law and statute and his fatherly wishes would pass on to her, and conveyed them to the man on whom it suited you to bestow them ? Shall those with whom we share our good things while we live be robbed by some praetor of goods and happiness when we are dead ? " I will not permit," the man tells us, " either legal action or occupation." [b] Will you then pluck the child's fringe from her dress,[c] and pull off the badges of her freedom as well as her fortune ? Does it surprise us that the people of Lampsacum drew the sword against a man like this ? Or that his departure from his province was a stealthy flight from Syracuse [d] ? Did we feel the wrongs of others as we feel our own, no trace of him would have been suffered to remain in our forum.[e] A father 114

[d] This town was fairly friendly with Verres, who ought to have been able to go away openly from it at least.

[e] *i.e.*, all his judgements would have been annulled.

114 relictum. Pater dat filiae, prohibes : leges sinunt, tamen te interponis. De suis bonis ita dat ut ab iure non abeat ; quid habes quod reprehendas ? Nihil, opinor. At ego concedo : prohibe, si potes, si habes qui te audiat, si potest tibi dicto audiens esse quisquam. Eripias tu voluntatem mortuis, bona vivis, ius omnibus ? Hoc populus Romanus non manu vindicasset, nisi te huic tempori atque huic iudicio reservasset ?

Posteaquam ius praetorium constitutum est semper hoc iure usi sumus : si tabulae testamenti non proferrentur, tum, uti quemque potissimum heredem esse oporteret, si is intestato mortuus esset, ita secundum eum possessio daretur. Quare hoc sit aequissimum facile est dicere ; sed in re tam usitata satis est ostendere omnes antea ius ita dixisse, et hoc

115 vetus edictum translaticiumque esse. XLV. Cognoscite hominis aliud in re vetere edictum novum, et simul, dum est unde ius civile discatur, adulescentes ei in disciplinam tradite ; mirum est hominis ingenium, mira prudentia. Minucius quidam mortuus est ante istum praetorem. Eius testamentum erat nullum ; lege hereditas ad gentem Minuciam veniebat. Si habuisset iste edictum, quod ante istum et postea omnes habuerunt, possessio Minuciae genti esset data : si quis testamento se heredem esse arbi-

---

[a] Each praetor takes it over from his predecessor's edict without question, and incorporates it in his own edict.

[b] There can have been no children or brothers of the deceased.

244

gives something to his daughter, you prohibit it; the laws allow it, yet you interfere! He makes, out of his own property, a perfectly legal gift : what fault can you find with that ? None, as I hold. But I will not stand in your way. Interfere, if you can, if you find anyone to listen to you, if anyone proves capable of obeying your orders. Are you to rob the dead of their power of choice ; the living, of their property ; living and dead, of their legal rights ? Would not the Roman nation have struck you down for this, had it not kept you for this present hour of judgement ?

Ever since praetor's law was first set up, we have always had the following provision in force : That if no written will is produced, possession shall be given to that person who would have had the best claim to inherit if the deceased had made no will. The equity of this may easily be shown : but it is enough to point out, in so every-day a matter, that all previous decisions had observed this principle, and that the clause stating it is ancient and is always taken over.[a] XLV. Now let us note another innovation by 115 which Verres' edict replaces the ancient usage : and at the same time let us decide to send the younger generation to him for training in civil law while there is still someone who can teach it to them; his ability and his legal knowledge are both really remarkable. Before he became praetor, a man named Minucius died. No will made by him was forthcoming, and by law the estate would go to the Minucian clan.[b] If Verres' edict had contained what the edicts of all previous and subsequent praetors have contained, possession would have been given to the clan accordingly ; and if anyone believed himself to be the real

traretur quod tum non exstaret, lege ageret in
hereditatem ; aut, pro praede litis vindiciarum cum
satis accepisset, sponsionem faceret et ita de hereditate certaret. Hoc, opinor, iure et maiores nostri et
nos semper usi sumus. Videte ut hoc iste correxerit.
116 Componit edictum his verbis ut quivis intellegere
possit unius hominis causa conscriptum esse, tantum
quod hominem non nominat ; causam quidem totam
perscribit, ius, consuetudinem, aequitatem, edicta
omnium neglegit. EX EDICTO URBANO. SI DE HERE-
DITATE AMBIGITUR . . . SI POSSESSOR SPONSIONEM NON
FACIET. Iam quid ad praetorem uter possessor sit ?
nonne id quaeri oportet, utrum possessorem esse
oporteat ? Ergo, quia possessor est, non moves
possessione ; si possessor non esset, non dares ? Nus-
quam enim scribis, neque tu aliud quicquam edicto
amplecteris nisi eam causam pro qua pecuniam
117 acceperas. Iam hoc ridiculum est : SI DE HEREDITATE
AMBIGITUR, ET TABULAE TESTAMENTI OBSIGNATAE NON
MINUS MULTIS SIGNIS QUAM E LEGE OPORTET AD ME PRO-
FERENTUR, SECUNDUM TABULAS TESTAMENTI POTISSIMUM
POSSESSIONEM DABO. Hoc translaticium est ; sequi
illud oportet, SI TABULAE TESTAMENTI NON PROFERENTUR.
Quid ait ? se ei daturum qui se dicat heredem esse.

---

^a These are two forms of procedure, both obscure to us
in some details, by which an action regarding the ownership
of property could be instituted. See the excursus in Long's
edition, pp. 194-198.

^b Verres apparently, in this clause, gave the party in
possession the right to bar any action against him by
another claimant. The method of doing so would be to
refuse *sponsionem facere*, " to make a contract," by which
each party to a suit agreed to pay up if the decision went
against him. Evidently Verres' friend was in possession of
Minucius's estate.

heir by the terms of the will not at the time forthcoming, he could sue for it directly, or else take
adequate security for the value of the property and
the intermediate returns from it and assert his claim
to it by the contract process.[a] That is the way in
which the law has been worked, if I am right, both
in our fathers' days and in our own. Let us see the
improvement made by Verres. He composed a 116
clause for his edict so worded that anyone can see
how it was framed to meet the case of one particular
person. Everything is there but the person's name.
He gives the whole case, indeed, in detail : what he
neglects is law, usage, equity, and all preceding edicts.
*Extract from the city edict. " If the succession to an
estate shall be disputed . . . unless the party in possession
shall agree to the contract proposed."* [b] Now how can
it affect the praetor which of the two parties *is* in
possession ? Is not the point to be settled which of
the two *ought* to be in possession ? You do not,
then, eject the man in possession, because he is in
possession : would you then refuse the same man
possession if he were not ? That point you nowhere
deal with ; nor does your edict provide for anything
else at all besides the case for which you got paid.
Here now is an absurdity. *" If the succession to an* 117
*estate shall be disputed, and if there shall be produced
before me a written will sealed with the full number of
seals* [c] *required by law, I will give possession in accordance
with the written will."* So far this is adopted from previous edicts : but now what should follow is " *If a
written will shall not be produced . . ."* [d] What does
Verres say ? That he will give possession to the man

---

[c] *i.e.*, witnessed by the full number of witnesses.
[d] The clause was evidently completed as in § 114.

Quid ergo interest proferantur necne ? si protulerit,
uno signo ut sit minus quam ex lege oportet, non des
possessionem : si omnino tabulas non proferet, dabis.
Quid nunc dicam ? neminem umquam hoc postea
alium edixisse ? Valde sit mirum neminem fuisse
qui istius se similem dici vellet. Ipse in Siciliensi
edicto hoc non habet ; exegerat enim iam mercedem ;
item ut illo edicto de quo ante dixi, in Sicilia de
hereditatum possessionibus dandis edixit idem quod
omnes Romae praeter istum. EX EDICTO SICILIENSI.
SI DE HEREDITATE AMBIGITUR . . . . .

118   XLVI. At, per deos immortales, quid est quod de
hoc dici possit ? Iterum enim iam quaero abs te,
sicut modo in illo capite Anniano de mulierum hereditatibus, nunc in hoc de hereditatum possessionibus,
cur ea capita in edictum provinciale transferre nolueris?
Utrum digniores homines existimasti eos qui habitant
in provincia quam nos qui aequo iure uteremur, an
aliud Romae aequum est, aliud in Sicilia ? Non
enim hoc potest hoc loco dici, multa esse in provinciis
aliter edicenda : non de hereditatum quidem possessionibus, non de mulierum hereditatibus. Nam in
utroque genere video non modo ceteros, sed te ipsum,
totidem verbis edixisse quot verbis edici Romae solet.

248

who *claims* to be heir ! What difference then does it
make whether the will is produced or not ?[a] Should
the claimant produce it, you would refuse possession
if it was deficient by one seal in the number legally
required : and yet will you give possession if the
man produces no written will at all ? What comment
is possible? That no subsequent praetor ever adopted
this clause in his edict ? It is truly astonishing that
no one should have felt inclined to have his character
compared to that of Verres. Nor does the clause
occur in his own Sicilian edict—of course, he had
got his money by then: as in the clause I spoke of
just now, so here ; his edict in Sicily, so far as concerns giving possession of inheritances, is identical
with those of all city praetors—except himself. *Extract from the Sicilian edict. If the succession to an
estate is disputed* . . .

XLVI. And what, in heaven's name, can be said 118
in defence of that ?[b] I ask you again, Verres, with
reference to this clause dealing with giving possession
of inheritances, what I asked you just now about
the clause dealing (for the benefit of Annius) with the
right of women to inherit : I ask why you would not
adopt those clauses in your provincial edict. Did
you consider that people who live in the provinces
deserved fairer treatment than we here ? Or is one
thing fair in Rome and another in Sicily ? It certainly cannot be argued, in this connexion, that a
provincial edict must show many changes : that does
not, in any case, apply to granting possession of inheritances, nor to the right of women to inherit.
For I note, under both heads, that not only all other
praetors, but you yourself too, have used word for
word the same language in your provincial edicts as

Quae Romae magna cum infamia pretio accepto edixeras, ea sola te, ne gratis in provincia male audires, ex edicto Siciliensi sustulisse video.

119   Et cum edictum totum eorum arbitratu, quam diu fuit designatus, componeret qui ab isto ius ad utilitatem suam nundinarentur, tum vero in magistratu contra illud ipsum edictum suum sine ulla religione decernebat. Itaque L. Piso multos codices implevit earum rerum in quibus ita intercessit, quod iste aliter atque ut edixerat decrevisset. Quod vos oblitos esse non arbitror, quae multitudo, qui ordo ad Pisonis sellam isto praetore solitus sit convenire; quem iste collegam nisi habuisset, lapidibus coopertus esset in foro. Sed eo leviores istius iniuriae videbantur quod erat in aequitate prudentiaque Pisonis paratissimum perfugium, quo sine labore, sine molestia, sine impensa, etiam sine patrono homines

120 uterentur. Nam, quaeso, redite in memoriam, iudices, quae libido istius in iure dicendo fuerit, quae varietas decretorum, quae nundinatio, quam inanes domus eorum omnium qui de iure civili consuli solent, quam plena atque referta Chelidonis; a qua muliere cum erat ad eum ventum et in aurem eius insusurratum, alias revocabat eos inter quos iam decreverat,

---

ᵃ One of the other praetors that year. An appeal, on such technical grounds, was possible from the decision of any magistrate to any other not lower in rank.

is regularly used at Rome. It is only the clauses which, to your great disgrace, you were bribed to insert in your edict at Rome—only these, I note, that you removed from your Sicilian edict, in order not to acquire a bad name in your province without being paid for it.

And just as, between his election and his entry 119 upon office, he composed the whole of his edict to suit those who were trafficking in justice with him to serve their own ends, so during the tenure of his office he had no scruple about giving decisions that contradicted the edict itself. The result was that Lucius Piso *a* filled a pile of note-books with records of the cases in which he vetoed decisions by Verres as inconsistent with Verres' own edict. I imagine you have not forgotten this—what a streaming crowd of people would regularly gather round Piso's judgement-seat during Verres' year of office. But for his having Piso for a colleague, Verres would have been buried in the Forum under a shower of stones. As it was, the wrongs he did appeared more tolerable because people found, in the equitable character and legal knowledge of Piso, an always available refuge, of which they could make use without trouble or un-pleasantness or expense or even an advocate's help. Pray recall to your memories, gentlemen, the wanton 120 character of Verres' administration of the law, the lack of uniformity in his decisions, the trafficking that went on ; how empty were the houses of all the experts in civil law whom it is the practice to consult, how densely crowded was the house of Chelidon. As often as that woman came up to him and whispered in his ear, he would call back the parties to a case that he had already judged, and alter his judgement ;

decretumque mutabat, alias inter aliquos contrarium
sine ulla religione decernebat ac proximis paulo ante
121 decreverat. Hinc illi homines erant qui etiam ridiculi inveniebantur ex dolore ; quorum alii, id quod
saepe audistis, negabant mirandum esse ius tam
nequam esse verrinum : alii etiam frigidiores erant,
sed quia stomachabantur ridiculi videbantur esse,
cum Sacerdotem exsecrabantur qui verrem tam
nequam reliquisset. Quae ego non commemorarem
(neque enim perfacete dicta neque porro hac severitate digna sunt) nisi vos illud vellem recordari, istius
nequitiam et iniquitatem tum in ore vulgi atque in
communibus proverbiis esse versatam.

122 XLVII. In plebem vero Romanam utrum superbiam prius commemorem an crudelitatem ? Sine
dubio crudelitas gravior est atque atrocior. Oblitosne
igitur hos putatis esse quem ad modum sit iste solitus
virgis plebem Romanam concidere ? Quam rem
etiam tribunus plebis in contione egit, cum eum quem
iste virgis ceciderat in prospectum populi Romani
produxit. Cuius rei recognoscendae faciam vobis suo
123 tempore potestatem. Superbia vero quae fuerit quis
ignorat ? quem ad modum is tenuissimum quemque
contempserit, despexerit, liberum esse numquam
duxerit ? P. Trebonius viros bonos et honestos complures fecit heredes ; in iis fecit suum libertum. Is

---

[a] *Ius Verrinum*, " Verres' administration of the law " :
ius verrinum, " pork gravy."
[b] Verres' predecessor, " Mr. Priest," who ought to have
sacrificed this particular animal.
252

at other times he would, without the least scruple,
deliver in one case a judgement directly opposed to
that which he had delivered in the previous case a
few minutes before. Hence those people whose in- 121
dignation went so far as to make them humorists :
some of these made the remark you have often heard
repeated, that *ius verrinum* ᵃ was of course poor stuff :
others were still sillier, only that their irritation
passed them off as good jesters, when they cursed
Sacerdos ᵇ for leaving such a miserable hog behind
him. I should not recall these jokes, which are not
particularly witty, nor, moreover, in keeping with
the serious dignity of this Court, were it not that I
would have you remember how Verres' offences
against morality and justice became at the time the
subject of common talk and popular catchwords.

XLVII. As to his behaviour towards ordinary 122
people in Rome, should I speak first of its snobbery
or its cruelty ? Cruelty is admittedly the more
terrible and savage quality. Well then, do you
think, gentlemen, that this audience has forgotten
Verres' way of having ordinary Roman folk flogged
till the blood ran ? The thing was brought before a
public meeting by a tribune of the plebs, who then
produced before the eyes of the Roman people a
man whom Verres had had flogged. This subject I
mean to give you an opportunity of considering in
its proper place.ᶜ His snobbery is doubtless already 123
familiar to you all, the contemptuous way in which
he looked down upon any poor man and treated him
as no better than a slave. Publius Trebonius bequeathed his property to several honest and respectable persons, one of whom was his own freedman.

ᵉ Verres' cruelty in Sicily is the subject of Book V.

A. Trebonium fratrem habuerat proscriptum. Ei cum cautum vellet, scripsit ut heredes iurarent se curaturos ut ex sua cuiusque parte ne minus dimidium ad A. Trebonium fratrem illum proscriptum perveniret. Libertus iurat ; ceteri heredes adeunt ad Verrem, docent non oportere se iurare facturos esse quod contra legem Corneliam esset, quae proscriptum iuvari vetaret. Impetrant ut ne iurent ; dat his possessionem. Id ego non reprehendo ; etenim erat iniquum homini proscripto egenti de fraternis bonis quicquam dari. Libertus, nisi ex testamento patroni 124 iurasset, scelus se facturum arbitrabatur ; itaque ei Verres possessionem hereditatis negat se daturum, ne posset patronum suum proscriptum iuvare, simul ut esset poena quod alterius patroni testamento obtemperasset. Das possessionem ei qui non iuravit ; concedo ; praetorium est. Adimis tu ei, qui iuravit ; quo exemplo ? Proscriptum iuvat ; lex est, poena est. Quid ad eum qui ius dicit ? Utrum reprehendis quod patronum iuvabat eum qui tum in miseriis erat, an quod alterius patroni mortui voluntatem conservabat, a quo summum beneficium acceperat ? Utrum horum reprehendis ? Et hoc

His brother Aulus Trebonius was among the outlawed; and wishing to provide for him, he stipulated
in his will that his heirs should swear to see to it that
at least half of their respective shares came to the
outlawed Aulus. The freedman did swear this; but
the other heirs approached Verres, and pointed out
that they ought not to swear to perform an action
that would violate the Cornelian law forbidding the
assistance of outlawed persons. Their request to be
exempted from taking the oath was granted; and
Verres gave them possession—an action that I will
not condemn, for it would indeed have been unfair
that an outlawed man in distress should have anything
out of his brother's estate given to him. The freedman had felt that he would be guilty of a crime if
he failed to swear as his old master's will required;
and because he did, Verres refused to give him 124
possession of his inheritance, that he might not be
able to help his old master who was outlawed, and
at the same time might be liable to punishment for
following the instructions in his other old master's
will. Well, Verres, you give possession to a man
who has *not* sworn the oath; I raise no objection;
a praetor has the right to do that. But you take that
right away from a man who *has* sworn it; what
precedent have you for that? Suppose he does help
the outlawed man—there is the law and its penalty.
What difference does it make to the praetor's decision? Do you condemn the freedman for being
willing to help his old master then in sore need? Or
for choosing to carry out the dying wishes of his
other old master to whom he owed everything?
Which of these two offences do you condemn? Yes,
and on that occasion this perfect gentleman, sitting

tum de sella vir optimus dixit : " Equiti Romano tam
locupleti libertinus sit homo heres ? " O modestum
ordinem, quod illinc vivus surrexit !

125 Possum sescenta decreta proferre in quibus, ut ego
non dicam, pecuniam intercessisse ipsa decretorum
novitas iniquitasque declarat. Verum ut ex uno de
ceteris coniecturam facere possitis, id quod priore
actione cognostis audite. C. Sulpicius Olympus fuit ;
XLVIII. is mortuus est C. Sacerdote praetore,
nescio an ante quam Verres praeturam petere coeperit.
Fecit heredem M. Octavium Ligurem ; Ligus hereditatem adiit ; possedit Sacerdote praetore sine ulla
controversia. Posteaquam Verres magistratum iniit,
ex edicto istius, quod edictum Sacerdos non habuerat,
Sulpicii patroni filia sextam partem hereditatis ab
Ligure petere coepit. Ligus non aderat. L. frater
eius causam agebat : aderant amici, propinqui.
Dicebat iste, nisi cum muliere decideretur, in possessionem se ire iussurum. L. Gellius causam Liguris
defendebat : docebat edictum eius non oportere in
eas hereditates valere quae ante eum praetorem
venissent ; si hoc tum fuisset edictum, fortasse
Ligurem hereditatem aditurum non fuisse. Aequa
postulatio, summa hominum auctoritas, pretio supe-
126 rabatur. Venit Romam Ligus ; non dubitabat quin,

in his chair of office, observed, " A freedman the
heir of a knight with a fortune like that ! " What
self-restraint the freedman class showed in letting
him leave his chair alive !

I could produce hundreds of his decisions whose 125
disregard for precedent and equity makes it plain,
without any comment from me, that money has had
a hand in them. But I will only ask you to listen to
a single one of them, which was put before you at
the first hearing : from it you may guess what the
rest must be. XLVIII. There was a man called
Gaius Sulpicius Olympus, who died during the
praetorship of Gaius Sacerdos, I rather think before
Verres began canvassing for the praetorship. He
left his property to Marcus Octavius Ligus ; Ligus
claimed the estate, and enjoyed undisputed possession of it so long as Sacerdos remained praetor.
After Verres had entered upon office, in accordance
with a clause in his edict that had not appeared in
the edict of Sacerdos, the daughter of the Sulpicius
whose freedman Sulpicius Olympus had been proceeded to claim from Ligus one-sixth of the estate.
Ligus not being in Rome, his brother Lucius appeared for him, supported by his friends and relatives.
Verres announced that unless they came to some
arrangement with the lady, he would make an order
for her to take possession. Lucius Gellius, who was
supporting Ligus, argued that Verres' edict could
not be held to apply to any estate inherited before
the date of his praetorship, and that had the present
regulation been in force then, Ligus might not have
chosen to claim the estate. The equity of this plea
and the respect due to those who urged it were no
match for money. Ligus arrived in Rome. He felt 126

si ipse Verrem convenisset, aequitate causae, auctoritate sua, commovere hominem posset. Domum ad eum venit, rem demonstrat, quam pridem sibi hereditas venisset docet ; quod facile homini ingenioso in causa aequissima fuit, multa quae quemvis commovere possent dixit ; ad extremum petere coepit ne usque eo suam auctoritatem despiceret gratiamque contemneret ut se tanta iniuria afficeret. Homo Ligurem accusare coepit, qui in re adventicia atque hereditaria tam diligens, tam attentus esset ; debere eum aiebat suam quoque rationem ducere ; multa sibi opus esse, multa canibus suis quos circa se haberet. Non possum illa planius commemorare quam ipsum Ligurem pro testimonio dicere audistis. 127 Quid est, Verres ? utrum ne his quidem testibus credetur, an haec ad rem non pertinent ? non credemus M. Octavio ? non L. Liguri ? quis nobis credet, cui nos ? quid est quod planum fieri testibus possit, si hoc non fit ? An id quod dicunt leve est ? Nihil levius quam praetorem urbanum hoc iuris in suo magistratu constituere, omnibus quibus hereditas venerit coheredem praetorem esse oportere. An vero dubitamus quo ore iste ceteros homines inferiores loco, auctoritate, ordine, quo ore homines rusticanos ex municipiis, quo denique ore, quos numquam liberos putavit, libertinos homines solitus sit appellare, qui

sure that, if he himself had an interview with Verres, the justice of his case and his personal influence would have an effect on the man. Calling on him at his house, he went into the facts, pointing out the length of time the estate had now been his; with the readiness of an intelligent man pleading a thoroughly just cause, he used a number of arguments that might have told with anyone; and finally proceeded to urge him not to think so little of his importance, or care so little for his goodwill, as to do him so grave an injustice. The fellow began at this to abuse Ligus for straining and exciting himself so much about a property that had only come to him by the chance of inheritance: Ligus ought to consider Verres' point of view as well as his own: Verres' own needs were considerable, and also those of the hounds he kept about him. I cannot tell the story more clearly than you have heard Ligus himself giving it in his evidence. What have you to say 127 then, Verres? Shall even these witnesses not be believed, or is their evidence irrelevant? Shall we not believe Marcus Octavius Ligus? or Lucius Ligus? Who then will believe *us*, or whom shall we believe? What *can* evidence prove, if it cannot prove this? Or is what they say no great matter? It is no less a matter than the claim set up by a city praetor, in the discharge of his office, that the praetor shall be co-inheritor with everyone who inherits an estate. Can we fail to picture the brazen way in which he would present his demands to all those other persons of lower station, rank, and importance, to those simple folk up from country towns, or to those freedmen whose freedom he never would recognize, when we

ob ius dicundum M. Octavium Ligurem, hominem ornatissimum loco, ordine, nomine, virtute, ingenio, copiis, poscere pecuniam non dubitavit?

128 XLIX. In sartis tectis vero quem ad modum se gesserit quid ego dicam? Dixerunt qui senserunt; sunt alii qui dicant; notae res ac manifestae prolatae sunt et proferentur. Dixit Cn. Fannius, eques Romanus, frater germanus Q. Titinii, iudicis tui, tibi se pecuniam dedisse. Recita. TESTIMONIUM CN. FANNII. Nolite Cn. Fannio dicenti credere, noli, inquam, tu, Q. Titini, Cn. Fannio, fratri tuo, credere; dicit enim rem incredibilem; C. Verrem insimulat avaritiae et audaciae, quae vitia videntur in quemvis potius quam in istum convenire. Dixit Q. Tadius, homo familiarissimus patris istius, non alienus a matris eius genere et nomine; tabulas protulit quibus pecuniam se dedisse ostendit. Recita. NOMINA Q. TADII. Recita. TESTIMONIUM Q. TADII. Ne Tadii quidem tabulis nec testimonio credemus? Quid igitur in iudiciis sequemur? Quid est aliud omnibus omnia peccata et maleficia concedere nisi hoc, hominum honestissimorum testimoniis et virorum bonorum tabulis non credere?

129 Nam quid ego de cotidiano sermone querimonia-

---

a The difference of family name between the two brothers is no doubt due to the adoption of one of them into another family.

hear that, from a man so distinguished as Marcus Octavius Ligus in position and rank and name, in character and ability and fortune, he did not hesitate to demand a bribe in return for his decision in court?

XLIX. His conduct in dealing with the mainten- 128 ance of public buildings I need hardly describe. Some of his victims have already described it, and there are others who can. Facts, notorious and convincing, have been produced, and more shall follow. The knight Gnaeus Fannius, own brother of the Quintus Titinius *a* who is one of your judges, has testified to his having paid you money. Read the evidence. *Evidence of Gnaeus Fannius.* Gentlemen, do not believe what Fannius says : Quintus Titinius, do not, I repeat, believe what Gnaeus Fannius your own brother says. For he says what is unbelievable ; he is attempting to charge Gaius Verres with unscrupulous greed for money—a charge that we feel is appropriate to anyone else rather than to him. We have heard Quintus Tadius, an intimate friend of Verres' father, and not unconnected, by birth and name, with Verres' mother : Tadius has produced his own accounts, showing that he has paid money to Verres. Read these. *Accounts of Quintus Tadius.* And this. *Evidence of Quintus Tadius.* Are we not to trust the accounts, or the evidence, even of Tadius ? What, then, do we mean to go upon in trying a case ? If we should set everyone free to commit every kind of offence and injury, how otherwise should we do it than by refusing to accept the evidence given by respectable persons, and the accounts kept by honourable gentlemen ?

And now how shall I deal with a thing that was 129 day after day the subject of indignant discussion

261

que populi Romani loquar, de istius impudentissimo furto, seu potius novo ac singulari latrocinio? Ausum esse in aede Castoris, celeberrimo clarissimoque monumento, quod templum in oculis cotidianoque aspectu populi Romani positum est, quo saepe numero senatus convocatur, quo maximarum rerum frequentissimae cotidie advocationes fiunt—in eo loco in sermone hominum audaciae suae monumentum aeternum relinquere?

130   L. Aedem Castoris, iudices, P. Iunius habuit tuendam de L. Sulla, Q. Metello consulibus. Is mortuus est; reliquit pupillum parvum filium. Cum L. Octavius C. Aurelius consules aedes sacras locavissent neque potuissent omnia sarta tecta exigere, neque ii praetores quibus erat negotium datum, C. Sacerdos et M. Caesius, factum est senatus consultum, quibus de sartis tectis cognitum et iudicatum non esset, uti C. Verres P. Caelius praetores cognoscerent et iudicarent. Qua potestate iste permissa sic abusus est[1] ut ex Cn. Fannio et ex Q. Tadio cognovistis, verum tamen cum esset omnibus in rebus apertissime impudentissimeque praedatus, hoc voluit clarissimum relinquere indicium latrociniorum suorum, de quo non audire aliquando sed videre cotidie possemus.

131 Quaesivit quis aedem Castoris sartam tectam deberet tradere. Iunium ipsum mortuum esse sciebat; scire

[1] *The words* sic abusus est *are Peterson's certain addition, being found in two MSS.*

---

a 80 B.C.   *b* 75 B.C.

throughout Rome—that impudent theft of his, or rather, that unheard of and extraordinary act of open robbery ? To think of the temple of Castor, that famous and glorious memorial of the past, that sanctuary which stands where the eyes of the nation may rest upon it every day, in which the Senate not seldom meets, and which is daily thronged with those who come to take counsel upon matters of high import : and then to think that there Verres has a memorial of his criminal audacity graven for ever upon the lips of men !

L. From the consulship of Lucius Sulla and Quintus 130 Metellus,[a] gentlemen, the contractor for the upkeep of the temple of Castor had been one Publius Iunius. He died, leaving a young son, not yet of age. Lucius Octavius and Gaius Aurelius during their consulship [b] had made contracts for temple maintenance, the execution of which they had not had time, in all cases, to certify, nor had the two praetors, Gaius Sacerdos and Marcus Caesius, to whom this duty had been assigned. The Senate therefore decreed that Gaius Verres and Publius Caelius, the new praetors, should examine and pronounce upon those contracts not already dealt with. How Verres misused the powers thus entrusted to him you have already learnt from Gnaeus Fannius and Quintus Tadius. But open and unashamed as all his depredations were, he chose to leave us an especially striking demonstration of his methods of robbery ; something that we might not hear of now and then, but daily see for ourselves. He inquired who was re- 131 sponsible for handing over the temple of Castor in good repair ; Iunius himself he knew was dead, and he wanted to know on whom the duty now devolved.

volebat ad quem illa res pertineret. Audit pupillum
esse filium. Homo, qui semper ita palam dictitasset,
pupillos et pupillas certissimam praedam esse prae-
toribus, optatum negotium sibi in sinum delatum esse
dicebat. Monumentum illa amplitudine, illo opere,
quamvis sartum tectum integrumque esset, tamen
aliquid se inventurum in quo moliri praedarique
132 posset arbitrabatur. L. Habonio[1] aedem Castoris
tradi oportebat : is casu pupilli Iunii tutor erat
testamento patris ; cum eo sine ullo intertrimento
convenerat iam quem ad modum traderetur. Iste ad
se Habonium vocat ; quaerit ecquid sit quod a pupillo
traditum non sit, quod exigi debeat. Cum ille, id
quod erat, diceret facilem pupillo traditionem esse ;
signa et dona comparere omnia ; ipsum templum
omni opere esse integrum : indignum isti videri coepit
ex tanta aede tantoque opere se non opimum praeda,
133 praesertim a pupillo, discedere. LI. Venit ipse in
aedem Castoris, considerat templum ; videt undique
tectum pulcherrime laqueatum, praeterea cetera nova
atque integra. Versat se ; quaerit quid agat. Dicit
ei quidam ex illis canibus quos iste Liguri dixerat esse
circa se multos, " Tu, Verres, hic quod moliare nihil
habes, nisi forte vis ad perpendiculum columnas
exigere." Homo omnium rerum imperitus quaerit
quid sit " ad perpendiculum " ; dicunt ei fere nullam
esse columnam quae ad perpendiculum esse possit.

[1] *There is fair MS. support for* Rabonius *as the true form
of the name.*

He was told that it was the son, who was still a
minor. He had always been in the habit of saying
openly that minors, male or female, were a praetor's
safest prey ; and here, he told himself, was a most
desirable piece of business put straight into his
hands. In so large and elaborate a building, even
were it in sound and good repair, he calculated on
finding some means of working a profitable job for
himself. The temple contract was to be transferred 132
to Lucius Habonius : this man, as it happened, was
by the will of Iunius made one of the boy's guardians,
and with him a quite comfortable settlement had
been reached *a* about the details of the transfer.
Verres told Habonius to come and see him, and asked
him whether his ward had failed in any detail of the
transfer that he should be required to make good.
Habonius replied, what was true, that his ward was
having no trouble about the transfer ; that no statues
or offerings were missing ; and that the building itself
was in sound condition throughout. Verres began to
feel that it would be a shame to abandon a great
elaborate building like that without lining his own
pockets richly—at a minor's expense, too. LI. He 133
went himself into the temple of Castor, and surveyed
the sacred edifice : he saw the whole roof beautifully
panelled, and everything else in fresh and sound condition. He turned round, and asked what he had
better do. Then one of the hounds, of whom he told
Ligus *b* he kept a large pack round him, observed,
" Look you, Verres, there is no job you can work
here, unless perhaps you would like to demand that
the pillars be made exactly plumb." The hopeless
ignoramus inquired what " plumb " signified : and
they told him that practically no pillar could possibly

"Nam mehercule," inquit, "sic agamus; columnae
134 ad perpendiculum exigantur." Habonius, qui legem
nosset, qua in lege numerus tantum columnarum
traditur, perpendiculi mentio fit nulla, et qui non
putaret sibi expedire ita accipere, ne eodem modo
tradendum esset, negat id sibi deberi, negat oportere
exigi. Iste Habonium quiescere iubet, et simul ei non-
nullam spem societatis ostendit; hominem modestum
et minime pertinacem facile coercet; columnas ita
se exacturum esse confirmat.

135 Nova res atque improvisa pupilli calamitas nuntiatur
statim C. Mustio, vitrico pupilli, qui nuper est mortuus, M. Iunio patruo, P. Titio tutori, homini
frugalissimo. Hi rem ad virum primarium, summo
officio ac virtute praeditum, M. Marcellum, qui erat
pupilli tutor, deferunt. Venit ad Verrem M.
Marcellus; petit ab eo pro sua fide ac diligentia
pluribus verbis ne per summam iniuriam pupillum
Iunium fortunis patriis conetur evertere. Iste, qui
iam spe atque opinione praedam illam devorasset,
neque ulla aequitate orationis neque auctoritate
M. Marcelli commotus est; itaque quem ad modum

266

be exactly plumb. " Why, damn it all," says Verres,
" let's do that ; let us demand that the pillars be
made exactly plumb." Habonius was familiar with 134
the wording of the contract, which merely gave an
inventory of the number of pillars and said nothing
about their being plumb ; and also he reckoned that
it would not pay him to take over the contract on
those conditions, since he might have to hand over
to his successor on the same conditions later on.
He therefore maintained that he had no right to
claim this, and that it ought not to be required.
Verres told Habonius to hold his tongue, at the
same time hinting that he would have some chance
of sharing in the profits. He had no trouble in suppressing this unassuming and easy-going person, and
stated definitely that he would make the requirement
about the pillars as mentioned.

This new and, for young Iunius, unexpectedly 135
disastrous development was promptly reported to
the boy's stepfather Gaius Mustius (recently deceased), to his uncle Marcus Iunius, and to another
of his guardians, an honest man named Publius
Titius. These three carried the matter to that
eminent and most trustworthy and excellent man
Marcus Marcellus, himself one of the guardians.
Marcellus went to see Verres, and, like the honourable and conscientious man he was, urged Verres at
considerable length not to think of so gross an injustice as to turn a boy like Iunius out of the property
his father had left him. Verres, who already had in
anticipation a vision of himself devouring his prey,
was untouched either by the fairness of the plea
or by the importance of the pleader, and answered
accordingly that he would insist on the thing being

267

136 ostendisset se id exacturum esse respondit. Cum
sibi omnes ad istum allegationes difficiles, omnes
aditus arduos ac potius interclusos viderent, apud
quem non ius, non aequitas, non misericordia, non
propinqui oratio, non amici voluntas, non cuiusquam
auctoritas, non gratia valeret, statuunt id sibi esse
optimum factu quod cuivis venisset in mentem,
petere auxilium a Chelidone, quae isto praetore non
modo in iure civili privatorumque omnium contro-
versiis populo Romano praefuit, verum etiam in his
sartis tectisque dominata est

137   LII. Venit ad Chelidonem C. Mustius, eques
Romanus, publicanus, homo cum primis honestus ;
venit M. Iunius, patruus pueri, frugalissimus homo
et castissimus : venit homo summo pudore, summo
officio, spectatissimus ordinis sui, P. Titius tutor. O
multis acerbam, o miseram atque indignam praeturam tuam ! Ut mittam cetera, quo tandem pudore
tales viros, quo dolore, meretricis domum venisse
arbitramini ? qui numquam ulla condicione istam
turpitudinem subissent, nisi officii necessitudinisque
ratio coegisset. Veniunt, ut dico, ad Chelidonem.
Domus erat plena ; nova iura, nova decreta, nova
iudicia petebantur : "mihi det possessionem, mihi ne
adimat, in me iudicium ne det, mihi bona addicat."
Alii nummos numerabant, ab aliis tabellae obsigna-

done as he had indicated. The guardians, perceiving 136
the difficulty of making any appeals to him, and
finding every pathway of approach steep, not to say
completely blocked, since he was a man with whom
neither law nor equity nor compassion, neither the
arguments of a relative nor the wishes of a friend
nor anyone's influence or goodwill, counted for anything at all—the guardians decided that their best
course (and the idea would have occurred to anyone)
was to ask the help of Chelidon, the woman who, so
long as Verres was praetor, not only controlled the
civil law and all the private controversies of the
nation, but also lorded it in all these matters of
maintenance contracts.

LII. Yes, they went to see Chelidon: Gaius 137
Mustius, knight and collector of revenue, as honourable a man as lives; the boy's uncle, the honest and
upright Marcus Iunius; and his guardian Publius
Titius, respectable and conscientious, than whom no
man of his rank is esteemed more highly. Ah, Verres,
how many there are to whom your praetorship has
brought pain and misery and shame! To speak of
nothing else, I bid you think simply of the feelings
of shame and disgust with which such men must have
entered the dwelling of a harlot. For no consideration
would they have brought themselves to stoop so low,
had not regard for duty and friendship compelled
them. They went, as I have said, to see Chelidon.
Her house was full: decisions, judgements, methods
of procedure—none ever heard of before—were being
applied for : " make him give me possession," " don't
let him take it from me," " don't let him pronounce
against me," " get him to award me the property."
Some were paying her cash, others were signing

bantur: domus erat non meretricio conventu sed
138 praetoria turba referta. Simul ac potestas primum
data est, adeunt hi quos dixi. Loquitur C. Mustius,
rem demonstrat, petit auxilium, pecuniam pollicetur.
Respondit illa, ut meretrix, non inhumaniter: libenter ait se esse facturam, et se cum isto diligenter
sermocinaturam; reverti iubet. Tum discedunt;
postridie revertuntur; negat illa posse hominem
exorari; permagnam eum dicere ex illa re pecuniam
confici posse.

LIII. Vereor ne quis forte de populo, qui priori
actione non adfuit, haec, quia propter insignem turpitudinem sunt incredibilia, fingi a me arbitretur.
139 Ea vos antea, iudices, cognovistis. Dixit iuratus
P. Titius, tutor pupilli Iunii; dixit M. Iunius tutor et
patruus: Mustius dixisset, si viveret, sed recenti re
de Mustio auditum est; dixit L. Domitius, qui cum
sciret me ex Mustio vivo audisse, quod eo sum usus
plurimum (etenim iudicium, quod prope omnium
fortunarum suarum C. Mustius habuit, me uno
defendente vicit), cum hoc, ut dico, sciret L. Domitius,
me scire ad eum res omnes Mustium solitum esse
deferre, tamen de Chelidone reticuit quoad potuit,
alio responsionem suam derivavit. Tantus in adu-
lescente clarissimo ac principe iuventutis pudor fuit
ut aliquam diu, cum a me premeretur, omnia potius

---

[a] When being cross-examined as a witness by Cicero.

promissory notes : the house was filled, not with a
courtesan's visitors, but with the crowd that attends a
praetor's court. As soon as they were allowed, the 138
gentlemen I have named approached the woman.
The speaker was Gaius Mustius ; he explained the
facts, asked for help, and promised her money. Her
reply, for a woman of that type, was not ill-natured :
she would gladly do her best, and would be sure to
talk to him about it—let them return later. They
left her, and returned the next day ; she then told
them that the man was inexorable, and that he said
there was a really big sum of money to be made out
of this business.

LIII. I am afraid that some of our audience who
were not present at the first hearing may suppose
that this story is my own invention, its exceptional
ugliness makes it so incredible. You, gentlemen, have 139
heard it all before. It has been told on oath by Publius
Titius, guardian of young Iunius. It has been told
by his guardian and uncle Marcus Iunius. It would
have been told by Mustius, if he were still alive, and
it has been heard recently from his lips. It has been
told by Lucius Domitius, who, though he knew I had
heard it from Mustius before the latter's death, since
I was very familiar with him—the fact is that Mustius,
with my sole support, won a case in which nearly the
whole of his fortune was involved—though, as I was
saying, Domitius knew this, and that I knew Mustius
to have been in the habit of reporting everything to
him, none the less he held his tongue about Chelidon
as long as he could, and made an evasive answer to
my question.[a] There was so much modesty in this
young noble of high rank and reputation, that for
some time, press him as I might, he made any answer

responderet quam Chelidonem nominaret; primo
necessarios istius ad eum allegatos esse dicebat,
deinde aliquando coactus Chelidonem nominavit.
140 Non te pudet, Verres, eius mulieris arbitratu gessisse
praeturam quam L. Domitius ab se nominari vix sibi
honestum esse arbitrabatur?

LIV. Reiecti a Chelidone capiunt consilium necessarium, ut suscipiant ipsi negotium. Cum Habonio
tutore, quod erat vix HS quadraginta milium, trans-
igunt HS ducentis milibus. Defert ad istum rem
Habonius : ut sibi videatur, satis grandem pecuniam
et satis impudentem esse. Iste, qui aliquanto plus
cogitasset, male accipit verbis Habonium, negat eum
sibi illa decisione satisfacere posse ; ne multa, loca-
141 turum se esse confirmat. Tutores hoc nesciunt ;
quod actum erat cum Habonio, putant id esse certis-
simum ; nullam maiorem pupillo metuunt calamitatem. Iste vero non procrastinat ; locare incipit, non
proscripta neque edicta die, alienissimo tempore,
ludis ipsis Romanis, foro ornato. Itaque renuntiat
Habonius illam decisionem tutoribus. Accurrunt
tamen ad tempus tutores ; digitum tollit Iunius
patruus. Isti color immutatus est ; vultus, oratio,
mens denique excidit. Quid ageret coepit cogitare.
Si opus pupillo redimeretur, si res abiret ab eo

---

[a] Of making the pillars plumb, or paying for its being
done.
[b] For the work of restoring the pillars.
272

rather than mention Chelidon's name, asserting to
begin with that the friends of Iunius had been sent to
see Verres, and only uttering Chelidon's name finally
when he could no longer help it. Do you feel no 140
shame, Verres, that your conduct as praetor has been
wholly governed by a woman whose very name
Domitius feels it hardly decent for him to mention ?

LIV. Rejected by Chelidon, they could do nothing
but resolve to undertake the obligation[a] themselves.
They agreed with the guardian Habonius to pay
£2000 for an operation whose real cost was barely
£400. Habonius reported this to Verres, observing
that in his opinion this was a fairly large and shameless sum. Verres, who had had a good deal more than
that in his mind, made some unpleasant remarks to
Habonius, and told him that he could not possibly
accept an arrangement like that ; and not to make a
long story of it, he declared that he was going to call
for tenders.[b] The guardians knew nothing of this ; 141
they imagined that their arrangement with Habonius
had quite settled the matter, and had no fear that
anything still worse might befall their ward. Verres
wasted no time ; he proceeded with the tenders
without any previous advertisement or announcement
of the day for tendering, at a most unsuitable time,
right in the middle of the Roman Games, with the
Forum all decorated. Habonius accordingly cancelled the agreement with the other guardians.
They hastened to the spot, nevertheless, at the day
fixed ; and Iunius, the uncle, made his bid. Verres
turned pale : his looks, his voice, his very power of
thought failed him. He began to wonder what to
do. If the ward were to secure the contract, and it
thus escaped the person whom he had himself put up

mancipe quem ipse apposuisset, sibi nullam praedam
esse. Itaque excogitat—quid? nihil ingeniose,
nihil ut quisquam possit dicere "improbe, verum
callide." Nihil ab isto vafrum, nihil veteratorium
exspectaveritis; omnia aperta, omnia perspicua
142 reperientur, impudentia, amentia, audacia. "Si
pupillo opus redimitur, mihi praeda de manibus
eripitur. Quod est igitur remedium? quod? ne
liceat pupillo redimere." Ubi illa consuetudo in
bonis praedibus praediisque vendundis omnium consulum, censorum, praetorum, quaestorum denique,
ut optima condicione sit is cuia res sit, cuium periculum? Excludit eum solum cui prope dicam soli
potestatem factam esse oportebat. Quid enim?
quisquam ad meam pecuniam me invito aspirat,
quisquam accedit? Locatur opus id quod ex mea
pecunia reficiatur; ego me refecturum dico; probatio futura est tua qui locas; praedibus et praediis
populo cautum est; et, si non putas cautum, scilicet
tu praetor in mea bona quos voles immittes, me ad
meas fortunas defendendas accedere non sines?

143   LV. Operae pretium est legem ipsam cognoscere;
dicetis eundem conscripsisse qui illud edictum de
hereditate. LEX OPERI FACIUNDO. QUAE PUPILLI IUNII ...

ᵃ Enforced sale by the State is meant. The law would
require purchasers to offer security for their ultimate
payment of the purchase-money.

ᵇ By the purchaser of the contract, for his power to
carry it out.

to secure it, there was no plunder for him to get.
He arrived at a plan : and what was it ?   Oh, nothing
ingenious ; nothing that anyone could describe as
" Dishonest, yes, but clever." You are to look for
no artful dodge, nothing of the wily old bird, from
Verres. You will find everything quite plain and
obvious, nothing but stupid reckless impudence.
" If the ward secures the contract, my prey is 142
snatched from my grasp. How do we stop that,
then ? How ? why, let us prohibit the ward from
bidding for it." What now becomes of the practice,
observed universally by consuls, censors, praetors,
and even quaestors, in selling property upon personal
and landed security *a*—the practice of allowing most
favoured treatment to the owner of the property,
who stands to lose by its sale ? Verres here excludes
from the right of bidding that person alone to whom
alone, one might almost say, the right should be
allowed. Why, what does this mean ? Can anyone
be hoping, or trying, to lay hands in spite of me upon
my own money ? Here is a contract to be made for
doing a repair for which I shall have to pay ; and I
undertake myself to do it. You, who let out the
contract, can see that the work is done properly :
personal and real security is given *b* to the state :
and even if you think the security insufficient, does
that mean that you, as praetor, may give anyone you
please leave to plunder my property, without allowing
me to make a move to protect my own pocket ?

LV. It is worth your while, gentlemen, to note 143
the text of the contract : you will recognize the
author of that clause in the edict relating to inheritance. *Text of the Contract. "In the matter of
the ward Iunius. . . ."* (Kindly read it more dis-

Dic, dic, quaeso, clarius. C. VERRES PRAETOR URBANUS
ADDIDIT. Corriguntur leges censoriae. Quid enim ?
Video in multis veteribus legibus, CN. DOMITIUS L.
METELLUS CENSORES ADDIDERUNT, L. CASSIUS CN. SER-
VILIUS CENSORES ADDIDERUNT ; vult aliquid eius modi
C. Verres. Dic, quid addidit ? recita. QUI DE L. MARCIO
M. PERPERNA CENSORIBUS . . . . SOCIUM NE ADMIT-
TITO, NEVE PARTEM DATO, NEVE REDIMITO. Quid ita ?
Ne vitiosum opus fieret ? at erat probatio tua. Ne
parum locuples esset ? at erat, et esset amplius si
144 velles, populo cautum praedibus et praediis. Hic te
si res ipsa, si indignitas iniuriae tuae non commovebat,
si pupilli calamitas, si propinquorum lacrimae, si D.
Bruti, cuius praedia suberant, periculum, si M.
Marcelli tutoris auctoritas apud te ponderis nihil
habebat, ne illud quidem animadvertebas, eius modi
fore hoc peccatum tuum quod tu neque negare posses
(in tabulas enim legem rettulisti) neque cum defensione aliqua confiteri ? Addicitur opus HS DLX. milibus,
cum tutores HS XL. milibus id opus ad illius iniquissimi
hominis arbitrium se effecturos esse clamarent.
145 Etenim quid erat operis ? Id quod vos vidistis. Omnes

---

^a It can only be conjectured that the complete clause
added by Verres prohibited in general terms the exact
action now taken by the guardians of Iunius.
276

tinctly.) *"Gaius Verres, city praetor, has further provided. . . ."* Improvements on the censors' forms of contract! Oh well, in a number of old contracts we find that sort of thing: "The censors Gnaeus Domitius and Lucius Metellus have further provided," "the censors Lucius Cassius and Gnaeus Servilius have further provided." Gaius Verres is after something of the same kind. Tell us then, what *is* this further provision: read it out. *"Any person who from the censors Lucius Marcius and Marcus Perperna*[a] *. . . must not take him as partner nor allow him to share in the undertaking nor himself secure the contract."* Why this arrangement? To prevent the work's being badly done? Well, you have the power of seeing to that. To ensure the contractor's having the necessary capital? Well, but security, personal and real, had been offered to the state, and more still would have been offered if you had required it. Here let me ask this. Even if the actual facts, 144 the shamefulness of the wrong you were doing, left you unmoved; if the ruin of that boy, and the tears of his kinsmen, and the risk to Decimus Brutus whose land was involved, and the personal authority of the boy's guardian Marcus Marcellus—if all this counted for nothing with you: yet did it not even occur to you that this piece of your misconduct was of a kind that you would be able neither to deny (having entered the contract in your books) nor, admitting it, to justify in any sort of way? The contract was let for £5600, though the guardians declared loudly that for £400 they were prepared to carry out the work so as to satisfy even that tyrannical rascal. How 145 much, after all, was there to do? Exactly what you yourselves, gentlemen, saw done. A scaffold was

277

illae columnae, quas dealbatas videtis, machina
apposita, nulla impensa deiectae iisdemque lapidibus
repositae sunt. Hoc tu HS DLX. milibus locavisti.
Atque in illis columnis dico esse quae a tuo redemptore commotae non sint; dico esse ex qua tantum
tectorium vetus deiectum sit et novum inductum.
Quod si tanta pecunia columnas dealbari putassem,
certe numquam aedilitatem petivissem.

146   LVI. At ut videatur tamen res agi et non eripi
pupillo : SI QUID OPERIS CAUSA RESCIDERIS, REFICITO.
Quid erat quod rescinderet, cum suo quemque loco
lapidem reponeret ? QUI REDEMERIT SATIS DET DAMNI
INFECTI EI QUI A VETERE REDEMPTORE ACCEPERIT.
Deridet, cum sibi ipsum iubet satis dare Habonium.
PECUNIA PRAESENS SOLVATUR. Quibus de bonis ?
Eius qui, quod tu HS DLX. milibus locasti, HS XL. milibus effecturum se esse clamavit. Quibus de bonis ?
Pupilli, cuius aetatem et solitudinem, etiamsi tutores
non essent, defendere praetor debuit. Tutoribus
defendentibus non modo patrias eius fortunas, sed
etiam bona tutorum ademisti. HOC OPUS BONUM SUO
147 CUIQUE FACITO. Quid est suo cuique ? Lapis aliqui

---

a Possibly *tectorium* here is " paint " or " whitewash."

b The aediles had the care of public buildings, and were
expected to spend their own money on them to some extent.

c *Damni infecti*, lit. " harm that is not done." The new
contractor for maintenance is to be secured against the
contractor for restoration doing damage which the new
contractor would have to make good.

278

moved up to each of those pillars that you can now
see freshly whitened ; they were taken down and
replaced, without further expense, stone for stone as
before. This was the undertaking for which your
contractor received £5600 ! Yes, and I assert that
of those pillars there are some that he never touched :
I assert that there is one from which he merely
scraped off the old stucco *a* and applied fresh. Well,
if I had supposed it cost so much to whiten pillars, I
should certainly never have been a candidate for the
aedileship.*b*

LVI. However, to give it the appearance of a 146
business arrangement and not a robbery of that boy,
we have the clause, " *Any portion of the structure
cut away in the course of the restoration must be
replaced.*" What was there to cut away, when he
simply put each stone back in its place ? " *The
contractor will be required to give security for possible
damage during restoration to the successor of the
original contractor.*" *c* A good joke, to require
Habonius to give security to himself ! " *The cost
shall be paid in cash.*" And from whose property ?
That of the person who declared distinctly that he
would do for £400 what you have paid your contractor £5600 to do ! From whose property, I ask
again ? That of a boy under age, whose tender years
and orphan condition called for the praetor's protection, even though he had had no guardians. He did
have guardians, who tried to protect him, and you,
Verres, have stolen not only his patrimony but the
property of the guardians too. " *The work must
be carried out soundly with the proper material for
each part of it.*" What do you mean by " *proper* 147
material for each part of it " ? A certain amount of

caedendus et apportandus fuit machina sua ; nam
illo non saxum, non materies advecta est ; tantum
operis in ista locatione fuit quantum paucae operae
fabrorum mercedis tulerunt, et manuspretium ma-
chinae. Utrum existimatis minus operis esse unam
columnam efficere ab integro novam nullo lapide
redivivo, an quattuor illas reponere ? Nemo dubitat
quin multo maius sit novam facere. Ostendam in
aedibus privatis, longa difficilique vectura, columnas
singulas ad impluvium HS xx. milibus non minus
148 magnas locatas. Sed ineptum est de tam perspicua
eius impudentia pluribus verbis disputare, praesertim
cum iste aperte tota lege omnium sermonem atque
existimationem contempserit, qui etiam ad extremum ascripserit REDIVIVA SIBI HABETO ; quasi quicquam redivivi ex opere illo tolleretur ac non totum
opus ex redivivis constitueretur.

At enim si pupillo redimi non licebat non necesse
erat rem ad ipsum pervenire ; poterat aliquis ad id
negotium de populo accedere. Omnes exclusi sunt
non minus aperte quam pupillus. Diem praestituit
operi faciundo Kalendas Decembres, locat circiter
Idus Septembres ; angustiis temporis excluduntur
149 omnes. LVII. Quid ergo ? Habonius istam diem
quomodo assequitur ? Nemo Habonio molestus est

marble had to be cut and brought to the right spot
by means of the proper appliance. That was all:
there was no stone and no timber brought there:
all that this contract involved was paying some
masons for a few days' work, plus the cost of the
scaffolding appliances. Which would you reckon the
bigger undertaking, gentlemen, to construct a single
complete new pillar without using any old stone
again, or to put four of those pillars back where they
were? Nobody can doubt that constructing one
new one is far the bigger thing. Now I will prove
to you that in a private house pillars just as large as
these, though they had to be brought a long way
over bad roads, have been erected round the rainpool
for £200 apiece. But it is silly, when his conduct is so 148
obviously shameless, to argue in great detail about it;
especially as by the whole wording of the contract
he openly showed his contempt for what everyone
would say or think, even adding at the end " *The
contractor may retain any unused old material*"—as if
any old material at all were taken away from that operation, when the whole thing was done with old material.

It may be suggested that it did not follow, if the
minor were not allowed to have the contract, that
the matter must come into the hands of Verres: any
member of the public might have undertaken the
business. No, they were all barred from it as
obviously as the minor himself. The day Verres
fixed for the undertaking to be completed was the
1st of December, and he let the contract about the
13th of September; everyone was barred by the
shortness of the time allowed. LVII. Well, but 149
then, how did Habonius keep within the time?
Nobody made any trouble for Habonius either on the

neque Kalendis Decembribus neque Nonis neque
Idibus ; denique aliquanto ante in provinciam iste
proficiscitur quam opus effectum est. Posteaquam
reus factus est, primo negabat se opus in acceptum
referre posse ; cum instaret Habonius, in me causam
conferebat, quod eum codicem obsignassem. Petit
a me Habonius et amicos allegat ; facile impetrat.
Iste quid ageret nesciebat ; si in acceptum non
rettulisset, putabat se aliquid defensionis habiturum ;
Habonium porro intellegebat rem totam esse pate-
facturum—tametsi quid poterat esse apertius quam
nunc est ? Ut uno minus teste ageret,[1] Habonio opus
in acceptum rettulit quadriennio post quam diem
150 operi dixerat. Hac condicione, si quis de populo
redemptor accessisset, non esset usus ; cum die
ceteros redemptores exclusisset, tum in eius arbitrium ac potestatem venire nolebant qui sibi ereptam
praedam arbitrarentur. Nunc ne argumentemur quo
ista pecunia pervenerit, facit ipse indicium. Primum
cum vehementius cum eo D. Brutus contenderet, qui
de sua pecunia HS DLX. milia numeravit, quod iam
iste ferre non poterat, opere addicto, praedibus
acceptis, de HS DLX milibus remisit D. Bruto HS CX.
milia. Hoc, si aliena res esset, certe facere non
potuisset. Deinde nummi numerati sunt Cornificio.
quem scribam suum fuisse negare non potest.

---

[1] ageret *is Peterson's emendation of the* MS. haberet.

---

[a] By alleging that he was ready to proceed against
Habonius for breach of contract.

[b] These two details are to show how fully the business
had (ostensibly) passed out of Verres' hands into those of
Habonius.

[c] The whole £5600.

1st of December, or a week later, or a fortnight later :
in fact Verres had left for his province some time
before the work was completed. After his prosecution, he first said for some time that he could not
certify that the work had been duly carried out ;
then, when Habonius pressed him, he referred him to
me, saying that I had the memorandum-book under
seal. Habonius asked me for it, and sent his friends
to support him : his request was granted at once.
Verres did not see what to do. If he refused to give
the certificate, he thought he might thus have some
sort of defence for himself [a] : but then he was aware
that Habonius was likely in that case to expose the
whole business—though what could be clearer than
it now is ? To have one less witness against him, he
gave Habonius his certificate—in the fourth year
after the date prescribed for the completion of the
work ! Had any contractor from the general public 150
come forward, he would not have enjoyed such
favourable treatment : all the other contractors were
not only barred by the time-limit, but afraid to trust
themselves to the discretion of a powerful person
who would be feeling that his prey had been torn
from his grasp. There is no need to argue where
that money must in fact have gone—he tells us himself. In the first place, when Decimus Brutus, who
had paid down that £5600 out of his own purse,
pressed him forcibly about it, he, not being able to
stand the pressure any longer, returned £1100 out
of the £5600 to Brutus, *after* the contract had been
let [b] and security accepted for its completion [b] :
which it is impossible to think that he would have
done if the affair no longer concerned him. Secondly,
the cash [c] was paid to Cornificius, who, as he cannot

Postremo ipsius Habonii tabulae praedam illam istius
fuisse clamant. Recita. NOMINA HABONII.

151 LVIII. Hic etiam priore actione Q. Hortensius
pupillum Iunium venisse praetextatum in vestrum
conspectum et stetisse cum patruo testimonium
dicente questus est, et me populariter agere atque
invidiam commovere, quod puerum producerem,
clamitavit. Quid erat, Hortensi, tandem in illo
puero populare, quid invidiosum ? Gracchi, credo,
aut Saturnini aut alicuius hominis eius modi pro-
duxeram filium, ut nomine ipso et memoria patris
animos imperitae multitudinis commoverem ? P.
Iunii erat, hominis de plebe Romana, filius, quem
pater moriens cum tutoribus et propinquis, tum legibus, tum aequitati magistratuum, tum iudiciis vestris
152 commendatum putavit. Hic istius scelerato nefarioque latrocinio bonis patriis fortunisque omnibus
spoliatus venit in iudicium, si nihil aliud, saltem ut
eum cuius opere ipse multos annos esset in sordibus
paulo tamen obsoletius vestitum videret. Itaque tibi,
Hortensi, non illius aetas sed causa, non vestitus sed
fortuna, popularis videbatur : neque te tam commovebat quod ille cum toga praetexta quam quod
sine bulla venerat. Vestitus enim neminem commovebat is quem illi mos et ius ingenuitatis dabat :

---

^a Against Verres.

^b Both were popular leaders and accounted martyrs in
the people's cause.

^c This was the convention for accused persons.

^d The mark of his *youth*.

^e The gold locket which free-born children wore, and
which young Iunius, it is suggested, has been reduced, by
poverty, to selling.

deny, was his own clerk. Finally, Habonius's own accounts proclaim the fact that the spoils fell to Verres. Read them aloud. *Accounts of Habonius.*

LVIII. I may add that in this connexion Hor- 151 tensius, during the first hearing, complained of the young Iunius having been brought into court for you to see, wearing his boy's dress, and having stood beside his uncle as the latter gave his evidence. Hortensius insisted loudly that I was playing to the gallery, and trying to arouse ill-feeling,[a] by thus bringing the boy forward. Now may I ask, Hortensius, what there was about the lad calculated to appeal to the public and excite its ill-will[a]? One would think I had brought forward the son of some man like Gracchus or Saturninus,[b] that his very name, and recollections of his father, might inflame the passions of the unsophisticated multitude. He was in fact the son of a very ordinary Roman called Publius Iunius ; and his dying father fancied that he had left him to the care, not only of his guardians and kinsmen, but also of the law, of the kindly justice of our magistrates, and of the courts of which you, gentlemen, are members. Despoiled, by that 152 criminal and wicked robber's hand, of his patrimony and his entire fortune, this boy has come into court for one purpose, if no other—to see the man who had made him go threadbare these many years now dressed himself, after all, a little more shabbily [c] still. So it was not his youth, Hortensius, but his cause, not his clothes but his misfortunes, that you thought would appeal to the public : you were less concerned by his coming here wearing a fringed toga[d] than by his not wearing his locket.[e] Nobody was much moved by seeing him wear the clothes that custom and the

quod ornamentum pueritiae pater dederat, indicium atque insigne fortunae, hoc ab isto praedone ereptum 153 esse graviter tum et acerbe homines ferebant. Neque erant hae lacrimae populares magis quam nostrae, quam tuae, Q. Hortensi, quam horum qui sententiam laturi sunt, ideo quod communis est causa, commune periculum : communi praesidio talis improbitas tamquam aliquod incendium restinguenda est. Habemus enim liberos parvos ; incertum est quam longa cuiusque nostrum vita futura sit ; consulere vivi ac prospicere debemus ut illorum solitudo et pueritia quam firmissimo praesidio munita sit. Quis est enim qui tueri possit liberum nostrorum pueritiam contra improbitatem magistratuum ? Mater, credo. Scilicet magno praesidio fuit Anniae pupillae mater, femina primaria ; minus, illa deos hominesque implorante, iste infanti pupillae fortunas patrias ademit. Tutoresne defendent ? Perfacile vero apud istius modi praetorem, a quo M. Marcelli tutoris in causa pupilli Iunii et oratio et voluntas et auctoritas repudiata est.

154 LIX. Quaerimus etiam quid iste in ultima Phrygia, quid in extremis Pamphyliae partibus fecerit, qualis in bello praedonum praedo ipse fuerit, qui in foro populi Romani pirata nefarius reperiatur ? Dubitamus quid iste in hostium praeda molitus sit, qui

privilege of free birth allowed him ; but the boy's jewel that his father had given him, the sign and token of his happier fortune—seeing how that robber had torn *this* from him, the people did then feel concern and distress indeed. And if the people wept 153 then, so did I, so did you, Hortensius, so did these who will presently give their verdict : and for this reason, that the cause concerns us all, and the danger threatens us all, and it is by the rescuing hands of us all that this wickedness must be extinguished like some destroying fire. For we are the fathers of little children, and no one of us can tell how long he has to live : we must take counsel, ere we die, and make provision that their lonely years of childhood may have as strong a rampart as we can build round them. For who can protect our children in their early years against the wickedness of our magistrates ? Their mothers, to be sure. And a strong defence indeed little Annia found her mother, great lady though the mother was ! Much she could do, with her cries for help to God and man, to stay Verres from robbing her infant daughter of all that the child's father had bequeathed her ! Will guardians save them ? An easy thing indeed, with a praetor such as this, with whom Marcus Marcellus pleaded for his ward Iunius, to find that his eloquence, his earnest wishes, his personal influence, all went for nothing !

LIX. Do we now ask how Verres has behaved in 154 distant Phrygia, or in the remote regions of Pamphylia ; or how in the war against the sea-robbers, he has played the robber himself : Verres, whose black deeds of piracy we find done here in the heart of Rome ? Can we doubt his jobbery over the plunder taken from our enemies, seeing how he has enriched

manubias sibi tantas ex L. Metelli manubiis fecerit,
qui maiore pecunia quattuor columnas dealbandas
quam ille omnes aedificandas locaverit? Exspectemus quid dicant ex Sicilia testes? Quis umquam
templum illud aspexit quin avaritiae tuae, quin iniuriae, quin audaciae testis esset? Quis a signo
Vertumni in circum maximum venit quin is uno quoque gradu de avaritia tua commoneretur? quam tu
viam tensarum atque pompae eius modi exegisti ut
tu ipse illa ire non audeas. Te putet quisquam, cum
ab Italia freto disiunctus esses, sociis temperasse,
qui aedem Castoris testem tuorum furtorum esse
volueris? quam populus Romanus cotidie, iudices
etiam tum cum de te sententiam ferent, videbunt.

155   LX. Atque etiam iudicium in praetura publicum
exercuit; non enim praetereundum est ne id quidem.
Petita multa est apud istum praetorem a Q. Opimio;
qui adductus est in iudicium, verbo quod cum esset
tribunus plebis intercessisset contra legem Corneliam,
re vera quod in tribunatu dixisset contra alicuius
hominis nobilis voluntatem. De quo iudicio si velim
dicere omnia, multi appellandi laedendique sint, id
quod mihi non est necesse. Tantum dicam, paucos
homines, ut levissime appellem, arrogantes hoc

---

a Consul in 119, and restorer of the temple of Castor,
where he dedicated trophies of the Dalmatian war.
b The contractor for the upkeep of this road bribed Verres
to let him scamp his work.

himself with spoil from the spoils that Lucius Metellus[a] took for us, and paid his contractor more money for whitening four of those pillars than Metellus paid for the building of them all ? Need we wait to hear what the witnesses from Sicily shall tell us ? Has anyone looked at that temple without becoming a witness to your rapacity and injustice and reckless wickedness ? Has anyone walked along the road from the statue of Vertumnus to the Circus Maximus without being reminded of your rapacious greed at every step he took ? The repair of that road, the route for sacred coaches and processions, you have enforced so thoroughly[b] that you would not risk going over it yourself. Is anyone expected to believe that, once salt water lay between you and Italy, you had any mercy on our allies, when you have not shrunk from letting Castor's temple be the witness of your thefts ? Upon that temple the eyes of Rome rest daily ; and upon it the eyes of your judges will rest, as they pronounce their verdict upon you.

LX. He conducted criminal as well as civil cases 155 during his praetorship ; and the following occurrence should not be passed unnoticed. A charge involving a fine was brought before him as praetor against Quintus Opimius, who was nominally prosecuted because, when tribune of the people, he had used his veto in violation of the Cornelian law, but really because, during his year of office, he had made a speech offensive to some man of high rank. If I chose to tell the full story of this trial, I should have to name, and cause pain to, a great many people. This my case does not require me to do ; and I will merely observe that a handful of arrogant persons (I cannot describe them more mildly), assisted by

adiutore Q. Opimium per ludum et iocum fortunis omnibus evertisse.

156 Is mihi etiam queritur quod a nobis ix. solis diebus prima actio sui iudicii transacta sit, cum apud ipsum tribus horis Q. Opimius, senator populi Romani, bona, fortunas, ornamenta omnia amiserit ? cuius propter indignitatem iudicii saepissime est actum in senatu ut genus hoc totum multarum atque eius modi iudiciorum tolleretur. Iam vero in bonis Q. Opimii vendendis quas iste praedas quam aperte, quam improbe fecerit, longum est dicere : hoc dico : nisi vobis id hominum honestissimorum tabulis planum fecero, fingi a me 157 hoc totum temporis causa putatote. Iam qui ex calamitate senatoris populi Romani, cum praetor iudicio eius praefuisset, spolia domum suam referre et manubias detrahere conatus sit, is ullam ab sese calamitatem poterit deprecari ?

LXI. Nam de subsortitione illa Iuniana iudicum nihil dico. Quid enim ? contra tabulas quas tu protulisti audeam dicere ? Difficile est ; non enim me tua solum et iudicum auctoritas sed etiam anulus aureus scribae tui deterret. Non dicam id quod probare difficile est : hoc dicam quod ostendam

---

ᵃ Probably this refers to the proposed practical repeal of Sulla's regulations limiting the activity of the tribunes : the law was to remain, but no action was to be taken against those who broke it.

ᵇ For the trial of Oppianicus. Iunius was accused of tampering with the ballot in order to secure a venial court. Verres as *praetor urbanus* had a general charge of all these ballots.

ᶜ *i.e.*, Verres' signature, which Cicero suggests was forged and sealed by his clerk.

290

Verres, with heartless levity brought Quintus Opimius to utter ruin.

Does Verres still complain of my unfairness in 156 dispatching the first hearing of his trial in nine days only, when Quintus Opimius, a senator of Rome, was completely stripped, by the court over which Verres presided, of property and money and personal treasures in three short hours ? a miscarriage of justice that has led to repeated motions in the Senate that all fines for this class of offence, and all prosecutions of this class, should be abolished.[a] And then again, in conducting the sale of Opimius's property, the amount of which Verres robbed him, and the naked and scandalous way in which he did it, would make a long story : but I tell you this, gentlemen— that unless I prove the fact to you, out of the ledgers of honest men, you may regard the whole thing as an invention of my own to meet the present emergency. And now shall the man who sought to profit by the 157 ruin of a senator of Rome at whose trial he had presided, and to carry home spoils and march off with trophies from such a source—shall this man have power to pray heaven to avert ruin in any shape from his own head ?

LXI. Enough ; for I make no reference to the notorious supplementary ballot[b] for members of the court over which Iunius presided. Why, how could I venture to throw doubt upon the records you have produced in court ? No light task that ; I am deterred from it not merely by respect for your character, Verres, and the character of the members of that court, but by your clerk's golden ring.[c] I will allege nothing so hard to prove as that. But I

multos ex te viros primarios audisse, cum diceres
ignosci tibi oportere quod falsum codicem protuleris ;
nam qua invidia C. Iunius conflagravit, ea, nisi pro-
158 vidisses, tibi ipsi tum pereundum fuisset.[1] Hoc modo
iste sibi et saluti suae prospicere didicit, referendo in
tabulas et privatas et publicas quod gestum non esset,
tollendo quod esset, et semper aliquid demendo,
mutando, interpolando. Eo enim usque progreditur
ut ne defensionem quidem maleficiorum suorum sine
aliis maleficiis reperire possit. Eius modi sortitionem
homo amentissimus suorum quoque iudicum fore
putavit per sodalem suum Q. Curtium, iudicem quae-
stionis suae : cui nisi ego vi populi atque hominum
clamore atque convicio restitissem, ex hac decuria
vestra, cuius mihi copiam quam largissime factam
oportebat, quos iste annuerat in suum consilium sine
causa subsortiebatur.

[1] conflagraret . . . fuisse *would improve the sense.*

[a] *Suae* refers to Curtius, not to Verres. Where no praetor
was available to preside over a *quaestio*, a president was
chosen from among the members of the court.
[b] Namely, the most honest men, who would be most
hostile to Verres. Cicero made Curtius resort to some
other panel to fill the vacancies in his court. He implies
that Curtius would have tampered with this ballot.

will repeat what I will show that many men of high standing have heard you say—that you ought to be forgiven for producing a forged record ; for the hatred against Gaius Iunius was so intense that, had you not taken precautions, you would then have been ruined yourself. This is the kind of precaution that Verres 158 has learnt to take for himself and his own safety : he takes records, private and official, inserts what never happened and erases what did, and is always scratching out or altering or interpolating something. Indeed he has gone so far that he cannot even avoid the consequences of his crimes except by committing fresh crimes. The insane scoundrel thought that he could manage a supplementary ballot of the same kind for the judges who were to try himself, by the help of Quintus Curtius, president of his own[a] criminal court. Had I not had the strong help of the people, who supported my resistance to this move with loud shouts of anger and abuse, Curtius would have proceeded to draw, by means of this supplementary ballot, upon your own panel, to which it was important for me to have the freest possible access, and would without the least justification have secured for his own court the men whom Verres selected for removal.[b]

ACTIONIS SECUNDAE IN C. VERREM
LIBER SECUNDUS

1   **I.** Multa mihi necessario, iudices, praetermittenda sunt, ut possim aliquo modo aliquando de his rebus quae meae fidei commissae sunt dicere. Recepi enim causam Siciliae; ea me ad hoc negotium provincia attraxit. Ego tamen, hoc onere suscepto et recepta causa Siciliensi, amplexus animo sum aliquanto amplius. Suscepi enim causam totius ordinis, suscepi causam rei publicae, quod putabam tum denique recte iudicari posse si non modo reus improbus adduceretur, sed etiam diligens et firmus accusator **2** ad iudicium veniret. Quo mihi maturius ad Siciliae causam veniendum est, relictis ceteris eius furtis atque flagitiis, ut et viribus quam integerrimis agere et ad dicendum temporis satis habere possim.

Atque antequam de incommodis Siciliae dico, pauca mihi videntur esse de provinciae dignitate, vetustate, utilitate dicenda. Nam cum omnium sociorum provinciarumque rationem diligenter habere

THE SECOND SPEECH AGAINST GAIUS VERRES: BOOK II

I. THERE is much, gentlemen, that I must inevitably 1 pass over, if I am to deal, sooner or later, to the best of my power, with the matters entrusted to my honourable keeping. For I promised to champion Sicily ; it is the province of Sicily that involved me in my present undertaking. And yet, though this is the burden I shouldered, though I did indeed promise to champion Sicily, my thoughts came to embrace a somewhat wider purpose. The fact is that I promised myself to champion the whole Senatorial order, nay, to champion Rome itself : feeling as I did that, if justice was to be done in this court, it was not enough for a guilty man to be prosecuted there ; a strong, conscientious man must appear there to prosecute him. And therefore I must not touch upon the rest 2 of Verres' robberies and outrages, but come without delay to the defence of Sicily, that I may be able to conduct it with the maximum of freshness and energy, and have time enough at my disposal for what I have to say.

But before I speak of Sicily's distresses, I feel that I should say a little of the high position of that province, of its antiquity, and of its practical import-ance. Your attentive consideration, due to the interests of all our allies and all our provinces, is

debetis, tum praecipue Siciliae, iudices, plurimis
iustissimisque de causis, primum quod omnium
nationum exterarum princeps Sicilia se ad amicitiam
fidemque populi Romani applicavit. Prima omnium,
id quod ornamentum imperii est, provincia est appel-
lata. Prima docuit maiores nostros quam praeclarum
esset exteris gentibus imperare. Sola fuit ea fide
benivolentiaque erga populum Romanum ut civitates
eius insulae, quae semel in amicitiam nostram venissent, numquam postea deficerent, pleraeque autem
et maxime illustres in amicitia perpetuo manerent.
3 Itaque maioribus nostris in Africam ex hac provincia
gradus imperii factus est ; neque enim tam facile opes
Carthaginis tantae concidissent nisi illud et rei fru-
mentariae subsidium et receptaculum classibus
nostris pateret. II. Quare P. Africanus, Carthagine
deleta, Siculorum urbes signis monumentisque
pulcherrimis exornavit, ut quos victoria populi Romani maxime laetari arbitrabatur, apud eos monu-
4 menta victoriae plurima collocaret. Denique ille
ipse M. Marcellus, cuius in Sicilia virtutem hostes,
misericordiam victi, fidem ceteri Siculi perspexerunt,
non solum sociis in eo bello consuluit, verum etiam
superatis hostibus temperavit. Urbem pulcherrimam Syracusas, quae cum manu munitissima esset
tum loci natura terra ac mari clauderetur, cum vi
consilioque cepisset, non solum incolumem passus est
esse, sed ita reliquit ornatam ut esset idem monu-

especially due, gentlemen, to those of Sicily, for
many strong reasons, the first of which is this, that
Sicily was the first of all foreign nations to become
the loyal friend of Rome. She was the first of all
to receive the title of province, the first such jewel
in our imperial crown. She was the first who made
our forefathers perceive how splendid a thing foreign
empire is. No other nation has equalled her in loyal
goodwill towards us : once the various states in the
island had embraced our friendship, they never
thereafter seceded from it ; and most of them, and
those the most notable, remained, without a break,
our firm friends. From this province therefore it 3
was that our forefathers took that great step in their
imperial career, the invasion of Africa : for the great
power of Carthage would never have been crushed
so readily had not Sicily been at our disposal, supplying us with corn and affording safe harbourage to
our fleets. II. This is why Scipio Africanus, after
the destruction of Carthage, richly adorned the
cities of Sicily with the finest statues and memorials,
intentionally setting up the most abundant memorials
of the triumph of Rome among those to whom, he
reckoned, that triumph gave most delight. Yes, 4
and Marcus Marcellus himself, known in Sicily as
terrible to his enemies, as merciful to the beaten,
as a faithful friend of all the rest—Marcellus not
only defended those who then fought for us, but in
the hour of victory spared those who fought against
us. When the noble city of Syracuse, strongly fortified by art, and defended by nature against assault
by land or sea, nevertheless fell before his strong
arm and military skill, he left it not merely unharmed,
but so richly adorned that it was a memorial alike

297

mentum victoriae, mansuetudinis, continentiae, cum homines viderent et quid expugnasset et quibus pepercisset et quae reliquisset. Tantum ille honorem habendum Siciliae putavit ut ne hostium quidem urbem ex sociorum insula tollendam arbitraretur.

5 Itaque ad omnes res sic illa provincia semper usi sumus ut, quicquid ex sese posset efferre, id non apud eos[1] nasci sed domi nostrae conditum putaremus. Quando illa frumentum quod deberet non ad diem dedit ? quando id quod opus esse putaret non ultro pollicita est ? quando id quod imperaretur recusavit ? Itaque ille M. Cato Sapiens cellam penariam rei publicae nostrae, nutricem plebis Romanae Siciliam nominabat. Nos vero experti sumus Italico maximo difficillimoque bello Siciliam nobis non pro penaria cella, sed pro aerario illo maiorum vetere ac referto fuisse ; nam sine ullo sumptu nostro coriis tunicis frumentoque suppeditando maximos exercitus nostros

6 vestivit, aluit, armavit. III. Quid ? illa quae forsitan ne sentimus quidem, iudices, quanta sunt ! quod multis locupletioribus civibus utimur, quod habent propinquam fidelem fructuosamque provinciam, quo facile excurrant, ubi libenter negotium gerant ; quos illa partim mercibus suppeditandis cum quaestu compendioque dimittit, partim retinet, ut arare, ut pascere, ut negotiari libeat, ut denique sedes ac domicilium collocare ; quod commodum non mediocre rei publicae est, tantum civium numerum

---

[1] nos *the Cluni MS., followed by Peterson, perhaps rightly*: " *not only* grown *on our own* soil *but already* stored *in our own* granaries."

of his victory, of his clemency, and of his self-control,
since men beheld the fortress he had captured, the
people he had spared, and the treasures he had left
unplundered. So much respect he reckoned due
to Sicily that the island of our friends was, he judged,
not to be deprived even of the city of our enemies.

And accordingly our relations with the province 5
for all purposes were always such that we looked upon
her various products not as growing on their soil, but
as already added to our stores at home. When has
she failed to pay us punctually her tribute of grain ?
When has she not spontaneously offered us what she
believed that we wanted ? When has she refused
to supply what was ordered of her ? Cato Sapiens
called her in consequence " the nation's storehouse,
the nurse at whose breast the Roman people is fed."
Nay, we in our time have found, in the critical days
of the great Italian war, how Sicily has been to us
no mere storehouse, but like the ancient and well-
filled State Treasury of our fathers' days, supplying
us with hides and shirts and grain, free of cost to
ourselves, to clothe, feed and equip our great armies.
III. Yes, and she does us services, great services, of 6
which we, gentlemen, I daresay, are not even aware.
Many of our citizens are the richer for having a
profitable field of enterprise in this loyal province
close at hand, which they can visit so easily, and where
they can carry on their business so freely. To some
of these Sicily supplies merchandise, and sends them
away enriched with profits : others she keeps with
her, to become, according to their preference, corn
farmers or stock farmers or business men, and in
short, to settle and make a home there. It is a
national advantage of no trifling kind that so large

tam prope ab domo tam bonis fructuosisque rebus
7 detineri. Et quoniam quasi quaedam praedia populi
Romani sunt vectigalia nostra atque provinciae, quem
ad modum vos propinquis vestris praediis maxime
delectamini, sic populo Romano iucunda suburbanitas
est huiusce provinciae.

Iam vero hominum ipsorum, iudices, ea patientia
virtus frugalitasque est ut proxime ad nostram
disciplinam illam veterem, non ad hanc quae nunc
increbruit, videantur accedere. Nihil ceterorum
simile Graecorum ; nulla desidia, nulla luxuries ;
contra summus labor in publicis privatisque rebus,
summa parsimonia, summa diligentia. Sic porro
nostros homines diligunt ut iis solis neque publicanus
8 neque negotiator odio sit. Magistratuum autem
nostrorum iniurias ita multorum tulerunt ut numquam ante hoc tempus ad aram legum praesidiumque
vestrum publico consilio confugerint ; tametsi et illum annum pertulerant qui sic eos afflixerat ut salvi
esse non possent, nisi C. Marcellus quasi aliquo fato
venisset, ut bis ex eadem familia salus Siciliae constitueretur, et postea M. Antonii infinitum illud imperium senserant. Sic a maioribus suis acceperant,
tanta populi Romani in Siculos esse beneficia ut etiam
iniurias nostrorum hominum perferendas putarent.

---

[a] 80 B.C., during which Lepidus, father of the triumvir,
was governor of Sicily.

[b] See *Divinatio* § 55. His wide general powers in 74
were like those conferred on Pompeius in 67 : but he failed
where Pompeius succeeded.

a number of Roman citizens should be kept so near
their own country, engaged in occupations so honest
and profitable. Our tributes and our provinces 7
constitute, in a sense, our nation's landed estates ;
and thus, just as you, gentlemen, gain most pleasure
from such of your estates as are close to Rome, so to
the nation there is something pleasant in the near-
ness of this province to the capital.

And then again, the character of the inhabitants is
such, so hardy and upright and honest, that it really
reminds us of the stern old Roman manners, rather
than of those which have come to prevail among us
to-day. They have none of the failings found elsewhere among Greeks ; they are neither slothful nor
self-indulgent ; on the contrary, they are highly
industrious, for their own and for the public good ;
plain-living and conscientious folk. Such, moreover,
is their attachment to our own people that among
them, and nowhere else, neither tax-collector nor
capitalist is an object of dislike. Acts of oppression, 8
again, on the part of Roman officials, they have borne
so patiently, time after time, that never before this
day have they, as a community, sought a refuge in
the sanctuary of the law and the stronghold of your
protection : and yet they had to live through that
awful year [a] which brought them so low that they
would certainly have been ruined but for the coming
of Gaius Marcellus, sent them, it would seem, by
destiny as the second Marcellus to be the saviour of
Sicily ; and after that they suffered under the
autocratic powers conferred on Marcus Antonius.[b]
It was an inherited tradition of theirs to regard Rome
as so great a benefactor of the Sicilians that they
must even endure oppression, if the oppressors were

9 In neminem civitates ante hunc testimonium publice
dixerunt. Hunc denique ipsum pertulissent, si
humano modo, si usitato more, si denique uno aliquo
in genere peccasset. Sed cum perferre non possent
luxuriem, crudelitatem, avaritiam, superbiam, cum
omnia sua commoda, iura, beneficia senatus populique
Romani unius scelere ac libidine perdidissent, hoc
statuerunt, aut istius iniurias per vos ulcisci ac
persequi, aut, si vobis indigni essent visi quibus opem
auxiliumque ferretis, urbes ac sedes suas relinquere,
quandoquidem agros iam ante istius iniuriis exagitati
10 reliquissent. IV. Hoc consilio a L. Metello legationes universae petiverunt ut quam primum isti
succederet ; hoc animo totiens apud patronos de
suis miseriis deplorarunt ; hoc commoti dolore
postulata consulibus, quae non postulata sed in istum
crimina viderentur esse, ediderunt. Fecerunt etiam
ut me, cuius fidem continentiamque cognoverant,
prope de vitae meae statu dolore ac lacrimis suis
deducerent, ut ego istum accusarem ; a quo mea
longissime ratio voluntasque abhorrebat ; quamquam
in hac causa multo plures partes mihi defensionis
11 quam accusationis suscepisse videor. Postremo

Romans. Verres is the first man against whom their 9 cities have officially sent witnesses to testify. They would, in fact, have endured even Verres in silence, if only his offences had been those of an ordinary man, offences of a recognized and usual type, or, indeed, of only a single sort, no matter what. But finding his luxury and his cruelty, his greed and his insolence, beyond their power of endurance ; finding all the privileges and rights and benefits ever granted them by the Roman senate and nation reft from them by this one unscrupulous scoundrel : they made up their minds to one of two things ; either to prosecute their oppressor, and secure revenge, if you would help them ; or else, if you should count them unworthy of receiving your aid and succour, to abandon their cities and their homes—their countryside they had already abandoned, driven from it like game by their oppressor. IV. This was the purpose of the entreaty 10 made by all their deputations to Lucius Metellus, that he would take over the government from Verres at the earliest possible moment ; this was the state of mind that led them to pour out their tale of woe so often into their Roman supporters' ears ; this was the distress that moved them to present to the consuls those petitions of theirs, which, it was plain, were not really petitions, but charges against that man yonder. And further, their distress and their lamentations succeeded in inducing myself, known to them as a man of honour and integrity, almost to abandon the fixed principle of my life in becoming the prosecutor of Verres, a step intensely repugnant to my ideas and my feelings : even though, in this particular case, I look upon myself as having undertaken the part of defender far more than that of prosecutor. And 11

homines ex tota provincia nobilissimi primique
publice privatimque venerunt ; gravissima atque
amplissima quaeque civitas vehementissime suas
iniurias persecuta est.

At quem ad modum, iudices, venerunt ? Videor
enim mihi liberius apud vos iam pro Siculis loqui
debere quam forsitan ipsi velint ; saluti enim potius
eorum consulam quam voluntati. Ecquem existimatis umquam ulla in provincia reum absentem contra
inquisitionem accusatoris tantis opibus, tanta cupiditate esse defensum ? Quaestores utriusque provinciae qui isto praetore fuerant cum fascibus mihi
12 praesto fuerunt ; his porro qui successerunt, vehementer istius cupidi, liberaliter ex istius cibariis
tractati, non minus acres contra me fuerunt. Videte
quid potuerit qui quattuor in una provincia quaestores
studiosissimos defensores propugnatoresque habuerit,
praetorem vero cohortemque totam sic studiosam ut
facile appareret non tam illis Siciliam, quam inanem
offenderant, quam Verrem ipsum, qui plenus deces-
serat, provinciam fuisse. Minari Siculis, si decre-
vissent legationes quae contra istum dicerent, minari,
si qui essent profecti ; aliis, si laudarent, benignissime
promittere ; gravissimos privatarum rerum testes,

lastly, men of the highest birth and the highest rank
have come to Rome, officially or as private persons,
from every part of the province ; every great and
important city of Sicily has flung itself eagerly into
the task of avenging its wrongs.

But in what circumstances, gentlemen, have they
thus come to us ? I feel that I must, at this point,
speak to you on behalf of these Sicilians with less
reserve than, it may be, they would themselves wish ;
I will aim at forwarding their deliverance rather than
their desires. Was ever an accused person, think
you, in any of our provinces, protected in his own
absence against a prosecutor's investigations by such
an expenditure of money and passionate effort ?
The quaestors of both divisions who had served under
him were on the spot to oppose me, supported by
lictors : and their successors, being his enthusiastic 12
supporters, and having been liberally dealt with by
him out of his fund for travelling expenses,[a] opposed
me with equal bitterness. Think of the power in the
hands of a man who had, in the one province, four
quaestors doing their utmost to shield and defend
him ; and the praetor, with all the praetor's staff,
doing so much for him that it was easy to see that
their field of operations had not been Sicily, which
they had found empty, but the governor of Sicily, who
had gone away full. They threatened the inhabitants
with vengeance if they appointed deputations to
give evidence against Verres, or if any of them left
for Rome : they made the most liberal promises
to others if only they would speak in his favour :
they took important witnesses, witnesses to private

---

[a] An ironical way of saying " bribed."

quibus nos praesentibus denuntiavimus, eos vi
custodiisque retinere.

13 V. Quae cum omnia facta sint, tamen unam solam
scitote esse civitatem, Mamertinam, quae publice
legatos qui istum laudarent miserit. Eius autem
legationis principem, civitatis nobilissimum civem,
C. Heium, iuratum dicere audistis isti navem onerariam maximam Messanae esse publice coactis operis
aedificatam ; idemque Mamertinorum legatus, istius
laudator, non solum istum bona sua, verum etiam
sacra deosque penates a maioribus traditos, ex aedibus
suis eripuisse dixit. Praeclara laudatio, cum duabus
in rebus legatorum una opera consumitur, in lau-
dando atque repetendo ! Atque ea ipsa civitas qua
ratione isti amica sit dicetur certo loco. Reperietis
enim, quae causae benivolentiae Mamertinis erga
istum sint, eas ipsas causas satis iustas esse dam-
nationis. Alia civitas nulla, iudices, publico consilio
14 laudat. Vis illa summi imperii tantum potuit apud
perpaucos homines, non civitates, ut aut levissimi
quidam ex miserrimis desertissimisque oppidis in-
venirentur qui iniussu populi ac senatus proficisce-
rentur, aut ii qui contra istum legati decreti erant,
et testimonium publicum mandataque acceperant, vi
ac metu retinerentur. Quod ego in paucis tamen usu

charges, men summoned in person by myself, and set guards to prevent them by force from leaving the country.

V. Now in spite of all this, let me inform you that 13 only one single city, that of the Mamertines, has sent an official deputation to speak in Verres' support : and the chief man of that very deputation, Gaius Heius, the most distinguished person in that city, has stated on oath in your hearing that a large cargo ship was built for Verres at Messana by workmen officially impressed ; and this same representative of the Mamertines and eulogist of Verres has charged Verres with not merely carrying off his personal property but plundering his home of the sacred vessels and household gods that were his family heirlooms. An impressive eulogy indeed, when the energies of those sent to deliver it are divided between praising the thief and denouncing his thefts ! You shall, more-over, be told when the time comes of the origin of Messana's attachment to Verres : and you will then see that the grounds for her citizens' goodwill towards him are in themselves sufficient grounds for his conviction. Of the other cities, not one, gentle-men, sends him official support. All the force of his 14 sovereign authority could only so far prevail with a handful of individuals—not cities—that in some cases certain unimportant inhabitants of unprosperous and decaying towns were found ready to go off to Rome without the authority of their town or town council, and in other cases persons who had been appointed to appear against him, and had been supplied with official evidence and instructions, were forced or frightened into staying at home. And after all, I am not sorry that in a few instances this has actually

307

venisse non moleste tuli, quo reliquae tot et tantae et
tam graves civitates, tota denique Sicilia plus auctoritatis apud vos haberet, cum videretis nulla vi retineri,
nullo periculo prohiberi potuisse quo minus experi-
rentur ecquid apud vos querimoniae valerent anti-
15 quissimorum fidelissimorumque sociorum. Nam quod
fortasse non nemo vestrum audierit, istum a Syracusanis publice laudari, id tametsi priore actione ex
Heraclii Syracusani testimonio cuius modi esset cognovistis, tamen vobis alio loco ut se tota res habeat,
quod ad eam civitatem attinet, demonstrabitur.
Intellegetis enim nullis hominibus quemquam tanto
odio quanto istum Syracusanis et esse et fuisse.

VI. At enim istum Siculi soli persequuntur : cives
Romani qui in Sicilia negotiantur, defendunt, diligunt,
salvum esse cupiunt. Primum, si ita esset, tamen vos
in hac quaestione de pecuniis repetundis, quae
sociorum causa constituta est lege iudicioque sociali,
16 sociorum querimonias audire oporteret. Sed intellegere potuistis priore actione cives Romanos honestissimos ex Sicilia plurimos maximis de rebus, et quas
ipsi accepissent iniurias et quas scirent esse aliis
factas, pro testimonio dicere. Ego hoc quod intellego,
iudices, sic confirmo. Videor mihi gratum fecisse
Siculis quod eorum iniurias meo labore, inimicitiis,
periculo sim persecutus : non minus hoc gratum me

occurred, since it must increase your respect for all
the many other great and important cities, in fact
for Sicily as a whole, showing you how these people
could be withheld by no force, turned back by no
peril, from discovering whether you feel any sort of
concern for the grievances of your oldest and most
loyal allies. As to the statement, which some of 15
you may have heard, that the Syracusans are giving
him an official eulogy, you know from the evidence of
the Syracusan Heraclius, given at the first hearing,
what that means ; you shall, however, have the
whole facts of the case, so far as Syracuse is concerned, put clearly before you later : and you will
certainly perceive that no man was ever hated so
heartily by any body of persons as that man was, and
is, hated by the people of Syracuse.

VI. It may be suggested that only the Sicilians are
his enemies, and that those Roman citizens who are
carrying on business in Sicily support him, like him,
and desire his acquittal. My first answer to that is
this : even were it so, yet the Extortion Court was
established for our allies ; the law was passed, the
procedure was set up, for our allies' benefit ; and
therefore it is the grievances of our allies to which
you, as members of this Court, must listen. But in 16
fact your attention was drawn, in the first hearing,
to the important evidence of a large number of
reputable Roman citizens from Sicily, showing both
the wrongs done to themselves and the wrongs they
knew had been done to others. I will tell this Court
one thing of whose truth I am sure, and it is this. I
believe myself to have gratified the Sicilians by my
endeavours to redress their wrongs at the cost of toil,
hostility, and danger to myself : I know that this

nostris civibus intellego fecisse, qui hoc existimant,
iuris libertatis rerum fortunarumque suarum salutem
17 in istius damnatione consistere. Quapropter de
istius praetura Siciliensi non recuso quin ita me
audiatis ut, si cuiquam generi hominum, sive Siculorum sive nostrorum civium, si cuiquam ordini, sive
aratorum sive pecuariorum sive mercatorum, probatus
sit, si non horum omnium communis hostis praedoque
fuerit, si cuiquam denique in re umquam ulla tempera-
verit, ut vos quoque ei temperetis.

Qui simul atque ei sorte provincia Sicilia obvenit,
statim Romae et ab urbe antequam proficisceretur,
quaerere ipse secum et agitare cum suis coepit
quibusnam rebus in ea provincia maximam uno anno
pecuniam facere posset. Nolebat in agendo discere
tametsi non provinciae rudis erat et tiro, sed Siciliae
paratus ad praedam meditatusque venire cupiebat.
18 O praeclare coniectum a vulgo in illam provinciam
omen communis famae atque sermonis, cum ex
nomine istius quid iste in provincia facturus esset
perridicule homines augurabantur! Etenim quis
dubitare posset—cum istius in quaestura fugam et
furtum recognosceret, cum in legatione oppidorum
fanorumque spoliationes cogitaret, cum videret in
foro latrocinia praeturae—qualis iste in quarto actu
improbitatis futurus esset? VII. Atque ut in-
tellegatis eum Romae quaesisse non modo genera

action of mine has been equally gratifying to our countrymen, who believe that the preservation of their rights and liberties, their property and fortunes, depends on the condemnation of the man now before you. And therefore I am content that you should 17 listen to my account of his governorship of Sicily on the understanding that, if he shall appear to have satisfied any description of person, Sicilian or Roman, cultivators or stock-farmers or traders or any class whatsoever; if he shall not appear equally the enemy and robber of all of them; if, in fact, you find that he has ever in any respect spared any of them—that then you in your turn shall spare him.

No sooner had the lot given him Sicily as his province than he proceeded, while still in Rome, before he left the city, to ask himself, and to discuss with his friends, by what methods he could make most money out of a single year in the province. He was not content to discover these methods on the spot, though he was no raw new-comer to the work of government; his prey being Sicily, he was anxious to arrive there with his designs thought out and prepared beforehand. Admirably indeed did popular rumour and the general 18 talk of the streets interpret the omens for that unhappy province, inferring with prophetic jests from his name Verres the manner in which he was likely to behave there ! Who, to be sure, could feel doubtful—considering his acts of desertion and theft as quaestor, thinking of his plunderings of towns and temples as assistant-governor, seeing in our Forum his deeds of brigandage as praetor—how he would perform the fourth act in the vicious drama of his life ? VII. And now, to show you that his researches at Rome included not only the general principles of

furandi sed etiam nomina certissima, accipite argumentum quo facilius de singulari eius impudentia existimare possitis.

19 Quo die Siciliam attigit (videte satisne paratus ex illo omine urbano ad everrendam provinciam venerit) statim Messana litteras Halaesam mittit, quas ego istum in Italia conscripsisse arbitror, nam simul atque e navi egressus est dedit : Halaesinus ad se Dio continuo veniret ; se de hereditate velle cognoscere quae eius filio a propinquo homine Apollodoro

20 Laphirone venisset. Ea erat, iudices, pergrandis pecunia. Hic est Dio, iudices, nunc beneficio Q. Metelli civis Romanus factus ; de quo multis viris primariis testibus multorumque tabulis vobis priore actione satis factum est HS deciens numerata esse ut eam causam in qua ne tenuissima quidem dubitatio posset esse isto cognoscente obtineret ; praeterea greges nobilissimarum equarum abactos, argenti vestisque stragulae domi quod fuerit esse direptum : ita HS deciens Q. Dionem quod hereditas ei venisset,

21 nullam aliam ob causam, perdidisse. Quid ? haec hereditas quo praetore Dionis filio venerat ? Eodem quo Anniae, P. Annii senatoris filiae, eodem quo M. Liguri senatori, C. Sacerdote praetore. Quid ? tum nemo molestus Dioni fuerat ? Non plus quam

---

^a *i.e.*, propraetor in Sicily and *praetor urbanus* in Rome respectively.

312

thieving but the precise names of his victims, let me put some evidence before you that may help you to appreciate the unique quality of his unscrupulous behaviour.

The day he landed in Sicily—mark how Rome's 19 prophetic interpretation of his name was borne out by his full preparations to sweep the province clean on arrival—he promptly sent off from Messana to Halaesa a letter which I conceive he had written in Italy, for he dispatched it the moment he had stepped ashore. In this letter he summoned Dio of Halaesa to appear before him without delay; he intended, he said, to investigate a legacy received by Dio's son from a relative, Apollodorus Laphiro. This legacy, 20 gentlemen, was a very large sum of money. Dio, you should know, has now the rank of a Roman citizen, conferred on him by Quintus Metellus; and it was he, as was made clear to you at the first hearing of this case by the personal and written evidence of a number of witnesses of high standing, by whom the sum of ten thousand pounds was paid over to secure from Verres a judgement in his favour on an issue admitting not the smallest shadow of doubt. Besides this, his herds of thoroughbred mares were taken from his fields, and his house plundered of all the silver and tapestries it contained. Thus Dio lost ten thousand pounds simply through having received a legacy. Now who was praetor[a] when this legacy came to Dio's 21 son? Why, the man who was praetor[a] when legacies[b] came to Annia the daughter of the senator Publius Annius and to the senator Marcus Ligus—Gaius Sacerdos was praetor. Then did no one make trouble for Dio at that time? No one, any more

[b] See i. 104 and 125.

Liguri, Sacerdote praetore. Quid ? ad Verrem quis
detulit ? Nemo, nisi forte existimatis ei quadruplatores ad fretum praesto fuisse. VIII. Ad urbem
cum esset, audivit Dioni cuidam Siculo permagnam
venisse hereditatem ; heredem statuas iussum esse
in foro ponere ; nisi posuisset, Veneri Erycinae esse
multatum. Tametsi positae essent ex testamento,
tamen putabat, quoniam Veneris nomen esset,
22 causam calumniae se reperturum. Itaque apponit
qui petat Veneri Erycinae illam hereditatem. Non
enim quaestor petit, ut est consuetudo, is qui Erycum
montem obtinebat : petit Naevius Turpio quidam,
istius excursor et emissarius, homo omnium ex illo
conventu quadruplatorum deterrimus, C. Sacerdote
praetore condemnatus iniuriarum. Etenim erat
eius modi causa ut ipse praetor, cum quaereret
calumniatorem, paulo tamen consideratiorem reperire
non posset. Hunc hominem Veneri absolvit, sibi
condemnat. Maluit videlicet homines peccare quam
deos, se potius a Dione quod non licebat quam
23 Venerem quod non debebatur auferre. Quid ego
hic nunc Sex. Pompeii Chlori testimonium recitem,
qui causam Dionis egit, qui omnibus rebus interfuit,
hominis honestissimi, tametsi civis Romanus virtutis
causa iam diu est, tamen omnium Siculorum primi
ac nobilissimi ? quid ipsius Q. Caecilii Dionis, hominis

---

^a *i.e.*, to the famous temple of Venus on Mt. Eryx in
Western Sicily.

^b Western Sicily.

^c Verres made Dio pay £10,000 to escape having the
whole legacy adjudged forfeit to Venus.

than for Ligus—so long as Sacerdos was praetor.
Then who laid an information against him before
Verres? No one, unless we are to suppose informers
were waiting for Verres on the quay. VIII. While
in or near Rome, Verres was told that a large legacy
had come to a Sicilian named Dio; that the legatee
was required to erect certain statues in the Forum;
and that failing such erection the legacy was forfeit
to Venus of Eryx.[a] Although they had been erected
as the will required, the mention of Venus suggested
to Verres sufficient opening for a false charge.
Accordingly, he put up a man to claim the legacy for 22
Venus of Eryx. No, the claim was not brought, as is
usual in such cases, by the quaestor of the division [b]
in which Mount Eryx lies: it was brought by a man
called Naevius Turpio, Verres' agent and emissary,
the most worthless of all the informers in that district,
a man who had been sentenced for assault during the
praetorship of Sacerdos. The case was indeed of such
a kind that the praetor himself, in casting about for
a dishonest claimant, could secure no one who was
even slightly more respectable than this man. Dio
won his case against Venus, but lost it against Verres.[c]
Our judge naturally would have earth do wrong rather
than heaven, and Dio be robbed immorally by him
rather than illegally by Venus.

Need I now read you the evidence of Sextus 23
Pompeius Chlorus, who was Dio's advocate and
directly acquainted with all the circumstances—a
man of the highest character, whose merit has long
earned him Roman citizenship, and is none the less
to be reckoned the most important and distinguished
of Sicilians? Or the evidence of the honoured and
honourable Quintus Caecilius Dio himself? Or that

probatissimi ac pudentissimi ? quid L. Caecilii, L.
Liguris, T. Manlii, L. Caleni ? quorum omnium testimoniis de hac Dionis pecunia confirmatum est.
Dixit hoc idem M. Lucullus, se de his Dionis incommodis pro hospitio quod sibi cum eo esset iam
24 ante cognosse. Quid ? Lucullus, qui tum in Macedonia fuit, melius haec cognovit quam tu, Hortensi,
qui Romae fuisti, ad quem Dio confugit, qui de
Dionis iniuriis gravissime per litteras cum Verre
questus es ? Nova tibi haec sunt, inopinata ? nunc
primum hoc aures tuae crimen accipiunt ? Nihil ex
Dione, nihil ex socru tua, femina primaria, Servilia,
vetere Dionis hospita, audisti ? Nonne multa mei
testes quae tu scis nesciunt ? nonne te mihi testem
in hoc crimine eripuit non istius innocentia sed legis
exceptio ? Recita. TESTIMONIA LUCULLI, CHLORI,
DIONIS. IX. Satisne vobis magnam pecuniam Venerius homo, qui e Chelidonis sinu in provinciam profectus esset, Veneris nomine quaesisse videtur ?

25   Accipite aliam in minore pecunia non minus impudentem calumniam. Sosippus et Philocrates fratres sunt Agyrinenses. Horum pater abhinc duo et
xx. annos est mortuus ; in cuius testamento, quodam
loco si commissum quid esset, multa erat Veneri.
Ipso vicensimo anno, cum tot interea praetores, tot
quaestores, tot calumniatores in provincia fuissent,

ᵃ The proper claimants on behalf of Venus (see § 22).

of Lucius Caecilius, Lucius Ligus, Titus Manlius, and Lucius Calenus? Everyone of these has testified to the facts about this money that Dio paid. There is similar evidence from Marcus Lucullus, who has stated that his earlier ties of hospitality with Dio led to his knowing what befell that unhappy man. And 24 further, did Lucullus, then in Macedonia, know more of all this than you did, Hortensius—you who were in Rome, you from whom Dio sought help, you who wrote to Verres earnestly protesting against Dio's wrongs? Is all this new and surprising to you? Does this charge now come to your ears for the first time? Did you hear nothing of it from Dio—nothing from that highly-respected lady your mother-in-law Servilia, so long Dio's guest and hostess? Are not many of the facts unknown to my witnesses and known to you? It is not your client's innocence, but the exemption the law gives you, that has deprived me of calling you yourself as a witness to the truth of this charge.—Read the evidence. *Evidence of Lucullus, Chlorus and Dio.* IX. Does the Court feel that this devotee of Venus, who came to his province fresh from Chelidon's arms, has used the name of Venus to secure enough for himself?

Let me now tell you of another false charge, not 25 less unscrupulous, though it involved a smaller sum of money. There are two brothers belonging to Agyrium, named Sosippus and Philocrates. Their father died twenty-two years ago. His will provided that, if a certain stipulation were not carried out, the estate should be forfeited to Venus. No less than twenty years later, after all the praetors and quaestors[a] and bringers of false charges who had meanwhile been in the province, the estate was

hereditas ab his Veneris nomine petita est. Causam
Verres cognoscit ; pecuniam per Volcatium accipit,
fere ad HS cccc. milia, ab duobus fratribus—multorum
testimonia audistis antea. Vicerunt Agyrinenses
fratres ita ut egentes inanesque discederent.

26   X. At enim ad Verrem pecunia ista non pervenit.
Quae est ista defensio ? utrum asseveratur in hoc
an temptatur ? mihi enim res nova est. Verres
calumniatorem apponebat, Verres adesse iubebat,
Verres cognoscebat, Verres iudicabat, pecuniae maximae dabantur, qui dabant causas obtinebant. Tu
mihi ita defendas : " Non est ista Verri numerata
pecunia "? Adiuvo te ; mei quoque testes idem
dicunt ; Volcatio dicunt sese dedisse. Quae vis erat
in Volcatio tanta ut HS cccc. milia duobus hominibus
auferret ? Ecquis Volcatio, si sua sponte venisset,
unam libellam dedisset ? Veniat nunc, experiatur
tecto recipiet nemo. At ego amplius dico. HS
quadringentiens cepisse te arguo contra leges, nego
tibi ipsi ullum nummum esse numeratum ; sed cum
ob tua decreta, ob edicta, ob imperata, ob iudicia
pecuniae dabantur, non erat quaerendum cuius manu
27 numerarentur, sed cuius iniuria cogerentur. Comites
illi tui delecti manus erant tuae ; praefecti, scribae,
accensi, medici, haruspices, praecones manus erant
tuae ; ut quisque te maxime cognatione, affinitate,

claimed from the brothers on behalf of Venus.
Verres tried the case; and nearly £4000 was paid
over to him, through Volcatius, by the two brothers
—you have already heard the evidence of a number
of witnesses. The Agyrian brothers won their case
—and left the court impoverished and broken men.

X. But, we are told, the money did not reach 26
Verres. What manner of defence is this? a serious
plea, or an experiment? I ask, for it is something
new in my experience. Verres put up the false
claimant, Verres summoned the defendants, Verres
tried the case, Verres pronounced judgement; a
large sum of money was paid; the payers won the
case. Is my opponent to reply: " The cash was not
paid to Verres?" Quite true; my own witnesses
endorse this statement; they tell us they paid it to
Volcatius. And who was Volcatius, that he should
be able to force £4000 out of two men? Would
anyone whom Volcatius approached on his own
responsibility have paid him one penny? Let him
approach somebody now, and see what happens:
no one will let him into his house. I will put the
matter more plainly. I am proving that you have
illegally acquired four *hundred* thousand pounds,
and I will say that not one shilling of this has been
directly paid to you personally; but since it was your
decrees and edicts, your orders and judgements, that
forced the money out of its owners, the point at issue
is not whose hands received the cash, but whose
tyranny compelled its payment. The members 27
of your select retinue were your hands; your
managers, secretaries, orderlies, doctors, sooth-
sayers, and criers were your hands; the more closely
a man was connected with you by any tie of blood,

319

necessitudine aliqua attingebat, ita maxime manus
tua putabatur ; cohors tota illa, quae plus mali
Siciliae dedit quam si centum cohortes fugitivorum
fuissent, tua manus sine controversia fuit. Quicquid
ab horum quopiam captum est, id non modo tibi
datum sed tua manu numeratum iudicari necesse est.
Nam si hanc defensionem probabitis, " Non accepit
ipse," licet omnia de pecuniis repetundis iudicia
tollatis. Nemo umquam reus tam nocens adducetur
qui ista defensione non possit uti. Etenim cum
Verres utatur, quis erit umquam posthac reus tam
perditus qui non ad Q. Mucii innocentiam referatur
si cum isto conferatur ? Neque nunc tam mihi isti
Verrem defendere videntur quam in Verre defensionis
temptare rationem.

28 Qua de re, iudices, magno opere vobis providen-
dum est ; pertinet hoc ad summam rem publicam
et ad existimationem ordinis nostri salutemque sociorum. Si enim innocentes existimari volumus, non
solum nos sed etiam nostros comites praestare
debemus. XI. Primum omnium opera danda est
ut eos nobiscum educamus qui nostrae famae capiti-
que consulant ; deinde, si in hominibus eligendis nos
spes amicitiae fefellerit, ut vindicemus, missos faciamus, semper ita vivamus ut rationem reddendam

---

a Here there is some play made with the military sense
of *manus* as well as of *cohors*.

b Because the loss of our *caput* (civic rights) would be the
penalty we might have to pay for their misconduct.

marriage, or friendship, the more he was reckoned
one of your hands ; the whole of the company that
formed your staff, a company that has done Sicily
more harm than if it had been a hundred companies
of revolted slaves, were undeniably your hands.[a]
Any sum appropriated by any of these persons must
inevitably be judged to have been not only paid
to you but paid in cash into your own hands. If this
Court is to accept " He did not receive the money
himself " as a valid defence, it may as well do away
with all judicial investigation of extortion. There
can never be any prosecution of any person, however
guilty, who will not be able to employ this line of
defence. Verres would employ it now ; and can the
guilt of any man who shall be prosecuted hereafter
be so black that we shall not, when we measure it
against the guilt of a Verres, class it with the innocence of a Scaevola ? But indeed I feel that in this
matter my opponents are aiming less at defending
Verres himself than at trying in the person of Verres
the effect of a new general line of defence.

Now here, gentlemen, is a danger against which 28
you must guard with care, a matter that vitally
concerns the nation's interests, the good name of our
Order and the welfare of our allies. If we would
have ourselves believed innocent, we must demon-
strate not only our own innocence, but that of the
persons who form our staff. In the first place, we
must do our best to take out with us men who
uphold the safety of our reputation and our existence
as citizens.[b] XI. In the next place, if having made
our choice we find our confidence in our friends
disappointed, we must punish them or dismiss them,
living in perpetual expectation of being called to

321

nobis arbitremur. Africani est hoc, hominis liberalissimi—verum tamen ea liberalitas est probanda quae
29 sine periculo existimationis est, ut in illo fuit : cum ab eo quidam vetus assectator ex numero amicorum non impetraret uti se praefectum in Africam duceret, et id ferret moleste, "Noli" inquit "mirari si tu hoc a me non impetras : ego iam pridem ab eo cui meam existimationem caram fore arbitror peto ut mecum praefectus proficiscatur, et adhuc impetrare non possum." Etenim re vera multo magis est petendum ab hominibus, si salvi et honesti esse volumus, ut eant nobiscum in provinciam, quam in beneficii loco deferendum. Sed tu, cum et tuos amicos in provinciam quasi in praedam invitabas, et cum iis ac per eos praedabare, et eos in contione anulis aureis donabas, non statuebas tibi non solum de tuis sed etiam de illorum factis rationem esse reddendam ?

30 Cum hos sibi quaestus constituisset magnos atque uberes ex his causis quas ipse instituerat cum consilio, hoc est cum sua cohorte, cognoscere, tum illud infinitum genus invenerat ad innumerabilem pecuniam corripiendam. XII. Dubium nemini est quin omnes omnium pecuniae positae sint in eorum potestate qui iudicia dant et eorum qui iudicant, quin nemo vestrum possit aedes suas, nemo fundum, nemo bona patria obtinere, si, cum haec a quopiam vestrum

account for our behaviour. Let me quote you a
saying of that very courteous gentleman Scipio
Africanus, only first observing that such courtesy is
truly admirable in one whose good name is as
secure as his was. One of his friends, an old adherent, 29
had asked to be taken to Africa as one of his cavalry
officers, and was much offended at being refused.
" Do not be surprised," said Scipio, " that I refuse
consent to your request. I have for some time
been asking a man, who would, as I believe, care
much for my honour, to go with me as one of my
officers ; and he has, so far, refused his consent."
And it is surely true that, if we would escape danger
and discredit, there is far more need to entreat men
to join our staff than to offer such a post as a favour.
Yet when you, Verres, invited your friends to join
your staff like members of a raiding party, when
you carried out your raids in their company or by
their means, when you presented them at public
gatherings with gold rings, did you not assume
that you would be called to account for their actions
as well as your own ?

Having now set on foot this method of making 30
for himself extensive and lucrative profits out of the
cases which he heard himself with the assistance of
his court—a court composed of his own staff—he
next hit upon another device with unlimited possi-
bilities of seizing vast sums of money. XII. It is
plain to us all that every man's whole fortune lies
at the mercy of those who appoint and those who
compose our courts ; that no man among you could
remain the owner of his house, or the owner of his
land, or the owner of his family property, if when
his title thereto in any case were disputed, a dis-

petita sint, praetor improbus, cui nemo intercedere
possit, det quem velit iudicem, iudex nequam et
31 levis quod praetor iusserit iudicet. Si vero illud
quoque accedet, ut praetor in ea verba iudicium det
ut vel L. Octavius Balbus iudex, homo et iuris et
officii peritissimus, non possit aliter iudicare,—si
iudicium sit eius modi : L. OCTAVIUS IUDEX ESTO : SI
PARET FUNDUM CAPENATEM, QUO DE AGITUR, EX IURE
QUIRITIUM P. SERVILII ESSE, NEQUE IS FUNDUS Q. CATULO
RESTITUETUR : non necesse erit L. Octavio iudici
cogere P. Servilium Q. Catulo fundum restituere,
aut condemnare eum quem non oporteat ? Eius
modi totum ius praetorium, eius modi omnis res
iudiciaria fuit in Sicilia per triennium Verre praetore.
Decreta eius modi : SI NON ACCIPIT QUOD TE DEBERE
DICIS, ACCUSES ; SI PETIT, DUCAS. C. Fuficium duci
iussit petitorem, L. Suettium, L. Racilium. Iudicia
eius modi : qui cives Romani erant, si Siculi essent,
cum Siculos eorum legibus dari oporteret ; qui
32 Siculi, si cives Romani essent. Verum, ut totum
genus amplectamini iudiciorum, prius iura Siculorum,
deinde istius instituta cognoscite.

---

^a The *formula* is of the normal type : the injustice lies in
the barefaced substitution of Catulus for Servilius in the
second clause. The formula would conclude with the normal
direction to inflict a stated penalty on Servilius.

honest praetor, exercising his authority without appeal, were to appoint the members of the court as he chose, and a worthless and irresponsible court were to give the verdict that the praetor said must be given. And if in addition to this the praetor 31 states the issue in such a form of words that not even a man so well versed in the law and in his duty as (shall we say) Lucius Octavius Balbus could, as a member of the court, alter the issue in his verdict— if the directions to the court are of this type, *Case to come before Lucius Octavius* : *If it shall appear that Publius Servilius is the lawful owner by Roman law of the estate at Capena in question And if the said estate shall not be restored to Quintus Catulus, etc.,ᵃ* will not Octavius, as judge of the Court, have to compel Servilius to " restore " the estate to Catulus, or failing that have to inflict an unjustified penalty ? It was in this fashion, during the three years of Verres' praetorship, that the whole administration of justice was directed by the praetor and carried out by the courts. The orders made were of this type: *If he refuses to be satisfied with receiving what you state is all you owe him, you are authorized to prosecute him ; and if he sues you further, to have him arrested.* Gaius Fuficius, Lucius Suettius, Lucius Racilius were plaintiffs whose arrest he thus ordered. His courts were composed, if the parties were Sicilians, of Roman citizens, though the law of the country required the appointment of Sicilians ; and of Sicilians, if the parties were Roman citizens. But 32 that you may be able to grasp the whole bearings of his judicial methods, let me first tell you about the legal rights of Sicily, and then about this man's innovations.

XIII. Siculi hoc iure sunt ut quod civis cum cive agat domi certet suis legibus ; quod Siculus cum Siculo non eiusdem civitatis, ut de eo praetor iudices ex P. Rupilii decreto, quod is de decem legatorum sententia statuit, quam illi legem Rupiliam vocant, sortiatur. Quod privatus a populo petit aut populus a privato, senatus ex aliqua civitate qui iudicet datur, cum alternae civitates reiectae sunt. Quod civis Romanus a Siculo petit, Siculus iudex, quod Siculus a cive Romano, civis Romanus datur. Ceterarum rerum selecti iudices ex conventu civium Romanorum proponi solent. Inter aratores et decumanos lege frumentaria, quam Hieronicam appellant, iudicia fiunt.

33 Haec omnia isto praetore non modo perturbata sed plane et Siculis et civibus Romanis erepta sunt. Primum suae leges : quod civis cum civi ageret, aut eum iudicem quem commodum erat, praeconem, haruspicem, medicum suum dabat ; aut, si legibus erat iudicium constitutum et ad civem suum iudicem venerant, libere civi iudicare non licebat. Edictum enim hominis cognoscite, quo edicto omnia iudicia redegerat in suam potestatem : SI QUI PERPERAM

---

[a] Proconsular governor of Sicily in 131, when this legislative commission drew up this legal " constitution " for Sicily.

[b] More literally " after a city on each side has been rejected." The praetor, it would seem, nominated the city council. If either party objected to his choice, he made another nomination. If the other party objected to this one, he made a third, which both were bound to accept.

[c] A periodical meeting of Roman citizens within a given area, for mutual convenience and business : the word may also signify the persons or the area.

XIII. The legal rights of the Sicilians are as
follows. Cases between two citizens of the same
city should be tried in that city's courts and by that
city's laws. For cases between two Sicilians of
different cities, the praetor should appoint a court,
choosing its members by lot in accordance with the
statutes known in Sicily as the Rupilian law, which
were enacted by Publius Rupilius*a* on the recommendation of the Commission of Ten. When an
individual sues a community or a community an
individual, the Council of some city is appointed to
try the case, each party being entitled to challenge
one Council thus proposed.*b* A Sicilian is appointed
to try any case where a Sicilian is sued by a Roman
citizen, and a Roman citizen to try any case where
a Roman citizen is sued by a Sicilian. In all other
cases the regular procedure is to nominate the
court from a panel*c* of Roman citizens resident in the
district ; except that cases between corn-farmers
and collectors of tithe are tried as is directed by the
corn laws known as the laws of Hiero.

All these rights, throughout this man's term of 33
office, were not simply disturbed but taken clean
away from Sicilians and Roman citizens alike. To
begin with the local law of each city : in cases
between two citizens of the same city, Verres would
either have them tried before anyone it suited him
to appoint—some crier or soothsayer or doctor
among his own following, or else, if the court was
legally composed and the litigants did appear before
a fellow-citizen of their own, the latter was allowed
no freedom in deciding the case. Listen to this
proclamation that the man made, bringing every
court in the land into subjection to his own will : *I*

IUDICASSET, SE COGNITURUM ; CUM COGNOSSET, ANIM-
ADVERSURUM. Idque cum faciebat, nemo dubitabat
quin, cum iudex alium de suo iudicio putaret iudicaturum, seque in eo capitis periculum aditurum,
voluntatem spectaret eius quem statim de capite
34 suo putaret iudicaturum. Selecti ex conventu aut
propositi ex negotiatoribus iudices nulli. Haec copia
quam dico iudicum cohors, non Q. Scaevolae—qui
tamen de cohorte sua dare non solebat—sed C.
Verris. Cuius modi cohortem putatis hoc principe
fuisse ? Sic,[1] ubi videtis edictum SI QUID PERPERAM
IUDICARIT SENATUS, eum quoque ostendam, si quando
sit datus, coactu istius quod non senserit iudicasse.
Ex lege Rupilia sortitio nulla, nisi cum nihil intererat
istius ; lege Hieronica iudicia plurimarum contro-
versiarum sublata uno nomine omnia ; de conventu
ac negotiatoribus nulli iudices. Quantam potestatem habuerit videtis : quas res gesserit cognoscite.

35 XIV. Heraclius est, Hieronis filius, Syracusanus,
homo in primis domi suae nobilis, et ante hunc
praetorem vel pecuniosissimus Syracusanorum, nunc,
nulla alia calamitate nisi istius avaritia atque iniuria,

---

[1] sicuti MSS.: sicubi *Peterson*.

---

[a] Apparently temporary, as distinguished from permanent,
residents in the district.
[b] *i.e.*, instead of the usual illegal substitute.

*will bring to justice any man who shall give a dishonest
legal decision, and will punish him accordingly.* That
meant, as everyone saw clearly, that the judge in
any case must expect his judgement itself to be
judged in turn, which might well mean his loss of all
his own rights, and that he would therefore, with
this hanging over him, follow out the wishes of a
man whom he expected shortly to sit in judgement
upon him. No judges were ever nominated from **34**
the district panel, or from among the business men [a]
in the place. It was the staff that, as I say, supplied
the judges; and not the staff of a Scaevola—
though it was not Scaevola's custom, in any case,
to draw upon his staff for this purpose—but the
staff of Gaius Verres, the character of which may
readily be inferred from that of its chief. In the
same way, where you find the proclamation *If any
Council shall give any dishonest legal decision, etc.*, I
shall prove that any Council too that was actually
appointed[b] was forced by Verres into giving decisions
of which it did not approve. No judges chosen by lot
as the Rupilian law enjoins, except when that man
had nothing to lose by it; all the numerous trials
that should have occurred in accordance with the
laws of Hiero swept away by a single order; no
judges taken from the district panel or from among
the business men. You see the extent of Verres'
powers: let me now tell you what use he made of
them.

XIV. Heraclius of Syracuse, the son of Hiero, is a **35**
man who holds the highest rank among his own people
and in the days before Verres' praetorship was perhaps
the wealthiest man in Syracuse; though his sole
disaster has been to encounter this greedy tyrant,

pauperrimus. Huic hereditas ad HS facile triciens
venit testamento propinqui sui Heraclii, plena domus
caelati argenti optimi multaeque stragulae vestis
pretiosorumque mancipiorum, quibus in rebus istius
cupiditates et insanias quis ignorat ? Erat in sermone res, magnam Heraclio pecuniam relictam ; non
solum Heraclium divitem, sed etiam ornatum supel-
36 lectile, argento, veste, mancipiis futurum. Audit
haec etiam Verres, et primo illo suo leniore artificio
Heraclium aggredi conatur, ut eum roget inspicienda
quae non reddat. Deinde a quibusdam Syracusanis
admonetur—hi autem quidam erant affines istius,
quorum iste uxores numquam alienas existimavit,
Cleomenes et Aeschrio, qui quantum apud istum et
quam turpi de causa potuerint ex reliquis criminibus
intellegetis—hi, ut dico, hominem admonent rem
esse praeclaram, refertam omnibus rebus ; ipsum
autem Heraclium hominem esse maiorem natu, non
promptissimum ; eum praeter Marcellos patronum,
quem suo iure adire aut appellare posset, habere
neminem ; esse in eo testamento quo ille heres esset
scriptus ut statuas in palaestra deberet ponere.
"Faciemus ut palaestritae negent ex testamento
esse positas, petant hereditatem, quod eam palaestrae
37 commissam esse dicant." Placuit ratio Verri : nam
hoc animo providebat, cum tanta hereditas in contro-
versiam venisset iudicioque peteretur, fieri non posse

---

[a] *Alienas* has the double sense of "strangers" and
"belonging to other people."
[b] The patroni of all Syracusans since the city's capture.

to-day he is the poorest. By the will of a kinsman of
his own name, he received a legacy amounting to a
clear £30,000 and including a house fully furnished
with fine engraved silver plate, with an abundance of
tapestries, and with valuable slaves ; and which of us
does not know this man's crazy passion for such things
as those ? It was common talk that Heraclius had
had a large sum left to him ; that he would be not only
wealthy, but richly supplied with furniture, plate,
woven fabrics and slaves. Verres too heard of this, 36
and made his first attack on Heraclius by his well-
known but comparatively mild method of asking him
for the loan of things to look at, with no intention of
returning them. It was then suggested to him by
certain citizens of Syracuse, Cleomenes and Aeschrio
—they were connected with him through their wives,
whom he always considered as quite his own[a]; and the
extent and disgraceful source of their influence with
him will appear plainly in connexion with other
charges—these persons, I say, pointed out to him that
the property was a very noble one, richly stocked with
all manner of good things; that Heraclius himself was
elderly and not very energetic ; that apart from the
Marcelli[b] he had no special protector whom he could
approach or call to his help ; and that in the will
leaving him the property there was a clause requiring
him to erect certain statues in the athletic park.
" Let us make the curators of the park declare that
the statues have not been erected in accordance with
the will, and let them claim the estate as being
forfeited to the park." The scheme pleased Verres : 37
he foresaw that, once the ownership of a great estate
like that became matter of dispute and a claim was
brought for its recovery, there was no doubt of his

ut sine praeda ipse discederet. Approbat consilium ;
auctor est ut quam primum agere incipiant, homi-
nemque id aetatis minime litigiosum quam tumul-
tuosissime adoriantur. Scribitur Heraclio dica. XV.
Primo mirantur omnes improbitatem calumniae :
deinde qui istum nossent partim suspicabantur, partim
plane videbant, adiectum esse oculum hereditati. Interea dies advenit quo die sese ex instituto ac lege Rupilia dicas sortiturum Syracusis iste edixerat. Paratus
ad hanc dicam sortiendam venerat ; tum eum docet
Heraclius non posse eo die sortiri, quod lex Rupilia
vetaret diebus xxx. sortiri dicam quibus scripta esset ;
dies xxx. nondum fuerant. Sperabat Heraclius, si
illum diem effugisset, ante alteram sortitionem Q.
Arrium, quem provincia tum maxime exspectabat,
38 successurum. Iste omnibus dicis diem distulit, et
eam diem constituit ut hanc Heraclii dicam sortiri
post dies xxx. ex lege posset. Posteaquam ea dies
venit, iste incipit simulare se velle sortiri. Heraclius
cum advocatis adit et postulat ut sibi cum palaestritis, hoc est cum populo Syracusano, aequo iure
disceptare liceat. Adversarii postulant ut in eam

---

[a] Lit. " would draw cases by lot," *i.e.* would select juries
by lot for the respective cases.
[b] *Sortiri* implies the procedure which Heraclius demands,
and which, as appears from the sequel, Verres from the
first intended not to employ.

securing some plunder by the time all was over. He approved the plan; he proposed their setting to work without delay, and launching the most violent attack possible against the by no means litigious old gentleman. Heraclius was formally sued. XV. At first there was general astonishment at the wickedness of the false claim; then those who knew Verres began either to suspect or to see distinctly that he had cast his eyes on the estate. Meanwhile the day drew near on which he had announced that he would proceed to the hearing of cases*a* at Syracuse, in accordance with the established practice of the Rupilian law. He had arrived in court ready to begin the hearing of this case, when Heraclius represented to him that the hearing could not begin that day, because the Rupilian law forbade the hearing of cases to begin within thirty days from the institution of the suit; and thirty days had not yet elapsed. Heraclius hoped that, if he could only escape that day, Quintus Arrius, for whom the province was then waiting eagerly, would succeed Verres before the case could come on again. Verres postponed the day for beginning the 38 whole session, and fixed a date late enough for him to begin the hearing of this suit against Heraclius after the legal thirty days had elapsed. When that day had arrived, he began a pretence of being willing to open it in the regular way.*b* Heraclius came forward with his supporters, and requested permission to plead his case against the curators—in effect, against the civic body of Syracuse—as citizen versus citizens.*c* His opponents requested that judges for this case should

c i.e., before a court chosen (*a*) by lot, (*b*) from among his fellow-citizens only.

rem iudices dentur, ex iis civitatibus quae in id forum
convenirent electi, qui Verri viderentur : Heraclius
contra, ut iudices e lege Rupilia dentur, ut ab institutis superiorum, ab auctoritate senatus, ab iure
39 omnium Siculorum ne recedatur. XVI. Quid ego
istius in iure dicundo libidinem et scelera demonstrem?
quis vestrum non ex urbana iuris dictione cognovit ?
quis umquam isto praetore Chelidone invita lege
agere potuit ? Non istum, ut non neminem, provincia corrupit : idem fuit qui Romae. Cum id
quod omnes intellegebant diceret Heraclius, ius
esse certum Siculis inter se quo iure certarent, legem
esse Rupiliam quam P. Rupilius consul de decem
legatorum sententia dedisset, hanc omnes semper
in Sicilia consules praetoresque servasse : negavit
se iudices e lege Rupilia sortiturum, quinque iudices,
quos commodum ipsi fuit, dedit.

40   Quid hoc homine facias ? quod supplicium dignum
libidine eius invenias ? Praescriptum tibi cum esset,
homo deterrime et impudentissime, quem ad modum
iudices inter Siculos dares ; cum imperatoris populi
Romani auctoritas, legatorum decem, summorum
hominum, dignitas, senatus consultum intercederet,
cuius consulto P. Rupilius de x. legatorum sententia
leges in Sicilia constituerat ; cum omnes ante te

be selected, at the discretion of Verres, from all the cities belonging to that assize district. Heraclius urged in reply that the judges should be appointed as directed by the Rupilian law ; that there should be no departure from the procedure, established by precedent and sanctioned by the Senate, to which all Sicilians alike were entitled. XVI. Need I give you 39 any proof of the criminal way in which this man administers the law as he chooses ? Did you not all see how he administered it in Rome ? Was the proper legal procedure available at any time for anyone during his term of office, if Chelidon willed otherwise ? Unlike some others, Verres was not morally ruined by his province—he was there what he had been in Rome. When Heraclius pleaded what all knew to be true, that Sicilians had fixed rights in their legal actions against one another ; that the Rupilian law was in existence, instituted by the consul Publius Rupilius on the recommendation of the Commission of Ten ; and that all consuls and all praetors in Sicily had maintained this law always : Verres thereupon announced that he would not cast lots as the Rupilian law directed, and appointed to try the case the five persons who suited him best.

How shall such a man be dealt with ? What fit 40 punishment can be found for behaviour so outrageous ? You barefaced ruffian ! When you found˙laid down for you the method of appointing courts for purely Sicilian cases ; when any other method was forbidden by the sanction of the chief magistrate of Rome, by the high authority of those ten eminent Commissioners, by that decree of the Senate instructing Rupilius to enact laws for Sicily in accord with the Commissioners' report ; when all your predecessors had strictly main-

praetorem Rupilias leges et in ceteris rebus et in
iudiciis maxime servassent : tu ausus es pro nihilo
prae tua praeda tot res sanctissimas ducere ? tibi
nulla lex fuit, nulla religio, nullus existimationis
pudor, nullus iudicii metus ? nullius apud te gravis
auctoritas, nullum exemplum quod sequi velles ?

41   Verum, ut institui dicere, quinque iudicibus nulla
lege, nullo instituto, nulla reiectione, nulla sorte, ex
libidine istius datis, non qui causam cognoscerent,
sed qui quod imperatum esset iudicarent, eo die
nihil actum est, adesse iubentur postridie. XVII.
Heraclius interea, cum omnes insidias fortunis suis
a praetore fieri videret, capit consilium de amicorum
et propinquorum sententia non adesse ad iudicium.
Itaque illa nocte Syracusis profugit. Iste postridie
mane, cum multo maturius quam umquam antea
surrexisset, iudices citari iubet. Ubi comperit
Heraclium non adesse, cogere incipit eos ut absentem
Heraclium condemnent. Illi eum commonefaciunt
ut, si sibi videatur, utatur instituto suo, nec cogat ante
horam decimam de absente secundum praesentem
42 iudicare ; impetrant. Interea sane perturbatus et
ipse et eius amici et consiliarii moleste ferre coeperunt Heraclium profugisse ; putabant absentis
damnationem, praesertim tantae pecuniae, multo
invidiosiorem fore quam si praesens damnatus esset.

tained the Rupilian statutes, and most strictly of all those that relate to judicial procedure : then could you dare to let all these solemn facts count for nothing when balanced against the prospect of plunder for yourself ? Could law and conscience, sense of shame and fear of judgement, be so utterly banished from your mind ? Could you let no man's opinion weigh with you, no man's actions make you follow his example ?

But to resume my narrative : defying the law and 41 the constitution, allowing no challenges and drawing no lots, he appointed these five judges, choosing the men he wanted, not to investigate the facts, but to give the verdict he bade them give. That day nothing was done ; they were summoned for the day following. XVII. Heraclius meanwhile, seeing that every sort of treacherous device to undo him was being employed by the chief magistrate, took the advice of his friends and kinsmen, and resolved not to appear in court. That night, accordingly, he fled from Syracuse. The following morning Verres rose much earlier than he had ever risen before, and ordered the court to be summoned. On learning that Heraclius was not present, he proceeded to direct the judges to find against the defendant by default. They requested him to be good enough to follow his own regular practice, and to wait till four o'clock before directing a judgement by default in favour of the party present ; and this he allowed. In the 42 interval he was a good deal upset, both he and his friends and counsellors beginning to feel troubled because of Heraclius's flight. They felt that a judgement against him by default, especially with so large a sum involved, would cause far more ill-feeling than if he had been present when the judgement was given.

Eo accedebat quod iudices e lege Rupilia dati non erant ; multo etiam rem turpiorem fore et iniquiorem visum iri intellegebant. Itaque hoc dum corrigere vult, apertior eius cupiditas improbitasque facta est. Nam illis quinque iudicibus uti sese negat ; iubet, id quod initio lege Rupilia fieri oportuerat, citari Heraclium et eos qui dicam scripserant ; ait se iudices ex lege velle sortiri. Quod ab eo pridie, cum multis lacrimis cum oraret atque obsecraret, Heraclius impetrare non potuerat, id ei postridie venit in mentem, ex lege Rupilia sortiri dicas oportere. Educit ex urna tres ; his ut absentem Heraclium condemnent imperat ; itaque condemnant.

43   Quae, malum, ista fuit amentia ! Ecquando te rationem factorum tuorum redditurum putasti ? ecquando his de rebus tales viros audituros existimasti ? Petatur hereditas ea, quae nulla debetur, in praedam praetoris ? interponatur nomen civitatis ? imponatur honestae civitati turpissima persona calumniae ? neque hoc solum, sed ita res agatur ut ne simulatio quidem aequitatis ulla adhibeatur ? Nam, per deos immortales, quid interest utrum praetor imperet vique cogat aliquem de suis bonis omnibus decedere, an huiusce modi iudicium det, quo iudicio

There was the further fact that the court had not been appointed as required by the Rupilian law, which they saw would make the affair much more discreditable and increase its appearance of unfairness. So he tried to put this straight, and the result was a still clearer revelation of his greed and wickedness. He now declared that he would not employ the five judges already mentioned; he gave orders for what ought, by the Rupilian law, to have been done at the outset, the summoning of Heraclius and those who were bringing the action; and he said that he was prepared to appoint the court by lot as the law directed. What all the tears and prayers and entreaties of Heraclius had not been able to extract from him the day before, now on the following day occurred to him—that it was his duty to appoint courts in accordance with the Rupilian law. He drew three names out of the urn; he ordered these persons to find against Heraclius by default; and they found against him accordingly.

O you knave, O you fool! Did you never look to **43** be called to account for your actions? Did you never expect that this honourable Court would hear this story told? Shall an estate be claimed from its lawful owner to become the prey of a governor? Shall the name of a city be dragged in, and an honoured community be forced to play the foul part of a dishonest claimant? And not only this, but shall the affair be so conducted that not even the pretence of justice is brought into it anywhere? For what difference does it make, in heaven's name, whether the governor orders and forcibly compels a man to hand over his whole property, or so organizes the legal proceedings against him that thereby,

indicta causa fortunis omnibus everti necesse sit?

44 XVIII. Profecto enim negare non potes te ex lege Rupilia sortiri iudices debuisse, cum praesertim Heraclius id postularet. Sin illud dices, te Heraclii voluntate ab lege recessisse, ipse te impedies, ipse tua defensione implicabere. Quare enim primum ille adesse noluit, cum ex eo numero iudices haberet quos postularat? deinde tu cur post illius fugam iudices alios sortitus es, si eos qui erant antea dati utriusque dederas voluntate? Deinde ceteras dicas omnes illo foro M. Postumius quaestor sortitus est; hanc solam tu illo conventu reperiere sortitus.

45   Ergo, inquiet aliquis, donavit populo Syracusano illam hereditatem. Primum, si id confiteri velim, tamen istum condemnetis necesse est; neque enim permissum est ut impune nobis liceat, quod alicui eripuerimus, id alteri tradere. Verum ex ista reperietis hereditate ita istum praedatum ut perpauca occulte fecerit; populum Syracusanum in maximam invidiam sua infamia, alieno praemio pervenisse; paucos Syracusanos, eos qui nunc se publice laudationis causa venisse dicunt, et tunc participes praedae fuisse et nunc non ad istius laudationem, sed ad communem litium aestimationem venisse. Posteaquam

the man's case unheard, he is stripped of all he
possesses ?   XVIII. Most certainly you cannot deny 44
that your duty was to appoint the court as the
Rupilian law enjoins ;   all the more so because
Heraclius applied for this to be done.   And if you
allege that you broke the law with his consent, you
will be blocking your own path, and entangling
yourself in your own defences.   For why, in the first
place, did Heraclius refuse to appear, if he had
judges from the class for which he applied ?   And
why did you in the next place appoint fresh judges
by lot after his flight, if those appointed before
were appointed with his approval as well as yours ?
And note further that all the other cases in that
district were tried by Marcus Postumius the
quaestor ;   this, it will be found, is the only case in
those assizes which you tried yourself.

Well, well, someone may tell me, he gave the 45
estate to the citizens of Syracuse.   Now to begin
with, even were I willing to allow this to be true,
you must declare the man guilty in spite of it, for
we are not given free leave to rob one man of a
thing and give it to another.   But you will in fact
find little concealment about the way in which he
plundered that estate ;   you will find that the
citizens of Syracuse have made themselves thoroughly
disliked, taking only the discredit while the profits
went elsewhere ;   and that a few individual Syracusans, being the persons who now tell us they are
here officially to testify to the man's merits, shared
in the plunder then, and have come here now, not to
testify to his merits, but to find themselves assessed
along with him for their share of the compensation
to be paid.   After judgement had been given

damnatus est absens, non solum illius hereditatis de
qua ambigebatur, quae erat HS triciens, sed omnium
bonorum paternorum ipsius Heraclii, quae non minor
erat pecunia, palaestrae Syracusanorum, hoc est
46 Syracusanis, possessio traditur. Quae est ista praetura ? Eripis hereditatem quae venerat a propinquo, venerat testamento, venerat legibus ; quae
bona is qui testamentum fecit huic Heraclio, aliquanto ante quam est mortuus, omnia utenda ac
possidenda tradiderat ; cuius hereditatis, cum ille
aliquanto ante te praetorem esset mortuus, controversia fuerat nulla, mentionem fecerat nemo. XIX.
Verum esto : eripe hereditatem propinquis, da
palaestritis, praedare in bonis alienis nomine civitatis,
everte leges, testamenta, voluntates mortuorum,
iura vivorum : num etiam patriis Heraclium bonis
exturbare oportuit ? Qui simul ac profugit, quam
impudenter, quam palam, quam acerbe, di immortales,
illa bona direpta sunt ! quam illa res calamitosa
Heraclio, quaestuosa Verri, turpis Syracusanis,
miseranda omnibus videbatur ! Nam illud quidem
statim curatur, ut quicquid caelati argenti fuit in
illis bonis ad istum deferatur, quicquid Corinthiorum
vasorum, stragulae vestis ; haec nemo dubitabat
quin non modo ex illa domo capta et oppressa, verum

against Heraclius by default, the park of Syracuse—
in other words, the people of Syracuse—received
possession not only of the estate in question, his
inherited estate, worth £30,000, but also of the
whole of his own family property, which was worth
at least as much more. There is the way to govern 46
a country ! You rob the man of an estate that had
been left to him by a relative, left to him by will,
left to him legally ; a property which Heraclius, the
maker of the will, some time before his death, had
conveyed complete to this Heraclius for his enjoyment and possession ; an inheritance concerning
which, though the testator had died long before you
came into office, no dispute whatsoever had occurred,
no suggestion of such a thing had been made by
anyone. XIX. But never mind that. Rob the
next-of-kin of the legacy, present it to the curators
of the park ; pounce upon another man's property
in the name of his fellow-citizens ; overthrow the
sanctions of law and the rights of bequest, the
wishes of the dead and the just claims of the living,
if you will : but must you also force Heraclius to
give up all that his own father left him ? No sooner
had he fled than it was all carried off ; and, God
help us, with what shameless publicity and cruelty !
What a picture ! Heraclius groaning under his
calamity, Verres gloating over his profits, the
Syracusans blushing with shame, men's hearts
everywhere filled with distress ! For one thing
was promptly seen to—the conveyance to Verres of
all the family engraved silver plate and Corinthian
brass and tapestries ; and no one could doubt that
such things would have to be gathered and brought
to him not only from that one captured and de-

ex tota provincia, ad istum comportari necesse esset. Mancipia quae voluit abduxit, alia divisit ; auctio facta est, in qua cohors istius invicta dominata est.
47 Verum illud est praeclarum. Syracusani qui praefuerant his Heraclii bonis verbo redigendis, re dispertiendis, reddebant eorum negotiorum rationem in senatu. Dicebant scyphorum paria complura, hydrias argenteas pretiosas, vestem stragulam multam, mancipia pretiosa data esse Verri. Dicebant quantum cuique eius iussu nummorum esset datum ; gemebant Syracusani, sed tamen patiebantur. Repente recitatur uno nomine HS ccc. iussu praetoris data. Fit maximus clamor omnium, non modo optimi cuiusque, neque eorum quibus indignum semper visum erat bona privati populi nomine per summam iniuriam erepta ; verum etiam ipsi illi auctores iniuriae et ex aliqua particula socii praedae ac rapinarum clamare coeperunt sibi ut haberet hereditatem. Tantus in curia clamor factus est ut
48 populus concurreret. XX. Res ab omni conventu cognita celeriter isti domum nuntiatur. Homo inimicus iis qui recitassent, hostis omnibus qui acclamassent, exarsit iracundia ac stomacho. Verum tamen fuit tum sui dissimilis. Nostis os hominis,

---

[a] The auction was a pretext for further appropriations by Verres. His staff, who would not have to pay, could always outbid genuine purchasers.

[b] As bribes to Verres' followers : these, and the presents (nominal or real) to Verres himself, are a condition of the town's being allowed to have the rest of the estate.

vastated house but from the length and breadth of
the province. He carried off such of the slaves as he
fancied, and sold the others in lots ; an auction
took place, at which his unconquerable followers
had everything at their mercy.[a] One incident
is truly impressive. The Syracusans who were in **47**
charge of this business of nominally selling and
really giving away this property of Heraclius submitted a report upon it to their Senate. They
stated that several pairs of goblets, some costly
silver jugs, a large quantity of fabrics, and some
valuable slaves, had been presented to Verres.
They stated the sums of money paid [b] by his orders
to various persons : groans were heard from the
citizens at this, but no protest was made. Suddenly
there was read out the single item of a payment of
£3000 made by the praetor's orders. This provoked
a loud and general uproar, and not only from all the
honest people, or those who had all the while felt
it to be horrible that a private person should with
such flagrant injustice be robbed of his property in
the name of the community : even the men who had
actually supported the outrage, and who to some
small extent had shared in the looting and plundering, began to call out, " Let him keep the estate for
himself." The uproar in the Senate-house was so
violent that a crowd of the townsfolk was attracted.
XX. The news spread through the district, and word **48**
of it was quickly brought to Verres' house   Filled
with personal spite against those who made the
report, and general hostility towards all who had
joined in the uproar, the fellow boiled over with
furious indignation. Nevertheless, he did not on
that occasion behave like his usual self. You know

nostis audaciam ; tamen tum rumore populi et
clamore et manifesto furto grandis pecuniae perturbatus est. Ubi se collegit, vocat ad se Syracusanos ; qui non posset negare ab illis pecuniam datam,
non quaesivit procul alicunde (neque enim probaret),
sed proximum, paene alterum filium, quem illam
pecuniam diceret abstulisse ; ostendit se reddere
coacturum. Qui posteaquam id audivit, habuit et
dignitatis et aetatis et nobilitatis suae rationem ;
verba apud senatum fecit, docuit ad se nihil pertinere,
de isto id quod omnes videbant neque ille quidem
obscure locutus est. Itaque illi Syracusani statuam
postea statuerunt ; et is, ut primum potuit, istum
49 reliquit de provinciaque decessit. Et tamen aiunt
eum queri solere non numquam se miserum quod
non suis, sed suorum, peccatis criminibusque prematur.
Triennium provinciam obtinuisti ; gener, lectus
adulescens, unum annum tecum fuit ; sodales, viri
fortes, legati tui primo anno te reliquerunt ; unus
legatus P. Tadius qui erat reliquus non ita multum
tecum fuit ; qui si semper una fuisset, tamen summa
cura cum tuae, tum multo etiam magis suae famae
pepercisset. Quid est quod tu alios accuses ? quid
est quam ob rem putes te tuam culpam non modo
derivare in aliquem sed communicare cum altero
50 posse ? Numerantur illa HS ccc. Syracusanis. Ea

---

[a] His son-in-law, not otherwise known.

his impudence ; you know his audacity : but he was
now thoroughly alarmed by the public talk and
clamour and the revelation of his theft of that huge
sum of money. Pulling himself together, he called
a meeting of the citizens. Unable to deny their
having paid that money, he did not look far afield,
since no one would have believed him, but fixed on
his nearest connexion,ᵃ almost a second son of his,
to accuse of appropriating the amount, and declared
that he would force him to pay it back. The other,
on hearing this, behaved as became his rank, age, and
birth. He made a speech in the Senate, showing
that he was clear of the business, and himself referred
not obscurely to what everyone knew to be the
truth about Verres. The Syracusans, owing to this,
later set up a statue in his honour ; and as soon as
he could he abandoned Verres and left the province.
And yet they tell us that Verres used now and then **49**
to complain of his ill-luck in suffering from misdeeds
and charges that concerned not him but those who
belonged to him !—You ruled Sicily for three years ;
and your excellent young son-in-law was there with
you for one year ; intimate friends, gentlemen of
honour, even your assistant-governors deserted you
in your first year ; Publius Tadius, the one assistant-
governor who did stay behind, spent comparatively
little time in your company, and if he had spent
all his time there would have taken great care not
to injure your reputation, and still more not to
injure his own. What ground have you for accusing
others ? What reason have you for believing that
you can transfer the blame of your offences to
someone else, or even share it with any second
person ? That £3000 was refunded to the Syra- **50**

quem ad modum ad istum postea per pseudothyrum revertantur tabulis vobis testibusque, iudices, planum faciam

XXI. Ex hac iniquitate istius et improbitate, iudices, quod praeda ex illis bonis ad multos Syracusanos invito populo senatuque Syracusano venerat, illa scelera per Theomnastum et Aeschrionem et Dionysodorum et Cleomenem invitissima civitate illa facta sunt : primum ut urbs tota spoliaretur, qua de re alius mihi locus ad dicendum est constitutus ; ut omnia signa iste per eos homines quos nominavi, omne ebur ex aedibus sacris, omnes undique tabulas pictas, deorum denique simulacra quae vellet auferret : deinde ut in curia Syracusis, quem locum illi βουλευτήριον nomine appellant, honestissimo loco et apud illos clarissimo, ubi illius ipsius M. Marcelli, qui eum Syracusanis locum, quem eripere belli ac victoriae lege posset, conservavit ac reddidit, statua ex aere facta est, ibi inauratam istius et alteram filio statuam ponerent, ut, dum istius hominis memoria maneret, senatus Syracusanus sine lacrimis et gemitu in curia 51 esse non posset. Per eosdem istius furtorum iniuriarum uxorumque socios istius imperio Syracusis Marcellia tolluntur, maximo gemitu luctuque civitatis ; quem illi diem festum cum recentibus beneficiis

---

a Or perhaps " led to."

b Theomnastus and his fellows : or perhaps the citizen body, under compulsion.

c See note on § 8.

cusans : how it subsequently came back to Verres by a back door I will show you, gentlemen, by means of documentary and personal evidence.

XXI. This piece of wicked injustice, gentlemen— this bestowal of that plundered property on a number of Syracusan individuals against the wishes of the Syracusan Senate and people—is well matched by [a] the crimes committed through Theomnastus and Aeschrio, Dionysodorus and Cleomenes, crimes which Syracuse resented bitterly. To begin with, as I intend to tell you in another part of my speech, the whole city was stripped of its treasures ; with the help of the persons whom I have named, he carried off from the temples in the city every statue, every ivory carving, every painting, and every sacred image on which he chose to lay his hands. And then, what happened in the Senate-house at Syracuse — the *bouleuterion,* as they call it there ? A revered spot, full of glorious memories for them ; a place where stands the bronze statue of the great Marcus Marcellus himself, the man who might, by the custom of war and conquest, have taken the place away from them, but instead of that protected and restored it. In that place they [b] erected a gilded statue of Verres, and another in honour of his son, that, so long as their memory of the man lasted, the senators of Syracuse might be unable to sit in their Senate-house without tears and groans. With the help of these same men, who shared with him thefts, outrages, and wives, and by his orders, the Marcellus Festival was suppressed at Syracuse, to the grief and distress of the whole community. This festival was being partly kept as an acknowledgement of the recent favours shown them by Gaius Marcellus,[c]

51

C. Marcelli debitum reddebant, tum generi, nomini, familiae Marcellorum maxima voluntate tribuebant. Mithridates in Asia, cum eam provinciam totam occupasset, Mucia non sustulit; hostis, et hostis in ceteris rebus nimis ferus et immanis, tamen honorem hominis deorum religione consecratum violare noluit. Tu Syracusanos unum diem festum Marcellis impertire noluisti, per quos illi adepti sunt ut ceteros

52 dies festos agitare possent. At vero praeclarum diem illis reposuisti Verria ut agerent, et ut ad eum diem quae sacris epulisque opus essent in complures annos locarentur. Iam in tanta istius impudentia remittendum aliquid videtur, ne omnia contendamus, ne omnia cum dolore agere videamur. Nam me dies, vox, latera deficiant si hoc nunc vociferari velim, quam miserum indignumque sit istius nomine apud eos diem festum esse qui se istius opera funditus exstinctos esse arbitrentur. O Verria praeclara! quo accessisti, quaeso, quo non attuleris tecum istum diem! Etenim quam tu domum, quam urbem adiisti, quod fanum denique, quod non eversum atque extersum reliqueris? Quare appellentur sane ista Verria, quae non ex nomine sed ex manibus naturaque tua constituta esse videantur.

53 XXII. Quam facile serpat iniuria et peccandi consuetudo, quam non facile reprimatur, videte, iudices.

---

[a] With allusion to *verrere* = " to sweep " (*cf.* §§ 18, 19): " the Spring Cleaning Festival."

and partly offered as a cordial tribute of respect
to the great Marcellus family as a whole. When
Mithridates overran Asia from end to end, he did not
suppress the Scaevola Festival; though he was our
enemy, and in all but this a most savage and inhuman
enemy, yet upon that memorial of human greatness,
hallowed by the sanctions of religion, he would lay
no hand. And then would such a man as you not let
the Syracusans offer a single day of festival to the
Marcelli, to whom alone they owe it that they have
been able to keep all their other festivals? Ah 52
yes, and truly glorious is the Verres Festival you
have given them to keep instead! What a day for
which to make contracts, years in advance, for
supplying the materials of its ceremonies and
banquets! Well, in dealing with impudence so
colossal, I feel that I must calm myself a little; the
strain must sometimes be relieved; indignation
must sometimes be imagined not to inspire my
words. The truth is that time, voice, and lung-power
would fail me, were I to seek now to express in
speech the pitiful shamefulness of this festival, kept
in Verres' honour by people who believe Verres
responsible for the utter ruin that has engulfed
them. Ha, the Verres Festival—splendid! Where,
I would know, have you ever gone without bringing
your feast-day along with you? What house or
town or sanctuary did you ever visit without verily
straining and draining it dry? Oh, by all means let
your festival be called the Verria *a*: we can see
that it was established to celebrate not your name
but your greedy hands and grasping character.

XXII. Now mark, gentlemen, how easily injustice 53
spreads, how hard it is to check the habit of doing

Bidis oppidum est tenue sane non longe a Syracusis.
Hic longe primus civitatis est Epicrates quidam.
Huic hereditas HS quingentorum milium venerat a
muliere quadam propinqua, atque ita propinqua ut
ea etiamsi intestata esset mortua Epicratem Bidi-
norum legibus heredem esse oporteret. Recens erat
illa res quam ante demonstravi de Heraclio Syracusano, qui bona non perdidisset nisi ei venisset hereditas. Huic quoque Epicrati venerat, ut dixi, hereditas.
54 Cogitare coeperunt eius inimici nihilo minus eodem
praetore hunc everti bonis posse quo Heraclius esset
eversus. Rem occulte instituunt, ad Verrem per eius
interpretes deferunt. Ita causa componitur ut item
palaestritae Bidenses peterent ab Epicrate hereditatem, quem ad modum palaestritae Syracusani ab
Heraclio petivissent. Numquam vos praetorem tam
palaestricum vidistis; verum ita palaestritas defendebat ut ab illis ipse unctior abiret.ᵃ Qui statim, quod
praesens esset, iubet cuidam amicorum suorum nu-
55 merari HS lxxx. Res occultari satis non potuit; per
quendam eorum qui interfuerant fit Epicrates certior.
Primo neglegere et contemnere coepit, quod causa
prorsus quod disputari posset nihil habebat. Deinde
cum de Heraclio cogitaret et istius libidinem nosset,
commodissimum putavit esse de provincia clam abire;
itaque fecit, profectus est Regium. XXIII. Quod
ubi auditum est, aestuare illi qui pecuniam dederant,

ᵃ Lit. " he would come away from them more anointed
(*i.e.* richer) than before "; alluding to the oiling practised
by athletes.

wrong. Bidis is a quite small town not far from
Syracuse. Much its most important citizen is a
certain Epicrates. This man inherited £5000 from a
female relative; so near a relative that, even had she
died intestate, Epicrates would by the laws of Bidis
have been her heir. It was not long after the affair,
already described to you, of Heraclius the Syracusan,
who was ruined simply by having a legacy left him.
This man Epicrates also, as I have said, had a legacy
left him. His enemies began to reflect that the 54
praetor under whom Heraclius had been ejected from
his property was still in office, and that it was equally
possible to eject Epicrates from his. Setting
secretly to work, they sent word of the business to
Verres through his agents. A lawsuit was concocted
in which the claimants were again curators of an
athletic park; those of Bidis were to claim the
legacy of Epicrates just as those of Syracuse had
claimed that of Heraclius. Never have you come
across a praetor so devoted to athletics; though his
patronage of these curators would usually, to be sure,
end in a financial success *a* for himself. He promptly
demanded a cash payment in advance of £800 to one
of his friends. The secret could not be kept properly, 55
and Epicrates received information through one of
the persons concerned. At first he was disposed not
to do anything about the matter or take it seriously,
his case being so overwhelmingly strong. Presently
he remembered Heraclius, and seeing what an unprincipled rascal Verres was, concluded that his best
plan was to leave the province secretly; he did so
accordingly, and went off to Regium. XXIII. This
becoming known, those who had paid the money were
much upset, believing that the action must drop if

putare nihil agi posse absente Epicrate. Nam
Heraclius tamen adfuerat, cum primo sunt dati
iudices : de hoc qui antequam aditum in ius esset,
antequam mentio denique controversiae facta esset
ulla, discessisset, putabant nihil agi posse. Homines
Regium proficiscuntur, Epicratem conveniunt; demon-
strant id quod ille sciebat, se HS LXXX. dedisse ; rogant
eum ut sibi id quod ab ipsis abisset pecuniae curet, ab
sese caveat, quemadmodum velit, de illa hereditate
56 cum Epicrate neminem esse acturum. Epicrates
homines multis verbis ab se male acceptos dimittit.
Redeunt illi Regio Syracusas ; queri cum multis, ut
fit, incipiunt se HS LXXX. nummum frustra dedisse.
Res percrebruit et in ore atque sermone omnium
coepit esse. Verres refert illam suam Syracusanam ;
ait se velle de illis HS LXXX. cognoscere ; advocat
multos. Dicunt Bidini Volcatio se dedisse ; illud non
addunt, iussu istius. Volcatium vocat, pecuniam
referri imperat. Volcatius animo aequissimo nummos affert, qui nihil amitteret, reddit inspectantibus
57 multis : Bidini nummos auferunt. Dicet aliquis,
Quid ergo in hoc Verrem reprehendis, qui non modo
ipse fur non est, sed ne alium quidem passus est esse ?
Attendite ; iam intellegetis hanc pecuniam, quae via
modo visa est exire ab isto, eam[1] semita revertisse.

---

[1] eadem *most MSS.*: eodem *Peterson*: eam *Mueller with
one good MS.*

Epicrates did not appear; for Heraclius had at least been in court when the judges in his case were first appointed; whereas Epicrates had gone off before the suit was instituted, in fact before anything about a counterclaim had been said, and so they believed that the action could not go forward. They set sail for Regium, and there saw Epicrates; they told him what he already knew, that they had paid over £800; they suggested that he should make good to them the sum they had themselves parted with, and take security from them, in whatever form he preferred, that no one should bring an action against him in connexion with the legacy. Epicrates made them a long 56 and angry reply, and turned them away. They went back from Regium to Syracuse, and began to bewail, in the hearing of a number of persons, as people will do, that they had paid away £800 for nothing. The story got about, and began to be mentioned and discussed everywhere. Verres revived his performance at Syracuse, said that he proposed to investigate this story of the £800, and summoned a number of persons to attend. The men from Bidis declared they had paid Volcatius the money—not adding "by Verres' orders." Verres sent for Volcatius and ordered repayment to be made. Volcatius, who was losing nothing by this, brought along the money very contentedly and repaid it before numerous witnesses; and the men from Bidis went off with it. "Well," 57 someone will say, "what fault have you to find with Verres here, where he has not only been no thief himself, but has even prevented theft by another man?" Wait; you will shortly be made aware that the money you have just seen escape him along the high road returned to him by a back lane. For what

355

Quid enim debuit praetor facere, cum consilio re
cognita cum comperisset suum comitem iuris, decreti,
iudicii corrumpendi causa—qua in re ipsius praetoris
caput existimatioque ageretur—pecuniam accepisse,
Bidinos autem pecuniam contra praetoris famam ac
fortunas dedisse ? non et in eum qui accepisset
animadvertisset, et in eos qui dedissent ? Tu qui
institueras in eos animadvertere qui perperam
iudicassent, quod saepe per imprudentiam fit, hos
pateris impune discedere qui ob tuum decretum, ob
tuum iudicium pecuniam aut dandam aut accipiendam
58 putarant ? XXIV. Volcatius idem apud te postea
fuit, eques Romanus, tanta accepta ignominia ; nam
quid est turpius ingenuo, quid minus libero dignum,
quam in conventu maximo cogi a magistratu furtum
reddere ? Qui si eo animo esset quo non modo eques
Romanus sed quivis liber debet esse, aspicere te
postea non potuisset ; inimicus, hostis esset tanta
contumelia accepta, nisi tecum tum collusisset et tuae
potius existimationi servisset quam suae. Qui quam
tibi amicus non modo tum fuerit quam diu tecum in
provincia fuit, verum etiam nunc sit cum iam a ceteris
amicis relictus es, et tu intellegis et nos existimare
possumus. An hoc solum argumentum est nihil isto
imprudente factum, quod Volcatius ei non succensuit ?
quod iste neque in Volcatium neque in Bidinos anim-
59 advertit ? Est magnum argumentum ; verum illud

356

was he bound to do as praetor, when he found, after investigation in court, that a member of his own staff had been bribed to secure an unjust verdict in a lawsuit—a thing that might mean the praetor's own disfranchisement and disgrace—and that the people of Bidis by giving the bribe had imperilled the praetor's representation and fortunes? Would he not have punished both the man who took the bribe and the men who gave it? You announced your intention of punishing those who should make improper awards, a thing often done inadvertently; do you let persons escape unpunished who have been capable of either giving or accepting bribes to upset your own ordinances and your own decisions? XXIV. Vol- 58 catius kept his position with you just as before, in spite of the shameful humiliation of his honour as a knight of Rome—for what can be more shameful for a gentleman, what more degrading for a free man, than to be forced by a magistrate to restore stolen goods before the eyes of a large audience? Had he had the feelings of a knight, nay, those of the humblest free man, he could not, after such treatment, have looked you in the face; he must have hated you, privately and publicly, for inflicting such disgrace upon him, had he not been your accomplice at the time and worked to uphold your honour more than his own. How close a friend of yours he has continued, not only as long as he was with you in Sicily, but even now when you are at last deserted by your other friends, you know well and we can infer. But have we no proof that he was in the whole secret except that Volcatius was not angry with him and he punished neither Volcatius or the people of Bidis? That proves much; but the final proof is this. To 59

maximum, quod illis ipsis Bidinis, quibus iste iratus
esse debuit, a quibus comperit, quod iure agere cum
Epicrate nihil possent etiamsi adesset, idcirco suum
decretum pecunia esse temptatum : iis, inquam,
ipsis non modo illam hereditatem quae Epicrati
venerat, sed, ut in Heraclio Syracusano, item in hoc
(paulo etiam atrocius, quod Epicrates appellatus
omnino non erat) bona patria fortunasque eius
Bidinis tradidit. Ostendit enim novo modo, si quis
quid de absente peteret, se auditurum. Adeunt
Bidini, petunt hereditatem ; procuratores postulant
ut se ad leges suas reiciat aut ex lege Rupilia dicam
scribi iubeat. Adversarii non audebant contra dicere;
exitus nullus reperiebatur. Insimulant hominem
fraudandi causa discessisse : postulant ut bona
60 possidere iubeat. Debebat Epicrates nullum nummum nemini ; amici si quis quid peteret iudicium se
passuros, iudicatum solvi satis daturos esse dicebant.
XXV. Cum omnia consilia frigerent, admonitu istius
insimulare coeperunt Epicratem litteras publicas corrupisse, a qua suspicione ille aberat plurimum ;
actionem eius rei postulant. Amici recusare ne quod
iudicium neve ipsius cognitio, illo absente, de existimatione eius constitueretur ; et simul idem illud

these very people of Bidis with whom he was bound
to be angry, whom he had found trying to secure by
bribery a corrupt decision from him just because they
had no legal case against Epicrates even if he should
appear—to these very people, I repeat, he gave
possession not merely of the legacy left to Epicrates,
but, treating him as he had treated Heraclius of
Syracuse (only a little more foully, since Epicrates
had never been summoned to appear at all), he gave
these people of Bidis the money and property inherited by Epicrates from his father. He showed in
a new way that he was ready to try any claims against
an absent man. The people of Bidis appeared and
claimed the legacy : Epicrates' representatives requested that he would either leave the case to be
settled by local law or direct a suit to be instituted as
required by the Rupilian law. The other side dared
not oppose this : they could see no way of escape.
Then they alleged that the defendant had absconded
to escape paying his creditors, and requested an order
for themselves to receive possession of his estate.
Epicrates owed no one a penny : his friends declared 60
that they would answer in court any claim made
against him, and would give guarantees for the payment of any such claim allowed by the court. XXV.
The whole conspiracy was hanging fire, when at
Verres' suggestion the plaintiffs started an allegation
that Epicrates had forged the public records—an
offence of which there was not the least ground for
suspecting him—and applied for permission to prosecute. His friends urged that in his absence no proceedings, no investigation by Verres affecting his
character should be allowed to take place, and at the
same time continued to reiterate their demand that

postulare non desistebant, ut se ad leges suas reiceret.
61 Iste amplam occasionem[1] nactus, ubi videt esse
aliquid quod amici absente Epicrate nollent defendere, asseverat se eius rei in primis actionem esse
daturum. Cum omnes perspicerent ad istum non
modo illos nummos qui per simulationem ab isto
exierant revertisse, sed multo etiam plures eum
postea nummos abstulisse, amici Epicratem defendere destiterunt. Iste Epicratis bona Bidinos omnia
possidere et sibi habere iussit ; ad illa HS D. milia
hereditaria accessit ipsius antiqua HS quindeciens
pecunia. Utrum res ab initio ita ducta est, an ad
extremum ita perducta, an ita parva est pecunia, an
is homo Verres, ut haec quae dixi gratis facta esse
videantur ?

62 Hic nunc de miseria Siculorum, iudices, audite.
Et Heraclius ille Syracusanus et hic Bidinus Epicrates
expulsi bonis omnibus Romam venerunt : sordidati,
maxima barba et capillo, Romae biennium prope
fuerunt. Cum L. Metellus in provinciam profectus
est, tum isti bene commendati cum Metello una proficiscuntur. Metellus, simul ac venit Syracusas,
utrumque rescidit, et de Epicrate et de Heraclio.
In utriusque bonis nihil erat quod restitui posset,
63 nisi si quid moveri loco non potuerat. XXVI. Fecerat hoc egregie primo adventu Metellus, ut omnes
istius iniurias, quas modo posset, rescinderet et irritas
faceret. Quod Heraclium restitui iusserat ac non
restituebatur, quisquis erat eductus senator Syra-

---

[1] *The best* MSS. *omit* occasionem, *the worst read* amplam
occasionem calumniae: amplam *if read alone (so Peterson,
Mueller) may be a substantive meaning* " hold " *or* " grasp."

Verres would refer the matter to be dealt with under their own laws. This gave Verres a good opening; **61** he had now found a charge against which Epicrates' friends were not ready to defend him in his absence, and declared that he would admit the case for trial at an early date. As everyone saw clearly not only that the cash with which he had ostensibly parted had come back to him, but that he had subsequently laid hands on a good deal more, Epicrates' friends abandoned his defence. Verres ordered the people of Bidis to have possession and ownership of the whole of Epicrates' property, his own original £15,000 as well as the £5000 legacy. Now had this business such an origin—was it so carried through to its conclusion—was the amount involved so small—is Verres so honest a man—that we can suppose the actions I have recounted to have been done for nothing?

Let me now show you, gentlemen, the unhappy **62** condition of these Sicilians. Deprived of all they had, both Heraclius of Syracuse and Epicrates of Bidis came to Rome; and there, wearing the mean clothes and the unshorn hair and beards of men in distress, they remained for nearly two years. When Lucius Metellus left for the province, they left with him, recommended strongly to his protection. As soon as he reached Syracuse, he cancelled both judgements, that against Epicrates and that against Heraclius. Nothing in either estate was left that could be restored, except what it had been impossible to remove; XXVI. but Metellus behaved admirably, **63** on his first arrival, in cancelling and annulling all the oppressive acts of Verres, so far as he could do so. His orders for the re-instatement of Heraclius not being obeyed, he ordered the arrest of all

cusanus ab Heraclio, duci iubebat, itaque permulti
ducti sunt. Epicrates quidem continuo restitutus est.
Alia iudicia Lilybaei, alia Agrigenti, alia Panhormi
restituta sunt. Census qui isto praetore sunt habiti
non servaturum se Metellus ostenderat : decumas
quas iste contra legem Hieronicam vendiderat sese
venditurum Hieronica lege edixerat. Omnia erant
Metelli eius modi ut non tam suam praeturam gerere
quam istius praeturam retexere videretur. Simul
64 atque ego in Siciliam veni, mutatus est. Venerat ad
eum illo biduo Laetilius quidam, homo non alienus a
litteris, itaque eo iste tabellario semper usus est. Is
epistulas complures attulerat, in his unam domo quae
totum immutarat hominem. Repente coepit dicere
se omnia Verris causa velle, sibi cum eo amicitiam
cognationemque esse. Mirabantur omnes hoc ei tum
denique in mentem venisse, posteaquam tam multis
eum factis decretisque iugulasset ; erant qui putarent
Laetilium legatum a Verre venisse qui gratiam
amicitiam cognationemque commemoraret. Ex illo
tempore a civitatibus laudationes petere, testes non
solum deterrere verbis sed etiam vi retinere coepit.
Quod nisi ego meo adventu illius conatus aliquantum
repressissem, et apud Siculos non Metelli sed Gla-
brionis litteris ac lege pugnassem, tam multos huc

Syracusan senators prosecuted on this account by Heraclius, and a number of them were arrested accordingly. Epicrates was re-instated promptly. At Lilybaeum, at Agrigentum, at Panhormus, various judgements were cancelled by restitution orders. Metellus gave notice that he would not regard as valid the assessments made during Verres' praetorship, and proclaimed his intention of selling in accordance with the law of Hiero the rights of tithe collection which Verres had sold in defiance of that law. All his actions were such that he seemed less to be doing his own work as praetor than undoing the work of his predecessor. No sooner had I reached Sicily than he became another man. Within 64 two days of that time he had had a visit from one Laetilius, a person not unversed in letters, and for that reason employed regularly by Verres to carry his mails. Laetilius had brought several letters, including one from home that had at once changed Metellus completely. He began forthwith to tell people that he was ready to do anything for Verres, that he was Verres' friend and kinsman. There was general surprise at his thinking of this at this late hour, after having officially done and ordered so much to wreck him ; some there were who suspected that Laetilius had been dispatched by Verres to remind Metellus that Verres was his well-wisher, friend, and relative. From that time onward he began to urge the different cities to furnish eulogies, and not only to intimidate my witnesses but forcibly to prevent their going. Had I not done something to counter his exertions by my visits, had I not, in dealing with the Sicilians, been armed with the written legal authority of Glabrio instead of that of

65 evocare non potuissem. XXVII. Verum quod institui
dicere, miserias cognoscite sociorum. Heraclius ille
et Epicrates longe mihi obviam cum suis omnibus
processerunt, venienti Syracusas egerunt gratias
flentes, Romam decedere mecum cupiverunt. Quod
erant mihi oppida complura etiam reliqua quae adire
vellem, constitui cum hominibus quo die mihi
Messanae praesto essent. Eo mihi nuntium mise-
runt se a praetore retineri. Quibus ego testimonium
denuntiavi, quorum edidi nomina Metello, cupi-
dissimi veniendi, maximis iniuriis affecti, adhuc non
venerunt. Hoc iure sunt socii ut iis ne deplorare
quidem de suis incommodis liceat.

66 Iam Heraclii Centuripini, optimi nobilissimique
adulescentis, testimonium audistis : a quo HS c.
milia per calumniam malitiamque petita sunt. Iste
poenis compromissisque interpositis HS cccc. milia
extorquenda curavit ; quodque iudicium secundum
Heraclium de compromisso factum erat, cum civis
Centuripinus inter duos cives diiudicasset, id irritum
iussit esse, eumque iudicem falso iudicasse iudicavit ;
in senatu esse, locis commodisque publicis uti vetuit ;
si quis eum pulsasset, edixit sese iudicium iniuriarum
non daturum ; quicquid ab eo peteretur, iudicem de
sua cohorte daturum, ipsi autem nullius actionem rei
67 sese daturum. Quae istius auctoritas tantum valuit

---

a Verres made the claimant quadruple his claim, and
both parties agree to submit the matter to an arbitrator.
Each party had to bind himself by an agreement (*com-
promissum*) to pay a certain sum as penalty (*poena*) if he
did not abide by the award.

Metellus, I should not have been able to secure the presence of so many of them at this trial. XXVII. But let us return to what I began to tell you of our allies' unhappy position. Heraclius and Epicrates, with all their friends, came out a long way to meet me, thanked me with tears as I approached Syracuse, and expressed their eagerness to go off to Rome with me. Having several towns still left which I wished to visit, I arranged a day with them for meeting me at Messana. They sent me word there that they were being detained by the praetor's orders. These witnesses, whom I have officially summoned, whose names I have given in to Metellus, who are most eager to come here and are the victims of outrageous injustice, have so far not arrived Our allies' rights do not even include permission to complain of their sufferings.

You have already heard the evidence of that young man of high character and position, Heraclius of Centuripa, against whom was brought a lying and malicious claim for £1000. Verres forced into the case arbitration agreements and penalties, and took steps to extract £4000 ; [a] and when the arbiter— a man of Centuripa, arbitrating between two of his fellow-citizens—decided in favour of Heraclius, Verres annulled the decision, and pronounced the arbiter guilty of making a false award. He forbade this man to appear in the Senate, attend town gatherings, or enjoy civic privileges ; and gave notice that he would allow no action for assault against anyone who might strike him, would appoint one of his staff to decide upon any claim brought against him, and would not allow the man himself to sue another man for anything. His authority

ut neque illum pulsaret quisquam, cum praetor in
provincia sua verbo permitteret, re hortaretur, neque
quisquam ab eo quicquam peteret, cum iste calumniae
licentiam sua auctoritate ostendisset ; ignominia
autem illa gravis tam diu in illo homine fuit quam diu
iste in provincia mansit. Hoc iniecto metu iudicibus
novo more, nullo exemplo, ecquam rem putatis esse
in Sicilia nisi ad nutum istius iudicatam ? Utrum id
solum videtur esse actum, quod est tamen actum, ut
haec Heraclio pecunia eriperetur ? an etiam illud, in
quo praeda erat maxima, ut nomine iudiciorum
omnium bona atque fortunae in istius unius essent
potestatem ?

68   XXVIII. Iam vero in rerum capitalium quaestioni-
bus quid ego unam quamque rem colligam et causam ?
Ex multis similibus ea sumam quae maxime improbitate excellere videbuntur.

Sopater quidam fuit Halicyensis, homo domi suae
cum primis locuples atque honestus. Is ab inimicis
suis apud C. Sacerdotem praetorem rei capitalis cum
accusatus esset, facile eo iudicio est liberatus. Huic
eidem Sopatro idem inimici ad C. Verrem, cum is
Sacerdoti successisset, eiusdem rei nomen detulerunt.
Res Sopatro facilis videbatur, et quod erat innocens
et quod Sacerdotis iudicium improbare istum ausurum
non arbitrabatur. Citatur reus ; causa agitur Syra-

was so far effective that nobody assaulted the man, in spite of the nominal permission and actual encouragement to do so given by the praetor to all those under him ; that nobody sued him for anything, in spite of Verres' official announcement of a free hand for false claimants ; but the man's painful humiliation lasted as long as Verres' term of office lasted. In the face of such unprecedented, such unheard-of intimidation of the courts of law, do you imagine that a single case was decided throughout Sicily except as Verres directed ? Do you suppose that the only thing which happened was what certainly did happen, the robbery of this money belonging to Heraclius ? That there was not also the further result, a highly profitable result for this robber, that he had, in the name of the law, every man's property and fortunes at his own sole disposal ?

XXVIII. And now to turn to his conduct of trials 68 for capital offences, I need not review the details of each several case ; I will select, out of a number of similar affairs, such as seem distinguished by exceptional wickedness.

Sopater of Halicyae was one of the wealthiest and most respected inhabitants of that town. Prosecuted by his enemies for a criminal offence in the praetorship of Gaius Sacerdos, he had no trouble, on that occasion, in securing an acquittal. When Verres succeeded Sacerdos, this same Sopater was prosecuted before him by these same enemies again on the same charge. He thought himself in little danger, both because he was not guilty, and because he could not suppose that Verres would venture to reverse the decision of Sacerdos. He was summoned to stand his trial, which took place at Syracuse. The

cusis : crimina tractantur ab accusatore ea quae erant
antea non solum defensione verum etiam iudicio
69 dissoluta. Causam Sopatri defendebat Q. Minucius,
eques Romanus in primis splendidus atque honestus,
vobisque, iudices, non ignotus. Nihil erat in causa
quod metuendum aut omnino quod dubitandum videretur. Interea istius libertus et accensus Timarchides, qui est, id quod ex plurimis testibus priore
actione didicistis, rerum huiusce modi omnium trans-
actor et administer, ad Sopatrum venit ; monet
hominem ne nimis iudicio Sacerdotis et causae suae
confidat ; accusatores inimicosque eius habere in
animo pecuniam praetori dare ; praetorem tamen ab
salute malle accipere, et simul malle, si fieri posset,
rem iudicatam non rescindere. Sopater, cum hoc illi
improvisum atque inopinatum accidisset, commotus
est sane, neque in praesentia Timarchidi quid
responderet habuit, nisi se consideraturum quid sibi
esset faciendum ; et simul ostendit se in summa
difficultate esse nummaria. Post ad amicos rettulit ;
qui cum ei fuissent auctores redimendae salutis, ad
Timarchidem venit. Expositis suis difficultatibus
hominem ad HS lxxx. perducit, eamque ei pecuniam
70 numerat. XXIX. Posteaquam ad causam dicendam
ventum est, tum vero sine metu, sine cura omnes
erant qui Sopatrum defendebant. Crimen nullum
erat, res erat iudicata, Verres nummos acceperat ;
quis posset dubitare quidnam esset futurum ? Res

charges put forward by the prosecutor were charges
that had previously been refuted not merely by the
arguments of the defence but by the verdict of the
court. Sopater was now defended by Quintus 69
Minucius, a most distinguished and respected
member of the equestrian order, not unknown to
the members of this Court. The case seemed to
offer no room for fear, or even for any kind of uncer-
tainty. While it was proceeding, Verres' freedman
attendant, Timarchides, who is, as numerous witnesses
informed you at the first hearing, the agent who
helps him to carry out all affairs of this kind, approached Sopater, warning him not to trust too
much to the decision of Sacerdos or the strength of
his own case ; his prosecutors and enemies were
proposing to offer the praetor money, which, however,
the latter would prefer to be paid for letting Sopater
off ; and at the same time he would rather, if he
could, avoid reversing the previous decision. Finding himself without warning in this unexpected
situation, Sopater was greatly perturbed, and had
no immediate answer ready for Timarchides, except
that he would think over what he had better do ;
observing at the same time that he was in great
financial difficulties. Later he told his friends what
had happened ; they undertook to buy his escape
for him, and he went back to Timarchides. After
stating fully the straits he was in, he bargained with
the man till he agreed to take £800, which sum he
paid him. XXIX. When the proceedings in court 70
began, all Sopater's supporters were now free from
fear and anxiety ; the charge was groundless, the
case had been judged, Verres had taken his money—
what doubt could there be of the result ? That day

illo die non peroratur; iudicium dimittitur. Iterum
ad Sopatrum Timarchides venit; ait accusatores
eius multo maiorem pecuniam praetori polliceri
quam quantum hic dedisset: proinde, si saperet,
videret. Homo, quamquam erat et Siculus et
reus, hoc est, et iure iniquo et tempore adverso,
ferre tamen atque audire diutius Timarchidem
non potuit. "Facite" inquit "quod vobis libet;
daturus non sum amplius." Idemque hoc amicis
eius et defensoribus videbatur; atque eo etiam
magis quod iste, quoquo modo se in ea quaestione
praebebat, tamen in consilio habebat homines honestos e conventu Syracusano, qui Sacerdoti quoque
in consilio fuerant tum cum est idem hic Sopater
absolutus. Hoc rationis habebant, facere eos nullo
modo posse ut eodem crimine, eisdem testibus, Sopatrum condemnarent idem homines qui antea absolvis-
71 sent. Itaque hac una spe ad iudicium venitur. Quo
posteaquam est ventum, cum in consilium frequentes
convenissent idem qui solebant, et hac una spe tota
defensio Sopatri niteretur, consilii frequentia et
dignitate, et quod erant, ut dixi, idem qui antea
Sopatrum eodem illo crimine liberarant, cognoscite
hominis apertam ac non modo non ratione sed ne
dissimulatione quidem tectam improbitatem et
audaciam. M. Petilium, equitem Romanum, quem
habebat in consilio, iubet operam dare, quod rei
privatae iudex esset. Petilius recusabat, quod suos

the pleadings were not completed before the court adjourned; after which Timarchides again approached Sopater, and told him that his accusers had offered the praetor a much larger sum than he had himself paid, and he would therefore be wise to think the matter over. Sopater was a Sicilian and a man on his trial; in a position, that is, politically inferior and immediately dangerous; but for all that, he could endure and listen to Timarchides no longer. " Do what you will," he replied; " I am not going to pay you anything more." This resolution was approved by his friends and advisers also, all the more because, let Verres behave in the trial as he might, there were on his council respectable men from the Syracuse district, who had also been serving in the same way under Sacerdos when this same Sopater had been acquitted. Sopater's friends argued that the men who had acquitted him previously could never agree to find him guilty now on the same charge and the same evidence as before; and they went into court trusting to this single hope. The court assembled; the council was well attended 71 by the usual persons; Sopater's whole hopes of a successful defence rested upon this good attendance of its reputable members, and on the fact which I mentioned, that these were the same persons as had before acquitted him on exactly the same charge. Remembering this, now observe the open and shameless wickedness of yonder man—wickedness cloaked neither by plausible argument nor even by any attempt at concealment. He told Marcus Petilius, a Roman knight sitting on his council, to go off to his duties as judge in a civil case. Petilius objected, because Verres was retaining on his

amicos, quos sibi in consilio esse vellet, ipse Verres
retineret in consilio. Iste homo liberalis negat se
quemquam retinere eorum qui Petilio vellent adesse.
Itaque discedunt omnes ; nam ceteri quoque impetrant ne retineantur, qui se velle dicebant alterutri
eorum qui tum illud iudicium habebant adesse.
Itaque iste solus cum sua cohorte nequissima
72 relinquitur. Non dubitabat Minucius, qui Sopatrum
defendebat, quin iste, quoniam consilium dimisisset,
illo die rem illam quaesiturus non esset, cum repente
iubetur dicere. Respondet "Ad quos ?" "Ad
me," inquit, "si tibi idoneus videor qui de homine
Siculo ac Graeculo iudicem." "Idoneus es," inquit,
"sed pervellem adessent ii qui adfuerant antea
causamque cognorant." "Dic," inquit, "illi adesse
non possunt." "Nam hercule," inquit Minucius, "me
quoque Petilius ut sibi in consilio adessem rogavit";
73 et simul a subselliis abire coepit. Iste iratus hominem verbis vehementioribus prosequitur, atque ei
gravius etiam minari coepit quod in se tantum
crimen invidiamque conflaret. XXX. Minucius, qui
Syracusis sic negotiaretur ut sui iuris dignitatisque
meminisset, et qui sciret se ita in provincia rem
augere oportere ut ne quid de libertate deperderet,
homini quae visa sunt, et quae tempus illud tulit et
causa, respondit ; causam sese dimisso atque ab-
legato consilio defensurum negavit. Itaque a subselliis discessit ; idemque hoc praeter Siculos ceteri

<hr />

a i.e., such of the Sicilians as Petilius did not ask for as
his assessors.

council friends of Petilius whose presence the latter desired on his own council. Our courteous gentleman replied that he would not retain any person who wished to attend Petilius. So off they all went; for the others [a] too asked and were granted permission to go, saying that they desired to support one or other of the parties in this other case. Thus Verres was left alone with the members of his rascally staff. Minucius, who was defending Sopater, was 72 assuming that Verres, having let his council go, did not mean to proceed with this business that day, when he was suddenly ordered to proceed with his speech. "To whom?" asked Minucius. "To me," was the reply, "if you think me qualified to try this little beast of a Sicilian Greek." "Certainly," said Minucius, "but I should be very glad to have those present who were present before and are acquainted with the case." "They cannot be present," said Verres; "go on." "Why, the truth is," said Minucius, "that Petilius has asked me too to be one of his council"; and with that he left his place to go. Verres n a rage pursued him with violent 73 language, and even began to threaten him savagely for conspiring thus to make people attack and hate him. XXX. Minucius, being a man who did not let his business interests at Syracuse make him forget his rights and responsibilities, and who was aware that his pursuit of wealth in Sicily ought not to mean any loss of his personal freedom, expressed with frankness what he felt about this case and the situation that had arisen, refusing to conduct the defence when the members of the court had been dismissed and packed off. He left his place accordingly; and Sopater's other friends and supporters,

74 Sopatri amici advocatique fecerunt. Iste, quamquam est incredibili importunitate et audacia, tamen
subito solus destitutus pertimuit et conturbatus est;
quid ageret, quo se verteret nesciebat. Si dimisisset eo tempore quaestionem, post, illis adhibitis
in consilium quos ablegarat, absolutum iri Sopatrum
videbat; sin autem hominem miserum atque innocentem ita condemnasset, cum ipse praetor sine
consilio, reus autem sine patrono atque advocatis
fuisset, iudiciumque C. Sacerdotis rescidisset, invidiam se sustinere tantam posse non arbitrabatur.
Itaque aestuabat dubitatione, versabat se utramque
in partem, non solum mente verum etiam corpore,
ut omnes qui aderant intellegere possent in animo
eius metum cum cupiditate pugnare. Erat hominum conventus maximus, summum silentium,
summa exspectatio quonam esset eius cupiditas
eruptura; crebro se accensus demittebat ad aurem
75 Timarchides. Tum iste aliquando "Age, dic!"
inquit. Reus orare atque obsecrare ut cum consilio
cognosceret. Tum repente iste testes citari iubet;
dicit unus et alter breviter; nihil interrogatur;
praeco DIXISSE pronuntiat. Iste, quasi metueret
ne Petilius privato illo iudicio transacto aut prolato
cum ceteris in consilium reverteretur, ita properans
de sella exsilit, hominem innocentem, a C. Sacerdote
absolutum, indicta causa, de sententia scribae medici
haruspicisque condemnat.

the Sicilians excepted, did likewise. Insolent and 74
unscrupulous beyond belief as Verres is, on finding
himself suddenly left behind alone he was overcome
with fright and confusion, unable to see what to do or
which way to turn. If he were to adjourn the trial
now, he saw that when the court met later, with
those members present whom he had got rid of,
Sopater would be acquitted; if on the other hand
he now condemned this unfortunate and guiltless
man, having himself presided without a council and
having left the accused without advocate or supporters,
and reversing thereby the decision of Sacerdos, he
felt that he would be unable to face the hatred that
such an action would entail. In an agony of in-
decision, he kept shifting first this way and then that,
not only mentally but physically, so that all those
present could see how fear was contending in his
mind with cupidity. There was a great crowd present
—dead silence—breathless anxiety as to what line
of attack his greed would adopt. His attendant
Timarchides kept bending down to whisper in his
ear. At last he said, " Come now, proceed ! " The 75
accused man prayed and besought him to try the
case before a court. Thereupon he abruptly ordered
the witnesses to be called; two or three of them
gave hurried evidence; there was no cross-examina-
tion; the court crier declared the case over. Verres
leapt up from his chair as eagerly as if he were
afraid that Petilius had finished or adjourned his
hearing of the civil suit and would reappear in
court with the others; and that innocent man,
whom Sacerdos had acquitted, and whose case had
not been tried, was, with the concurrence of a clerk,
an apothecary, and a soothsayer, pronounced Guilty.

76 XXXI. Retinete, retinete hominem in civitate, iudices ; parcite et conservate, ut sit qui vobiscum res iudicet, qui in senatu sine ulla cupiditate de bello et pace sententiam ferat. Tametsi minus id quidem nobis, minus populo Romano laborandum est, qualis istius in senatu sententia futura sit. Quae enim eius auctoritas erit ? quando iste sententiam dicere audebit aut poterit ? quando autem homo tantae luxuriae atque desidiae nisi Februario mense aspirabit in curiam ? Verum veniat sane ; decernat bellum Cretensibus, liberet Byzantios, regem appellet Ptolomaeum ; quae vult Hortensius, omnia dicat et sentiat : minus haec ad nos, minus ad vitae nostrae discrimen, minus ad fortunarum nostrarum periculum

77 pertinent. Illud est capitale, illud formidolosum, illud optimo cuique metuendum, quod iste, ex hoc iudicio si aliqua vi se eripuerit, in iudicibus sit necesse est, sententiam de capite civis Romani ferat, sit in eius exercitu signifer qui imperium iudiciorum tenere vult. Hoc populus Romanus recusat, hoc ferre non potest : clamat permittitque vobis ut, si istis hominibus delectemini, si ex eo genere splendorem ordini atque ornamentum curiae constituere velitis, habeatis sane istum vobiscum senatorem : etiam de vobis iudicem, si vultis, habeatis : de se homines, si qui extra istum ordinem sunt, quibus ne reiciendi quidem amplius quam trium iudicum praeclarae leges Corneliae

---

a The regular month for receiving petitions from subject or foreign communities, which venal senators could secure bribes to support (see Book I. § 90).

b Current pieces of foreign business, not of the highest importance.

c Hortensius : see *Actio prima*, § 35.

XXXI. Save Verres, gentlemen! save him for **76** Rome! spare him, and keep him safe! You need such a man on the Bench. You need him in the Senate, to give his disinterested voice for peace or war. This latter consideration, to be sure, of how his voice will be given in the Senate, concerns us, and concerns the country, comparatively little. For how much weight will his opinion have? When will he have the courage, or the ability, to utter it? And when, unless it be in February,[a] will such an indolent profligate come near the House? But let him attend, by all means; let him declare war on Crete, let him award the Byzantines freedom and Ptolemy his royal title;[b] let him say, and let him think, whatsoever Hortensius will have him say and think. Such matters are of comparatively small import for us, for the safety of our lives, for the security of our fortunes. The fatal thing, the terrible thing, **77** the thing that all honest men must fear, is the certainty that Verres, if violence shall somehow secure his escape from his judges now, will be one of our judges, that his verdict will control the liberties of Roman citizens, that he will hold a commission in the army of the man[c] who aspires to the command of our law-courts. It is against this that Romans protest; it is to this that they cannot submit. If you, they cry, delight in such a man as this, if you choose to select persons of this type to add lustre to your order and distinction to your House, you may keep him, by all means, as a fellow-senator; nay, if you will have it so, you may keep him as a judge— to judge yourselves; but we who are not members of your order, we whom the great laws of Sulla do not permit even to challenge more than three of our

faciunt potestatem, hunc hominem tam crudelem, tam
78 sceleratum, tam nefarium nolunt iudicare. XXXII.
Etenim si illud est flagitiosum, quod mihi omnium
rerum turpissimum maximeque nefarium videtur, ob
rem iudicandam pecuniam accipere, pretio habere addictam fidem et religionem, quanto illud flagitiosius,
improbius, indignius, eum a quo pecuniam ob absol-
vendum acceperis condemnare, ut ne praedonum
quidem praetor in fide retinenda consuetudinem
conservet! Scelus est accipere ab reo : quanto
magis ab accusatore, quanto etiam sceleratius ab
utroque! Fidem cum proposuisses venalem in provincia, valuit apud te plus is qui pecuniam maiorem
dedit : concedo ; forsitan aliquis aliquando eius modi
quidpiam fecerit. Cum vero fidem ac religionem
tuam iam alteri addictam pecunia accepta habueris,
postea eandem adversario tradideris maiore pecunia,
utrumque falles, et trades cui voles, et ei quem
79 fefelleris ne pecuniam quidem reddes ? Quem mihi
tu Bulbum, quem Staienum ? quod umquam huiusce
modi monstrum aut prodigium audivimus aut vidimus,
qui cum reo transigat, post cum accusatore decidat,
honestos homines, qui causam norint, ableget a
consilioque dimittat, ipse solus reum absolutum a quo
pecuniam acceperit condemnet, pecuniamque non
reddat ? Hunc hominem in iudicum numero habebimus ? hic alteram decuriam senatoriam iudex

---

[a] A senator might challenge six.
[b] Two notoriously venal judges in the trial of Oppianicus
some years before.
[c] *Decuria*, a section of the album (" White Book ") of
senators eligible for service as members of Criminal Courts.

judges,ᵃ we refuse to be judged by this cruel and infamous scoundrel. XXXII. For indeed, if it is a 78 wicked thing—and to me it seems the foulest and vilest thing in the world—that a judge should accept a bribe, that he should make money the master of his honour and his conscience, how much more wicked and vicious and shameful still it is that he should condemn a man from whom he has taken money to acquit him ; that he, a magistrate, should have even less care to keep his pledged word than is customary among a gang of bandits ! It is a crime to take money from an accused man : how much worse to take it from his prosecutor, how much worse still to take it from them both ! You exposed your honour for sale in your province, and the man swayed you most who paid you best ; well, never mind—there may now and then have been some-one who did something of the same description. But when your honour and conscience is already another man's property and the price is already paid, will you then transfer that honour and conscience to his opponent who pays you more ? Will you cheat them both and choose your own purchaser, and not even give your victim his money back ? Talk not 79 to me of Bulbus or Staienus ᵇ ; what such unnatural prodigy have we ever seen or heard of as this man who makes one bargain with the accused and then concludes another with the accuser, who banishes and expels from his court the respectable men who know the facts, condemns unsupported the already acquitted man whose money he has taken, and refuses to give that money back ? Shall we have such a man as this among our judges ? Shall this man's name appear again in a panel ᶜ of senators ?

obtinebit? hic de capite libero iudicabit? huic iu-
dicialis tabella committetur? quam iste non modo
cera verum etiam sanguine, si visum erit, notabit.

80   XXXIII. Quid enim horum se negat fecisse?
illud videlicet unum, quod necesse est, pecuniam
accepisse. Quidni iste neget? At eques Romanus,
qui Sopatrum defendit, qui omnibus eius consiliis
rebusque interfuit, Q. Minucius, iuratus dicit pecuniam datam, iuratus dicit Timarchidem dixisse
maiorem pecuniam ab accusatoribus dari. Dicent
hoc multi Siculi, dicent omnes Halicyenses, dicet
etiam praetextatus Sopatri filius, qui ab isto homine
crudelissimo patre innocentissimo pecuniaque patria
81 privatus est. Verum si de pecunia testibus planum
facere non possem, illud negare posses aut nunc
negabis, te consilio tuo dimisso, viris primariis qui in
consilio C. Sacerdoti fuerant tibique esse solebant
remotis de re iudicata iudicavisse? teque eum quem
C. Sacerdos adhibito consilio causa cognita absol-
visset eundem remoto consilio causa incognita con-
demnasse? Cum haec confessus eris, quae in foro
palam Syracusis in ore atque in oculis provinciae gesta
sunt, negato tum sane, si voles, te pecuniam accepisse;
reperies, credo, aliquem qui, cum haec quae palam
gesta sunt videat, quaerat quid tu occulte egeris,

---

^a Referring perhaps to the scandal mentioned in the
Actio prima, § 40.

Shall a free man's status depend on *his* verdict?
Shall the tablet to record the verdict be put into
his hands—a tablet that he will be ready to smear,
if the fancy takes him, not with mere wax *a* but
with the blood of men.

XXXIII. For which of these charges does he deny? 80
only one, doubtless, the one that he must deny—that
he received the money. Deny this? Of course he
denies it. But the Roman knight Quintus Minucius,
who defended Sopater, who knew of all that Sopater
did and meant to do, has sworn that the money was
paid, and has sworn that Timarchides said that the
prosecutors were offering more money still. That is
what many in Sicily will say; what every man at
Halicyae will say; what, moreover, Sopater's young
son will say, whom that ruffian's cruelty has robbed of
his innocent father, and of the money his father would
have left him. But even if I could not bring evidence 81
to prove the facts about the money, could you deny,
or will you now deny, that you first dismissed your
council and got rid of the reputable persons who had
sat on the council of Sacerdos and had been regularly
sitting on yours, and then pronounced judgement on
an issue already judged? That you took a man whom
Sacerdos, supported by his council, had first tried
fairly and then acquitted, and with your council dismissed and no trial held at all declared him guilty?
When you have confessed to having done this thing
that was done openly, in the market-place of Syracuse,
in full view of the province, then by all means deny, if
you care to deny, that you took the man's money;
you may, of course, possibly find someone who, having
seen what happened in the daylight, is yet not sure of
what you did in the dark, or someone who cannot

381

aut qui dubitet utrum malit meis testibus an tuis defensoribus credere.

82 Dixi iam ante me non omnia istius quae in hoc genere essent enumeraturum, sed electurum ea quae maxime excellerent. XXXIV. Accipite nunc aliud eius facinus nobile et multis locis saepe commemoratum, et eius modi ut in uno omnia maleficia inesse videantur. Attendite diligenter ; invenietis enim id facinus natum a cupiditate, auctum per stuprum, crudelitate perfectum atque conclusum.

83 Sthenius est, hic qui nobis assidet, Thermitanus, antea multis propter summam virtutem summamque nobilitatem, nunc propter suam calamitatem atque istius insignem iniuriam, omnibus notus. Huius hospitio Verres cum esset usus, et cum apud eum non solum Thermis saepenumero fuisset sed etiam habitasset, omnia domo eius abstulit quae paulo magis animum cuiuspiam aut oculos possent commovere. Etenim Sthenius ab adulescentia paulo studiosius haec compararat, supellectilem ex aere elegantiorem, et Deliacam et Corinthiam, tabulas pictas, etiam argenti bene facti, prout Thermitani hominis facultates ferebant, satis. Quae, cum esset in Asia adulescens, studiose, ut dixi, comparabat, non tam suae delectationis causa quam ad invitationes adventusque nostrorum hominum, amicorum atque

84 hospitum. Quae posteaquam iste omnia abstulit, alia rogando, alia poscendo, alia sumendo, ferebat Sthenius ut poterat ; angebatur animi necessario quod

quite decide whether he had rather believe my witnesses or your supporters.

I have already said that I do not mean to enumerate 82 all Verres' achievements of this sort, but to choose out the most remarkable. XXXIV. Let me tell you now of another notorious crime of his, the story of which has spread widely and often been told ; a crime that seems to comprehend in itself every kind of evil action. I ask for your close attention to the tale of this crime, which was, as you will see, engendered by greed, nourished by lust, and finally completed by cruelty.

The gentleman who is sitting near me is Sthenius of 83 Thermae, whose high rank and character once made his name familiar to many of us, and whose unhappy fate and notable sufferings at Verres' hands have made it now familiar to us all. Though Verres had enjoyed his hospitality, though he had not only repeatedly been to see him at Thermae but actually stayed in his house, he carried off from it every object in which anyone could feel or see any degree of unusual beauty. The truth is that Sthenius had all his life been a rather keen collector of such things—Delian and Corinthian bronze of special elegance, pictures, and even finely-wrought silver, of which he had, considering what the means of a man of Thermae would allow, a good stock. As a young man in Asia he had, as I said, been a keen collector of these things ; less with a view to his own enjoyment than to enable him to invite, and be ready to receive, our own people as his friends and guests. When Verres had carried all his treasures off, having 84 asked for some, demanded others, and helped himself to the rest, Sthenius bore his loss as well as he could. He was, of course, distressed at the almost bare and

domum eius exornatam atque instructam fere iam
iste reddiderat nudam atque inanem : verum tamen
dolorem suum nemini impertiebat : praetoris iniurias
85 tacite, hospitis placide ferendas arbitrabatur. Interea
iste cupiditate illa sua nota atque apud omnes per-
vagata, cum signa quaedam pulcherrima atque antiquissima Thermis in publico posita vidisset, adamavit ;
a Sthenio petere coepit ut ad ea tollenda operam
suam profiteretur seque adiuvaret. Sthenius vero
non solum negavit, sed etiam ostendit fieri id nullo
modo posse ut signa antiquissima, monumenta P.
Africani, ex oppido Thermitanorum incolumi illa
civitate imperioque populi Romani tollerentur.

86   XXXV. Etenim ut simul Africani quoque humani-
tatem et aequitatem cognoscatis, oppidum Himeram
Carthaginienses quondam ceperant, quod fuerat in
primis Siciliae clarum et ornatum. Scipio, qui hoc
dignum populo Romano arbitraretur, bello confecto
socios sua per nostram victoriam recuperare, Siculis
omnibus Carthagine capta quae potuit restituenda
curavit. Himera deleta, quos cives belli calamitas
reliquos fecerat, ii se Thermis collocarant in isdem
agri finibus neque longe ab oppido antiquo ; hi se
patrum fortunam ac dignitatem recuperare arbitrabantur cum illa maiorum ornamenta in eorum oppido
87 collocabantur.   Erant signa ex aere complura : in his
eximia pulchritudine ipsa Himera, in muliebrem

---

a The younger.   *b* In 408 b.c.
c In 146 b.c. ; the third Punic War.

384

empty state to which Verres had by now reduced his well fitted and furnished home ; still, he shared his unhappiness with nobody; the outrages of a governor must, he felt, be borne in silence, and those of a guest with calmness. Verres, in the meantime, with the 85 cupidity for which he is notorious all over the world, fell in love with certain very fine and ancient statues which he saw standing in some public part of Thermae, and began pressing Sthenius to promise him his assistance in getting hold of them. Sthenius, however, refused ; and more than that, pointed out that these ancient statues, memorials of Scipio Africanus,[a] could not by any possibility be carried away from the town of Thermae so long as Thermae and the Roman Empire remained intact.

XXXV. What he meant—if I may, incidentally, 86 illustrate the sympathy and fair-mindedness of the hero of Africa—was this. Long ago,[b] the Carthaginians captured the town of Himera, till then one of the most famous and most richly adorned towns in Sicily. The honour of Rome, it seemed to Scipio, demanded that, when the war [c] was over, our triumph should lead to our allies recovering what belonged to them; and after the capture of Carthage he saw to it that restitution was made, so far as might be, to all the Sicilians. Now after the destruction of Himera, those of its citizens who had survived the horrors of war had settled at Thermae, within the territory of the ancient city, and not far away from it ; and as they watched their ancestral treasures being set up in their town, they felt themselves beginning to regain the prosperity and importance enjoyed by their forefathers. There were several bronze statues; among others, 87 one of exceptional beauty, the figure of a woman

385

figuram habitumque formata, ex oppidi nomine et
fluminis. Erat etiam Stesichori poetae statua,
senilis, incurva, cum libro, summo, ut putant, artificio
facta ; qui fuit Himerae, sed et est et fuit tota
Graecia summo propter ingenium honore et nomine.
Haec iste ad insaniam concupiverat. Etiam, quod
paene praeterii, capella quaedam est, ea quidem mire,
ut etiam nos, qui rudes harum rerum sumus, intellegere
possumus, scite facta et venuste. Haec et alia Scipio
non neglegenter abiecerat, ut homo intellegens Verres
auferre posset, sed Thermitanis restituerat : non quo
ipse hortos aut suburbanum aut locum omnino ubi ea
poneret nullum haberet ; sed quod, si domum abstulisset, non diu Scipionis appellarentur, sed eorum
ad quoscumque illius morte venissent ; nunc iis locis
posita sunt ut mihi semper Scipionis fore videantur
itaque dicantur.

88 XXXVI. Haec cum iste posceret agereturque ea
res in senatu, Sthenius vehementissime restitit,
multaque, ut in primis Siculorum in dicendo copiosus
est, commemoravit : urbem relinquere Thermitanis
esse honestius quam pati tolli ex urbe monumenta
maiorum, spolia hostium, beneficia clarissimi viri,
indicia societatis populi Romani atque amicitiae.

wearing woman's dress, representing Himera herself,
whose name is that of both town and river. There
was also a statue of the poet Stesichorus, represented
as an old man leaning forward and holding a book;
this is reckoned a very fine work of art; its subject
lived at Himera, but is, and always has been, honoured
and renowned for his genius throughout the Greek
world. Both these Verres had been seized with a
frantic craving to acquire. There is also—I had
nearly forgotten it—the figure of a she-goat, and this
certainly is, as even we who know little of such things
can tell, a wonderfully clever and charming bit of
work. These and other such objects Scipio had not
thrown carelessly aside for a connoisseur like Verres
to appropriate, but had returned them to their owners,
the people of Thermae; not because he was without
a garden in Rome, or an estate near it, or a place of
some kind somewhere in which to put them; but
because, if he took them away home, they would be
called Scipio's for a short while only, and thereafter
be known as the property of those who inherited
them at his death: standing where they do, I feel
that they will be Scipio's always; and so indeed are
they described.

XXXVI. When Verres demanded these treasures, 88
the matter was discussed in the local Senate. Sthenius
there attacked the proposal violently, reminding his
hearers of the facts in a long speech, delivered with
the fluency for which he is distinguished among
Sicilians. Better, he said, for them to abandon
Thermae than to allow the removal from Thermae of
those memorials of their fathers, those trophies of
victory, those gifts of their illustrious benefactor,
those tokens of their alliance and friendship with the

Commoti animi sunt omnium ; repertus est nemo
quin mori diceret satius esse. Itaque hoc adhuc
oppidum Verres invenit prope solum in orbe ter-
rarum unde nihil eius modi rerum de publico per
vim, nihil occulte, nihil imperio, nihil gratia, nihil
pretio posset auferre. Verum hasce eius cupiditates
exponam alio loco ; nunc ad Sthenium revertar.
89 Iratus iste vehementer Sthenio et incensus hospitium
ei renuntiat, domo eius emigrat—atque adeo exit,
nam iam ante emigrarat. Eum autem statim inimicissimi Sthenii domum suam invitant, ut animum eius
in Sthenium inflammarent ementiendo aliquid et
criminando. Hi autem erant inimici Agathinus,
homo nobilis, et Dorotheus, qui habebat in matri-
monio Callidamam, Agathini eius filiam ; de qua iste
audierat, itaque ad generum Agathini migrare maluit.
Una nox intercesserat cum iste Dorotheum sic
diligebat ut diceres omnia inter eos esse communia,
Agathinum ita observabat ut aliquem affinem atque
propinquum ; contemnere etiam signum illud Himerae iam videbatur, quod eum multo magis figura
90 et liniamenta hospitae delectabant. XXXVII. Itaque hortari homines coepit ut aliquid Sthenio periculi crearent criminisque confingerent. Dicebant
se illi nihil habere quod dicerent. Tum iste iis
aperte ostendit et confirmavit eos in Sthenium quicquid vellent, simul atque ad se detulissent, probaturos.

---

a His furniture (*i.e.*, his host's treasures) had already been
sent off.

Roman nation. All his hearers were deeply stirred ;
none but declared that death were a better fate.
And this is consequently almost the only town in the
world from which Verres has so far found it impossible
to carry off any publicly-owned treasure of this sort,
either by stealth, or by force, or by the exercise of
authority, or by favour, or by purchase. However, I
will tell elsewhere the tale of his voracity in such
matters, and will now go back to Sthenius. Inflamed **89**
with violent anger against Sthenius, he renounced his
hospitality and moved out of his house—or rather,
stepped out of it, for he had *moved* ª out of it already.
He was promptly invited by the chief enemies of
Sthenius to stay with them ; they meant to increase
his resentment against Sthenius by concocting some
lying charge against the man. These enemies were
a man of some note named Agathinus, and Dorotheus,
who was married to Callidama the daughter of
Agathinus ; Verres had heard of this lady, and chose
the son-in-law's house as his new abode for that reason.
After one night there he was so fond of Dorotheus
that one would have supposed they had all things in
common, and was paying Agathinus the attentions
due to a near connexion ; it would even appear that
he no longer cared much for the statue of Himera, the
shape and features of his hostess gave him so much
greater satisfaction. XXXVII. The result was that **90**
he began encouraging these people to do something to
ruin Sthenius and rig up some sort of charge against
him. They told him that they could think of nothing
to say. Thereupon he informed them, openly and
positively, that any charge they chose to bring before
him against Sthenius they would succeed in proving
as soon as they had brought it. At this they delayed

Itaque illi non procrastinant; Sthenium statim
educunt, aiunt ab eo litteras publicas esse corruptas.
Sthenius postulat ut, cum secum sui cives agant de
litteris publicis corruptis, eiusque rei legibus Thermitanorum actio sit ; senatusque et populus Romanus
Thermitanis, quod semper in amicitia fideque man-
sissent, urbem agros legesque suas reddidisset ;
Publiusque Rupilius postea leges ita Siculis ex senatus consulto de decem legatorum sententia dedisset
ut cives inter sese legibus suis agerent ; idemque hoc
haberet Verres ipse in edicto : ut de his omnibus
91 causis se ad leges reiceret. Iste homo omnium
aequissimus atque a cupiditate remotissimus se
cogniturum esse confirmat ; paratum ad causum
dicendam venire hora nona iubet. Non erat obscurum quid homo improbus ac nefarius cogitaret ;
neque enim ipse satis occultarat, nec mulier tacere
potuerat. Intellectum est id istum agere ut, cum
Sthenium sine ullo argumento ac sine teste damnasset,
tum homo nefarius de homine nobili atque id aetatis
suoque hospite virgis supplicium crudelissime sumeret. Quod cum esset perspicuum, de amicorum
hospitumque suorum sententia Thermis Sthenius
Romam profugit ; hiemi fluctibusque sese committere maluit quam non istam communem Siculorum
tempestatem calamitatemque vitaret.

92   XXXVIII. Iste homo certus et diligens ad horam

390

no longer, but promptly issued a summons against Sthenius, and alleged that he had forged an official document. Sthenius made application as follows: Whereas he was charged, by his fellow-citizens, with forging an official document; and whereas the laws of Thermae provided a form of trial for that offence; and whereas the Senate and People of Rome, considering the unbroken amity and loyalty of the people of Thermae, had restored to them their city, their lands, and their own laws; and whereas the right of citizens to proceed against one another under their own laws was thereafter laid down in the laws made for the Sicilians by Publius Rupilius, in conformity with a decree of the Senate and the recommendations of the Commission of Ten; and whereas Verres in his Edict had confirmed this right: That on all the aforesaid grounds Verres would send his case for trial under the laws of the city. But this paragon of disinterested **91** impartiality announced that he would try the case himself, and ordered Sthenius to appear with his defence ready by the middle of the afternoon. The rascal's immoral plan was not obscure; for he had not kept it quite secret himself, nor had that woman succeeded in holding her tongue. It was seen that his purpose was, with no support of proof or evidence, to pronounce Sthenius guilty, and then to inflict, upon this elderly man of high standing, who had been the scoundrel's own host, the merciless punishment of flogging. This being obvious, Sthenius took the advice of his friends and intimates, and fled from Thermae to Rome, ready to face the rough waves of winter, if so he might escape the hurricane that was devastating all the land of Sicily.

XXXVIII. Our punctual and business-like Verres **92**

nonam praesto est; Sthenium citari iubet. Quem
posteaquam videt non adesse, dolore ardere atque
iracundia furere coepit; Venerios domum Sthenii
mittere, equis circum agros eius villasque dimittere.
Itaque dum exspectat quidnam sibi certi afferatur,
ante horam tertiam noctis de foro non discedit.
Postridie mane descendit; Agathinum ad sese vocat,
iubet eum de litteris publicis in absentem Sthenium
dicere. Erat eius modi causa ut ille ne sine adversario quidem apud inimicum iudicem reperire posset
93 quid diceret; itaque tantum verbo posuit Sacerdote
praetore Sthenium litteras publicas corrupisse. Vix
ille hoc dixerat cum iste pronuntiat STHENIUM LIT-
TERAS PUBLICAS CORRUPISSE VIDERI ; et haec praeterea
addidit homo Venerius, novo modo, nullo exemplo,
OB EAM REM HS D. VENERI ERYCINAE DE STHENII BONIS
SE EXACTURUM ; bonaque eius statim coepit vendere ;
et vendidisset, si tantulum morae fuisset quo minus
94 ei pecunia illa numeraretur. Ea posteaquam numerata est, contentus hac iniquitate non fuit; palam
de sella ac tribunali pronuntiat SI QUIS ABSENTEM
STHENIUM REI CAPITALIS REUM FACERE VELLET, SESE
EIUS NOMEN RECEPTURUM ; et simul ut ad causam
accederet nomenque deferret Agathinum, novum
affinem atque hospitem, coepit hortari. Tum ille

arrived in the afternoon at the hour appointed, and
ordered Sthenius to be summoned. Finding that his
victim was absent, in a wild outburst of disappointed
fury he dispatched police-messengers to the house of
Sthenius, and sent others off on horseback to make
the round of his estates and farm-houses ; and he
waited so long for news from these men that the
evening was half gone before he left the court-
house. The next morning he arrived early, sent
for Agathinus, and bade him prosecute Sthenius for
forgery in his absence. The case was so weak that,
even though Sthenius was not there to reply and
was being tried by his personal enemy, Agathinus
could think of no arguments to submit ; he there- 93
fore merely stated in so many words that during
the praetorship of Sacerdos Sthenius had forged an
official document. The words were hardly out of
his mouth when Verres pronounced sentence,
" Sthenius is found guilty of forgery of an official
document " : to which this devotee of Venus added,
without any usage or precedent to support him, " I
will exact as penalty the payment of £5000 from
the estate of Sthenius to Our Lady of Eryx ; "
whereupon he took steps at once to have the belong-
ings of Sthenius sold up ; and sold up they would
have been, had there been the smallest delay in
paying him that £5000. The payment completed, 94
he was not satisfied with this outrage of justice.
From his chair of office on the tribunal he announced
publicly that if anyone should think fit to prosecute
Sthenius in absence on a capital charge, permission
to prosecute would be granted ; and with that he
began urging his new host and connexion, Agathinus,
to come forward and undertake such a prosecution.

clare omnibus audientibus se id non esse facturum,
neque se usque eo Sthenio esse inimicum ut eum rei
capitalis affinem esse diceret. Hic tum repente
Pacilius quidam, homo egens et levis, accedit; ait,
si liceret, absentis nomen deferre se velle. Iste
vero et licere et fieri solere, et se recepturum; itaque
defertur.   Edicit statim ut Kalendis Decembribus
adsit Sthenius Syracusis.

95   Hic, qui Romam pervenisset, satisque feliciter
anni iam adverso tempore navigasset, omniaque
habuisset aequiora et placabiliora quam animum
praetoris atque hospitis, rem ad amicos suos detulit;
quae, ut erat acerba atque indigna, sic videbatur
omnibus. XXXIX. Itaque in senatu continuo Cn.
Lentulus et L. Gellius consules faciunt mentionem
placere statui, si patribus conscriptis videretur, NE
ABSENTES HOMINES IN PROVINCIIS REI FIERENT RERUM
CAPITALIUM; causam Sthenii totam et istius crudelitatem et iniquitatem senatum docent   Aderat in
senatu Verres pater istius, et flens unum quemque
senatorum rogabat ut filio suo parceret; neque
tamen multum proficiebat, erat enim summa voluntas
senatus. Itaque sententiae dicebantur, CUM STHE-
NIUS ABSENS REUS FACTUS ESSET, DE ABSENTE IUDICIUM
NULLUM FIERI PLACERE, ET, SI QUOD ESSET FACTUM, ID

Agathinus replied, in a loud voice which all could hear, that he would not do so, that he was not so bitter an enemy to Sthenius as to allege him to be connected with a capital offence. Upon this, without warning, one Pacilius, a man of no position or character, stepped forward and professed himself ready, if it was allowable, to prosecute Sthenius in his absence. Verres replied that it was both allowable and usual, and that permission should be granted; and it was done accordingly. Verres at once gave notice summoning Sthenius to appear at Syracuse on the 1st day of December.

Sthenius had reached Rome, after a voyage 95 which, considering that the stormy season had begun, was quite satisfactory, and had been in all ways calmer and more agreeable than the temper of his guest the praetor. He reported the attack on him to his friends, all of whom considered it a cruel piece of injustice, as indeed it was. XXXIX. The immediate result was that the consuls Gnaeus Lentulus and Lucius Gellius moved the following resolution in the Senate, *That in the opinion of this House the prosecution of persons in their absence on capital charges should be prohibited in the provinces,* and gave the Senate a full account of the case of Sthenius and Verres' iniquitous cruelty. The elder Verres, this man's father, was in the House, and with tears in his eyes kept beseeching one senator after another to have mercy on his son, but without much success, so strong was the feeling in the Senate. Speeches were made supporting the motion *That whereas Sthenius has been prosecuted in his absence, it is agreed that no trial of him in his absence shall take place, and that if any*

96 RATUM ESSE NON PLACERE. Eo die transigi nihil potuit,
quod et id temporis erat et ille pater istius invenerat
homines qui dicendo tempus consumerent. Postea
senex Verres defensores atque hospites omnes
Sthenii convenit ; rogat eos atque orat ne oppugnent
filium suum ; de Sthenio ne laborent ; confirmat iis
curaturum se esse ne quid ei per filium suum noceretur,
se homines certos eius rei causa in Siciliam et terra
et mari esse missurum. Et erat spatium dierum fere
triginta ante Kalendas Decembres, quo die iste ut
97 Syracusis Sthenius adesset edixerat. Commoventur
amici Sthenii ; sperant fore ut patris litteris nuntiis-
que filius ab illo furore revocetur. In senatu postea
causa non agitur. Veniunt ad istum domestici
nuntii litterasque a patre afferunt ante Kalendas
Decembres, cum isti etiam tum de Sthenio in integro
tota res esset ; eodemque ei tempore de eadem re
litterae complures a multis eius amicis ac necessariis
afferuntur. XL. Hic iste, qui prae cupiditate neque
officii sui neque periculi neque pietatis neque humanitatis rationem habuisset umquam, neque in eo quod
monebatur auctoritatem patris neque in eo quod
rogabatur voluntatem anteponendam putavit libidini
suae, mane Kalendis Decembribus ut edixerat
98 Sthenium citari iubet.—Si abs te istam rem parens

such trial has already taken place, it shall be invalid.
No final decision could be reached that day, both 96
because it was so late, and because Verres' father
secured certain members to spin out the proceedings
with long speeches. When the House rose, the old
gentleman asked all the supporters and intimate
friends of Sthenius to come and see him, and urgently
entreated them not to continue the attack on his son.
" You need not," he told them, " be anxious about
Sthenius. I give you my word that I will see to it
that no harm comes to him through my son ; I will
for this purpose send him word in Sicily by responsible
messengers, both overland and by water." It was,
certainly, some thirty days yet to the 1st of December,
the day Verres had officially fixed for the appearance
of Sthenius at Syracuse. The appeal succeeded ;
the friends of Sthenius felt sure that the father's 97
letters and messengers would make the son give up
his insane purpose. The question was not discussed
any further in the Senate. The messengers from
home reached Verres, bringing his father's letters,
before the 1st of December, while he had as yet taken
no irrevocable steps regarding Sthenius ; and at
the same time a number of letters on the same
subject reached him from a number of his friends
and acquaintances. XL. And then this man, whose
passions had always blinded him to considerations
of morality and prudence, of duty towards others
and feeling for others, resolved neither to heed his
father's warnings nor to defer to his father's wishes,
because they interfered with his own desires. On
the morning of the 1st of December, in accordance
with his notice, he ordered Sthenius to be summoned into court.—Had your father made that 98

tuus alicuius amici rogatu benignitate aut ambitione
adductus petisset, gravissima tamen apud te voluntas
patris esse debuisset ; cum vero abs te tui capitis
causa peteret hominesque certos domo misisset,
hique eo tempore ad te venissent cum tibi in integro
tota res esset, ne tum quidem te potuit, si non pietatis,
at salutis tuae ratio ad officium sanitatemque re-
ducere ?—Citat reum ; non respondit. Citat accusatorem ; attendite, quaeso, iudices, quanto opere istius
amentiae fortuna ipsa adversata sit, et simul videte
qui Sthenii causam casus adiuverit ; citatus accusator,
M. Pacilius, nescio quo casu non respondit, non
99 adfuit. Si praesens Sthenius reus esset factus, si
manifesto in maleficio teneretur, tamen, cum accusator non adesset, Sthenium condemnari non
oporteret. Etenim, si posset reus absente accusatore condemnari, non ego a Vibone Veliam parvulo
navigio inter fugitivorum ac praedonum ac tua tela
venissem, quo tempore omnis illa mea festinatio
fuit cum periculo capitis, ob eam causam, ne tu
ex reis eximerere si ego ad diem non adfuissem.
Quod igitur tibi erat in tuo iudicio optatissimum,
me cum citatus essem non adesse, cur Sthenio
non putasti prodesse oportere, cum eius accusator
non adfuisset ? Itaque fecit ut exitus principio

request of you at the instance of some friend, and
from motives of kindliness or self-interest, even so
you should have paid the utmost respect to a parent's
wishes ; and when he asked you to do it to save yourself from ruin, and sent responsible messengers to
you from home for the purpose, who reached you
at a time when you had not finally committed yourself, could you not even so be recalled to duty and
common sense by respect, if not for your father, at
least for your own safety ?—He summoned the
accused ; there was no answer. He summoned the
prosecutor ; and I would bid you mark, gentlemen,
how mightily Fortune herself fought against this
madman, and note at the same time how chance
helped the cause of Sthenius : the prosecutor,
Marcus Pacilius, by some chance or other did not
answer, did not appear. Now if Sthenius had been 99
there to meet the charge in person, had his guilt
been manifest and undeniable, even so, with no
prosecutor there, it would have been wrong to
convict him. Why, if it were possible for an accused
man to be convicted with his prosecutor absent, I
should never have made that voyage in a small boat
from Vibo to Velia, risking the murderous assaults
of revolted slaves and pirates—and your own ; I
hurried forward the whole of my journey then at
the risk of my life, simply in order that my failure
to appear at the time appointed should not mean
your liberation from the ranks of the accused. You
could have desired nothing better in your own trial
than that I should not be there when called upon :
why did you not hold that Sthenius had a right to
the same advantage when *his* prosecutor failed to
appear ? And so the last stage of his proceedings

simillimus reperiretur : quem absentem reum fecerat, eum absente accusatore condemnat.

100   XLI. Nuntiabatur illi primis illis temporibus id quod pater quoque ad eum pluribus verbis scripserat, agitatam rem esse in senatu ; etiam in contione tribunum plebis de causa Sthenii M. Palicanum esse questum ; postremo me ipsum apud hoc collegium tribunorum plebis, cum eorum omnium edicto non liceret Romae quemquam esse qui rei capitalis condemnatus esset, egisse causam Sthenii, et cum rem ita exposuissem quem ad modum nunc apud vos, docuissemque hanc damnationem duci non oportere, x tribunos plebis hoc statuisse, idque de omnium sententia pronuntiatum esse, NON VIDERI STHENIUM IMPEDIRI EDICTO QUO MINUS EI LICERET ROMAE ESSE.

101 Cum haec ad istum afferrentur, pertimuit aliquando et commotus est ; vertit stilum in tabulis suis, quo facto causam omnem evertit suam ; nihil enim sibi reliqui fecit quod defendi aliqua ratione posset. Nam si ita defenderet, " Recipi nomen absentis licet ; hoc fieri in provincia nulla lex vetat," mala et improba defensione, verum aliqua tamen uti videretur ; postremo illo desperatissimo perfugio uti posset, se imprudentem fecisse, existimasse id licere ; quamquam haec perditissima defensio est, tamen aliquid

---

a They published every year an official list of outlawed persons.

was like the first. He had allowed Sthenius to be prosecuted when Sthenius himself was absent; and now, when the prosecutor was absent, he pronounced Sthenius guilty.

XLI. News was brought to him very soon after- 100 wards, and his father had told him too, in a long letter, that his action had been discussed in the Senate; further, that a tribune of the people, Marcus Palicanus, had denounced the proceedings against Sthenius at a public meeting; and lastly, that I myself had approached the corporation of tribunes, had pleaded the case of Sthenius as affected by their corporate proclamation banishing from Rome all persons convicted of capital offences,[a] had set the facts before them (as I have just set them before yourselves), and had argued that this sentence ought not to be treated as a valid conviction; whereupon all ten tribunes had agreed, and a resolution had been carried unanimously, *That in the opinion of this body the proclamation of banishment from Rome does not apply to Sthenius.* When 101 this news reached Verres, he was at last thoroughly frightened and upset; and then he applied the blunt end of his style[b] to his records, thereby making an end of all his chances of acquittal, for he has left himself no loop-hole for any sort of defence. For if he were to plead thus, "The prosecution of an absent person is legal, there is no law to forbid this in the provinces," it would be held a weak and immoral line of defence, but still a defence of a kind; or as a last desperate resort he might have pleaded that he acted in ignorance, thinking it was legal; this would be a quite hopeless defence, but at least it

[b] To erase what was written.

dici videretur. Tollit ex tabulis id quod erat, et facit coram delatum esse.

102   XLII. Hic videte in quot se laqueos induerit, quorum ex nullo se umquam expediet. Primum, ipse in Sicilia saepe et palam de loco superiore dixerat, et in sermone multis demonstrarat, licere nomen recipere absentis, se exemplo fecisse quod fecisset. Haec eum dictitasse priore actione et Sex. Pompeius Chlorus dixit, de cuius virtute antea commemoravi, et Cn. Pompeius Theodorus, homo et Cn. Pompeii clarissimi viri iudicio plurimis maximisque in rebus probatissimus et omnium existimatione ornatissimus, et Posides Macro Soluntinus, homo summa nobilitate, existimatione, virtute ornatissimus ; et hac actione quam voletis multi dicent, et qui ex isto ipso audierunt viri primarii nostri ordinis, et alii qui interfuerunt cum absentis nomen reciperetur. Deinde Romae, cum res esset acta in senatu, omnes istius amici, in his etiam pater eius hoc defendebat, licere fieri, saepe esse factum, istum quod fecisset aliorum exemplo institutoque fecisse.

103 Dicit praeterea testimonium tota Sicilia, quae in communibus postulatis civitatum omnium consulibus edidit, rogare atque orare patres conscriptos ut statuerent ne absentium nomina reciperentur.

would have some show of reason. He expunged the true statement from the records, and made them read that Sthenius was present when prosecuted.

XLII. And now observe the number of different 102 nooses he has thus put round his neck—from none of which will he ever get it free. First, he himself in Sicily had frequently, publicly and officially stated, and had argued in many private conversations, that to allow the prosecution of a person in his absence was legal, that he had precedent for doing what he had done. Evidence that he had repeatedly said this was given at the first hearing by Sextus Pompeius Chlorus, of whose high character I have already spoken ; by Gnaeus Pompeius Theodorus, a man whose conduct of many important affairs has won the full approval of the eminent Gnaeus Pompeius, and whose reputation everywhere stands very high ; and by Posides Macro of Solus, a man of the highest standing, reputation, and character. Similar evidence shall be given at this hearing by as many witnesses as you care to hear, both by leading members of our own Order who heard the above statement from his own lips, and by others who were present when he allowed the prosecution of Sthenius in absence. Next, when this affair was brought up in the Senate at Rome, all his friends, including his father, pleaded just this on his behalf—that his action was legal, that it had often been done before, that he had a precedent set up by other persons for doing what he did. Further, all Sicily 103 testifies to this fact, in the general petition addressed to the consuls by all her cities, wherein she prays and entreats this honourable House to decree the prohibition of all prosecutions of absent persons. You

Qua de re Cn. Lentulum, patronum Siciliae, clarissimum adulescentem, dicere audistis Siculos, cum se causam quae sibi in senatu pro his agenda esset docerent, de Sthenii calamitate questos esse, propterque hanc iniuriam quae Sthenio facta esset eos statuisse ut hoc quod dico postularetur.

104 Quae cum ita essent, tantane amentia praeditus atque audacia fuisti ut in re tam clara, tam testata, tam abs te ipso pervulgata, tabulas publicas corrumpere auderes ? At quem ad modum corrupisti ? nonne ita ut omnibus nobis tacentibus ipsae tuae te tabulae condemnare possent ? Cedo, quaeso, codicem ; circumfer, ostende. Videtisne totum hoc nomen, coram ubi facit delatum, esse in litura ? Quid fuit istic antea scriptum ? quod mendum ista litura correxit ? Quid a nobis, iudices, exspectatis argumenta huius criminis ? Nihil dicimus ; tabulae sunt in medio, quae se corruptas atque interlitas esse

105 clamant. Ex istis etiam tu rebus effugere te posse confidis, cum te nos non opinione dubia sed tuis vestigiis persequamur, quae tu in tabulis publicis expressa ac recentia reliquisti ? Is mihi etiam Sthenium litteras publicas corrupisse causa incognita iudicavit, qui defendere non poterit se non in ipsius Sthenii nomine litteras publicas corrupisse ?

106 XLIII. Videte porro aliam amentiam ; videte ut, dum expedire sese vult, induat. Cognitorem ascribit Sthenio ; quem ? Cognatum aliquem aut propin

have heard what that distinguished young champion of Sicily, Gnaeus Lentulus, had to tell you about this : that when the Sicilians were putting before him the issue on which he was to support their interests in the Senate, they denounced the treatment of the unhappy Sthenius, and that it was precisely this wrong done to Sthenius that made them resolve to present the petition I speak of. In the face of all this, how could 104 you be possessed with such frantic recklessness as to alter an official document that stated a fact so clearly true, so fully confirmed, and by your own action so widely known ? And how did you effect the alteration ? Why, in such a fashion that your own tablets would be enough to convict you without a word said by any of us here. Let us have the volume, please ; carry it round, and show it to the Court. Do you see, gentlemen, how the whole passage that states that Sthenius was there when prosecuted is written over an erasure ? What was written there before ? what was the slip corrected by that erasure ? Why should this Court feel that *we* must prove this charge ? We hold our tongues ; the documents are before you, proclaiming themselves altered and interpolated. Do you think to escape our pursuit here, where we are 105 tracking you with the help not of vague conjectures but of your own footprints, left clear and fresh on this official document ? Do I find that the man who without trial convicted Sthenius of altering an official record is a man who cannot deny that, dealing with this same Sthenius, he has altered an official record himself ?

XLIII. Next note another piece of folly; note how, 106 trying to free himself, he entangles himself further. He assigns Sthenius an attorney ; and who is it ?

quum? Non. Thermitanum aliquem, honestum hominem ac nobilem? Ne id quidem. At Siculum, in
quo aliquis splendor dignitasque esset? Neminem.
Quid igitur? Civem Romanum. Cui hoc probari
potest? Cum esset Sthenius civitatis suae nobilissi-
mus, amplissima cognatione, plurimis amicitiis, cum
praeterea tota Sicilia multum auctoritate et gratia
posset, invenire neminem Siculum potuit qui pro se
cognitor fieret? Hoc probabis? An ipse civem
Romanum maluit? Cedo cui Siculo, cum is reus
fieret, civis Romanus cognitor factus umquam sit.
Omnium praetorum litteras qui ante te fuerunt pro-
fer, explica: si unum inveneris, ego hoc tibi, quem
ad modum in tabulis scriptum habes, ita gestum
107 esse concedam. At, credo, Sthenius hoc sibi amplum
putavit, eligere ex civium Romanorum numero, ex
amicorum atque hospitum suorum copia, quem
cognitorem daret. Quem delegit? quis in tabulis
scriptus est? C. Claudius C. F. Palatina. Non
quaero quis hic sit Claudius, quam splendidus, quam
honestus, quam idoneus propter cuius auctoritatem
et dignitatem Sthenius ab omnium Siculorum consuetudine discederet et civem Romanum cognitorem
daret. Nihil horum quaero; fortasse enim Sthenius
non splendorem hominis sed familiaritatem secutus
est. Quid? si omnium mortalium Sthenio nemo
inimicior quam hic C. Claudius cum semper tum
in his ipsis rebus et temporibus fuit, si de litteris
corruptis contra venit, si contra omni ratione pug-

Some kinsman or connexion of his ? No. Some respectable and important citizen of Thermae ? Not that either. Some other Sicilian, then, of appreciable prominence and worth ? No one of the kind. Then who is it ? A Roman citizen. Now who will let that pass ? Sthenius was the most important man in his community ; his family was extensive, his friendships numerous ; in addition, his influence and popularity made him count for much all through Sicily : could he then find no Sicilian to stand attorney for him ? Will you make us believe that ? Or did he himself prefer a Roman citizen ? Quote me a single case of an accused Sicilian whose attorney has been a Roman citizen. Go through the records of all the praetors who have preceded you, and if you find one such case, I will admit that what you have written in that record is what did happen. But we are to suppose, perhaps, 107 that Sthenius thought it would look well to choose out of the ranks of our Roman citizens—out of his large circle of friends and guests—someone to be his attorney. Whom, then, did he choose ? Whose name appears in the record ? " Gaius Claudius, son of Gaius Claudius, of the Palatine tribe." Now I will not ask who this Claudius is, how eminent or respected he is, or how far his influence and merit might properly lead Sthenius to disregard the regular Sicilian custom and offer a Roman citizen as his attorney. I will ask no such questions ; for I daresay Sthenius was guided in his choice not by the man's eminence but by his friendship for himself. Well then, if it is true that no man living was a more bitter enemy of Sthenius than this Claudius, his enemy always, but most of all in this affair and at this time ; if he appeared against Sthenius in this forgery charge, and fought against

navit, utrum potius pro Sthenio inimicum cognitorem esse factum an te ad Sthenii periculum inimici eius nomine abusum esse credemus?

108 XLIV. Ac ne qui forte dubitet cuius modi totum sit negotium, tametsi iam dudum omnibus istius improbitatem perspicuam esse confido, tamen paulum etiam attendite. Videtis illum subcrispo capillo, nigrum, qui eo vultu nos intuetur ut sibi ipsi peracutus esse videatur, qui tabulas tenet, qui scribit, qui monet, qui proximus est. Is est C. Claudius, qui in Sicilia sequester istius, interpres, confector negotiorum, prope collega Timarchidi numerabatur, nunc obtinet eum locum ut vix Apronio illi de familiaritate concedere videatur, et[1] qui se non Timarchidi sed
109 ipsius Verris collegam et socium esse dicebat. Dubitate etiam, si potestis, quin eum iste potissimum ex omni numero delegerit cui hanc cognitoris falsi improbam personam imponeret, quem et huic inimicissimum et sibi amicissimum esse arbitraretur. Hic vos dubitabitis, iudices, tantam istius audaciam, tantam crudelitatem, tantam iniuriam vindicare? Dubitabitis exemplum illorum iudicum sequi qui damnato Cn. Dolabella damnationem Philodami Opuntii resciderunt, quod is non absens reus factus esset, quae res iniquissima et acerbissima est, sed

---

[1] *The* MSS. *read* et *for* ei, *which is Benedict's conjecture;* et *makes very fair sense:* Claudius *was considered nearly on a level with Timarchides, but thought and described himself as higher still.*

him with every weapon available ; shall we prefer to
believe that Sthenius's enemy became his attorney in
order to save him, or that *you* have made a false use of
that enemy's name in order that Sthenius might be
ruined ?

XLIV. Now to remove any possible doubt as to the 108
meaning of the whole business, although I feel sure
that this man's wickedness has long been transparent
to all of you, I ask your attention a little further.
You observe yonder person with delicate curls and
dark complexion, who is looking at us with what
he is pleased to consider a very sharp expression,
handling documents, writing notes, making sugges-
tions, sitting close to Verres.   That is Claudius, who
in Sicily was Verres' agent and go-between and
business manager, and had an official rank nearly on a
level with Timarchides, and who is now so highly
placed that he would seem to enjoy the great man's
confidence hardly less than the notable Apronius ;
who used to call himself the official equal and
coadjutor not of Timarchides but of Verres himself.
You may hesitate, if you still can, to conclude that 109
Verres chose him specially out of all the rest to play
the wicked part of counterfeit attorney simply
because he looked upon him as the worst enemy of
Sthenius and his own best friend.   And now will you
hesitate, gentlemen, to inflict the punishment that all
this insolence, this inhumanity, this tyranny of his
deserves ?   Will you hesitate to follow the precedent
set by the court which upon the conviction of Gnaeus
Dolabella annulled the conviction of Philodamus of
Opus because he had been prosecuted, not in his
absence—nothing so unjust and cruel as that—but

cum ei legatio iam Romam a suis civibus esset data? Quod illi iudices multo in leviore causa statuerunt aequitatem secuti, vos id statuere in gravissima causa, praesertim aliorum auctoritate iam confirmatum, dubitabitis?

110   XLV. At quem hominem, C. Verres, tanta tam insigni iniuria affecisti? quem hominem absentem de litteris corruptis causa incognita condemnasti? cuius absentis nomen recepisti? quem absentem non modo sine crimine et sine teste verum etiam sine accusatore damnasti? Quem hominem? di immortales! non dicam amicum tuum, quod apud homines clarissimum est, non hospitem, quod sanctissimum est; nihil enim minus libenter de Sthenio commemoro, nihil aliud in eo quod reprehendi possit invenio, nisi quod homo frugalissimus atque integerrimus te, hominem plenum stupri flagitii sceleris, domum suam invitavit; nisi quod qui C. Marii, Cn. Pompeii, C. Marcelli, L. Sisennae, tui defensoris, ceterorum virorum fortissimorum hospes fuisset atque esset, ad eum numerum clarissimorum hominum tuum quoque nomen ascripsit.

111 Quare de hospitio violato et de tuo isto scelere nefario nihil queror: hoc dico, non iis qui Sthenium norunt, hoc est, nemini eorum qui in Sicilia fuerunt; nemo enim ignorat quo hic in civitate

after being appointed by his fellow-citizens member
of a deputation to visit Rome? Equity induced that
court to take that decision on grounds comparatively
weak: will you hesitate to take a similar decision
when the grounds for it are very strong, especially now
that it is supported by the authority of a precedent?

XLV. Yes, Verres, and what manner of man is 110
it to whom you have done so great and conspicuous
a wrong? Who is this whom, absent and untried,
you have pronounced guilty of forgery? Who is
this whom you have allowed, in his absence, to be
prosecuted? Who is this whom you have convicted,
in his absence, not only without any speech or
evidence for the prosecution, but without even the
presence of the prosecutor? Who is this man?
God help me, I will not say that you were bound to
him by friendship, which is the most glorious thing
in the world, nor by hospitality, which is the most
sacred; for there is nothing that I am more unwilling to record of Sthenius, nor can I observe any
other thing in him that is open to censure, than
that so upright and honest living a man as he is
invited to his house a licentious and filthy criminal
like yourself; than that, having been or still being
the host of Gaius Marius, Gnaeus Pompeius, Gaius
Marcellus, Lucius Sisenna, your present supporter,
and all those other gallant gentlemen, he has added
to that roll of illustrious persons your name also. I 111
do not therefore denounce the violation of hospitality
and your abominable crime in violating it. What
I have to say is this, and I say it, not to those who
know Sthenius, not, in other words, to anyone who
has ever been in Sicily—for all such persons know
how pre-eminent he is in his own city, and how

sua splendore, qua apud omnes Siculos dignitate
atque existimatione sit : sed ut illi quoque qui in
ea provincia non fuerunt intellegere possint in quo
homine tu statueris exemplum eius modi, quod
cum propter iniquitatem rei tum etiam propter
hominis dignitatem acerbum omnibus atque in-
112 tolerandum videretur. XLVI. Estne Sthenius is
qui, omnes honores domi suae facillime cum adeptus
esset, amplissime ac magnificentissime gessit ; qui
oppidum non maximum maximis ex pecunia sua locis
communibus monumentisque decoravit ; cuius de
meritis in rem publicam Thermitanorum Siculosque
universos fuit aenea tabula fixa Thermis in curia, in
qua publice erat de huius beneficiis scriptum et
incisum ? quae tabula tum imperio tuo revulsa, nunc
a me tamen deportata est, ut omnes huius honores
inter suos et amplitudinem possent cognoscere.
113 Estne hic qui apud Cn. Pompeium, clarissimum
virum, cum accusatus esset, quod propter C. Marii
familiaritatem et hospitium contra rem publicam
sensisse eum inimici et accusatores eius dicerent,
cumque magis invidioso crimine quam vero ar-
cesseretur, ita a Cn. Pompeio absolutus est ut in
eo ipso iudicio Pompeius hunc hospitio suo dig-
nissimum statueret ? ita porro laudatus defensus-
que ab omnibus Siculis ut idem Pompeius non
ab homine solum, sed etiam a provincia tota,

---

[a] Evidently a cautious allusion to proceedings in the
time of the Sullan proscriptions.

great his worth and reputation are in the eyes of all
Sicilians ; but I would enable even those persons
who have never been in the province to know the
character of the man whom you have chosen to
mark by treatment which all, whether they looked to
the injustice of the deed itself or to the high merit
of the sufferer, accounted an intolerable piece of
brutality. XLVI. Can Sthenius be the man who 112
attained with ease all the posts of authority in his
own city, and discharged their responsibilities with
splendid liberality ? the man who at his own cost
adorned his little town by erecting splendid
public buildings and works of art, whose services
to the state of Thermae and to the Sicilians
generally are attested by a bronze tablet set up
in the Senate-house at Thermae, engraved with an
inscription officially recording his benefactions ?
Which tablet, torn down by your orders at the time,
I have none the less now brought over here, that all
men might learn of the honours and the greatness
which he has achieved among his own people. Can 113
this be the man who was denounced to the illustrious
Gnaeus Pompeius, on the ground, as his enemies
who denounced him argued, that his relations of
friendship and hospitality with Gaius Marius proved
him to have been disloyal to his country *a*—a charge
that, however false, had much power to excite
ill-will against him ; and who nevertheless was
acquitted of the charge by Pompeius, in terms that
of themselves declared him fully worthy to be host
or guest of Pompeius himself ? and who, moreover,
was eulogized and defended by all the Sicilians so
warmly that Pompeius felt himself to be earning,
by that acquittal, not only the man's own gratitude

413

se huius absolutione inire gratiam arbitraretur? Postremo, estne hic qui et animum in rem publicam habuit eius modi, et tantum auctoritate apud suos cives potuit, ut perficeret in Sicilia solus te praetore, quod non modo Siculus nemo, sed ne Sicilia quidem tota potuisset, ut ex oppido Thermis nullum signum, nullum ornamentum, nihil ex sacro, nihil de publico attingeres, cum praesertim et essent

114 multa praeclara et tu omnia concupisses? Denique nunc vide quid inter te, cuius nomine apud Siculos dies festi agitantur et praeclara illa Verria celebrantur, cui statuae Romae stant inauratae, a communi Siciliae, quem ad modum inscriptum videmus, datae —vide, inquam, quid inter te et hunc Siculum, qui abs te est patrono Siciliae condemnatus, intersit. Hunc civitates ex Sicilia permultae testimonio suo legationibusque ad eam rem missis publice laudant: te, omnium Siculorum patronum, una Mamertina civitas, socia furtorum ac flagitiorum tuorum, publice laudat—ita tamen novo more ut legati laedant, legatio laudet; ceterae quidem civitates publice litteris, legationibus, testimoniis accusant, queruntur, arguunt; si tu absolutus sis, se funditus eversas esse arbitrantur.

115 XLVII. Hoc de homine ac de huius bonis etiam in Eryco monte monumentum tuorum flagitiorum crudelitatisque posuisti, in quo Sthenii Thermitani

but that of the whole province ? Finally, can this be
the man who had so much love for his city, and so
much power over his fellow-citizens, that he achieved
what no one else in Sicily achieved throughout your
praetorship, what was beyond the power not only
of any other single Sicilian but of all Sicily together
—he kept your hands off every statue and every
work of art, everything sacred to the gods, or owned
by the state ; and that although there were many
things of high merit there, and you had resolved
to have them all ? And now compare with yourself, 114
in whose honour the people of Sicily keep holiday and
celebrate the sublime Festival of Verres—yourself,
gilt statues of whom are set up in Rome, the joint
offering (so the inscription informs us) of the Sicilian
population—compare with yourself, I repeat, this
Sicilian who has been condemned as a criminal by
you, the champion of Sicily. His merits are attested,
directly and officially, through the mouths of deputies
sent here for that purpose, by one Sicilian city
after another. You, the champion of all Sicily, have
your merits officially attested by one city alone, the
city of the Mamertines, your partner in robbery
and rascality—though, what is unusual, while the
deputation lauds your virtues the deputies lash
your vices ; whereas all the other cities officially send
us letters and deputations and witnesses to accuse
and denounce and convict you, and are persuaded
that your acquittal would mean their own complete
destruction.

XLVII. At the expense of this man, and of this 115
man's estate you have actually set up on Mount
Eryx a memorial of your barbarous wickedness
that bears the name of Sthenius of Thermae upon it.

nomen ascriptum est Vidi argenteum Cupidinem cum lampade. Quid tandem habuit argumenti aut rationis res quam ob rem in eo potissimum Sthenianum praemium poneretur? Utrum hoc signum cupiditatis tuae, an tropaeum necessitudinis atque hospitii, an amoris indicium esse voluisti? Faciunt hoc homines quos in summa nequitia non solum libido et voluptas, verum etiam ipsius nequitiae fama delectat, ut multis in locis notas ac vestigia suorum 116 flagitiorum relinqui velint. Ardebat amore illius hospitae, propter quam hospitii iura violarat; hoc non solum sciri tum, verum etiam commemorari semper volebat; itaque ex illa ipsa re quam accusante Agathino gesserat Veneri potissimum deberi praemium statuit, quae illam totam accusationem iudiciumque conflarat. Putarem te gratum in deos si hoc donum Veneri non de Sthenii bonis dedisses sed de tuis: quod facere debuisti, praesertim cum tibi illo ipso anno a Chelidone venisset hereditas.

117 Hic ego, si hanc causam non omnium Siculorum rogatu recepissem; si hoc a me muneris non universa provincia poposcisset; si me animus atque amor in rem publicam existimatioque offensa nostri ordinis ac iudiciorum non hoc facere coegisset; atque haec una causa fuisset, quod amicum atque hospitem meum Sthenium, quem ego in quaestura mea singulariter

---

I have seen it—a silver Cupid, holding a torch.
Now may I ask what justification or reason there
was for applying the profit made out of Sthenius
for *that* particular purpose ? Did you intend this
statue to be a symbol of cupidity, or a token of
friendship and hospitality, or a record of your amour ?
It is the way of those men who take delight not
only in the sensual excitement of vicious excess,
but also in their reputation as vicious persons, to
like leaving behind them everywhere the marks
and footprints of their evil deeds. Inflamed with 116
desire for his hostess, he had for her sake profaned
the tie that bound him to his former host ; this
fact he wished to have not merely known at the
time but remembered for ever ; so he decided that
out of the fortune which, with the help of the woman's
father as prosecutor, he had so nobly won,[a] a fee was
specially due to the goddess of Love, whose work
the whole underhand business of the prosecution
and trial was. I could believe you grateful to heaven
if you had made this offering to Venus not out of
the property of Sthenius but out of your own ; that
is what you ought to have done ; especially as that
very year you had had a legacy from Chelidon.

And now let me say this. Even had I not been 117
persuaded to undertake this case by the whole
Sicilian people ; had the province not united to
entreat me to do it thus much service ; had my loyal
devotion to my country, had the cloud that rests on
the good name of our Order and of these courts of
law, not compelled me to do as I am doing ; had
my sole motive been that you have treated my
friend and host Sthenius, for whom I felt, during
my quaestorship, the warmest friendship and the

dilexissem, de quo optime existimassem, quem in
provincia existimationis meae studiosissimum cupidis-
simumque cognossem, tam crudeliter scelerate nefarieque tractasses :—tamen digna causa videretur
cur inimicitias hominis improbissimi susciperem, ut
118 hospitis salutem fortunasque defenderem. Fecerunt
hoc multi apud maiores nostros ; fecit etiam nuper
homo clarissimus Cn. Domitius, qui M. Silanum consularem virum accusavit propter Aegritomari Trans-
alpini hospitis iniurias. Putarem me idoneum qui
exemplum sequerer humanitatis atque officii, pro-
poneremque spem meis hospitibus ac necessariis quo
tutiorem sese vitam meo praesidio victuros esse
arbitrarentur. Cum vero in communibus iniuriis
totius provinciae Sthenii quoque causa contineatur,
multique uno tempore a me hospites atque amici
publice privatimque defendantur, profecto vereri
non debeo ne quis hoc quod facio non existimet
me summi officii ratione impulsum coactumque
suscepisse.

XLVIII. Atque ut aliquando de rebus ab isto
cognitis iudicatisque et de iudiciis datis dicere de-
sistamus, et, quoniam facta istius in his generibus
infinita sunt, nos modum aliquem et finem orationi
nostrae criminibusque faciamus, pauca ex aliis
119 generibus sumemus. Audistis ob ius dicendum Q.
Varium dicere procuratores suos isti centum et
triginta milia nummum dedisse ; meministis Q.

highest respect, and to whom, I knew well, my own reputation in the province was an object of earnest solicitude—that you have treated that man with the abominable and wicked brutality which I have described :—even then I should feel the protection of this kind friend's happiness and fortune a sufficient reason for incurring this foul scoundrel's enmity. In the days of our forefathers, many have acted thus ; 118 and thus, not long since, did the eminent Gnaeus Domitius act, when he prosecuted the ex-consul Marcus Silanus for the wrong done to his former host, Aegritomarus of Transalpine Gaul. I should feel that I might well copy so humane and upright an action. I should offer those who have given me hospitality and friendship some reason to think that they will live lives of greater security because I am here to protect them. But when I find that the case of Sthenius is but one detail in the general catalogue of a whole province's wrongs, and that I am simultaneously defending, as citizens and as individuals, not one but many of my old hosts and friends, then, surely, I need not be afraid of being supposed to have undertaken to do what I am doing from any motive, or under any obligation, beyond the recognition of what is my bounden duty.

XLVIII. Now I cannot prolong indefinitely my tale of the cases Verres tried, the sentences he pronounced, the proceedings he authorized. His misdeeds of this kind are without number ; but my list of charges must be cut short, or my speech will never be done. I will therefore select a few instances of other kinds. You 119 have heard the statement of Quintus Varius that his agents paid Verres £1300 to secure a favourable decision; you remember the evidence that Varius

419

Varii testimonium, remque hanc totam C. Sacerdotis, hominis ornatissimi, testimonio comprobari. Scitis Cn. Sertium, M. Modium, equites Romanos, sescentos praeterea cives Romanos multosque Siculos dixisse se isti pecuniam ob ius dicendum dedisse. De quo crimine quid ego disputem, cum id totum positum sit in testibus ? quid porro argumenter, qua de re dubitare nemo possit ? An hoc dubitabit quisquam omnium, quin is venalem in Sicilia iurisdictionem habuerit qui Romae totum edictum atque omnia decreta vendiderit ? et quin is ab Siculis ob decreta interponenda pecuniam acceperit qui M. Octavium Ligurem pecuniam ob ius dicendum poposcerit ? Quod enim iste praeterea genus pecuniae cogendae praeteriit ? quod non ab omnibus aliis praeteritum excogitavit ? Ecqua res apud civitates Siculas expetitur, in qua aut honos aliquis sit aut potestas aut procuratio, quin eam rem tu ad tuum quaestum nundinationemque hominum traduxeris ? XLIX. Dicta sunt priore actione et privatim et publice testimonia ; legati Centuripini Halaesini Catinenses Panhormitanique dixerunt, multarum praeterea civitatum, iam vero privatim plurimi. Quorum ex testimoniis cognoscere potuistis tota Sicilia per triennium neminem ulla in civitate senatorem factum esse gratis, neminem ut leges eorum sunt suffragiis, neminem nisi istius imperio aut

---

[a] Orders for the possession of disputed property pending the final settlement of the dispute.

gave, and how the facts of the whole case are
established by the evidence of the eminent Gaius
Sacerdos. You are aware that the Roman knights
Gnaeus Sertius and Marcus Modius, scores of other
Roman citizens, and a large number of Sicilians, have
stated that they paid Verres money to secure favourable decisions. Need I discuss this kind of charge,
when it is so wholly a matter of the evidence of
witnesses? Need I labour to prove the facts where
their truth can be questioned by nobody? Will
anyone at all question the fact that he offered his
judicial decisions for sale there in Sicily, when we
know that he did sell his edict entire, and his judicial
orders wholesale, here in Rome? Or that he accepted
money from Sicilians for making provisional orders,ᵃ
when he demanded money from Marcus Octavius
Ligus for pronouncing a final judgement? Why, what 120
further methods of extorting money has he neglected?
What possible methods, neglected by everyone else,
has he not devised?—Is there any object of ambition
in the cities of Sicily, any post of any honour or power
or responsibility, that you have not converted to your
own profit by your trafficking in human beings?
XLIX. The evidence of this, both official and unofficial, has been given at the first hearing; given by
official deputies from Centuripa, from Halaesa, from
Catina, from Panhormus, from many other cities; and
given also by a host of unofficial witnesses. The
evidence of these persons has sufficed to show you,
gentlemen, that throughout Sicily for three years the
rank of senator has never, in one single city, been
conferred free of charge, never by the method of
election which their laws prescribe, never otherwise
than by Verres' spoken or written orders; that in

421

litteris ; atque in his omnibus senatoribus cooptandis non modo suffragia nulla fuisse, sed ne genera quidem spectata esse ex quibus in eum ordinem cooptari liceret, neque census neque aetates neque cetera 121 Siculorum iura valuisse ; quicumque senator voluerit fieri, quamvis puer, quamvis indignus, quamvis ex eo loco ex quo non liceret, si is pretio apud istum idoneos vinceret,[1] factum esse semper ; non modo Siculorum nihil in hac re valuisse leges, sed ne ab senatu quidem populoque Romano datas. Quas enim leges sociis amicisque dat is qui habet imperium a populo Romano, auctoritatem legum dandarum ab senatu, eae debent et populi Romani et senatus existimari.

122   Halaesini, pro multis et magnis suis maiorumque suorum in rem publicam nostram meritis atque beneficiis suo iure, nuper, L. Licinio Q. Mucio consulibus, cum haberent inter se controversias de senatu cooptando, leges ab senatu nostro petiverunt. Decrevit senatus honorifico senatus consulto ut iis C. Claudius Appii filius Pulcher praetor de senatu cooptando leges conscriberet. C. Claudius, adhibitis omnibus Marcellis qui tum erant, de eorum sententia leges Halaesinis dedit, in quibus multa sanxit de aetate hominum, ne qui minor triginta annis natus ; de quaestu, quem qui fecisset ne legeretur ; de censu,

---

[1] *The MSS. show a variety of readings here, of which the two oldest seem to be* idoneus vinceret *and* idoneus esset. *The emendation in the text is supported by Madvig and others, and is Mueller's reading.*

---

[a] 95 B.C.

[b] These traditional patrons of Sicily were an important branch of the Claudian clan.

filling all those senatorial vacancies there have not
only been no elections, but not even any attention paid
to the legal qualifications for membership, that neither
wealth, nor age, nor any other qualification recognized
in Sicily, has been of any value; that anyone who 121
wished to become a senator, however young or incapable or disqualified by his legal standing, had only
to pay Verres a larger bribe than more suitable people
offered, and a senator he invariably became; and that
in this matter it was not only the local Sicilian laws
that were completely set aside, but even the laws
given by the Senate and Roman People; by them, I
say, for when laws are given to our allies and friends
by a man who has received his military power from
the People and his legislative authority from the
Senate, those laws must be held to be the gift of both
the People and the Senate.

The people of Halaesa were made independent in 122
recognition of the many valuable services and benefits
rendered to Rome by themselves and their ancestors;
but not long ago, in the consulship of Lucius Licinius
and Quintus Mucius,[a] owing to an internal dispute
regarding the way of filling vacancies in their Senate,
they asked the Roman Senate to legislate for them.
The Senate honoured them by passing a decree
appointing the praetor Gaius Claudius Pulcher (son
of Appius Claudius) to draw up for them regulations
for filling the aforesaid vacancies. Claudius, having
secured the help of all the contemporary members of
the Marcellus family,[b] in accordance with their advice
provided Halaesa with regulations, laying down a
number of points, such as the age of candidates (those
under thirty were excluded), the professions dis-
qualifying for membership, the property qualification,

de ceteris rebus. Quae omnia ante istum praetorem et nostrorum magistratuum auctoritate et Halaesinorum summa voluntate valuerunt. Ab isto et praeco qui voluit istum ordinem pretio mercatus est, et pueri annorum senum septenumque denum senatorium nomen nundinati sunt ; et quod Halaesini, antiquissimi et fidelissimi socii atque amici, Romae impetrarant, ut apud se ne suffragiis quidem fieri liceret, id pretio ut fieri posset effecit.

123   L. Agrigentini de senatu cooptando Scipionis leges antiquas habent, in quibus et illa eadem sancta sunt et hoc amplius : cum Agrigentinorum duo genera sint, unum veterum, alterum colonorum quos T. Manlius praetor ex senatus consulto de oppidis Siculorum deduxit Agrigentum, cautum est in Scipionis legibus ne plures essent in senatu ex colonorum numero quam ex vetere Agrigentinorum. Iste, qui omnia iura pretio exaequasset omniumque rerum dilectum atque discrimen pecunia sustulisset, non modo illa quae erant aetatis ordinis quaestusque permiscuit, sed etiam in his duobus generibus civium

124 novorum veterumque turbavit. Nam cum esset ex veterum numero quidam senator demortuus, et cum ex utroque genere par numerus reliquus esset, veterem cooptari necesse erat legibus, ut is amplior numerus esset. Quae cum ita se res haberet, tamen ad istum emptum venerunt illum locum senatorium non solum veteres verum etiam novi. Fit ut pretio

and all such other points. All these regulations, supported by our magistrates and thoroughly approved by the inhabitants, were faithfully observed until Verres became praetor. Verres was bribed to sell the title to an auctioneer who wanted it; from Verres boys of sixteen and seventeen purchased the rank of senator. The right to prohibit such things, even by election, had been granted, at Rome, to our old and faithful friend and ally Halaesa; and Verres made such things possible to those who bribed him!

L. Agrigentum has ancient laws, made by Scipio, 123 controlling elections to its Senate; these contain the same provisions as those mentioned, and the following one besides. There are two classes of Agrigentines; one comprises the old population, the other the settlers from Sicilian towns whom, by order of our Senate, the praetor Titus Manlius established in Agrigentum. In view of this, the laws of Scipio provided that the number of settlers in the Senate should not exceed that of the original inhabitants. Verres, always a leveller of privileges when bribed, and ready to remove distinctions and discriminations everywhere if paid to do it, not only blotted out all those of age, rank, and profession, but also made confusion of that concerning the two classes of citizens, the new and the old. A senator belonging to the old 124 class died; and since an equal number of senators of either class then remained, the election in his place of a member of the old class was legally necessary, in order that this class might be in the majority. In spite of this, the would-be purchasers of this place in the Senate who now approached Verres included members of the new class as well as of the old. The

novus vincat litterasque a praetore afferat Agrigentum. Agrigentini ad istum legatos mittunt, qui eum
leges doceant consuetudinemque omnium annorum
demonstrent, ut iste intellegeret ei se illum locum
vendidisse cui ne commercium quidem esse oporteret.
Quorum oratione iste, cum pretium iam accepisset,
125 ne tantulum quidem commotus est. Idem fecit
Heracleae. Nam eo quoque colonos P. Rupilius
deduxit, legesque similes de cooptando senatu et
de numero veterum ac novorum dedit. Ibi non
solum iste ut apud ceteros pecuniam accepit, sed
etiam genera veterum ac novorum numerumque
permiscuit. LI. Nolite exspectare, dum omnes
obeam oratione mea civitates : hoc uno complector
omnia, neminem isto praetore senatorem fieri
potuisse nisi qui isti pecuniam dedisset.
126 Hoc idem transfero in magistratus, curationes,
sacerdotia ; quibus in rebus non solum hominum
iura sed etiam deorum immortalium religiones omnes
repudiavit. Syracusis lex est de religione, quae in
annos singulos Iovis sacerdotem sortito capi iubeat,
quod apud illos amplissimum sacerdotium putatur ;
127 cum suffragiis tres ex tribus generibus creati sunt,
res revocatur ad sortem. Perfecerat iste imperio ut
pro suffragio Theomnastus familiaris suus in tribus
illis renuntiaretur ; in sorte, cui imperare non
poterat,[1] exspectabant homines quidnam acturus

---

[1] potuerat *the best* MSS., *followed by Peterson ; but the
sense thus given seems impossibly grotesque.*

result was that a new man offered most, succeeded, and came back to Agrigentum with an order from the praetor. The Agrigentines sent Verres a deputation, to tell him what the law was, and to point out that it had been observed without a break, so that he might be aware that he had sold the place to a man who ought not to have been allowed even to bargain for it. Having already received his bribe, he was not affected in the smallest degree by what they said. At Hera- 125 clea he behaved in the same way. Settlers had been established there too, by Publius Rupilius, who had instituted similar laws to regulate elections to the Senate and the proportion between the old citizens and the new. There this man not only took his money as he did everywhere else, but also ignored the distinction of the old from the new class, and the proportion between them. LI. You must not expect me to deal with every city in turn ; let me observe comprehensively that so long as Verres was praetor no man could become a senator unless he had first paid Verres money.

The same thing may be said of magistracies, 126 directorships, and priesthoods, in dealing with which he trampled down not only the rights of men but all the commandments of the powers above. At Syracuse there is a religious ordinance requiring the annual appointment, by lot, of the priest of Jupiter, whose office is the most important priesthood they have ; one candidate is nominated for it, by election, 127 from each of the three divisions of the citizens, and then the lot decides between these. Verres, using his official power to influence the election, succeeded in having his crony Theomnastus returned as one of the three candidates ; and people wondered what he would do with the lot, which was not amenable to his

esset. Homo, id quod erat facillimum, primo vetat sortiri, iubet extra sortem Theomnastum renuntiari. Negant id Syracusani per religiones sacrorum ullo modo fieri posse ; fas denique negant esse. Iubet iste sibi legem recitari. Recitatur : in qua scriptum erat, ut, quot essent renuntiati, tot in hydriam sortes conicerentur ; cuium nomen exisset, ut is haberet id sacerdotium. Iste homo ingeniosus et peracutus " Optime " inquit, " nempe, scriptum ita est, *quot renuntiati erunt*. Quot ergo " inquit " sunt renuntiati ? " Respondent "Tres." " Numquid igitur oportet nisi tres sortes conici, unam educi ? " " Nihil." Conici iubet tres in quibus omnibus scriptum esset nomen Theomnasti. Fit clamor maximus, cum id universis indignum ac nefarium videretur. Ita Iovis illud sacerdotium amplissimum per hanc rationem Theomnasto datur.

128   LII. Cephaloedi mensis est certus, quo mense sacerdotem maximum creari oporteat. Erat eius honoris cupidus Artemo quidam, Climachias cognomine, homo sane locuples et domi nobilis ; sed is fieri nullo modo poterat si Herodotus quidam adesset ; ei locus ille atque honos in illum annum ita deberi putabatur ut ne Climachias quidem contra diceret. Res ad istum defertur, et istius more deciditur— toreumata sane nota ac pretiosa auferuntur. Hero-

orders. The man first tried the simple plan of forbidding the lot, ordering Theomnastus to be returned
as appointed without it. The Syracusans replied that
this could not possibly be done without invalidating
the sacred rites; that it would, in fact, be an act of
sin. He told them to read him the text of the law;
they did so. One clause directed the placing in an
urn of as many lots as there were candidates nominated; the man whose name came out of the urn was
to hold the priesthood. "Very good," observed the
highly acute and ingenious Verres, "the expression is
So many candidates as shall be nominated; quite so;
well, how many *have* been nominated?" "Three,"
was the reply. "Then nothing is required except to
put three lots in and draw one out?" "Nothing."
He thereupon ordered three lots to be put in, each
one inscribed with the name of Theomnastus; whereupon there was a great cry of indignation at what
everyone held a shameful piece of wickedness. And
that is the way in which the most high-priesthood of
Jupiter was conferred upon Theomnastus.

LII. At Cephaloedium there is a fixed month in 128
which the office of high-priest has to be filled. This
position was coveted by one Artemo, surnamed
Climachias, who was admittedly a man of wealth
and of high rank in his own town; however, his
appointment was out of the question if a certain
Herodotus appeared as candidate, a man whose
claims to this position of authority for the coming
year were so strongly supported that Climachias
himself could not oppose them. The matter was
reported to Verres and settled in his customary
fashion—there was a transfer of some quite famous
and valuable chased silver work. Herodotus, who

dotus Romae erat ; satis putabat se ad comitia
tempore venturum si pridie venisset. Iste, ne aut
alio mense ac fas erat comitia haberentur aut Hero-
doto praesenti honos adimeretur (id quod iste non
laborabat, Climachias minime volebat), excogitat—
dixi iamdudum, non est homo acutior quisquam, nec
fuit—excogitat, inquam, quem ad modum mense
illo legitimo comitia haberentur nec tamen Herodotus
129 adesse posset. Est consuetudo Siculorum ceterorum-
que Graecorum, quod suos dies mensesque con-
gruere volunt cum solis lunaeque ratione, ut non
numquam, si quid discrepet, eximant unum aliquem
diem, aut summum biduum, ex mense, quos illi
exaeresimos dies nominant ; item non numquam
uno die longiorem mensem faciunt aut biduo. Quae
cum iste cognosset novus astrologus, qui non tam
caeli rationem quam caelati argenti duceret, eximi
iubet non diem ex mense, sed ex anno unum dimidia-
tumque mensem, hoc modo ut, quo die verbi causa
esse oporteret Idus Ianuarias, eo die Kalendas
Martias proscriberet ; itaque fit, omnibus recusanti-
bus et plorantibus. Dies is erat legitimus comitiis
habendis ; eo modo sacerdos Climachias renuntiatus
130 est. Herodotus cum Roma revertitur, diebus, ut
ipse putabat, quindecim ante comitia, offendit eum
mensem qui consequitur mensem comitialem, comitiis iam abhinc triginta diebus habitis. Tunc Cepha-
loeditani fecerunt intercalarium xlv.[1] dies longum,

---

[1] xxxv *the mss.* : *but 45 days are actually needed.*

---

[a] *Novus* may mean that he was a recent recruit to the
study, or that his methods were novel, or perhaps both.

was at Rome, took it that the day before the election would be time enough for him to arrive. But Verres, to avoid both holding the election in an unlawful month and having Herodotus there when his office was taken from him (not that the latter point troubled Verres, but Climachias was much against it), devised a plan—there is, I said some time ago, no sharper man alive, nor ever was — a plan for holding the election in the lawful month and yet not having Herodotus there. It is the custom of the 129 Sicilian as of all other Greeks, as they like to secure the agreement of their days of the month with the motions of the sun and moon, to correct an occasional discrepancy by shortening a month by some one day, or two days at most, days which they term " eliminated " ; also they sometimes lengthen a month by one day, or by two days. When this was discovered by our new *a* student of astronomy, who was thinking more of the silver plate than of the silver moon, he gave orders, not for shortening the month by a day, but for shortening the year by a month and a half, so that (for instance) the day which ought to be reckoned as the 13th of January would by his orders be publicly announced to be the 1st of March ; and this, to the discontentment and dismay of everyone, was what happened. The 1st of March was the lawful day for the election, and so it came about that Climachias was duly returned as high-priest elect. Herodotus on his return from 130 Rome, fifteen days, as he imagined, before the election, found himself in the month following the election month, and the election over for a month already. The people of Cephaloedium subsequently introduced a supplementary month of forty-five days,

ut reliqui menses in suam rationem reverterentur. Hoc si Romae fieri posset, certe aliqua ratione expugnasset iste ut dies xxxv. inter binos ludos tollerentur, per quos solos iudicium fieri posset.

131 LIII. Iam vero censores quem ad modum isto praetore in Sicilia creati sint operae pretium est cognoscere. Ille enim est magistratus apud Siculos qui diligentissime mandatur a populo propter hanc causam, quod omnes Siculi ex censu quotannis tributa conferunt, in censu habendo potestas omnis aestimationis habendae summaeque faciendae censori permittitur. Itaque et populus cui maxime fidem suarum rerum habeat maxima cura deligit, et propter magnitudinem potestatis hic magistratus **a** 132 populo summa ambitione contenditur. In ea re iste nihil obscure facere voluit, non in sortitione fallere, neque dies de fastis eximere. Nihil sane vafre nec malitiose facere conatus est, sed, ut studia cupiditatesque honorum atque ambitiones ex omnibus civitatibus tolleret, quae res evertendae rei publicae solent esse, ostendit sese in omnibus civitatibus 133 censores esse facturum. Tanto mercatu praetoris indicto, concurritur undique ad istum Syracusas; flagrabat domus tota praetoria studio hominum et cupiditate : nec mirum, omnibus comitiis tot civitatum unam in domum revocatis, tantaque ambitione

---

ᵃ The Roman games, ending September 18, and the Games of Sulla's victory, beginning October 26. As September had twenty-nine days, the free period seems to consist of thirty-six days, not thirty-five. See *Actio prima*, § 31. Perhaps we should read *xxxvi* for *xxxv*.

so that the remaining months might fall at the
right time as before. Had this been possible at
Rome, Verres would certainly have somehow pushed
through the removal of the thirty-five days, between
the two festival periods,[a] in which alone his trial
could take place.

LIII. And now it is worth our while to observe 131
how censors were appointed in Sicily during his
praetorship. For the censorship is, of all offices,
the one which in Sicily the citizens take most care
to entrust to the right man, because all Sicilians
pay their annual tribute in proportion to their
assessed wealth, and in making the assessment the
censor is entrusted with complete power to value
each property and fix the amount due. Consequently
the community exercises the greatest care in selecting
the person who is to be trusted so largely with its
property, and on the other hand the competition
for the office is especially keen in the community
because of the great power conferred by it. Verres 132
decided that his dealings with this matter should
be quite open ; he would resort to no dishonest
drawing of lots or cutting days out of the calendar.
He certainly tried to do nothing underhand or
fraudulent here ; with the purpose of banishing
from all his cities those eager and covetous desires
for office that are the ruin of so many states, he
announced that he would himself appoint the censors
in every city. Upon the praetor's declaring his 133
great market open, there was a general rush to see
him at Syracuse ; his official residence was a seething
mass of excited human cupidity ; nor was this
surprising, when the polling-stations of all those
cities were concentrated in a single house, and the

provinciae totius in uno cubiculo inclusa. Exquisitis palam pretiis et licitationibus factis, discribebat censores binos in singulas civitates Timarchides. Is suo labore suisque accessionibus, huius negotii atque operis molestia, consequebatur ut ad istum sine ulla sollicitudine summa pecuniae referretur. Iam hic Timarchides quantum pecuniam fecerit plane adhuc cognoscere non potuistis; verum tamen priore actione quam varie, quam improbe praedatus esset multorum testimoniis cognovistis.

134   LIV. Sed ne miremini qua ratione hic tantum apud istum libertus potuerit, exponam vobis breviter quid hominis sit, ut et istius nequitiam qui illum secum habuerit, eo praesertim numero ac loco, et calamitatem provinciae cognoscatis. In mulierum corruptelis, et in omni eius modi luxuria atque nequitia, mirandum in modum reperiebam hunc Timarchidem ad istius flagitiosas libidines singularemque nequitiam natum atque aptum fuisse, investigare, adire, appellare, corrumpere, quidvis facere in eius modi rebus quamvis callide, quamvis audacter, quamvis impudenter; eundem mira quaedam excogitasse genera furandi; nam ipsum Verrem tantum avaritia semper hiante atque imminente fuisse, ingenio et cogitatione nulla, ut quicquid sua sponte faciebat, item ut vos Romae cognovistis, eripere potius quam fallere vide-

135 retur. Haec vero huius erat ars et malitia miranda,

fierce ambitions of an entire province shut up in a single room. Prices were openly ascertained and offers openly made, after which the two censors for each state were assigned by Timarchides. This person, by doing the work and interviewing the candidates himself, and bearing the unpleasantness of so laborious a piece of business, achieved the conveyance of all the profits to Verres without troubling him at all. How large the profits made by this man Timarchides were you have not so far had the opportunity of learning exactly ; but still you did learn, at the first hearing, from the evidence of many witnesses, in how many rascally ways he plundered his victims.

LIV. Now you may wonder how this freedman 134 gained so much control of Verres' affairs ; and therefore I will tell you briefly the sort of man he is, that you may appreciate both the iniquity of Verres in giving him a place on his staff, a place, moreover, of high rank and consideration, and also the disastrous consequences for the province. In the seduction of women, and all such licentious wickedness, I learnt that this fellow Timarchides was remarkedly well constituted and adapted to further the evil debauches of this prince of scoundrels, to track out and visit and accost and pervert, and do anything else that such affairs demand, with unlimited cunning, boldness, and effrontery. I learnt, too, his remarkable skill in working out methods of stealing ; for Verres had no quality but the greed that hung with ever-open mouth over his prey, no ingenuity or power of thought, so that any theft of his own devising was seen, as you have seen in Rome, to involve more violence than trickery. But this fellow's amazing 135

quod acutissime[1] tota provincia quid cuique accidisset, quid cuique opus esset, indagare et odorari solebat; omnium adversarios, omnium inimicos diligenter cognoscere, colloqui, attemptare; ex utraque parte causas voluntates perspicere, facultates et copias; quibus opus esset metum offerre, quibus expediret spem ostendere; accusatorum et quadruplatorum quicquid erat habebat in potestate; quod cuique negotii conflare volebat nullo labore faciebat; istius omnia decreta, imperia, litteras peritissime et

136 callidissime venditabat. Ac non solum erat administer istius cupiditatum, verum etiam ipse sui meminerat, neque solum nummos si qui isti exciderant tollere solebat, ex quibus pecuniam maximam fecit, sed etiam voluptatum flagitiorumque istius ipse reliquias colligebat. Itaque in Sicilia non Athenionem, qui nullum oppidum cepit, sed Timarchidem fugitivum omnibus oppidis per triennium scitote regnasse, in Timarchidi potestate sociorum populi Romani antiquissimorum atque amicissimorum liberos, matres familias, bona fortunasque omnes fuisse. Is igitur, ut dico, Timarchides in omnes civitates accepto pretio censores dimisit: comitia isto praetore censorum ne simulandi quidem causa fuerunt.

137 LV. Iam hoc impudentissime: palam, licebat enim videlicet legibus, singulis censoribus denarii treceni[2] ad statuam praetoris imperati sunt. Censores cxxx.

---

[1] accuratissime *Peterson, with good* MS. *support.*
[2] treceni *is Mueller's emendation, adopted by Peterson, of* MSS. trecenti.

skill and rascality consisted in the clever way in which he would track or smell out the misfortunes and necessities of everyone in the province ; take the trouble to find out everyone's opponents and enemies, and talk to them and lure them on; explore the aims and feelings and available resources of both sides ; threaten where it was necessary, and encourage where it was desirable. All the professional and mercenary prosecutors were in his power ; when he wanted to work up trouble for anyone, he did it with perfect ease ; decrees, orders, written authorities from Verres he would place on the market with the most accomplished skill. Nor 136 did he merely help to satisfy the greed of his master ; he bore himself in mind too ; and it was not only that he used to pick up any coins that Verres might have let drop, and thus made a large sum of money for himself ; he used also to collect the leavings of Verres' licentious pleasures. You must know, therefore, that for these three years it was not Athenio, who never captured a town, but Timarchides who was the real slave king over all the towns of Sicily ; that the wives and the children, the goods and the money of Rome's oldest and closest allies were at the mercy of Timarchides. Well, it was this Timarchides who, as I have said, received the bribes and distributed censors to the various cities : so long as Verres was praetor there was not even a pretence made of appointing censors by election.

LV. Then here is a piece of impudence. Orders 137 were given openly—for the act, we must not doubt, was legal—that each of the censors should contribute £12 towards a statue of their praetor. One hundred and thirty censors were appointed ; they

facti sunt ; pecuniam illam ob censuram contra leges
clam dederunt ; haec denarium xxxix. milia palam
salvis legibus contulerunt in statuam. Primum, quo
tantam pecuniam? Deinde, quam ob rem censores
ad statuam tibi conferebant? Ordo aliqui censorum
est, collegium, genus aliquod hominum? Nam aut
publice civitates istos honores habent, aut, si homines,[1]
ut aratores, ut mercatores, ut navicularii : censores
quidem qui magis quam aediles ? Ob beneficium ?
Ergo hoc fatebere, abs te haec petita esse (nam empta
non audebis dicere) ? te eos magistratus hominibus
beneficii, non rei publicae causa permisisse ? Hoc
cum tute fateare, quisquam dubitabit quin tu istam
apud populos provinciae totius invidiam atque
offensionem non ambitionis neque beneficiorum col-
locandorum, sed pecuniae conciliandae causa susceperis ?

138   Itaque illi censores fecerunt idem quod in nostra
re publica solent ii qui per largitionem magistratus
adepti sunt : dederunt operam ut ita potestatem gererent ut illam lacunam rei familiaris exple-
rent. Sic census habitus est te praetore ut eo censu
nullius civitatis res publica posset administrari ;
nam locupletissimi cuiusque censum extenuarant,
tenuissimi auxerant. Itaque in tributis imperandis
tantum oneris plebi imponebatur ut, etiamsi homines
tacerent, res ipsa illum censum repudiaret ; id quod

---

[1] *This is Peterson's emendation of* aut si generatim homines.

made those other secret and illegal payments to secure their appointment, and these open and not illegal subscriptions towards the statue amounted to £1560. Why so much money, in the first place? And in the next place, why should your statue be subscribed for by censors? Do the censors in any way constitute an order, a corporate body, a definite class of persons? Honours of this kind are either officially conferred by communities, or else, if by individuals, by definite classes of individuals, such as farmers, or merchants, or shipowners; but why by censors, any more than by aediles? In return for favours received? I see; then will you confess that these posts were begged from you —"bought" is more than you will dare to admit— that you conferred them on people as favours, instead of in the public interest? When you yourself confess to as much as that, can there be any question that you accepted the hatred and resentment of the whole population of the province, not to gain popularity or bestow judicious favours, but to make money?

Naturally, the behaviour of these censors was like **138** that of those members of our own government who have acquired their offices by bribery; they took care to discharge their functions so as to fill up the hole made in their finances. The assessment made during your praetorship was made in a way that brought the financial administration in every city to a standstill. For all the wealthiest men had their assessments reduced, while the poorest had theirs increased; and the demands of the tribute imposed in consequence such a burden upon the humbler classes that even if no one had said anything the facts of the case would have exposed the conduct of this assessment, as we need only glance at

intellegi facillime re ipsa potest. LVI. Nam L. Metellus, qui, posteaquam ego inquirendi causa in Siciliam veni, repente Laetilii adventu istius non modo amicus verum etiam cognatus factus est—is, quod videbat istius censu stari nullo modo posse, eum censum observari iussit qui viro fortissimo atque innocentissimo Sex. Peducaeo praetore habitus esset. Erant enim tum censores legibus facti, delecti a suis civitatibus ; quibus, si quid commisissent, poenae legibus erant constitutae. Te autem praetore, quis censor aut legem metueret, qua non tenebatur, quoniam creatus lege non erat, aut animadversionem tuam, cum id quod abs te emerat vendidisset? Teneat iam sane meos testes Metellus, cogat alios laudare, sicut in multis conatus est ; modo haec faciat quae facit. Quis enim umquam tanta a quoquam contumelia, quis tanta ignominia affectus est ? Quinto quoque anno Sicilia tota censetur ; erat censa praetore Peducaeo ; quintus annus cum in te praetorem incidisset, censa denuo est ; postero anno L. Metellus mentionem tui census fieri vetat, censores dicit de integro sibi creari placere, interea Peducaeanum censum observari iubet. Hoc si tuus inimicus tibi fecisset, tamen, si animo aequo provincia tulisset, inimici iudicium grave videretur. Fecit amicus recens et cognatus voluntarius ; aliter enim,

the facts to see at once.   LVI. For Lucius Metellus,
the very man whom, after I had come to Sicily to
collect evidence, the arrival of Lucius Laetilius
turned suddenly into the friend and even the cousin
of Verres—Metellus, I say, finding it wholly out
of the question to adhere to Verres' assessment,
ordered the employment of the assessment made in
the praetorship of the gallant and incorruptible
Sextus Peducaeus.   Yes, for then the censors were
chosen legally, elected by their own cities, and
subject, if they misconducted themselves, to penalties
fixed by law.   But under you, what censor need **139**
be afraid either of the law, by which, not having
been lawfully appointed, he was not bound, or of
being punished by you for selling to others what
you had sold to him ?   Now let Metellus detain my
witnesses, by all means ; let him force others to
eulogize the accused, as in many cases he has tried
to do ;   I will only ask him to do what he is doing.
For did ever one man inflict upon another such an
insult, such a humiliation as this ?   Every four years
the whole of Sicily is assessed ;   it was assessed
when Peducaeus was praetor ;   the fourth year
following found you praetor, and it was assessed
again ;   and the year after that Metellus forbids
any reference to your assessment, tells us that
he has decided to have an entirely fresh appointment of censors, and meanwhile orders the use
of the assessment made by Peducaeus.   Had this
been done by your personal enemy, even so, if
the province were satisfied, your enemy's verdict
upon you would have been a serious matter.   It
was done in fact by your new friend, your volunteer
cousin ;   it was done because he could not do other-

si provinciam retinere, si salvus ipse in provincia
140 vellet esse, facere non potuit. LVII. Exspectas
etiam quid hi iudicent ? Si tibi magistratum ab-
rogasset, minore ignominia te affecisset quam cum
ea quae magistratu gessisti sustulit atque irrita
iussit esse. Neque in hac re sola fuit eius modi, sed,
antequam ego in Siciliam veni, in maximis rebus
ac plurimis. Nam et Heraclio Syracusanos tuos illos
palaestritas bona restituere iussit, et Epicrati Bidinos,
et pupillo Drepanitano A. Claudium ; et, nisi mature
Laetilius in Siciliam cum litteris venisset, minus xxx.
diebus Metellus totam triennii praeturam tuam
rescidisset.

141 Et quoniam de ea pecunia quam tibi ad statuam
censores contulerunt dixi, non mihi praetermittendum
videtur ne illud quidem genus pecuniae conciliatae
quam tu a civitatibus statuarum nomine coegisti.
Video enim eius pecuniae summam esse pergrandem,
ad HS viciens ; tantum conficietur ex testimoniis et
litteris civitatum. Et iste hoc concedit nec potest
aliter dicere : quare cuius modi putamus esse illa
quae negat, cum haec tam improba sint quae fatetur ?
Quid enim vis constitui ? consumptam esse omnem
istam pecuniam in statuis ? Fac ita esse : tamen hoc
ferendum nullo modo est, tantam a sociis pecuniam
auferri ut omnibus in angiportis praedonis improbissimi statua ponatur, qua vix tuto transiri posse

wise, if he meant to remain governor of Sicily or even to live there in safety. LVII. After this, need 140 you wait to hear the verdict of this court? Had Metellus deprived you of your office, he would have inflicted a lesser disgrace upon you than by thus cancelling your official proceedings and declaring them null and void. Nor was this the only matter in which he acted thus; he had done the like before I reached Sicily, in other matters of high importance. He had ordered those curators of yours at Syracuse to make restitution to Heraclius, and those at Bidis to Epicrates, and Aulus Claudius to his ward at Drepanum; and if Laetilius had not been so quick in reaching Sicily with that letter, Metellus would have nullified the whole of your three years of office in less than a month.

Having referred to the money subscribed by the 141 censors for your statue, I think I should also say something of the method of making money whereby you extracted it, ostensibly for providing statues, from the various cities. The total amount is, I observe, very large, not less than £20,000; the personal and written evidence supplied by the cities will show it to come to fully as much as that. Verres indeed admits so much, nor can he help admitting it; and when the offences he does not deny are so serious, what are we to think of the offences he does deny? Why, to what conclusion would you have us come? That all this money was spent on statues? Suppose that true: it remains quite intolerable that our allies should be robbed of enough money to set up a statue of this buccaneering ruffian in every alley-way, in places where, one would think, it was hardly

142 videatur. LVIII. Verum ubi tandem aut in quibus
statuis ista tanta pecunia consumpta est ? Consume-
tur, inquies. Scilicet exspectemus legitimum illud
quinquennium ; si hoc intervallo non consumpserit,
tum denique nomen eius de pecuniis repetundis
statuarum nomine deferemus. Reus est maximis
plurimisque criminibus in iudicium vocatus, HS viciens
ex hoc uno genere captum videmus : si condemnatus
eris, non, opinor, id ages ut ista pecunia in quinquen-
nio consumatur in statuis ; sin absolutus eris, quis
erit tam amens qui te ex tot tantisque criminibus
elapsum post quinquennium statuarum nomine
arcessat ? Ita si neque adhuc consumpta est ista
pecunia et est perspicuum non consumptum iri, licet
iam intellegamus inventam esse rationem quare et
iste HS viciens ex hoc uno genere conciliarit et ceperit,
et ceteri, si hoc a vobis erit comprobatum, quam volent
magnas hoc nomine pecunias capere possint ; ut iam
videamur non a pecuniis capiendis homines absterrere,
sed, cum genera quaedam pecuniarum capiendarum
comprobarimus, honesta nomina turpissimis rebus im-
143 ponere. Etenim si C Verres HS c. milia populum,
verbi gratia Centuripinum, poposcisset, eamque ab
iis pecuniam abstulisset, non, opinor, esset dubium
quin eum, cum id planum fieret, condemnari necesse
esset. Quid ? si eundem populum HS cc. milia
poposcit, eaque coegit atque abstulit, num idcirco
absolvetur, quod ascriptum est eam pecuniam datam

safe to go. LVIII. But where, on what statues, 142
has all that money of yours in fact been spent ? It
will be so spent, you will answer. We are to wait, I
take it, for the five legal years of grace to elapse ;
and if he has not so spent it meanwhile, then will
come our time to prosecute him for extortion in
connexion with these statues ! He stands here
charged now with a great number of serious offences ;
and we find that, under this one head, he has laid
hold of twenty thousand pounds. If you are found
guilty, it will not, I imagine, be your object to have
this money spent on statues within the next five years;
and if you are acquitted, no one will be such a fool,
after your escape from all these grave charges, as to
arraign you five years later for your behaviour
about the statues. So, if the money has not yet been
spent, and if it is also obvious that it is not going
to be spent, we can now see that a method has been
discovered whereby Verres, in this one department,
collected and stole £20,000, and whereby all other
governors, if this one's conduct receives your sanction,
will be able to steal as large sums as they choose on
the same pretext ; so that we shall palpably not be
deterring people from stealing, but, by our sanction
of stealing of particular kinds, applying respectable
names to villainous actions. For surely, if Verres 143
had simply demanded the sum of a thousand pounds
from, shall we say, the people of Centuripa, and
taken that sum away from them, there could really
be no doubt that the proof of this fact must lead to
his conviction. Well then, now that he has, from
those very people, demanded, extracted, and taken
away two thousand pounds, he will surely not be
acquitted simply because a note has been added

statuarum nomine ? Non, opinor ; nisi forte id
agimus, non ut magistratibus nostris moram acci-
piendi, sed ut sociis causam dandi afferre videamur.

Quod si quem statuae magno opere delectant, et si
quis earum honore et gloria ducitur, is haec tamen
constituat necesse est : primum, averti pecuniam
domum non placere ; deinde, ipsarum statuarum
modum quendam esse oportere ; deinde illud, certe
144 ab invitis exigi non oportere. LIX. Ac de aver-
tenda pecunia quaero abs te utrum ipsae civitates
solitae sint statuas tibi faciendas locare ei cui possent
optima conditione locare, an aliquem procuratorem
praeficere qui statuis faciendis praeesset, an tibi, an
cui tu imperasses, adnumerare pecuniam. Nam si
per eos statuae fiebant a quibus tibi iste honos habebatur, audio ; sin Timarchidi pecunia numerabatur,
desine, quaeso, simulare te, cum in manifestissimo
furto teneare, gloriae studiosum ac monumentorum
fuisse.

Quid vero ? modum statuarum haberi nullum placet ?
145 Atqui habeatur necesse est. Etenim sic considerate.
Syracusana civitas, ut eam potissimum nominem,
dedit ipsi statuam—est honos ; et patri—bella haec
pietatis et quaestuosa simulatio ; et filio—ferri hoc
potest, hunc enim puerum non oderant. Verum
quotiens et quot nominibus a Syracusanis statuas
auferes ? Ut in foro statuerent abstulisti, ut in curia,

that this money was paid for statues ? No, I think not ; unless, of course, our object is not to discourage our officials from taking such payments but **to** encourage our allies to make them.

Now a man may take great pleasure in these statues, and be attracted by the honour and glory they confer ; but for all that there are certain facts that he must accept. The money for them must not be applied to his private ends ; the number of actual statues must not exceed a certain limit ; and certainly they must not be exacted from unwilling donors. LIX. On the first point, I should like to 144 ask you whether the cities themselves usually either let the contracts for making the statues to the contractor who in each case made the most satis-factory tender, or appointed some agent to super-intend their making ; or whether they paid the money in cash to you or to some person at your orders. For if the making of the statues was carried out by the persons who paid you that honour, well and good ; but if the fact is that the money for them was paid in cash to Timarchides, kindly drop this pretence of a thirst for monumental fame, now that you stand plainly convicted of being a thief.

And then again, can an unlimited number of statues be approved ? Why, it cannot possibly. Look at 145 the matter thus. The city of Syracuse, if I may select it for mention, gave a statue of himself—that was in honour of him ; one of his father—that was a pretty, and remunerative, pretence that he was a good son ; and one of his son—that may be tolerated, for they had no aversion to the boy. But how often, and on how many pretexts, do you mean to get statues out of the Syracusans ? You got one out of

coegisti ; ut pecuniam conferrent in eas statuas quae
Romae ponerentur imperasti : ut idem darent
homines aratorum nomine—dederunt ; ut idem pro
parte in commune Siciliae conferrent—etiam id contulerunt. Una civitas cum tot nominibus pecuniam
contulerit, idemque hoc civitates ceterae fecerint,
nonne res ipsa vos admonet ut putetis modum aliquem
huic cupiditati constitui oportere ? Quid ? si hoc voluntate sua nulla civitas fecit, si omnes imperio, metu,
vi, malo adductae tibi pecuniam statuarum nomine
contulerunt, per deos immortales, num cui dubium
esse poterit quin, etiamsi statuerit accipere ad statuas
licere, idem tamen statuat eripere certe non licere ?

146 Primum igitur in hanc rem testem totam Siciliam
citabo, quae mihi una voce statuarum nomine magnam pecuniam per vim coactam esse demonstrat.
Nam legationes omnium civitatum in postulatis communibus, quae fere omnia ex tuis iniuriis nata sunt,
etiam hoc ediderunt, UT STATUAS NE CUI, NISI CUM IS
DE PROVINCIA DECESSISSET, POLLICERENTUR. LX. Tot
praetores in Sicilia fuerunt, totiens apud maiores
nostros Siculi senatum adierunt, totiens hac memoria :
tamen huiusce novi postulati genus atque principium
147 tua praetura attulit. Quid enim tam novum non
solum re sed genere ipso postulandi ? Nam cetera

them to be erected in their market-place, you extorted another for their senate-house, you ordered a subscription for those to be set up in Rome ; the same persons were to pay as corn-farmers—they paid ; the same again, as sharing in the contribution from Sicily as a whole—and they subscribed again. When you find, gentlemen, that one city has subscribed under all these headings, and that all the other cities have done the same, does not this simple fact urge you to recognize the need for some limit to be imposed on this passion for fame ? But if it is further true that no city has done this of its own free will, that they all subscribed, nominally for your statues, under the pressure of command, intimidation, violence and ill-treatment—then, God help us, it should surely be plain enough to any man that, even if he has made up his mind that it is permissible to accept money for statues, he must also make up his mind that it is certainly not permissible to take that money by force. Well, in the first place, I will call the whole of Sicily 146 as a witness to this fact ; her united voice proves the forcible collection of a great sum of money for the nominal purpose of these statues. The embassies of all her cities, in that general petition nearly all of whose clauses have their origin in your acts of tyranny, have included the clause, " That they should not promise statues to any official unless and until he has left his province." LX. How many praetors have governed Sicily ! How often the Sicilians have approached the Senate, in our fathers' times and within our own memory ! And yet it is *your* praetorship that is the source and origin of this novel petition. The novelty is remarkable in the mere form of the 147 petition as well as in its substance. For the other

quae sunt in isdem postulatis de iniuriis tuis sunt nova,
sed tamen non novo modo postulantur. Rogant et
orant Siculi patres conscriptos ut nostri magistratus
posthac decumas lege Hieronica vendant. Tu primus
contra vendideras : audio. Ne in cellam quod
imperatur aestiment : hoc quoque propter tuos ternos
denarios nunc primum postulatur, sed genus ipsum
postulandi non est novum. Ne absentis nomen
recipiatur : ex Sthenii calamitate et tua natum est
iniuria. Cetera non colligam. Sunt omnia Siculorum postulata eius modi ut crimina collecta in unum
te reum esse videantur ; quae tamen omnia novas
iniurias habent, sed postulationum formulas usitatas :
hoc postulatum de statuis ridiculum esse videatur ei
148 qui rem sententiamque non perspiciat. Postulant
enim, non uti ne cogantur statuere. Quid igitur ? ut
ipsis ne liceat. Quid est hoc ? Petis a me, quod in
tua potestate est, ut id tibi facere ne liceat : pete
potius ne quis te invitum polliceri aut facere cogat.
" Nihil egero " inquit ; " negabunt enim omnes se
coegisse ; si me salvum esse vis, mihi impone istam
vim ut omnino mihi ne liceat polliceri. Ex tua
praetura primum haec est nata postulatio ; qua cum
utuntur, hoc significant atque adeo aperte ostendunt,

---

requests in the petition, referring to the wrongs you did, are new themselves, but there is nothing new in the way in which they are put. Thus the Sicilians humbly entreat your honourable House that our governors shall in future sell the rights of collecting tithe as is provided by the law of Hiero. You were the first to do otherwise—well, let us pass on. They ask that governors shall not require fixed money payments instead of supplies demanded for their households. Here too is a request made now for the first time, due to your 3-denarius exaction [a]; however, there is nothing strange in the actual form of the request. They ask that no prosecution of absent persons be allowed; this arises from the ruin of Sthenius and the wrong done him by you. I will not deal with the other points. All the petitions of these Sicilians are such as to look like a collection of charges directed against you and you only. But though they refer to novel kinds of oppression, the form of their wording is familiar; whereas this petition regarding statues must seem absurd to anyone who does not perceive its real meaning. For they ask not that no 148 one else should oblige them to erect the statues, but that they should not be allowed to do so of themselves. What can this mean? You are asking me not to allow you to do a thing which it is in your power to do or not do; ask me rather that no one shall compel you to promise or do it against your will. "That is of no use to me" is the reply, "for they will all say they did not compel me; if you would save me, apply compulsion to me, so that I am simply not allowed to make the promise." You, Verres, are the praetor whose rule has given rise to this petition, in making which they imply, nay, they declare openly,

sese ad statuas tuas pecuniam, metu ac malo coactos, invitissimos contulisse.

149   Quid ? si hoc non dicant, tibi non necesse sit ipsi id confiteri ?   Vide et perspice qua defensione sis usurus ;   nam intelleges hoc tibi de statuis confitendum esse.   LXI. Mihi enim renuntiatur ita constitui a tuis patronis, hominibus ingeniosis, causam tuam, et ita eos abs te institui et doceri : ut quisque ex provincia Sicilia gravior homo atque honestior testimonium vehementius dixerit, sicuti multi primarii viri multa dixerunt, te statim hoc istis tuis defensoribus dicere, " Inimicus est propterea quod arator est."   Itaque uno genere, opinor, circumscribere habetis in animo genus hoc aratorum, quod eos infenso animo atque inimico venisse dicatis quia fuerit in decumis iste vehementior.   Ergo aratores inimici omnes et adversarii sunt ?   nemo eorum est, quin perisse te cupiat ?   Omnino praeclare te habes cum is ordo atque id hominum genus quod optimum atque honestissimum est, a quo uno et summa rei publicae et illa provincia maxime contine-

150 tur, tibi est inimicissimum ?   Verum esto ;   alio loco de aratorum animo et iniuriis videro ;   nunc, quod mihi abs te datur, id accipio, eos tibi esse inimicissimos. Nempe ita dicis, propter decumas.   Concedo : non quaero iure an iniuria sint inimici.   Quid ergo ? illae quid sibi statuae equestres inauratae volunt, quae populi Romani oculos animosque maxime offendunt, propter aedem Volcani ?   Nam inscriptum esse video

---

that they subscribed for your statues quite against their will, under the stress of fear and ill-treatment.

Why, if they did not say so, would you not have to 149 confess to it yourself? Look carefully at your intended line of defence, and you will see at once that you have to make this confession about the statues. LXI. I am informed that your case is being prepared by your able advocates, that they are being primed and instructed by you, on the following lines. Whenever any notably impressive and respectable witness from Sicily has given his evidence with unusual heat, as a number of important persons have to a large extent done, you promptly say to your counsel, " He hates me because he is a farmer."—I gather, then, that you gentlemen *a* mean to class all the members of this farmer class together, declaring that they have come here full of spite and hostility because Verres was especially forcible in handling the corn-tithes. Well then, the farmers are all your enemies and opponents, are they? They all desire your ruin, do they? All is well, you think, when the best and most respectable division of the human race, the class by which, more than by any other, both the empire as a whole and that particular province are held together, is your mortal enemy? But let that pass; I will 150 deal elsewhere with the farmers' feelings and the farmers' wrongs; for the present, I accept your admission that they are your mortal enemies. Naturally, you say, because of the tithes. Yes, yes, very well: I do not ask whether you deserve their enmity or not. Now then, what is the meaning of those gilt equestrian statues near the temple of Vulcan that are so particularly offensive to the eyes and feelings of Rome? I observe that an inscription

quandam ex his statuis aratores dedisse. Si honoris
causa statuam dederunt, inimici non sunt ; credamus
testibus ; tum enim honori tuo, nunc iam religioni
suae consulunt. Sin autem metu coacti dederunt,
confiteare necesse est te in provincia pecunias
statuarum nomine per vim ac metum coegisse. Utrum
tibi commodum est elige.

151   LXII. Equidem libenter hoc iam crimen de statuis
relinquam, ut mihi tu illud concedas quod tibi honestissimum est, aratores tibi ad statuam honoris tui
causa voluntate sua contulisse. Da mihi hoc, iam tibi
maximam partem defensionis praecideris ; non enim
poteris aratores tibi iratos esse atque inimicos dicere.
O causam singularem ! o defensionem miseram ac
perditam ! nolle hoc accipere reum ab accusatore, et
eum reum qui praetor in Sicilia fuerit, aratores ei
statuam sua voluntate statuisse, aratores de eo bene
existimare, amicos esse, salvum cupere ! Metuit ne
hoc vos existimetis ; obruitur enim aratorum testi-
152 moniis. Utar eo quod datur. Certe hoc vobis ita
iudicandum est, eos, qui isti inimicissimi sunt, ut ipse
existimari vult, ad istius honores atque monumenta
pecuniam voluntate sua non contulisse. Atque ut
hoc totum facillime intellegi possit, quem voles eorum
testium quos produxero, qui ex Sicilia testes sunt,

states that one of these statues was presented by the
farmers. If they gave this statue to do you honour,
they are not your enemies; let us, then, believe
their evidence; they were thinking of your honour
then, they are thinking of their consciences now.
If, on the other hand, they were frightened into
giving it, you have to admit that you, as governor,
extorted the money, nominally for statues, by
violence and intimidation. Choose the alternative
that suits you!

LXII. I should be glad, for my part, to drop this 151
charge about the statues at this point, if you would
only grant me what would be most to your credit, that
the farmers subscribed for the statue of their own
accord to do you honour. Allow me this and instantly
you have cut away the main prop of your defence,
being then unable to allege that the farmers are
angry and hostile. What an amazing position, what
a miserable and hopeless line of defence! That the
accused man, after being the governor of Sicily,
should have to deny, when his accuser is willing
to allow, that the farmers, of all people, have set up a
statue to him of their own free will, that the farmers
think well of him, feel friendly towards him, and hope
for his escape! Your believing this is what he is
afraid of; for it is the evidence of the farmers that is
crushing him. I will stress, then, what he does let 152
you believe. You must certainly conclude that the
persons who are, as he would have you suppose, his
deadly enemies have not subscribed money to honour
and commemorate him of their own free will. And
to make the whole matter clear without more ado, you,
Verres, shall ask any one you please of the witnesses
I shall call who come from Sicily, Roman citizen or

sive togatum sive Siculum, rogato, et eum qui
tibi inimicissimus esse videbitur, qui se spoliatum
abs te dicet, ecquid suo nomine in tuam statuam
contulerit: neminem reperies qui neget; etenim
153 omnes dederunt. Quemquam igitur putas dubita-
turum quin is quem tibi inimicissimum esse oporteat, qui abs te gravissimas iniurias acceperit,
pecuniam statuae nomine dederit vi atque imperio
adductus, non officio ac voluntate? Et huius ego
pecuniae, iudices, quae permagna est impudentissimeque coacta ab invitis, non habui rationem
neque habere potui, quantum ab aratoribus, quantum ab negotiatoribus qui Syracusis, qui Agrigenti,
qui Panhormi, qui Lilybaei negotiantur, esset co-
actum. Eam iam[1] intellegitis ipsius quoque con-
fessione ab invitissimis coactam esse.

154 LXIII. Venio nunc ad civitates Siciliae, de quibus
facillime iudicium fieri voluntatis potest. An etiam
Siculi inviti contulerunt? Non est probabile. Etenim
sic C. Verrem praeturam in Sicilia gessisse constat ut,
cum utrisque satis facere non posset, et Siculis et
togatis, officii potius in socios quam ambitionis in cives
rationem duxerit. Itaque eum non solum PATRONUM
istius insulae sed etiam SOTERA inscriptum vidi Syracusis. Hoc quantum est? Ita magnum ut Latine
uno verbo exprimi non possit. Is est nimirum SOTER

---

[1] eam iam *Peterson for MS.* quoniam *or* ut iam: *other
proposals are* et iam (*poor sense*) *and* quam iam.

Sicilian—yes, even the man you shall regard as your deadliest enemy, the man who shall declare that you robbed him—whether he personally subscribed for your statue ; and you will find nobody who says No, for every one of them did subscribe. Then will anyone 153 doubt, do you think, that a man who is bound to be your deadly enemy, who has sustained the heaviest wrongs at your hands, paid the money supposed to be for your statue because he was ordered and forced to pay it, and not because he wished to pay it or felt he ought to pay it ? The amount of this money, gentlemen, of this vast sum that has been so brazenly extorted from unwilling givers, I have neither calculated nor been able to calculate—how much was extorted from the farmers, and how much from the business men carrying on business at Syracuse and Agrigentum, at Panhormus and Lilybaeum. What you do know by now, from his own confession as well as otherwise, is that it was extorted from persons who were entirely unwilling to pay it.

LXIII. Let us now consider the Sicilian cities, the 154 test of whose willingness may be applied very easily. Or—were even the Sicilians unwilling to subscribe ? We can hardly believe that ! It is surely well understood that Gaius Verres, governor of Sicily, finding it impossible to satisfy both parties, both Sicilians and Romans, let his actions be directed rather by his sense of duty towards our allies than by his desire for the goodwill of our own citizens. That is why an inscription which I have seen in Syracuse describes him as not merely the island's advocate but also as its *Soter*. And what does this word mean ? It means so much that it cannot be rendered by any single Latin word ; *Soter* in fact

qui salutem dedit. Huius nomine etiam dies festi
agitantur, pulchra illa Verria, non quasi Marcellia,
sed pro Marcelliis, quae illi istius iussu sustulerunt.
Huius fornix in foro Syracusis est, in quo nudus filius
stat, ipse autem ex equo nudatam ab se provinciam
prospicit. Huius statuae locis omnibus, quae hoc
demonstrare videantur, prope modum non minus
multas statuas istum posuisse Syracusis quam
abstulisse. Huic etiam Romae videmus in basi
statuarum maximis litteris incisum A COMMUNI
155 SICILIAE DATAS. Quam ob rem qui hoc probare potes
cuiquam, tantos honores habitos esse ab invitis?
LXIV. Hic tibi etiam multo magis quam paulo ante
in aratoribus videndum et considerandum est quid
velis. Magna res est utrum tibi Siculos publice
privatimque amicos an inimicos existimari velis. Si
inimicos, quid te futurum est? quo confugies? ubi
nitere? Modo aratorum, honestissimorum hominum
ac locupletissimorum, et Siculorum et civium Romanorum, maximum numerum abs te abalienasti: nunc
de Siculis civitatibus quid ages? Dices tibi Siculos
esse amicos? qui poteris? qui, quod nullo in homine
antea fecerant, ut in eum publice testimonium
dicerent, cum praesertim ex ea provincia condemnati sint complures qui ibi praetores fuerunt, duo soli
absoluti, hi nunc veniunt cum litteris, veniunt cum
mandatis, veniunt cum testimoniis publicis. Qui, si
te publice laudarent, tamen id more potius suo quam

signifies "the Giver of Deliverance." He is, moreover, commemorated by the celebration of a festival,
that noble Festival of Verres, which does not copy
but takes the place of the Festival of the Marcelli,
abolished by them at his command. In the market-
place at Syracuse rises his arch of honour, above
which stands the naked figure of his son, and he
himself on horseback surveys his province, stripped
naked by him. His statues are everywhere, as if to
prove that he set up nearly as many statues in
Syracuse as he carried away from it. Even in Rome
we see him glorified by the inscription, cut in huge
letters on the pedestal of his statues, *Presented by the
united people of Sicily*. In the face of all this, how 155
can you make anyone believe that people have
honoured you thus highly against their will? LXIV.
And here you must consider, as with the farmers
just now, but a good deal more carefully still, what
line you mean to take. It will matter a great deal
whether you choose to have the Sicilians, individually
and collectively, regarded as your friends or as your
enemies. If as your enemies, what becomes of you?
What refuge will you find, what ground to stand on?
You have just quarrelled with the farmers, the
respectable and wealthy farmers, Sicilian and Roman
alike; how will you deal now with the Sicilian
cities? Will you declare the Sicilians your friends?
And how can you? Never before have they gone
so far as to give evidence against anyone officially,
in spite of the fact that a number of former governors
of the province have been convicted and only two
acquitted; yet now here they are, with official letters,
official instructions, official evidence. Were they
giving you official eulogies, we should think it was

merito tuo facere viderentur, hi, cum de tuis factis
publice conqueruntur, nonne hoc indicant, tantas esse
iniurias ut multo maluerint de suo more decedere
156 quam de tuis moribus non dicere ?   Confitendum est
igitur tibi necessario Siculos inimicos esse, qui quidem
in te gravissima postulata consulibus ediderint, et me
ut hanc causam salutisque suae defensionem susciperem obsecrarint ; qui cum a praetore prohiberen-
tur, a quattuor quaestoribus impedirentur, omnium
minas atque omnia pericula prae salute sua levia
duxerint ; qui priore actione ita testimonia graviter
vehementerque dixerint ut Artemonem Centuripinum legatum et publice testem Q. Hortensius
accusatorem, non testem, esse diceret.   Etenim ille
cum propter virtutem et fidem cum Androne, homine
honestissimo et certissimo, tum etiam propter eloquentiam legatus a suis civibus electus est, ut posset
multas istius et varias iniurias quam apertissime vobis
planissimeque explicare.

LXV. Dixerunt Halaesini, Catinenses, Tyndaritani, Hennenses, Herbitenses, Agyrinenses, Netini,
Segestani — enumerare omnes non est necesse.
Scitis quam multi et quam multa priore actione
157 dixerint : nunc et illi et reliqui dicent.   Omnes
denique hoc in hac causa intellegent, hoc animo esse
Siculos ut, si in istum animadversum non sit, sibi

more their own practice than your merits that made
them do it; and as they are in fact officially denouncing your conduct, are they not showing us
that their wrongs are so heavy that they have much
preferred abandoning their own practice to being
silent about your practices? You are, therefore, 156
obliged to admit the Sicilians to be your enemies;
and in truth they have presented to the consuls a
petition that is a strong attack upon you, and have
besought me to undertake this case and defend them
from destruction; in spite of their praetor's prohibition and the obstacles put in their way by their four
quaestors, they have made light of all threats from
those persons and all dangers to themselves, if only
they may so escape that destruction; and at the
first hearing they gave their evidence with such
impressive vehemence that Hortensius accused
Artemo, the deputy and official witness from Centuripa, of being not a witness but a prosecutor. It
is indeed true that Artemo was chosen deputy by
his fellow-citizens, along with the respectable and
trustworthy Andro, partly for his honourable and
upright character, but partly also for his eloquence,
that through him the many different wrongs done by
Verres might be put before this Court in the clearest
and most convincing way possible.

LXV. Halaesa, Catina, Tyndaris, Henna, Herbita,
Agyrium, Netum, Segesta—all these have spoken;
no need to complete the list; you know how many
spoke at the first hearing, and how much they had
to say. These shall speak again now, and the others
too. And finally, there is one thing in this case 157
which all men shall perceive, that the temper of the
Sicilians is such that, if no punishment be inflicted

relinquendas domos ac sedes suas et ex Sicilia de-
cedendum atque adeo fugiendum esse arbitrentur.
Hos homines tu persuadebis ad honorem atque amplitudinem tuam pecunias maximas voluntate sua
contulisse ?   Credo, qui te in tua civitate incolumem
esse nollent, hi monumenta tuae formae ac nominis
in suis civitatibus esse cupiebant.   Res declarabit ut
cupierint.   Iamdudum enim mihi nimium tenuiter
Siculorum erga te voluntatis argumenta colligere
videor, utrum statuas voluerint tibi statuere an
coacti sint.

158   De quo homine auditum est umquam, quod tibi
accidit, ut eius in provincia statuae, in locis publicis
positae, partim etiam in aedibus sacris, per vim et per
universam multitudinem deicerentur ?   Tot homines
in Asia nocentes, tot in Africa, tot in Hispania, Gallia,
Sardinia, tot in ipsa Sicilia fuerunt :   ecquo de homine
hoc umquam audivistis ?   Novum est, iudices ;   in
Siculis quidem et in omnibus Graecis monstri simile.
Non crederem hoc de statuis nisi iacentes revulsasque
vidissem, propterea quod apud omnes Graecos hic
mos est, ut honorem hominibus habitum in monumentis eius modi nonnulla religione deorum consecrari
159 arbitrentur.   Itaque Rhodii, qui prope soli bellum
illud superius cum Mithridate rege gesserint, omnesque eius copias acerrimumque impetum moenibus,
litoribus classibusque suis exceperint, tamen, cum ei
462

upon yonder man, they see nothing for it but to desert their homes and dwellings, and to take their departure, or rather flight, from Sicily. Are these the men of whom you will persuade us that they freely subscribed vast sums of money to honour and glorify you? A likely tale, that while they would not have you go unpunished in your own country, they desired to have memorials of your appearance and illustrious name in theirs! What they did desire the facts will show. Indeed I feel that I have been marshalling too long, and in too great detail, my proofs of the Sicilians' feeling towards you, asking whether they wished to erect statues to you or were made to do it.

Have we ever heard that what happened to you 158 happened to any other man—that his statues in his province, statues set up in public places, and some of them even in sacred edifices, were attacked and thrown down by a united multitude? Think of all the bad rulers that Asia has had, that Africa has had, that Spain and Gaul and Sardinia have had, that Sicily herself has had; yet has this court ever heard this told of any one of them? It is an unheard-of act, gentlemen; and for Sicilians, for any Greeks at all, to behave thus is a sort of monstrosity. I should not believe this about the statues had I not seen them lying there, wrenched off their pedestals; for it is the way of all Greeks to fancy that, in memorials of this kind, the honour bestowed on men is hallowed with a measure of divine consecration. Thus it was that the Rhodians, who maintained the 159 first war against King Mithridates almost single-handed, whose walls and coasts and fleets faced his whole army and the main brunt of his attack, none

regi inimici praeter ceteros essent, statuam eius, quae
erat apud ipsos in celeberrimo urbis loco, ne tum
quidem in ipsis urbis periculis attigerunt. Ac forsitan
vix convenire videretur, quem ipsum hominem
cuperent evertere, eius effigiem simulacrumque
servare ; sed tamen videbam, apud eos cum essem,
et religionem esse quandam in his rebus a maioribus
traditam, et hoc disputari, cum statua se eius habuisse
temporis rationem quo posita esset, cum homine eius
quo gereret bellum atque hostis esset. LXVI. Videtis igitur consuetudinem religionemque Graecorum,
quae monumenta hostium in bello ipso soleat
defendere, eam summa in pace praetoris populi
160 Romani statuis praesidio non fuisse. Tauromenitani,
quorum est civitas foederata, homines quietissimi, qui
maxime ab iniuriis nostrorum magistratuum remoti
consuerant esse praesidio foederis, hi tamen istius
evertere statuam non dubitaverunt ; qua abiecta
basim tamen in foro manere voluerunt, quod gravius
in istum fore putabant si scirent homines statuam eius
a Tauromenitanis esse deiectam, quam si nullam
umquam positam esse arbitrarentur. Tyndaritani
deiecerunt in foro, et eadem de causa equum inanem
reliquerunt. Leontinis, misera in civitate atque inani,
tamen istius in gymnasio statua deiecta est. Nam
quid ego de Syracusanis loquar ? quod non est pro-

the less, though they hated that king as no other people did, laid no hand upon the statue of him that stood in the most frequented part of their city, not even when that city was in actual danger. It might perhaps seem hardly fitting, when they were eager for the overthrow of the man himself, to preserve the image and likeness of him. But I found, when I was among them, that they have an inherited sense of the sanctity, as it were, of such things ; and they argued thus, that with the statue they had thought of the time when it was set up ; with the man, of the time when he was fighting them and was their enemy. LXVI. And now you see that the traditional reverence of the Greeks, which commonly protects the memorials of their enemies while they are actually at war with them, has yet, in a time of profound peace, been no protection to the statues of a governor representing the Roman People. The people of Tauromenium, a treaty 160 state, are a most inoffensive body of persons, whom their treaty has regularly shielded from any contact with oppression on the part of our officials ; yet they have thrown down Verres' statue without hesitation; and after knocking it over they decided to keep the pedestal in their market-place, thinking that the knowledge of the overthrow of his statue by the people of Tauromenium would tell more heavily against him than the belief that none had ever been set up. The people of Tyndaris overthrew his statue in their market-place, and from the same motive left the horse there riderless. At Leontini, wretched and poverty-stricken place though it is, his statue in the gymnasium was thrown down nevertheless. Need I speak of what the Syracusans did ? The act

prium Syracusanorum, sed et illorum et commune conventus illius ac prope totius provinciae. Quanta illuc multitudo, quanta vis hominum convenisse dicebatur tum cum statuae sunt illius deiectae et eversae ! At quo loco ! celeberrimo ac religiosissimo, ante ipsum Serapim, in primo aditu vestibuloque templi ! Quod nisi Metellus hoc tam graviter egisset atque illam rem imperio edictoque prohibuisset, vestigium statuarum istius in tota Sicilia nullum esset relictum.

161 Atque ego hoc non vereor, ne quid horum non modo impulsu verum omnino adventu meo factum esse videatur. Omnia ista ante facta sunt non modo quam ego Siciliam verum etiam quam iste Italiam attigit. Dum ego in Sicilia sum, nulla statua deiecta est. Postea quam illinc decessi quae sunt gesta cognoscite. LXVII. Centuripinorum senatus decrevit populusque iussit ut, quae statuae C. Verris ipsius et patris et filii essent, eas quaestores demoliendas locarent, dumque ea demolitio fieret, senatores ne minus triginta adessent. Videte gravitatem civitatis et dignitatem. Neque eas in urbe sua statuas esse voluerunt quas inviti per vim atque imperium dedissent, neque eius hominis in quem ipsi cum gravissimo testimonio publice, quod numquam antea, Romam mandata legatosque misissent ; et id gravius esse putarunt si publico consilio quam si per vim

162 multitudinis factum esse videretur. Cum hoc con-

ᵃ Or perhaps " crowded."

was not theirs alone, it was shared by the district, almost by the whole province. What a swarming multitude of people assembled there, we have been told, on the day when his statues were knocked over and thrown down! And think of the actual spot, the famous *a* and sacred spot facing Serapis himself, close to the entrance doorway of his temple! In fact, had Metellus not dealt severely with these proceedings, and by direct order and proclamation put a stop to such actions, not one vestige of this fellow's statues would have been left from end to end of Sicily.

Nor am I afraid that any of these doings will be 161 found to have been due to my instigation, or indeed to anything connected with my visit. They were all over not merely before I reached Sicily but before Verres reached Italy. All the time I was in Sicily, not one statue was thrown down. Now let me tell you what happened after I came away. LXVII. At Centuripa it was decreed by the Senate and confirmed by the people that the quaestors should contract for the demolition of the statues of Verres and Verres' father and Verres' son, and that not less than thirty senators should be in attendance while the demolition was proceeding. Observe the sober dignity with which this community behaved. They would not have those statues in their city, the statues which they had been ordered and forced to present against their will, the statues of a man against whom they had sent to Rome, what they had never sent before, an officially instructed deputation to give their solemn testimony; and they held that their action would have greater weight if it were seen to be the work of considered official policy, and not of mob violence. When 162

silio statuas Centuripini publice sustulissent, audit
Metellus; graviter fert; evocat ad se Centuripinorum
magistratus et decem primos; nisi restituissent
statuas vehementer minatur. Illi ad senatum
renuntiant; statuae, quae istius causae nihil prod-
essent, reponuntur; decreta Centuripinorum quae
de statuis erant facta non tolluntur.

Hic ego aliud alii concedo: Metello, homini
sapienti, prorsus non possum ignoscere si quid stulte
facit. Quid? ille hoc putabat Verri criminosum fore,
si statuae eius essent deiectae, quod saepe vento aut
aliquo casu fieri solet? Non erat in hoc neque
crimen ullum neque reprehensio. Ex quo igitur
crimen atque accusatio nascitur? ex hominum
163 iudicio et voluntate. LXVIII. Ego, si Metellus
statuas Centuripinos reponere non coegisset, haec
dicerem: Videte, iudices, quantum et quam acerbum
dolorem sociorum atque amicorum animis inusserint
istius iniuriae, cum Centuripinorum amicissima ac
fidelissima civitas, quae tantis officiis cum populo
Romano coniuncta est ut non solum rem publicam
nostram sed etiam in quovis homine privato nomen
ipsum Romanum semper dilexerit, ea publico consilio
atque auctoritate iudicarit C. Verris statuas esse in
urbe sua non oportere. Recitarem decreta Centuripinorum; laudarem illam civitatem, id quod veris-
468

the people of Centuripa had by this deliberate official action removed the statues, Metellus heard of it, and was very angry; sending for the magistrates and ten chief citizens of Centuripa, he threatened them with savage penalties if they failed to put the statues back. These men reported this to their Senate, whereupon the statues, which could do Verres' cause no good, were replaced; but the decree which the people of Centuripa had passed about the statues was not rescinded.

Now there are some persons for whom certain allowances must be made; but I simply cannot excuse foolishness on the part of a sensible man like Metellus. Why, did he think that Verres' case would be damaged by the mere overthrowing of his statues, a kind of thing for which the wind, or some accident, is often responsible? There was no ground here for prosecution, or even for criticism. What does give ground, then, for a prosecutor's attacks? The judgements, and the feelings, of human beings. LXVIII. 163 If Metellus had *not* forced the people of Centuripa to replace those statues, I should be addressing you thus: Look, gentlemen, how deep and bitter a resentment must have been burnt into the souls of our friends and allies by yonder man's oppression, when this entirely friendly and loyal city Centuripa, which is bound to the people of Rome by devotion so splendid that its affection is given, not only to Rome as a whole, but to any and every individual who but bears the name of " Roman "—when this city, with the deliberate authority of its government, has pronounced that statues of Gaius Verres should not be left within its walls. I should recite to you the decrees that Centuripa passed; I should sing the praises of the

sime possem ; commemorarem decem milia civium
esse Centuripinorum, fortissimorum fidelissimorumque sociorum ; eos omnes hoc statuisse, monumentum
164 istius in sua civitate nullum esse oportere. Haec
tum dicerem, si statuas Metellus non reposuisset :
velim quaerere nunc ex ipso Metello quidnam sua
vi et auctoritate mihi ex hac oratione praeciderit.
Eadem opinor omnia convenire. Neque enim, si maxime statuae deiectae essent, ego eas vobis possem
iacentes ostendere : hoc uno uterer, civitatem tam
gravem iudicasse statuas C. Verris demoliendas. Hoc
mihi Metellus non eripuit ; haec etiam addidit, ut
quererer, si mihi videretur, tam iniquo iure sociis
atque amicis imperari ut iis ne in suis quidem beneficiis libero iudicio uti liceret ; vos rogarem ut coniecturam faceretis qualem in his rebus in me L. Metellum fuisse putaretis, in quibus rebus obesse mihi
posset, cum in hac re tam aperta cupiditate fuerit,
in qua nihil obfuit. Sed ego Metello non irascor, neque ei suam purgationem eripio, qua ille apud omnes
utitur, ut nihil malitiose neque consulto fecisse
videatur.

165 LXIX. Iam igitur est ita perspicuum ut negare
non possis nullam tibi statuam voluntate cuiusquam
datam, nullam pecuniam statuarum nomine nisi vi
expressam et coactam. Quo quidem in crimine non

city, as I very honestly might; I should remind you that the citizens of Centuripa, our honoured and loyal allies, are ten thousand in number, and that every one of them has made up his mind that no memorial of Verres must exist in their land. That is how I should address you, if Metellus had not put those statues back; and now I should like Metellus himself to say from what part of such an address his violent exercise of authority has debarred me. In my view, not one word need be changed. However completely the statues had been overthrown, I could not show you them lying prostrate; I could only argue from the one fact, that this important city pronounced judgement that the statues of Gaius Verres should be demolished. Of this argument Metellus has not robbed me; indeed, he has given me others; for I might, if I chose, protest against the oppressive orders given to these allies and friends of ours, whereby they are not even allowed to judge for themselves what acts of benevolence they shall perform; and I might ask you to guess how Metellus must have treated me in matters where he had power to hinder me, seeing the frank partisanship that he has displayed in this matter where he has not hindered me at all. However, I will not quarrel with Metellus, nor rob him of what all men grant him, his special immunity from being supposed ever to act with a deliberately evil purpose.

LXIX. Well, Verres, it is plain by now, too transparently plain for you to deny it, that no single statue was voluntarily given you by anyone, nor any money for providing statues that was not extracted and extorted by force. Now in discussing this charge I do

illud solum intellegi volo, te ad statuas HS viciens
coegisse, sed multo etiam illud magis, quod simul
demonstratum est quantum odium in te aratorum,
quantum omnium Siculorum sit et fuerit. In quo
quae vestra defensio futura sit coniectura assequi non
queo. "Oderunt Siculi : togatorum enim causa
166 multa feci." At hi quidem acerrimi inimici sunt.
"Inimicos habeo cives Romanos, quod sociorum commoda ac iura defendi." At socii in hostium numero
sese abs te habitos queruntur. "Aratores inimici
sunt propter decumas." Quid? qui agros immunes
liberosque arant, cur oderunt ? Cur Halaesini ? cur
Centuripini? cur Segestani? cur Halicyenses? Quod
genus hominum, quem numerum, quem ordinem
proferre possum qui te non oderit, sive civium Romanorum sive Siculorum ? Ut, etiamsi causas cur
te oderint non possim dicere, tamen illud dicendum
putem, quem omnes mortales oderint, eum vobis
167 quoque odio esse oportere. An hoc dicere audebis,
utrum de te aratores, utrum denique Siculi universi
bene existiment, aut quo modo existiment, ad rem
id non pertinere ? Neque tu hoc dicere audebis,
nec, si cupias, licebit ; eripiunt enim tibi istam
orationem contemnendorum Siculorum atque aratorum statuae illae equestres, quas tu paulo ante
quam ad urbem venires poni inscribique iussisti, ut
omnium inimicorum tuorum animos accusatorumque
168 tardares. Quis enim tibi molestus esset, aut quis ap-

not wish to insist only that you extorted £20,000 for
statues. Much more important is what this demon-
strates, the strength of the hatred that has been felt
and still is felt for you, by the farmers and by all the
people of Sicily. And here I cannot guess what your
line of defence is to be. " The Sicilians hate me,
yes ; for I have acted largely in the interests of the
Roman section " ? Why, it is these who are your 166
savagest enemies. " I have made enemies of the
Roman citizens by protecting the interests and rights
of our allies " ? Why, our allies are denouncing you
for treating them as if we were at war with them.
" The farmers are my enemies on account of the
tithe " ? What about those farmers, then, whose land
is exempt, free from tithe—why do they hate you ?
why do the farmers of Halaesa and Centuripa and
Segesta and Halicyae hate you ? What type or
grade or class of men can I mention that does not hate
you, whether they are Romans or Sicilians ? So
much so that, even if I could not say for what reasons
they do hate you, I feel that I might well say one
thing, that a man who is hated by all human beings
cannot but be an object of hatred to this Court. Or 167
will you dare to say, that the question whether the
farmers, whether indeed the Sicilians as a whole,
think well of you, or what they do think of you, is
irrelevant ? You will not dare to say that ; nor can
you if you would ; all talk about the unimportance of
the Sicilians or the farmers is barred for you by those
equestrian statues which you caused to be erected
and provided with inscriptions, a little while before
your return to Rome, hoping thus to check the fierce
attacks of all your enemies and accusers—for who 168
would annoy you, or dare to call you to account, when

pellare te auderet, cum videret statuas ab negotiatoribus, ab aratoribus, a communi Siciliae positas ?
Quod est aliud in illa provincia genus hominum ?
nullum. Ergo ab universa provincia, generatimque a
singulis eius partibus, non solum diligitur sed etiam
ornatur. Quis hunc attingere audeat ? Potes igitur
dicere nihil tibi obesse oportere aratorum, negotia-
torum Siculorumque omnium testimonia, cum eorum
nominibus in statuarum inscriptione oppositis omnem
te speraris invidiam atque infamiam tuam posse
exstinguere ? an quorum tu auctoritate statuas
cohonestare tuas conatus es, eorum ego dignitate
accusationem meam comprobare non potero ?

169   Nisi forte quod apud publicanos gratiosus fuisti, in
ea re spes te aliqua consolatur. Quae gratia ne quid
tibi prodesse posset ego mea diligentia perfeci, ut
etiam obesse deberet tu tua sapientia curasti.
Etenim rem totam, iudices, breviter cognoscite.
LXX. In scriptura Siciliae pro magistro est quidam
L. Carpinatius, qui et sui quaestus causa, et fortasse
quod sociorum interesse arbitrabatur, bene penitus in
istius familiaritatem sese dedit. Is cum praetorem
circum omnia fora sectaretur neque ab eo umquam
discederet, in eam iam venerat consuetudinem in
vendendis istius decretis et iudiciis transigendisque
negotiis ut prope alter Timarchides numeraretur ;
170 hoc erat etiam capitalior, quod idem pecunias iis

---

a Rents of state lands.
b i.e., of the company of revenue contractors. The
magister or Chairman of Directors would live in Rome :
Carpinatius was one of many sub-managers who directed
operations in the various districts.

he saw those statues, erected by the merchants, by the
farmers, by united Sicily ? What other class of
persons is there in the province ? Why, none. Very
well, here is the province as a whole, and here are the
several classes that compose it, not merely liking the
man, but doing him honour. Now who will dare to
touch him ! Is it possible, then, for you to say that
the evidence of the farmers, the merchants and all
the Sicilians must not be allowed to tell against you,
when, by shielding yourself with these men's names
inscribed upon your statues, you have been expecting
to blot out all the odium and infamy that has come
upon you ? You sought the support of their word,
to make your statues respectable—may I not have
the support of their worth, to make my arguments
convincing ?

Perhaps, however, you derive some sort of confid- 169
ence and comfort from having been popular with the
revenue contractors ? My watchfulness has made it
impossible for this popularity at all to help your case ;
and your intelligence has taken effective steps to
make it actually tell against you. Let me in a few
words, gentlemen, put the whole story before you.
LXX. For collecting the pasture rents *a* of Sicily the
working director *b* is one Lucius Carpinatius. This
man, both for his own profit and possibly also with
an eye to the shareholders' interests, worked his way
very thoroughly into intimacy with Verres. He used
to follow the praetor round from one market town to
another, never leaving him ; and before long had
become so closely connected with him, marketing his
decrees and decisions, and putting through his pieces
of jobbery, that he was looked on as a second
Timarchides, but even more deadly, from his custom 170

qui ab isto aliquid mercabantur faenori dabat. Ea autem faeneratio erat eius modi, iudices, ut etiam is quaestus huic cederet; nam quas pecunias ferebat iis expensas quibuscum contrahebat, eas aut scribae istius aut Timarchidi aut etiam isti ipsi referebat acceptas. Idem praeterea pecunias istius extraordinarias grandes suo nomine faenerabatur.

171 Hic primo Carpinatius, antequam in istius familiaritatem tantam pervenisset, aliquotiens ad socios litteras de istius iniuriis miserat. Canuleius vero, qui in portu Syracusis operas dabat, furta quoque istius permulta nominatim ad socios perscripserat, ea quae sine portorio Syracusis erant exportata; portum autem et scripturam eadem societas habebat. Ita factum est ut essent permulta quae ex societatis litteris dicere in istum et proferre possemus.

172 Verum accidit ut Carpinatius, qui iam cum isto summa consuetudine, praeterea re ac ratione coniunctus esset, crebras postea litteras ad socios de istius summis officiis in rem communem beneficiisque mitteret. Etenim cum iste omnia quaecumque Carpinatius postulabat facere ac decernere solebat, tum ille etiam plura scribebat ad socios, ut, si posset, quae antea scripserat, ea plane exstingueret. Ad extremum vero, cum iste iam decedebat, eius modi

---

[a] *i.e.*, on the " received " side of the account.
[b] The accounts showed that Verres himself was lending money to his victims.
[c] *i.e.*, he was director of the collection of harbour dues.
476

of lending money at interest to those who wanted to buy something from Verres. And this system of loans was so managed, gentlemen, that the profits even from this source came to our friend here ; for the sums that Carpinatius entered as paid to those to whom he made the loans he re-entered [a] as received from Verres' secretary, or from Timarchides, or even from Verres himself [b] ; besides which, he also lent in his own name large sums of Verres' money not entered in the accounts at all. In the early days, before 171 establishing this close connexion with Verres, Carpinatius had several times written to the company complaining of wrongs done by Verres ; and Canuleius, whose work had to do with the harbour [c] at Syracuse, sent the company a detailed list of numerous thefts Verres had committed in the matter of goods exported from Syracuse without paying the export tax, the same company being contractors for harbour dues as for pasture rents. The result was to provide us with a number of points from the company's records to quote and bring up against Verres.

But it so happened that Carpinatius, being before 172 long closely associated with Verres as his regular intimate—and by substantial reasons as well—subsequently wrote a number of letters to the company about the great services that Verres had been good enough to render to the company's interests. And indeed, by the time that Verres was regularly doing and ordering whatever Carpinatius asked of him, the latter was writing even more frequently to the company, hoping that if possible, the effect of his earlier letters would be completely wiped out. Finally, when Verres was about to

litteras ad eos misit ut huic frequentes obviam prodirent, gratias agerent, facturos se si quid imperasset
studiose pollicerentur. Itaque socii fecerunt vetere
instituto publicanorum, non quo istum ullo honore
dignum arbitrarentur, sed quod sua interesse putabant se memores gratosque existimari ; gratias isti
egerunt, Carpinatium saepe ad se de eius officiis
173 litteras misisse dixerunt. LXXI. Iste cum respondisset ea se libenter fecisse, operasque Carpinatii
magno opere laudasset, dat amico suo cuidam negotium, qui tum magister erat eius societatis, ut
diligenter caveret atque prospiceret ne quid esset in
litteris sociorum quod contra caput suum atque
existimationem valere posset. Itaque ille, multitudine sociorum remota, decumanos convocat, rem
defert. Statuunt illi atque decernunt ut eae litterae
quibus existimatio C. Verris laederetur removerentur,
operaque daretur ne ea res C. Verri fraudi esse posset.
174 Si ostendo hoc decrevisse decumanos, si planum facio
hoc decreto remotas esse litteras, quid exspectatis
amplius ? Possumne magis rem iudicatam afferre,
magis reum condemnatum in iudicium adducere ?
At quorum iudicio condemnatum ? nempe eorum
quos ii qui severiora iudicia desiderant arbitrantur res

---

[a] Lit. " tithe-contractors " evidently the wealthiest and
most influential section of the company, in which the
pasture-rents and harbour-dues contracts were a subsidiary
undertaking : see § 175.

leave Sicily, he wrote urging them to assemble in force and meet him on his arrival, to express their thanks, and to promise to execute zealously any commands he might have for them. The company accordingly observed the traditional practice of revenue-contractors, not because they thought he deserved any marks of respect, but because they felt it would pay them not to seem forgetful or ungrateful; they expressed their thanks to him, and told him that Carpinatius had frequently written to them about the services he had done them. LXXI. He replied that it had been a pleasure to 173 him, and spoke in high terms of the good work of Carpinatius; and then he instructed one of his friends, who was at the time chairman of that company, to take the utmost care and precaution that the company's records should contain nothing that could possibly endanger his position or his character. Accordingly the chairman, after the main body of shareholders had dispersed, called a meeting of the directors *a* and put this before them. This meeting passed a resolution that all records damaging to the reputation of Gaius Verres should be expunged, and that care should be taken to stop this action from being injurious to the said Gaius Verres. If I prove that the directors did pass this 174 resolution, if I establish the fact that in accordance with this resolution the records were expunged, what more would this Court have? Could I bring forward any issue more clearly decided in advance, or prosecute any person more clearly convicted in advance? Convicted, and by whose judgement? Why, by that of the persons who, if those who long for the restoration of severer tribunals are right, should

iudicare oportere [publicanorum iudicio][1]; quos videlicet nunc populus iudices poscit, de quibus, ut eos
iudices habeamus, legem ab homine non nostri generis,
non ex equestri loco profecto, sed nobilissimo, pro-
175 mulgatam videmus. Decumani, hoc est principes
et quasi senatores publicanorum, removendas de
medio litteras censuerunt. Habeo ex iis qui ad-
fuerunt quos producam, quibus hoc committam,
homines honestissimos ac locupletissimos, istos
ipsos principes equestris ordinis, quorum splendore vel maxime istius qui legem promulgavit oratio
et causa nititur. Venient in medium, dicent
quid statuerint. Profecto, si recte homines novi,
non mentientur; litteras enim communes de
medio removere potuerunt, fidem suam et religionem removere non possunt. Ergo equites Romani,
qui te suo iudicio condemnarunt, horum iudicio
condemnari noluerunt. Vos nunc utrum illorum iudicium an voluntatem sequi malitis considerate.

176 LXXII. Ac vide quid te amicorum tuorum studium,
quid tuum consilium, quid sociorum voluntas adiuvet.
Dicam paulo promptius; neque enim iam vereor ne
quis hoc me magis accusatorie quam libere dixisse
arbitretur. Si istas litteras non decreto decu-

---

[1] *All MSS. have the bracketed words, which modern editors
agree to suspect.*

---

[a] Lucius Aurelius Cotta.
[b] *i.e.*, to have used an unfair, mean, ungentlemanly line
of argument—viz. that " worse remains behind."

be the members of these tribunals; the persons
whose appointment thereto we are told the nation
is now demanding; the persons whose appointment
thereto we see directed in a measure that is proposed
not by a man of my own type, not by a man of
equestrian antecedents, but by a man of most
ancient nobility.[a] The tithe-contractors, in other 175
words the principal, we might almost say the
senatorial, section of the revenue-contractors, agreed
to doing away with those records. I have some of
them who were at the meeting, whom I will call
upon, and whom I will entrust with this matter, men
of high standing and great substance, those very
leaders of the equestrian order upon whose illustrious
character the proposer of the measure most insisted
and most rested his appeal. They will appear before
you; they will tell you what they agreed to do;
and it is certain that, if I know them rightly, they
will tell you the truth; for they could do away
with the records of their company, but they cannot
do away with their own honour and conscience. So
it comes to this: the Roman knights, whose own
verdict pronounced this man guilty, did not wish to
have him pronounced guilty by the verdict of this
Court; it is now for this Court to consider whether
it will rather be guided by their verdict or by
their wishes.

LXXII. And now ask yourself, Verres, how much 176
good the devotion of your friends, or your own
designs, or the benevolence of your business allies
can do you. I will speak with some little boldness,
for I have now no fear of being thought to have
spoken more like a prosecutor than like a fair-
minded man.[b] If the directors had not made away

481

manorum magistri removissent, tantum possem in
te dicere quantum in litteris invenissem : nunc,
decreto isto facto litterisque remotis, tantum mihi
licet dicere quantum possum, tantum iudici suspicari
quantum velit. Dico te maximum pondus auri,
argenti, eboris, purpurae, plurimam vestem Meliten-
sem, plurimam stragulam, multam Deliacam supellectilem, plurima vasa Corinthia, magnum numerum
frumenti, vim mellis maximam Syracusis exportasse :
his pro rebus quod portorium non esset datum, litteras
ad socios misisse L. Canuleium, qui in portu operas
177 daret. Satisne magnum crimen hoc videtur ? Nullum, opinor, maius. Qui id defendet Hortensius ?
Postulabit ut litteras Canuleii proferam ? Crimen
eius modi nisi litteris confirmetur inane esse dicet ?
Clamabo litteras remotas esse de medio, decreto
sociorum erepta mihi esse istius indicia ac monumenta furtorum. Aut hoc contendat numquam esse
factum, aut omnia tela excipiat necesse est. Negas
esse factum ? Placet mihi ista defensio ; descendo ;
aequa enim contentio, aequum certamen proponitur.
Producam testes, et producam plures eodem tempore ; quoniam tum cum actum est una fuerunt,
nunc quoque una sint ; cum interrogabuntur, obli-
gentur non solum iuris iurandi atque existimationis

with those records as agreed by the tithe-contractors,
I should be able to accuse you only of such misconduct as I had found actually recorded ; as it is,
that resolution having been carried and the records
made away with, it is open to me to say the worst
I can of you, and to each member of this court to
suspect the worst he will of you. I assert that you
exported from Syracuse a great weight of gold,
silver, ivory, and purple fabrics, a great deal of
Maltese cloth and tapestries, a quantity of Delian
wares, a large number of Corinthian vessels, a large
quantity of corn and an immense amount of honey ;
and that Lucius Canuleius, the agent for harbour
business, wrote to his company complaining that no
export tax had been paid on these goods. Does this 177
seem a serious enough charge ? I can conceive none
more serious. What defence to it will Hortensius
make ? Will he demand that I should produce
this letter from Canuleius ? Will he maintain that a
charge of that kind is harmless unless backed by
documentary evidence ? I reply indignantly that
the documents have been done away with, that by
the resolution of the company the tokens and records
of that man's pilferings have been snatched from
my hands. Either he must contend that this never
happened, or he must be ready to face every such
assault. Do you say it did not happen ? Good,
that is the line to take ; I am ready for you ; here
is a fair field for us, and no favour. I will now
bring forward my witnesses ; and I will bring
forward a number of them together ; they were
with one another when the thing was done, let them
be so now. When they are examined, they will be
bound to speak truth, not only by the risk of perjury

178 periculo, sed etiam communi inter se conscientia. Si
planum fit hoc ita quem ad modum dico esse factum,
num poteris dicere, Hortensi, nihil in istis fuisse
litteris quod Verrem laederet? Non modo id non
dices, sed ne illud quidem tibi dicere licebit, tantum
quantum ego dicam non fuisse. Ergo hoc vestro
consilio et gratia perfecistis, ut, quem ad modum
paulo ante dixi, et mihi summa facultas ad accusandum daretur, et iudici libera potestas ad credendum.

179   LXXIII. Quod cum ita sit, nihil fingam tamen.
Meminero me non sumpsisse quem accusarem, sed
recepisse quos defenderem ; vos ex me causam non
a me prolatam, sed ad me delatam, audire oportere ;
me Siculis satis esse facturum si quae cognovi in
Sicilia, quae accepi ab ipsis, diligenter exposuero ;
populo Romano, si nullius vim, nullius potentiam
pertimuero ; vobis, si facultatem vere atque honeste
iudicandi fide et diligentia mea fecero ; mihimet, si
ne minimum quidem de meo curriculo vitae, quod

180 mihi semper propositum fuit, decessero. Quapropter nihil est quod metuas ne quid in te confingam.
Etiam quod laetere habes ; multa enim quae scio a
te esse commissa, quod aut nimium turpia aut parum
credibilia sunt, praetermittam ; tantum agam de hoc
toto nomine societatis. Ut iam scire possis, quaeram
decretumne sit. Cum id invenero, quaeram re-

and infamy, but by their partnership in knowledge
of the facts. If it is thus established that the thing **178**
happened as I say it did, you will hardly be able to
argue, Hortensius, that there was nothing in those
documents to damage Verres. Not only will you not
say that, but it will not even be possible for you to
maintain that what I allege is not true in every
detail. Well then, your schemes and favours have
succeeded, as I said just now, in giving me a free
hand to bring charges and each member of this
court full power to believe them.

LXXIII. In spite of this, I will invent nothing. **179**
I will bear in mind that I have undertaken not a
prosecution of my own accord but a defence at the
request of others ; that you, gentlemen, are to hear
me pleading a case not instigated by me but submitted to me ; that I shall be doing my duty by the
Sicilians if I conscientiously set forth such facts as
I learnt in their country and heard from their own
lips ; my duty by my own nation, if I refuse to be
terrified by any man's violence or any man's power ;
my duty by this court, if my honesty and assiduity
enable its members to pronounce a true and upright
decision ; my duty to myself, if I adhere rigidly to
the principles of conduct by which my career has
always been regulated. And therefore there is no **180**
reason for you, Verres, to fear my inventing charges
against you. Nay, you may in one respect con-
gratulate yourself : there are many crimes of yours
known to me about which, because they are either
too foul or too incredible, I shall keep silence. I
will simply deal with this affair of the revenue company as a whole. Not to keep you in suspense, I
will ask—Was that resolution agreed to ? When

motaene sint litterae ? Cum id quoque constabit,
vos iam hoc, me tacito, intellegetis : si illi qui hoc
istius causa decreverunt equites Romani nunc idem
in eum iudices essent, istum sine dubio condemnarent,
de quo litteras eas quae istius furta indicarent et ad
se missas et suo decreto remotas scirent esse. Quem
igitur ab iis equitibus Romanis qui istius causa
cupiunt omnia, qui ab eo benignissime tractati sunt,
condemnari necesse esset, is a vobis, iudices, ulla via
aut ratione absolvi potest ?

181   Ac ne forte ea quae remota de medio atque erepta
nobis sunt omnia ita condita fuisse atque ita abdite
latuisse videantur ut haec diligentia quam ego a me
exspectari maxime puto nihil eorum investigare,
nihil assequi potuerit : quae consilio aliquo aut ratione
inveniri potuerunt inventa sunt, iudices ; manifestis
in rebus hominem iam teneri videbitis. Nam quod
in publicanorum causis vel plurimum aetatis meae
versor vehementerque illum ordinem observo, satis
commode mihi videor eorum consuetudinem usu
182 tractandoque cognosse. LXXIV. Itaque ut hoc comperi, remotas esse litteras societatis, habui rationem
eorum annorum per quos iste in Sicilia fuisset : deinde

486

I have arrived at that fact, I will ask—Were the
documents destroyed? That also being established,
I need say no more, for the court will at once be
convinced of this—that if those same knights who then
passed that resolution in order to help Verres were
sitting here now as judges to try him, they would
without question find him guilty, since they know
that the letters giving information of his robberies
were written to them and were destroyed in accordance with their resolution. Those knights, who
feel so warmly towards him, and have been treated
with so much consideration by him, would be unable
to avoid convicting him; and in view of this, gentlemen, can there possibly be any way open, or any
justification, for his not being convicted by you?

And further, lest it should by some chance be 181
thought that the proofs, thus made away with and
torn from my grasp, have all of them been so well
stowed away, and hidden away, and kept dark, that
the assiduous efforts which I feel sure are expected
of me have failed to track down or lay hold of any of
them, I will say, gentlemen, that what it was reasonably possible for intelligence and foresight to discover has been discovered; you shall now behold
the man caught red-handed. Having been concerned
for perhaps the greater part of my life in cases
connected with revenue-contractors, and having
observed the customs of this section of the community with close attention, I believe I may say that
practical experience has given me a fairly intimate
acquaintance with them. LXXIV. When therefore 182
I found that the company's records had been made
away with, I noted the years during which Verres
had been in Sicily, and then looked to see, what

quaesivi, quod erat inventu facillimum, qui per eosdem
annos magistri illius societatis fuissent, apud quos
tabulae fuissent. Sciebam enim hanc magistrorum
qui tabulas haberent consuetudinem esse, ut cum
tabulas novo magistro traderent, exempla litterarum
ipsi habere non nollent. Itaque ad L. Vibium,
equitem Romanum, virum primarium, quem reperiebam magistrum fuisse eo ipso anno qui mihi maxime
quaerendus erat, primum veni. Sane homini praeter
opinionem improviso incidi. Scrutatus sum quae
potui et quaesivi omnia ; inveni duos solos libellos,
a L. Canuleio missos sociis ex portu Syracusis, in
quibus erat scripta ratio mensium complurium rerum
exportatarum istius nomine sine portorio ; itaque
183 obsignavi statim. Erant[1] haec ex eodem genere
quod ego maxime genus ex sociorum litteris reperire
cupiebam ; verum tantum inveni, iudices, quod apud
vos quasi exempli causa proferre possem. Sed tamen
quicquid erit in his libellis, quantulumcumque videbitur esse, hoc quidem certe manifestum erit : de
ceteris ex hoc coniecturam facere debebitis. Recita
mihi, quaeso, hunc primum libellum, deinde illum
alterum. LIBELLI CANULEIANI.

Non quaero unde cccc. amphoras mellis habueris,
unde tantum Melitensium, unde quinquaginta tri-
cliniorum lectos, unde tot candelabra ; non, inquam,
iam quaero unde haec habueris, sed quo tantum tibi
opus fuerit, id quaero. Omitto de melle ; sed
tantumne Melitensium, quasi etiam amicorum uxores,

---

[1] *Peterson conjectures* Non erat haec (*no MS. has* non,
but erat *is in one early one*) ; *but* tantum inveni *in the next
sentence can mean* " *I found only so much* . . ."

was quite easy to discover, who during those years had been the company's directors and had had charge of the accounts. I knew it was the way of directors in charge of accounts, when handing these over to their successors, rather to like keeping copies of the documents for themselves. Knowing this, I first paid a visit to Lucius Vibius, a prominent member of the equestrian order who had, I found, been director in the very year that most called for investigation. My unexpected visit took him altogether by surprise. I examined everything I could, and asked questions about everything. I found just two papers, sent to the company by Canuleius from the port of Syracuse, which contained a return for several months of goods exported on behalf of Verres, that had paid no export tax; these papers I therefore put under seal at once. They were of the sort that I was **183** especially anxious to discover among the company's records; but what I had come upon was only enough to produce before you as a specimen of the rest. Still, whatever these papers may contain, and however little that may seem to be, one thing at least will be obvious, that from what you see you are bound to draw inferences about the rest. Kindly read us this paper first, and then that one. *Papers written by Canuleius.*

Now I do not ask you where you got those 400 casks of honey, or all that Maltese cloth, or those 50 dining-room couches, or all those chandeliers. I do not, I repeat, at present ask where you got them all; what I do ask is what you wanted them all for. Never mind the honey; but why so much Maltese cloth, as if you meant to have enough over to equip all your friends' wives; and why so many

tantum lectorum, quasi omnium istorum villas
184 ornaturus esses? LXXV. Et cum haec paucorum
mensium ratio in his libellis sit, facite ut vobis triennii
totius veniat in mentem. Sic contendo : ex his
parvis libellis, apud unum magistrum societatis
repertis, vos iam coniectura assequi posse cuius modi
praedo iste in illa provincia fuerit, quam multas
cupiditates, quam varias, quam infinitas habuerit,
quantam pecuniam non solum numeratam verum
etiam in huiusce modi rebus positam confecerit.
185 Quae vobis alio loco planius explicabuntur : nunc
hoc attendite. His exportationibus quae recitatae
sunt scribit HS LX. socios perdidisse ex vicensima
portorii Syracusis. Pauculis igitur mensibus, ut hi
pusilli et contempti libelli indicant, furta praetoris,
quae essent HS duodeciens, ex uno oppido solo
exportata sunt. Cogitate nunc, cum illa Sicilia sit,
hoc est insula quae undique exitus maritimos habeat,
quid ex ceteris locis exportatum putetis ; quid
Agrigento, quid Lilybaeo, quid Panhormo, quid
Thermis, quid Halaesa, quid Catina, quid ex ceteris
oppidis ; quid vero Messana, quem iste sibi locum
maxime tutum arbitrabatur, ubi animo semper
soluto liberoque erat, quod sibi iste Mamertinos
delegerat ad quos omnia quae aut diligentius ser-
vanda aut occultius exportanda erant deportaret. His
inventis libellis ceteri remoti et diligentius sunt
reconditi ; nos tamen, ut omnes intellegant hoc

couches, as if you meant to furnish all their country houses? LXXV. Moreover, the return contained 184 in these papers is for a few months only; so you must allow, gentlemen, for the full three years. My contention is that, from these brief papers found in the hands of a single director of the company, you can fairly infer the nature of the man's piratical career in the province, the number and variety and boundless extent of his greedy desires, and the amount of money he secured, not only in cash but also invested in such forms as those here mentioned. The story of all this shall be told in clearer detail 185 later on; for the moment I ask you to note this point. On the export transactions mentioned in what has been read the writer states that the company has lost £600, due from the 5 per cent tax on exports from Syracuse. In a few short months, therefore, as these contemptible scraps of paper inform us, our praetor exported contraband goods to the value of £12,000 from one town alone. Now ask yourselves, the country being Sicily, an island with ports of departure all round it, the probable amount thus exported from the other localities— from Agrigentum, from Lilybaeum, from Panhormus, from Thermae, from Halaesa, from Catina, from all the other towns, and particularly from Messana, which he reckoned the safest spot for him, and in which he always felt easy and comfortable, having chosen the Mamertines as his consignees for everything that might need to be guarded with special care or sent out of the country with special secrecy After the detection of these papers, all the rest were carried off and stowed away with particular care; however, we on this side, wishing everyone to

nos sine cupiditate agere, his ipsis libellis contenti
sumus.

186 LXXVI. Nunc ad sociorum tabulas accepti et
expensi, quas removere honeste nullo modo potuerunt, et ad amicum tuum Carpinatium reverte-
mur. Inspiciebamus Syracusis a Carpinatio con-
fectas tabulas societatis, quae significabant multis
nominibus eos homines versuram a Carpinatio fecisse
qui pecunias Verri dedissent. Quod erit vobis luce
clarius, iudices, cum eos ipsos produxero qui dederunt; intellegetis enim illa tempora per quae,
cum essent in periculo, pretio sese redemerunt cum
societatis tabulis non solum consulibus verum etiam
187 mensibus convenire. Cum haec maxime cognosce-
remus et in manibus tabulas haberemus, repente
aspicimus lituras eius modi quasi quaedam vulnera
tabularum recentia. Statim suspicione offensi ad
ea ipsa nomina oculos animumque transtulimus.
Erant acceptae pecuniae c. VERRUCIO c. f. ; sic
tamen ut usque ad alterum R litterae constarent
integrae, reliquae omnes essent in litura. Alterum,
tertium, quartum, permulta erant eiusdem modi
nomina. Cum manifesto res flagitiosa litura tabularum atque insignis turpitudo teneretur, quaerere incipimus de Carpinatio quisnam is esset Verrucius quicum tantae pecuniae rationem haberet.
Haerere homo, versari, rubere. Quod lege ex-
492

appreciate the reasonable spirit in which we are dealing with this matter, are satisfied with these papers before us.

LXXVI. We will now go back to the company's 186 accounts of receipts and expenditure, which they had no respectable means of suppressing, and to your friend Carpinatius. I was at Syracuse looking through the company's accounts kept by Carpinatius, in which a number of items showed that persons who had paid sums of money to Verres had borrowed for the purpose from Carpinatius—a fact that will be clearer than daylight to you, gentlemen, the moment I bring forward the actual persons who made these payments ; for you will see that the dates at which they bought release from their critical situations by bribery correspond, not only year for year but month for month, with the company's accounts. While noting these particular facts, with 187 the accounts open in my hands, I suddenly caught sight of some erasures that suggested recent injuries to the tablets. As soon as this suspicion struck me, I transferred my eyes and attention to these special items. There were sums entered as received from *Gaius Verrucius son of Gaius d⁰* ; but whereas up to the second "r" the letters were plainly untouched, all after that were written over an erasure ; and there was a second, a third, a fourth, a large number of items of the same character. Since these erasures on the tablets manifestly indicated some conspicuously villainous and dirty proceeding, I proceeded to ask Carpinatius who this Verrucius was with whom he had such extensive money transactions. The man hesitated, shuffled, went red in the face. As the law exempts the accounts of

cipiuntur tabulae publicanorum quo minus Romam deportentur, ut res quam maxime clara et testata esse posset, in ius ad Metellum Carpinatium voco, tabulasque societatis in forum defero. Fit maximus concursus hominum, et, quod erat Carpinatii nota cum isto praetore societas ac faeneratio, summe exspectabant omnes quidnam in tabulis 188 teneretur. LXXVII. Rem ad Metellum defero, me tabulas perspexisse sociorum ; in his tabulis magnam rationem C. Verrucii permultis nominibus esse ; meque hoc perspicere ex consulum mensiumque ratione, hunc Verrucium neque ante adventum C. Verris neque post decessionem quicquam cum Carpinatio rationis habuisse. Postulo ut mihi respondeat qui sit is Verrucius, mercator an negotiator an arator an pecuarius, in Sicilia sit an iam decesserit. Clamare omnes ex conventu neminem umquam in Sicilia fuisse Verrucium. Ego instare ut mihi responderet quis esset, ubi esset, unde esset : cur servus societatis qui tabulas conficeret semper in Verrucii nomine certo 189 ex loco mendosus esset. Atque haec postulabam, non quo illum cogi putarem oportere ut ad ea mihi responderet invitus, sed ut omnibus istius furta, illius flagitium, utriusque audacia perspicua esse posset. Itaque illum in iure metu conscientiaque peccati mutum atque exanimatum ac vix vivum

revenue-contractors from liability to removal to
Rome, and as I wished to have the facts cleared up and
corroborated as far as I could, I brought an action
against Carpinatius before Metellus, and took the
company's accounts along to the court-house. A
large crowd gathered; and since Carpinatius was
notorious as a partner of Governor Verres and as a
money-lender, there was great and general curiosity
to know what the account-books contained. LXXVII.
I stated my charge before Metellus, saying that I 188
had inspected the company's accounts; that they
included a large one, with a great many entries,
under the name of Gaius Verrucius; and that by
comparing the months and years I had discovered
that no such Verrucius had kept any sort of account
with Carpinatius either before the arrival of Gaius
Verres or after his departure. I demanded therefore that Carpinatius should tell me who this Verrucius
was, merchant or banker or arable or pastoral farmer,
and whether he was still in Sicily or had gone away.
The whole audience shouted that there had never
been in Sicily anyone called Verrucius. I insisted
that he should answer me and say who this was,
where he was, and where he came from, and why
the company's slave who wrote up the accounts,
when he wrote the name of Verrucius, always went
wrong at one particular point. And I did not make 189
these demands because I thought it right that he
should be forced to answer my questions against
his will; my purpose was to make quite plain to
everyone the peculations of Verres, the misconduct
of Carpinatius, and the audacity of them both. So
I left the man there before the praetor, speechless
and dazed and half dead with the terrors of his

relinquo; tabulas in foro, summa hominum frequentia,
exscribo; adhibentur in scribendo ex conventu viri
primarii, litterae lituraeque omnes assimulatae et
190 expressae de tabulis in libros transferuntur. Haec
omnia summa cura et diligentia recognita et collata
et ab hominibus honestissimis obsignata sunt.

Si Carpinatius tum mihi respondere noluit, responde
tu mihi nunc, Verres, quem esse hunc tuum paene
gentilem Verrucium putes. Fieri non potest ut,
quem video te praetore in Sicilia fuisse, et quem ex
ipsa ratione intellego locupletem fuisse, eum tu in
tua provincia non cognoveris. Atque adeo, ne hoc
aut longius aut obscurius esse possit, procedite in
medium atque explicate descriptionem imaginemque
tabularum, ut omnes mortales istius avaritiae
non iam vestigia sed ipsa cubilia videre possint.
191 LXXVIII. Videtis VERRUCIUM? videtis primas litteras integras? videtis extremam partem nominis,
codam illam Verrinam tamquam in luto demersam
esse in litura? Sic habent se tabulae, iudices, ut
videtis. Quid exspectatis? quid quaeritis amplius?
Tu ipse, Verres, quid sedes? quid moraris? Nam
aut exhibeas nobis Verrucium necesse est aut te
Verrucium esse fateare.

Laudantur oratores veteres, Crassi illi et Antonii,
quod crimina diluere dilucide, quod copiose reorum
causas defendere solerent. Nimirum illi non ingenio

guilty conscience, and proceeded to make a copy of
the accounts, there in the market-place with a great
crowd looking on. Men of position in the district
helped with the writing, and every letter and erasure
was transferred, reproduced exactly, from the
accounts to my books. The whole thing was then 190
examined and compared with scrupulous care, and
signed and sealed by certain gentlemen of high
standing.

If Carpinatius would not answer me then, will you
answer me now, Verres, and say who you suppose
this Verrucius is who is almost one of your own clan?
I see the man was in Sicily during your praetorship,
and the account is enough to show me that he was
rich, so it is out of the question that you in your
own province were not acquainted with him. Or
rather, for the sake of brevity and clearness, step
forward, gentlemen, and unroll this facsimile tran-
script of the accounts, so that instead of following
out the tracks of his voracity the world may now
see it at home in its lair. LXXVIII. Do you see the 191
word VERRUCIUS? Do you see how the first letters
are all right? Do you see the last part of the name,
how the tail-bit there is sunki n the erasure like a
pig's tail in mud? Well, gentlemen, the accounts
are what you see they are; what are you waiting
for, what more would you have? You yourself,
Verres, why are you sitting there doing nothing?
Either you must show us Verrucius, you know, or
you must confess that Verrucius is you.

Famous orators of the past, like Crassus and
Antonius, were celebrated for their brilliant way of
undermining the prosecutor's case and bringing up
a mass of arguments to support the accused. But

solum his patronis sed fortuna etiam praestiterunt.
Nemo enim tum ita peccabat ut defensioni locum
non relinqueret ; nemo ita vivebat ut nulla eius vitae
pars summae turpitudinis esset expers ; nemo ita in
manifesto peccato tenebatur ut, cum impudens
fuisset in facto, tum impudentior videretur si negaret.

192 Nunc vero quid faciat Hortensius ? Avaritiaene
crimina frugalitatis laudibus deprecetur ? At hominem flagitiosissimum, libidinosissimum nequissimum-
que defendit. An ab hac eius infamia ac[1] nequitia
vestros animos in aliam partem fortitudinis commemoratione traducat ? At homo inertior, ignavior,
magis vir inter mulieres, impura inter viros mulier-
cula, proferri non potest. At mores commodi. Quis
contumacior ? quis inhumanior ? quis superbior ?
At haec sine cuiusquam malo. Quis acerbior, quis
insidiosior, quis crudelior umquam fuit ? In hoc
homine atque in eius modi causa quid facerent omnes
Crassi et Antonii ? Tantum, opinor, Hortensi : ad
causam non accederent, neque in alterius impudentia
sui pudoris existimationem amitterent. Liberi enim
ad causas solutique veniebant, neque committebant
ut, si impudentes in defendendo esse noluissent,
ingrati in deserendo existimarentur.

---

[1] ac (*Mueller's conjecture*) *is in no* MS.

---

[a] It is implied that Hortensius is hampered by being
under obligations to Verres.

the fact is that they had not only better brains than the advocates of to-day but also better luck. For in those days no man was such an offender that no grounds were left for a defence of him ; no man lived so evil a life that every part of it was utterly foul ; no man was caught misconducting himself so unmistakably that the shamelessness of his act would be thought less than the shamelessness of his denying it. But in this case, what is Hortensius to 192 do ? Is he to palliate the charges of greed against his client by eulogizing his respectability ? Why, that client is an immoral, licentious, filthy scoundrel. Is he to divert your attention from his scandalous immorality by dwelling upon his bravery ? Why, a lazier man, a greater coward, a fellow who so plays the man among women and the degraded contemptible woman among men, is not to be produced anywhere. Is it said that he is good-natured ? No one is more rude and unfeeling and overbearing. Is it said that his bad points do no hurt to anyone ? No one was ever more harsh and treacherous and brutal. With such a client, and with such a case, what would any Crassus or Antonius do ? So much as this, surely, Hortensius : they would not undertake the case at all, nor lose their name as men of honour for the sake of a man who sticks at nothing. For they always came into court with their hands free and unshackled, and never so committed themselves that they could only avoid the shamelessness of defending a scoundrel by being thought ungrateful for refusing to defend him.[a]

INDEX OF NAMES

The references are to the pages of the Latin text.

INDEX OF NAMES

INDEX OF NAMES

INDEX OF NAMES

Printed in Great Britain by R. & R. CLARK, LIMITED, *Edinburgh*

THE LOEB CLASSICAL LIBRARY

VOLUMES ALREADY PUBLISHED

LATIN AUTHORS

AMMIANUS MARCELLINUS. J. C. Rolfe. 3 Vols.

APULEIUS : THE GOLDEN ASS (METAMORPHOSES). W. Adlington (1566). Revised by S. Gaselee.

ST. AUGUSTINE : CITY OF GOD. 7 Vols. Vol. I. G. E. McCracken. Vol. II. W. M. Green. Vol. III. D. Wiesen. Vol. IV. P. Levine. Vol. V. E. M. Sanford and W. M. Green. Vol. VI. W. C. Greene. Vol. VII. W. M. Green.

ST. AUGUSTINE, CONFESSIONS OF. W. Watts (1631). 2 Vols.

ST. AUGUSTINE : SELECT LETTERS. J. H. Baxter.

AUSONIUS. H. G. Evelyn White. 2 Vols.

BEDE. J. E. King. 2 Vols.

BOETHIUS : TRACTS AND DE CONSOLATIONE PHILOSOPHIAE. Rev. H. F. Stewart and E. K. Rand. Revised by S. J. Tester.

CAESAR : ALEXANDRIAN, AFRICAN AND SPANISH WARS. A. G. Way.

CAESAR : CIVIL WARS. A. G. Peskett.

CAESAR : GALLIC WAR. H. J. Edwards.

CATO AND VARRO : DE RE RUSTICA. H. B. Ash and W. D. Hooper.

CATULLUS. F. W. Cornish ; TIBULLUS. J. B. Postgate ; and PERVIGILIUM VENERIS. J. W. Mackail.

CELSUS : DE MEDICINA. W. G. Spencer. 3 Vols.

CICERO : BRUTUS AND ORATOR. G. L. Hendrickson and H. M. Hubbell.

CICERO : DE FINIBUS. H. Rackham.

CICERO : DE INVENTIONE, etc. H. M. Hubbell.

CICERO : DE NATURA DEORUM AND ACADEMICA. H. Rackham.

CICERO : DE OFFICIIS. Walter Miller.

CICERO : DE ORATORE, etc. 2 Vols. Vol. I : DE ORATORE, Books I and II. E. W. Sutton and H. Rackham. Vol. II : DE ORATORE, Book III ; DE FATO ; PARADOXA STOICORUM ; DE PARTITIONE ORATORIA. H. Rackham.

CICERO : DE REPUBLICA, DE LEGIBUS. Clinton W. Keyes.

THE LOEB CLASSICAL LIBRARY

NEMESIANUS, AVIANUS, with " Aetna," " Phoenix " and other poems. J. Wight Duff and Arnold M. Duff.

OVID : THE ART OF LOVE AND OTHER POEMS. J. H. Mozley.

OVID : FASTI. Sir James G. Frazer.

OVID : HEROIDES AND AMORES. Grant Showerman. Revised by G. P. Goold.

OVID : METAMORPHOSES. F. J. Miller. 2 Vols. Vol. I. Revised by G. P, Goold.

OVID : TRISTIA AND EX PONTO. A. L. Wheeler.

PETRONIUS. M. Heseltine ; SENECA : APOCOLOCYNTOSIS. W. H. D. Rouse. Revised by E. H. Warmington.

PHAEDRUS AND BABRIUS (Greek). B. E. Perry.

PLAUTUS. Paul Nixon. 5 Vols.

PLINY : LETTERS, PANEGYRICUS. B. Radice. 2 Vols.

PLINY : NATURAL HISTORY. 10 Vols. Vols. I-V. H. Rackham. Vols. VI-VIII. W. H. S. Jones. Vol. IX. H. Rackham. Vol. X. D. E. Eichholz.

PROPERTIUS. H. E. Butler.

PRUDENTIUS. H. J. Thomson. 2 Vols.

QUINTILIAN. H. E. Butler. 4 Vols.

REMAINS OF OLD LATIN. E. H. Warmington. 4 Vols. Vol. I (Ennius and Caecilius). Vol. II (Livius, Naevius, Pacuvius, Accius). Vol. III (Lucilius, Laws of the XII Tables). Vol. IV (Archaic Inscriptions).

SALLUST. J. C. Rolfe.

SCRIPTORES HISTORIAE AUGUSTAE. D. Magie. 3 Vols.

SENECA : APOCOLOCYNTOSIS. Cf. PETRONIUS.

SENECA : EPISTULAE MORALES. R. M. Gummere. 3 Vols.

SENECA : MORAL ESSAYS. J. W. Basore. 3 Vols.

SENECA : NATURALES QUAESTIONES. T. H. Corcoran. 2 Vols.

SENECA : TRAGEDIES. F. J. Miller. 2 Vols.

SENECA THE ELDER. M. Winterbottom. 2 Vols.

SIDONIUS : POEMS AND LETTERS. W. B. Anderson. 2 Vols.

SILIUS ITALICUS. J. D. Duff. 2 Vols.

STATIUS. J. H. Mozley. 2 Vols.

SUETONIUS. J. C. Rolfe. 2 Vols.

TACITUS : AGRICOLA AND GERMANIA. M. Hutton ; DIALOGUS. Sir Wm. Peterson. Revised by R. M. Ogilvie, E. H. Warmington, M. Winterbottom.

TACITUS : HISTORIES AND ANNALS. C. H. Moore and J. Jackson. 4 Vols.

TERENCE. John Sargeaunt. 2 Vols.

TERTULLIAN : APOLOGIA AND DE SPECTACULIS. T. R. Glover; MINUCIUS FELIX. G. H. Rendall.

VALERIUS FLACCUS. J. H. Mozley.

VARRO: DE LINGUA LATINA. R. G. Kent. 2 Vols.
VELLEIUS PATERCULUS AND RES GESTAE DIVI AUGUSTI.
F. W. Shipley.
VIRGIL. H. R. Fairclough. 2 Vols.
VITRUVIUS: DE ARCHITECTURA. F. Granger. 2 Vols.

GREEK AUTHORS

ACHILLES TATIUS. S. Gaselee.
AELIAN: ON THE NATURE OF ANIMALS. A. F. Scholfield.
3 Vols.
AENEAS TACTICUS, ASCLEPIODOTUS AND ONASANDER. The
Illinois Greek Club.
AESCHINES. C. D. Adams.
AESCHYLUS. H. Weir Smyth. 2 Vols.
ALCIPHRON, AELIAN AND PHILOSTRATUS: LETTERS. A. R.
Benner and F. H. Fobes.
APOLLODORUS. Sir James G. Frazer. 2 Vols.
APOLLONIUS RHODIUS. R. C. Seaton.
THE APOSTOLIC FATHERS. Kirsopp Lake. 2 Vols.
APPIAN: ROMAN HISTORY. Horace White. 4 Vols.
ARATUS. *Cf.* CALLIMACHUS: HYMNS AND EPIGRAMS.
ARISTIDES. C. A. Behr. 4 Vols. Vol. I.
ARISTOPHANES. Benjamin Bickley Rogers. 3 Vols. Verse
trans.
ARISTOTLE: ART OF RHETORIC. J. H. Freese.
ARISTOTLE: ATHENIAN CONSTITUTION, EUDEMIAN ETHICS.
VIRTUES AND VICES. H. Rackham.
ARISTOTLE: THE CATEGORIES. ON INTERPRETATION. H. P.
Cooke; PRIOR ANALYTICS. H. Tredennick.
ARISTOTLE: GENERATION OF ANIMALS. A. L. Peck.
ARISTOTLE: HISTORIA ANIMALIUM. A. L. Peck. 3 Vols.
Vols. I and II.
ARISTOTLE: METAPHYSICS. H. Tredennick. 2 Vols.
ARISTOTLE: METEOROLOGICA. H. D. P. Lee.
ARISTOTLE: MINOR WORKS. W. S. Hett. "On Colours,"
"On Things Heard," "Physiognomics," "On Plants,"
"On Marvellous Things Heard," "Mechanical Prob-
lems," "On Invisible Lines," "Situations and Names of
Winds," "On Melissus, Xenophanes, and Gorgias."
ARISTOTLE: NICOMACHEAN ETHICS. H. Rackham.
ARISTOTLE: OECONOMICA AND MAGNA MORALIA. G. C.
Armstrong. (With METAPHYSICS, Vol. II.)
ARISTOTLE: ON THE HEAVENS. W. K. C. Guthrie.

ARISTOTLE : ON THE SOUL, PARVA NATURALIA, ON BREATH. W. S. Hett.

ARISTOTLE : PARTS OF ANIMALS. A. L. Peck : MOVEMENT AND PROGRESSION OF ANIMALS. E. S. Forster.

ARISTOTLE : PHYSICS. Rev. P. Wicksteed and F. M. Cornford. 2 Vols.

ARISTOTLE : POETICS ; LONGINUS ON THE SUBLIME. W. Hamilton Fyfe ; DEMETRIUS ON STYLE. W. Rhys Roberts.

ARISTOTLE : POLITICS. H. Rackham.

ARISTOTLE : POSTERIOR ANALYTICS. H. Tredennick ; TOPICS. E. S. Forster.

ARISTOTLE : PROBLEMS. W. S. Hett. 2 Vols.

ARISTOTLE : RHETORICA AD ALEXANDRUM. H. Rackham. (With PROBLEMS, Vol. II.)

ARISTOTLE : SOPHISTICAL REFUTATIONS. COMING-TO-BE AND PASSING-AWAY. E. S. Forster ; ON THE COSMOS. D. J. Furley.

ARRIAN : HISTORY OF ALEXANDER AND INDICA. 2 Vols. Vol. I. P. Brunt. Vol. II. Rev. E. Iliffe Robson.

ATHENAEUS : DEIPNOSOPHISTAE. C. B. Gulick. 7 Vols.

BABRIUS AND PHAEDRUS (Latin). B. E. Perry.

ST. BASIL : LETTERS. R. J. Deferrari. 4 Vols.

CALLIMACHUS : FRAGMENTS. C. A. Trypanis ; MUSAEUS : HERO AND LEANDER. T. Gelzer and C. Whitman.

CALLIMACHUS : HYMNS AND EPIGRAMS, AND LYCOPHRON. A. W. Mair ; ARATUS. G. R. Mair.

CLEMENT OF ALEXANDRIA. Rev. G. W. Butterworth.

COLLUTHUS. *Cf.* OPPIAN.

DAPHNIS AND CHLOE. *Cf.* LONGUS.

DEMOSTHENES I : OLYNTHIACS, PHILIPPICS AND MINOR ORATIONS : I-XVII AND XX. J. H. Vince.

DEMOSTHENES II : DE CORONA AND DE FALSA LEGATIONE. C. A. and J. H. Vince.

DEMOSTHENES III : MEIDIAS, ANDROTION, ARISTOCRATES, TIMOCRATES, ARISTOGEITON. J. H. Vince.

DEMOSTHENES IV-VI : PRIVATE ORATIONS AND IN NEAERAM. A. T. Murray.

DEMOSTHENES VII : FUNERAL SPEECH, EROTIC ESSAY, EXORDIA AND LETTERS. N. W. and N. J. DeWitt.

DIO CASSIUS : ROMAN HISTORY. E. Cary. 9 Vols.

DIO CHRYSOSTOM. 5 Vols. Vols. I and II. J. W. Cohoon. Vol. III. J. W. Cohoon and H. Lamar Crosby. Vols. IV and V. H. Lamar Crosby.

DIODORUS SICULUS. 12 Vols. Vols. I-VI. C. H. Oldfather. Vol. VII. C. L. Sherman. Vol. VIII. C. B. Welles. Vols.

6

THE LOEB CLASSICAL LIBRARY

MANETHO. W. G. Waddell; PTOLEMY: TETRABIBLOS. F. E. Robbins.

MARCUS AURELIUS. C. R. Haines.

MENANDER. F. G. Allinson.

MINOR ATTIC ORATORS. 2 Vols. K. J. Maidment and J. O. Burtt.

MUSAEUS: HERO AND LEANDER. *Cf.* CALLIMACHUS: FRAGMENTS.

NONNOS: DIONYSIACA. W. H. D. Rouse. 3 Vols.

OPPIAN, COLLUTHUS, TRYPHIODORUS. A. W. Mair.

PAPYRI. NON-LITERARY SELECTIONS. A. S. Hunt and C. C. Edgar. 2 Vols. LITERARY SELECTIONS (Poetry). D. L. Page.

PARTHENIUS. *Cf.* LONGUS.

PAUSANIAS: DESCRIPTION OF GREECE. W. H. S. Jones. 4 Vols. and Companion Vol. arranged by R. E. Wycherley.

PHILO. 10 Vols. Vols. I-V. F. H. Colson and Rev. G. H. Whitaker. Vols. VI-X. F. H. Colson. General Index. Rev. J. W. Earp.
Two Supplementary Vols. Translation only from an Armenian Text. Ralph Marcus.

PHILOSTRATUS: THE LIFE OF APOLLONIUS OF TYANA. F. C. Conybeare. 2 Vols.

PHILOSTRATUS: IMAGINES; CALLISTRATUS: DESCRIPTIONS. A. Fairbanks.

PHILOSTRATUS AND EUNAPIUS: LIVES OF THE SOPHISTS. Wilmer Cave Wright.

PINDAR. Sir J. E. Sandys.

PLATO: CHARMIDES, ALCIBIADES, HIPPARCHUS, THE LOVERS, THEAGES, MINOS AND EPINOMIS. W. R. M. Lamb.

PLATO: CRATYLUS, PARMENIDES, GREATER HIPPIAS, LESSER HIPPIAS. H. N. Fowler.

PLATO: EUTHYPHRO, APOLOGY, CRITO, PHAEDO, PHAEDRUS. H. N. Fowler.

PLATO: LACHES, PROTAGORAS, MENO, EUTHYDEMUS. W. R. M. Lamb.

PLATO: LAWS. Rev. R. G. Bury. 2 Vols.

PLATO: LYSIS, SYMPOSIUM, GORGIAS. W. R. M. Lamb.

PLATO: REPUBLIC. Paul Shorey. 2 Vols.

PLATO: STATESMAN, PHILEBUS. H. N. Fowler; ION. W. R. M. Lamb.

PLATO: THEAETETUS AND SOPHIST. H. N. Fowler.

PLATO: TIMAEUS, CRITIAS, CLITOPHO, MENEXENUS, EPISTULAE. Rev. R. G. Bury.

PLOTINUS. A. H. Armstrong. 6 Vols. Vols. I-III.

THE LOEB CLASSICAL LIBRARY

PLUTARCH : MORALIA. 16 Vols. Vols. I-V. F. C. Babbitt.
Vol. VI. W. C. Helmbold. Vol. VII. P. H. De Lacy and
B. Einarson. Vol. VIII. P. A. Clement, H. B. Hoffleit.
Vol. IX. E. L. Minar, Jr., F. H. Sandbach, W. C.
Helmbold. Vol. X. H. N. Fowler. Vol. XI. L. Pearson,
F. H. Sandbach. Vol. XII. H. Cherniss, W. C. Helmbold.
Vol. XIII, Parts 1 and 2. H. Cherniss. Vol. XIV. P. H.
De Lacy and B. Einarson. Vol. XV. F. H. Sandbach.

PLUTARCH : THE PARALLEL LIVES. B. Perrin. 11 Vols.

POLYBIUS. W. R. Paton. 6 Vols.

PROCOPIUS : HISTORY OF THE WARS. H. B. Dewing. 7 Vols.

PTOLEMY : TETRABIBLOS. *Cf.* MANETHO.

QUINTUS SMYRNAEUS. A. S. Way. Verse trans.

SEXTUS EMPIRICUS. Rev. R. G. Bury. 4 Vols.

SOPHOCLES. F. Storr. 2 Vols. Verse trans.

STRABO : GEOGRAPHY. Horace L. Jones. 8 Vols.

THEOPHRASTUS : CHARACTERS. J. M. Edmonds ; HERODES,
etc. A. D. Knox.

THEOPHRASTUS : DE CAUSIS PLANTARUM. G. K. K. Link and
B. Einarson. 3 Vols. Vol. I.

THEOPHRASTUS : ENQUIRY INTO PLANTS. Sir Arthur Hort.
2 Vols.

THUCYDIDES. C. F. Smith. 4 Vols.

TRYPHIODORUS. *Cf.* OPPIAN.

XENOPHON : ANABASIS. C. L. Brownson.

XENOPHON : CYROPAEDIA. Walter Miller. 2 Vols.

XENOPHON : HELLENICA. C. L. Brownson.

XENOPHON : MEMORABILIA AND OECONOMICUS. E. C. Marchant ; SYMPOSIUM AND APOLOGY. O. J. Todd.

XENOPHON : SCRIPTA MINORA. E. C. Marchant and G. W.
Bowersock.

CAMBRIDGE, MASS.　　　　　　LONDON
HARVARD UNIV. PRESS　　　WILLIAM HEINEMANN LTD.